READINGS IN ENVIRONMENTAL IMPACT

Edited by

Peter E. Black

Lee P. Herrington

SUNY at Syracuse
College of Environmental
Science and Forestry

MSS Information Corporation
655 Madison Avenue, New York, N.Y. 10021

This is a custom-made book of readings prepared for the courses taught by the editors, as well as for related courses and for college and university libraries. For information about our program, please write to:

MSS INFORMATION CORPORATION
655 Madison Avenue
New York, New York 10021

MSS wishes to express its appreciation to the authors of the articles in this collection for their cooperation in making their work available in this format.

Library of Congress Cataloging in Publication Data

Black, Peter E   comp.
  Readings in environmental impact.

  1. Environmental law — United States — Addresses, essays, lectures. 2. Environmental policy — United States — Addresses, essays, lectures. 3. Environmental impact statements — Addresses, essays, lectures.
I. Herrington, Lee Pierce, joint comp. II. Title.
KF3775.A75B55   353.008′232   74-13079
ISBN 0-8422-5201-0
ISBN 0-8422-0451-2 (pbk.)

CONTENTS

5

PREFACE

The readings in this collection were assembled for our undergraduate course for seniors in Resources Management at the State University of New York College of Environmental Science and Forestry. It presumes that the student has had considerable background in ecology, and is intended to provide only a portion of the readings for the course, the remainder being in current articles and actual environmental impact statements. Almost all of the readings might be useable for a graduate-level course along with Anderson's *NEPA and the Courts* (Johns Hopkins University Press) and appropriate background ecological references, if needed.

We think it impractical to include all the appropriate historical perspective that is necessary to understand the National Environmental Policy Act of 1969 in this collection, and therefore only acknowledge its existence with the 100-year-old quote from George Perkins Marsh.

Peter E. Black
Lee P. Herrington
Syracuse, New York, 1974

SECTION I

THE NATIONAL ENVIRONMENTAL
POLICY ACT IN PERSPECTIVE

... an early statement on environmental impact.

"But it is certain that man has reacted upon organized and
inorganic nature, and thereby modified ... the material structure
of his earthly home ... We cannot always distinguish between the
results of man's actions and the effects of purely geological or
cosmical causes. ... But man is everywhere a disturbing agent.
Wherever he plants his foot, the harmonies of nature are turned to
discords. ... Man ... extends his action over vast spaces, his
revolutions are swift and radical, and his devastations are, for
an almost incalculable time after he has withdrawn the arm that
gave the blow, irreparable. ... But our inability to assign
definite values to these causes of the disturbance of natural
arrangements is not a reason for ignoring the existence of
such causes in any general view of the relations between man and
nature, and we are never justified in assuming a force to be
insignificant because its measure is unknown, or even because no
physical effect may be traced to its origin."

The Earth as Modified by Human Action
by George Perkins Marsh, 1874

The National Environmental Policy Act of 1969, Public Law 91-190 January 1, 1970 (42 U.S.C. 4321-4347)

An Act to establish a national policy for the environment, to provide for the establishment of a Council on Environmental Quality, and for other purposes.

Be it enacted by the Senate and House of Representatives of the United States of America in Congress assembled, That this Act may be cited as the "National Environmental Policy Act of 1969."

Purpose

SEC. 2. The purposes of this Act are: To declare a national policy which will encourage productive and enjoyable harmony between man and his environment; to promote efforts which will prevent or eliminate damage to the environment and biosphere and stimulate the health and welfare of man; to enrich the understanding of the ecological systems and natural resources important to the Nation; and to establish a Council on Environmental Quality.

Title i

Declaration of National Environmental Policy

SEC. 101. (a) The Congress, recognizing the profound impact of man's activity on the interrelations of all components of the natural environment, particularly the profound influences of population growth, high-density urbanization, industrial expansion, resource exploitation, and new and expanding

FOURTH ANNUAL REPORT, Council on Environmental Quality (U.S. Government Printing Office: 496-584 O-73-29) pp. 408-412.

11

technological advances and recognizing further the critical importance of restoring and maintaining environmental quality to the overall welfare and development of man, declares that it is the continuing policy of the Federal Government, in cooperation with State and local governments, and other concerned public and private organizations, to use all practicable means and measures, including financial and technical assistance, in a manner calculated to foster and promote the general welfare, to create and maintain conditions under which man and nature can exist in productive harmony, and fulfill the social, economic, and other requirements of present and future generations of Americans.

(b) In order to carry out the policy set forth in this Act, it is the continuing responsibility of the Federal Government to use all practicable means, consistent with other essential considerations of national policy, to improve and coordinate Federal plans, functions, programs, and resources to the end that the Nation may—

(1) Fulfill the responsibilities of each generation as trustee of the environment for succeeding generations;

(2) Assure for all Americans safe, healthful, productive, and esthetically and culturally pleasuring suroundings;

(3) Attain the widest range of beneficial uses of the environment without degradation, risk to health or safety, or other undesirable and unintended consequences;

(4) Preserve important historic, cultural, and natural aspects of our national heritage, and maintain, wherever possible, an environment which supports diversity, and variety of individual choice;

(5) Achieve a balance between population and resource use which will permit high standards of living and a wide sharing of life's amenities; and

(6) Enhance the quality of renewable resources and approach the maximum attainable recycling of depletable resources.

(c) The Congress recognizes that each person should enjoy a healthful environment and that each person has a responsibility to contribute to the preservation and enhancement of the environment.

Sec. 102. The Congress authorizes and directs that, to the fullest extent possible: (1) the policies, regulations, and public laws of the United States shall be interpreted and administered in accordance with the policies set forth in this Act, and (2) all agencies of the Federal Government shall—

(A) Utilize a systematic, interdisciplinary approach which will insure the integrated use of the natural and social sciences and the environmental design arts in planning and in decisionmaking which may have an impact on man's environment;

(B) Identify and develop methods and procedures, in consultation with the Council on Environmental Quality established by title II of this Act, which will insure that presently unquantified environmental amenities and values may be given appropriate consideration in decisionmaking along with economic and technical considerations;

(C) Include in every recommendation or report on proposals for legislation and other major Federal actions significantly affecting the quality of the human environment, a detailed statement by the responsible official on—

(i) The environmental impact of the proposed action,

(ii) Any adverse environmental effects which cannot be avoided should the proposal be implemented,

(iii) Alternatives to the proposed action,

(iv) The relationship between local short-term uses of man's environment and the maintenance and enhancement of long-term productivity, and

(v) Any irreversible and irretrievable commitments of resources

12

which would be involved in the proposed action should it be implemented.

Prior to making any detailed statement, the responsible Federal official shall consult with and obtain the comments of any Federal agency which has jurisdiction by law or special expertise with respect to any environmental impact involved. Copies of such statement and the comments and views of the appropriate Federal, State, and local agencies, which are authorized to develop and enforce environmental standards, shall be made available to the President, the Council on Environmental Quality and to the public as provided by section 552 of title 5, United States Code, and shall accompany the proposal through the existing agency review processes;

(D) Study, develop, and describe appropriate alternatives to recommended courses of action in any proposal which involves unresolved conflicts concerning alternative uses of available resources;

(E) Recognize the worldwide and long-range character of environmental problems and, where consistent with the foreign policy of the United States, lend appropriate support to initiatives, resolutions, and programs designed to maximize international cooperation in anticipating and preventing a decline in the quality of mankind's world environment;

(F) Make available to States, counties, municipalities, institutions, and individuals, advice and information useful in restoring, maintaining, and enhancing the quality of the environment;

(G) Initiate and utilize ecological information in the planning and development of resource-oriented projects; and

(H) Assist the Council on Environmental Quality established by title II of this Act.

Sec. 103. All agencies of the Federal Government shall review their present statutory authority, administrative regulations, and current policies and procedures for the purpose of determining whether there are any deficiencies or inconsistencies therein which prohibit full compliance with the purposes and provisions of this Act and shall propose to the President not later than July 1, 1971, such measurers as may be necessary to bring thier authority and policies into conformity with the intent, purposes, and procedures set forth in this Act.

Sec. 104. Nothing in section 102 or 103 shall in any way affect the specific statutory obligations of any Federal agency (1) to comply with criteria or standards of environmental quality, (2) to coordinate or consult with any other Federal or State agency, or (3) to act, or refrain from acting contingent upon the recommendations or certification of any other Federal or State agency.

Sec. 105. The policies and goals set forth in this Act are supplementary to those set forth in existing authorizations of Federal agencies.

Title ii

Council on Environmental Quality

Sec. 201. The President shall transmit to the Congress annually beginning July 1, 1970, an Environmental Quality Report (hereinafter referred to as the "report") which shall set forth (1) the status and condition of the major natural, manmade, or altered environmental classes of the Nation, including, but not limited to, the air, the aquatic, including marine, estuarine, and fresh water, and the terrestrial environment, including, but not limited to, the forest, dryland, wetland, range, urban, suburban and rural environment; (2) current and foreseeable trends in the quality, management and utilization of such environments and the effects of those trends on the social, economic, and other requirements of the Nation; (3) the adequacy of available natural resources for fulfilling human and economic requirements of the Nation in the

13

light of expected population pressures; (4) a review of the programs and activities (including regulatory activities) of the Federal Government, the State and local governments, and nongovernmental entities or individuals with particular reference to their effect on the environment and on the conservation, development and utilization of natural resources; and (5) a program for remedying the deficiencies of existing programs and activities, together with recommendations for legislation.

SEC. 202. There is created in the Executive Office of the President a Council on Environmental Quality (hereinafter referred to as the "Council"). The Council shall be composed of three members who shall be appointed by the President to serve at his pleasure, by and with the advice and consent of the Senate. The President shall designate one of the members of the Council to serve as Chairman. Each member shall be a person who, as a result of his training, experience, and attainments, is exceptionally well qualified to analyze and interpret environmental trends and information of all kinds; to appraise programs and activities of the Federal Government in the light of the policy set forth in title I of this Act; to be conscious of and responsive to the scientific, economic, social, esthetic, and cultural needs and interests of the Nation; and to formulate and recommend national policies to promote the improvement of the quality of the environment.

SEC. 203. The Council may employ such officers and employees as may be necessary to carry out its functions under this Act. In addition, the Council may employ and fix the compensation of such experts and consultants as may be necessary for the carrying out of its functions under this Act, in accordance with section 3109 of title 5, United States Code (but without regard to the last sentence thereof).

SEC. 204. It shall be the duty and function of the Council—

(1) To assist and advise the President in the preparation of the Environmental Quality Report required by section 201;

(2) To gather timely and authoritative information concerning the conditions and trends in the quality of the environment both current and prospective, to analyze and interpret such information for the purpose of determining whether such conditions and trends are interfering, or are likely to interfere, with the achievement of the policy set forth in title I of this Act, and to compile and submit to the President studies relating to such conditions and trends;

(3) To review and appraise the various programs and activities of the Federal Government in the light of the policy set forth in title I of this Act for the purpose of determining the extent to which such programs and activities are contributing to the achievement of such policy, and to make recommendations to the President with respect thereto;

(4) To develop and recommend to the President national policies to foster and promote the improvement of environmental quality to meet the conservation, social, economic, health, and other requirements and goals of the Nation;

(5) To conduct investigations, studies, surveys, research, and analyses relating to ecological systems and environmental quality;

(6) To document and define changes in the natural environment, including the plant and animal systems, and to accumulate necessary data and other information for a continuing analysis of these changes or trends and an interpretation of their underlying causes;

(7) To report at least once each year to the President on the state and condition of the environment; and

(8) To make and furnish such studies, reports thereon, and recommendations with respect to matters of policy and legislation as the President may request.

SEC. 205. In exercising its powers, functions, and duties under this Act, the Council shall—

14

(1) Consult with the Citizens' Advisory Committee on Environmental Quality established by Executive Order No. 11472, dated May 29, 1969, and with such representatives of science, industry, agriculture, labor, conservation organizations, State and local governments and other groups, as it deems advisable; and

(2) Utilize, to the fullest extent possible, the services, facilities and information (including statistical information) of public and private agencies and organizations, and individuals, in order that duplication of effort and expense may be avoided, thus assuring that the Council's activities will not unnecessarily overlap or conflict with similar activities authorized by law and performed by established agencies.

SEC. 206. Members of the Council shall serve full time and the Chairman of the Council shall be compensated at the rate provided for Level II of the Executive Schedule Pay Rates (5 U.S.C. 5313). The other members of the Council shall be compensated at the rate provided for Level IV of the Executive Schedule Pay Rates (5 U.S.C. 5315).

SEC. 207. There are authorized to be appropriated to carry out the provisions of this Act not to exceed $300,000 for fiscal year 1970, $700,000 for fiscal year 1971, and $1 million for each fiscal year thereafter.

Approved January 1, 1970.

The Environmental Quality Improvement Act of 1970, Public Law 91-224, April 3, 1970 (42 U.S.C. 4371-4374)

Title ii—Environmental Quality
(of the Water Quality Improvement Act of 1970)

Short Title

Sec. 201. This title may be cited as the "Environmental Quality Improvement Act of 1970."

Findings, Declarations, and Purposes

Sec. 202. (a) The Congress finds—
(1) That man has caused changes in the environment;
(2) That many of these changes may affect the relationship between man and his environment; and
(3) That population increases and urban concentration contribute directly to pollution and the degradation of our environment.

(b)(1) The Congress declares that there is a national policy for the environment which provides for the enhancement of environmental quality. This policy is evidenced by statutes heretofore enacted relating to the prevention, abatement, and control of environmental pollution, water and land resources, transportation, and economic and regional development.

(2) The primary responsibility for implementing this policy rests with State and local governments.

(3) The Federal Government encourages and supports implementation of this policy through appropriate regional organizations established under existing law.

FOURTH ANNUAL REPORT, Council on Environmental Quality (U.S. Government Printing Office: 496-584 O-73-29) pp. 413-415.

(c) The purposes of this title are—

(1) To assure that each Federal department and agency conducting or supporting public works activities which affect the environment shall implement the policies established under existing law; and

(2) To authorize an Office of Environmental Quality, which, notwithstanding any other provision of law, shall provide the professional and administrative staff for the Council on Environmental Quality established by Public Law 91–190.

Office of Environmental Quality

SEC. 203. (a) There is established in the Executive Office of the President an office to be known as the Office of Environmental Quality (hereafter in this title referred to as the "Office"). The Chairman of the Council on Environmental Quality established by Public Law 91–190 shall be the Director of the Office. There shall be in the Office a Deputy Director who shall be appointed by the President, by and with the advice and consent of the Senate.

(b) The compensation of the Deputy Director shall be fixed by the President at a rate not in excess of the annual rate of compensation payable to the Deputy Director of the Bureau of the Budget.

(c) The Director is authorized to employ such officers and employees (including experts and consultants) as may be necessary to enable the Office to carry out its functions under this title and Public Law 91–190, except that he may employ no more than 10 specialists and other experts without regard to the provisions of title 5, United States Code, governing appointments in the competitive service, and pay such specialists and experts without regard to the provisions of chapter 51 and subchapter 111 of chapter 53 of such title relating to classification and General Schedule pay rates, but no such specialist or expert shall be paid at a rate in excess of the maximum rate for GS–18 of the General Schedule under section 5330 of title 5.

(d) In carrying out his functions the Director shall assist and advise the President on policies and programs of the Federal Government affecting environmental quality by—

(1) Providing the professional and administrative staff and support for the Council on Environmental Quality established by Public Law 91–190;

(2) Assisting the Federal agencies and departments in appraising the effectiveness of existing and proposed facilities, programs, policies, and activities of the Federal Government, and those specific major projects designated by the President which do not require individual project authorization by Congress, which affect environmental quality;

(3) Reviewing the adequacy of existing systems for monitoring and predicting environmental changes in order to achieve effective coverage and efficient use of research facilities and other resources;

(4) Promoting the advancement of scientific knowledge of the effects of actions and technology on the environment and encourage the development of the means to prevent or reduce adverse effects that endanger the health and well-being of man;

(5) Asssisting in coordinating among the Federal departments and agencies those programs and activities which affect, protect, and improve environmental quality;

(6) Assisting the Federal departments and agencies in the development and interrelationship of environmental quality criteria and standards established through the Federal Government;

(7) Collecting, collating, analyzing, and interpreting data and information on environmental quality, ecological research, and evaluation.

(e) The Director is authorized to contract with public or private agencies, institutions, and organizations and with individuals without regard to sec-

17

tions 3618 and 3709 of the Revised Statutes (31 U.S.C. 529; 41 U.S.C. 5) in carrying out his functions.

Report

Sᴇᴄ. 204. Each Environmental Quality Report required by Public Law 91–190 shall, upon transmittal to Congress, be referred to each standing committee having jurisdiction over any part of the subject matter of the Report.

Authorization

Sᴇᴄ. 205. There are hereby authorized to be appropriated not to exceed $500,000 for the fiscal year ending June 30, 1970, not to exceed $750,000 for the fiscal year ending June 30, 1971, not to exceed $1,250,000 for the fiscal year ending June 30, 1972, and not to exceed $1,500,000 for the fiscal year ending June 30, 1973. These authorizations are in addition to those contained in Public Law 91–190.

Approved April 3, 1970.

Preparation of Environmental Impact Statements: Guidelines*

On May 2, 1973, the Council on Environmental Quality published in the FEDERAL REGISTER, for public comment, a proposed revision of its guidelines for the preparation of environmental impact statements. Pursuant to the National Environmental Policy Act (P.L. 91–190, 42 U.S.C. 4321 et seq.) and Executive Order 11514 (35 FR 4247) all Federal departments, agencies, and establishments are required to prepare such statements in connection with their proposals for legislation and other major Federal actions significantly affecting the quality of the human environment. The authority for the Council's guidelines is set forth below in § 1500.1. The specific policies to be implemented by the guidelines is set forth below in § 1500.2.

The Council received numerous comments on its proposed guidelines from environmental groups, Federal, State, and local agencies, industry, and private individuals. Two general themes were presented in the majority of the comments. First, the Council should increase the opportunity for public involvement in the impact statement process. Second, the Council should provide more detailed guidance on the responsibilities of Federal agencies in light of recent court decisions interpreting the Act. The proposed guidelines have been revised in light of the specific comments relating to these general themes, as well as other comments received, and are now being issued in final form.

The guidelines will appear in the Code of Federal Regulations in Title 40, Chapter V, at Part 1500. They are being codified, in part, because they affect State and local governmental agencies, environmental groups, industry, and private individuals, in addition to Federal agencies, to which they are specifically directed, and the resultant need to make them widely and readily available.

---

*38 Fed. Reg. 20550–20562, August 1, 1973.

FOURTH ANNUAL REPORT, Council on Environmental Quality, (U.S. Government Printing Office: 496-584 O-73-29) pp. 416-439.

19

AUTHORITY: National Environmental Act (P.L. 91–190, 42 U.S.C. 4321 et seq.) and Executive Order 11514.

§ 1500.1 Purpose and authority.

(a) This directive provides guidelines to Federal departments, agencies, and establishments for preparing detailed environmental statements on proposals for legislation and other major Federal actions significantly affecting the quality of the human environment as required by section 102(2)(C) of the National Environmental Policy Act (P.L. 91–190, 42 U.S.C. 4321 et. seq.) (hereafter "the Act"). Underlying the preparation of such environmental statements is the mandate of both the Act and Executive Order 11514 (35 FR 4247) of March 5, 1970, that all Federal agencies, to the fullest extent possible, direct their policies, plans and programs to protect and enhance environmental quality. Agencies are required to view their actions in a manner calculated to encourage productive and enjoyable harmony between man and his environment, to promote efforts preventing or eliminating damage to the environment and biosphere and stimulating the health and welfare of man, and to enrich the understanding of the ecological systems and natural resources important to the Nation. The objective of section 102(2)(C) of the Act and of these guidelines is to assist agencies in implementing these policies. This requires agencies to build into their decisionmaking process, beginning at the earliest possible point, an appropriate and careful consideration of the environmental aspects of proposed action in order that adverse environmental effects may be avoided or minimized and environmental quality previously lost may be restored. This directive also provides guidance to Federal, State, and local agencies and the public in commenting on statements prepared under these guidelines.

(b) Pursuant to section 204(3) of the Act the Council on Environmental Quality (hereafter "the Council") is assigned the duty and function of reviewing and appraising the programs and activities of the Federal Government, in the light of the Act's policy, for the purpose of determining the extent to which such programs and activities are contributing to the achievement of such policy, and to make recommendations to the President with respect thereto. Section 102(2)(B) of the Act directs all Federal agencies to identify and develop methods and procedures, in consultation with the Council, to insure that unquantified environmental values be given appropriate consideration in decisionmaking along with economic and technical considerations; section 102(2)(C) of the Act directs that copies of all environmental impact statements be filed with the Council; and section 102(2)(H) directs all Federal agencies to assist the Council in the performance of its functions. These provisions have been supplemented in sections 3(h) and (i) of Executive Order 11514 by directions that the Council issue guidelines to Federal agencies for preparation of environmental impact statements and such other instructions to agencies and requests for reports and information as may be required to carry out the Council's responsibilities under the Act.

§ 1500.2 Policy.

(a) As early as possible and in all cases prior to agency decision concerning recommendations or favorable reports on proposals for (1) legislation significantly affecting the quality of the human environment (see §§ 1500.5(i) and 1500.12) (hereafter "legislative actions") and (2) all other major Federal actions significantly affecting the quality of the human environment (hereafter "administrative actions"), Federal agencies will, in consultation with other appropriate Federal, State and local agencies and the public assess in detail the potential environmental impact.

(b) Initial assessments of the environmental impacts of proposed action should be undertaken concurrently with initial technical and economic studies and, where required, a draft environmental impact statement prepared and circulated for comment in time to accompany the proposal through the existing agency review processes for such action. In this process, Federal agencies shall:

(1) Provide for circulation of draft environmental statements to other Federal, State, and local agencies and for their availability to the public in accordance with the provisions of these guidelines; (2) consider the comments of the agencies and the public; and (3) issue final environmental impact statements responsive to the comments received. The purpose of this assessment and consultation process is to provide agencies and other decisionmakers as well as members of the public with an understanding of the potential environmental effects of proposed actions, to avoid or minimize adverse effects wherever possible, and to restore or enhance environmental quality to the fullest extent practicable. In particular, agencies should use the environmental impact statement process to explore alternative actions that will avoid or minimize adverse impacts and to evaluate both the long- and short-range implications of proposed actions to man, his physical and social surroundings, and to nature. Agencies should consider the results of their environmental assessments along with their assessments of the net economic, technical and other benefits of proposed actions and use all practicable means, consistent with other essential considerations of national policy, to restore environmental quality as well as to avoid or minimize undesirable consequences for the environment.

§ 1500.3 Agency and OMB procedures.

(a) Pursuant to section 2(f) of Executive Order 11514, the heads of Federal agencies have been directed to proceed with measures required by section 102 (2)(C) of the Act. Previous guidelines of the Council directed each agency to establish its own formal procedures for (1) identifying those agency actions requiring environmental statements, the appropriate time prior to decision for the consultations required by section 102 (2)(C) and the agency review process for which environmental statements are to be available, (2) obtaining information required in their preparation, (3) designating the officials who are to be responsible for the statements, (4) consulting with and taking account of the comments of appropriate Federal, State and local agencies and the public, including obtaining the comment of the Administrator of the Environmental Protection Agency when required under section 309 of the Clean Air Act, as amended, and (5) meeting the requirements of section 2(b) of Executive Order

11514 for providing timely public information on Federal plans and programs with environmental impact. Each agency, including both departmental and subdepartmental components having such procedures, shall review its procedures and shall revise them, in consultation with the Council, as may be necessary in order to respond to requirements imposed by these revised guidelines as well as by such previous directives. After such consultation, proposed revisions of such agency procedures shall be published in the FEDERAL REGISTER no later than October 30, 1973. A minimum 45-day period for public comment shall be provided, followed by publication of final procedures no later than forty-five (45) days after the conclusion of the comment period. Each agency shall submit seven (7) copies of all such procedures to the Council. Any future revision of such agency procedures shall similarly be proposed and adopted only after prior consultation with the Council and, in the case of substantial revision, opportunity for public comment. All revisions shall be published in the FEDERAL REGISTER.

(b) Each Federal agency should consult, with the assistance of the Council and the Office of Management and Budget if desired, with other appropriate Federal agencies in the development and revision of the above procedures so as to achieve consistency in dealing with similar activities and to assure effective coordination among agencies in their review of proposed activities. Where applicable, State and local review of such agency procedures should be conducted pursuant to procedures established by Office of Management and Budget Circular No. A–85.

(c) Existing mechanisms for obtaining the views of Federal, State, and local agencies on proposed Federal actions should be utilized to the maximum extent practicable in dealing with environmental matters. The Office of Management and Budget will issue instructions, as necessary, to take full advantage of such existing mechanisms.

§ 1500.4 Federal agencies included; effect of the Act on existing agency mandates.

(a) Section 102(2)(C) of the Act applies to all agencies of the Federal Government. Section 102 of the Act provides that "to the fullest extent possible: (1) The policies, regulations, and public laws of the United States shall be interpreted and administered in accordance

21

with the policies set forth in this Act;" and section 105 of the Act provides that "the policies and goals set forth in this Act are supplementary to those set forth in existing authorizations of Federal agencies." This means that each agency shall interpret the provisions of the Act as a supplement to its existing authority and as a mandate to view traditional policies and missions in the light of the Act's national environmental objectives. In accordance with this purpose, agencies should continue to review their policies, procedures, and regulations and to revise them as necessary to ensure full compliance with the purposes and provisions of the Act. The phrase "to the fullest extent possible" in section 102 is meant to make clear that each agency of the Federal Government shall comply with that section unless existing law applicable to the agency's operations expressly prohibits or makes compliance impossible.

§ 1500.5   Types of actions covered by the Act.

(a) "Actions" include but are not limited to:

(1) Recommendations or favorable reports relating to legislation including requests for appropriations. The requirement for following the section 102 (2)(C) procedure as elaborated in these guidelines applies to both (i) agency recommendations on their own proposals for legislation .(see § 1500.12); and (ii) agency reports on legislation initiated elsewhere. In the latter case only the agency which has primary responsibility for the subject matter involved will prepare an environmental statement.

(2) New and continuing projects and program activities: directly undertaken by Federal agencies; or supported in whole or in part through Federal contracts, grants, subsidies, loans, or other forms of funding assistance (except where such assistance is solely in the form of general revenue sharing funds, distributed under the State and Local Fiscal Assistance Act of 1972, 31 U.S.C. 1221 et. seq. with no Federal agency control over the subsequent use of such funds); or involving a Federal lease, permit, license certificate or other entitlement for use.

(3) The making, modification, or establishment of regulations, rules, procedures, and policy.

§ 1500.6   Identifying major actions significantly affecting the environment.

(a) The statutory clause "major Federal actions significantly affecting the

quality of the human environment" is to be construed by agencies with a view to the overall, cumulative impact of the action proposed, related Federal actions and projects in the area, and further actions contemplated. Such actions may be localized in their impact, but if there is potential that the environment may be significantly affected, the statement is to be prepared. Proposed major actions, the environmental impact of which is likely to be highly controversial, should be covered in all cases. In considering what constitutes major action significantly affecting the environment, agencies should bear in mind that the effect of many Federal decisions about a project or complex of projects can be individually limited but cumulatively considerable. This can occur when one or more agencies over a period of years puts into a project individually minor but collectively major resources, when one decision involving a limited amount of money is a precedent for action in much larger cases or represents a decision in principle about a future major course of action, or when several Government agencies individually make decisions about partial aspects of a major action. In all such cases, an environmental statement should be prepared if it is reasonable to anticipate a cumulatively significant impact on the environment from Federal action. The Council, on the basis of a written assessment of the impacts involved, is available to assist agencies in determining whether specific actions require impact statements.

(b) Section 101(b) of the Act indicates the broad range of aspects of the environment to be surveyed in any assessment of significant effect. The Act also indicates that adverse significant effects include those that degrade the quality of the environment, curtail the range of beneficial uses of the environment, and serve short-term, to the disadvantage of long-term, environmental goals. Significant effects can also include actions which may have both beneficial and detrimental effects, even if on balance the agency believes that the effect will be beneficial. Significant effects also include secondary effects, as described more fully, for example, in § 1500.8(a) (iii)(B). The significance of a proposed action may also vary with the setting, with the result that an action that would have little impact in an urban area may be significant in a rural setting or vice versa. While a precise definition of environmental "significance," valid in all contexts, is not possible, effects to be considered in assessing significance in-

22

clude, but are not limited to, those outlined in Appendix II of these guidelines.

(c) Each of the provisions of the Act, except section 102(2)(C), applies to all Federal agency actions. Section 102(2)(C) requires the preparation of a detailed environmental impact statement in the case of "major Federal actions significantly affecting the quality of the human environment." The identification of major actions significantly affecting the environment is the responsibility of each Federal agency, to be carried out against the background of its own particular operations. The action must be a (1) "major" action, (2) which is a "Federal action," (3) which has a "significant" effect, and (4) which involves the "quality of the human environment." The words "major" and "significantly" are intended to imply thresholds of importance and impact that must be met before a statement is required. The action causing the impact must also be one where there is sufficient Federal control and responsibility to constitute "Federal action" in contrast to cases where such Federal control and responsibility are not present as, for example, when Federal funds are distributed in the form of general revenue sharing to be used by State and local governments (see § 1500.5(ii)). Finally, the action must be one that significantly affects the quality of the human environment either by directly affecting human beings or by indirectly affecting human beings through adverse effects on the environment. Each agency should review the typical classes of actions that it undertakes and, in consultation with the Council, should develop specific criteria and methods for identifying those actions likely to require environmental statements and those actions likely not to require environmental statements. Normally this will involve:

(i) Making an initial assessment of the environmental impacts typically associated with principal types of agency action.

(ii) Identifying on the basis of this assessment, types of actions which normally do, and types of actions which normally do not, require statements.

(iii) With respect to remaining actions that may require statements depending on the circumstances, and those actions determined under the preceding paragraph (C)(4)(ii) of this section as likely to require statements, identifying: (a) what basic information needs to be gathered; (b) how and when such information is to be assembled and analyzed; and (c) on what bases environ-

mental assessments and decisions to prepare impact statements will be made. Agencies may either include this substantive guidance in the procedures issued pursuant to § 1500.3(a) of these guidelines, or issue such guidance as supplemental instructions to aid relevant agency personnel in implementing the impact statement process. Pursuant to § 1500.14 of these guidelines, agencies shall report to the Council by June 30, 1974, on the progress made in developing such substantive guidance.

(d) (1) Agencies should give careful attention to identifying and defining the purpose and scope of the action which would most appropriately serve as the subject of the statement. In many cases, broad program statements will be required in order to assess the environmental effects of a number of individual actions on a given geographical area (e.g., coal leases), or environmental impacts that are generic or common to a series of agency actions (e.g., maintenance or waste handling practices), or the overall impact of a large-scale program or chain of contemplated projects (e.g., major lengths of highway as opposed to small segments). Subsequent statements on major individual actions will be necessary where such actions have significant environmental impacts not adequately evaluated in the program statement.

(2) Agencies engaging in major technology research and development programs should develop procedures for periodic evaluation to determine when a program statement is required for such programs. Factors to be considered in making this determination include the magnitude of Federal investment in the program, the likelihood of widespread application of the technology, the degree of environmental impact which would occur if the technology were widely applied, and the extent to which continued investment in the new technology is likely to restrict future alternatives. Statements must be written late enough in the development process to contain meaningful information, but early enough so that this information can practically serve as an input in the decision-making process. Where it is anticipated that a statement may ultimately be required but that its preparation is still premature, the agency should prepare an evaluation briefly setting forth the reasons for its determination that a statement is not yet necessary. This evaluation should be periodically updated, particularly when significant new information becomes available concerning the

23

potential environmental impact of the program. In any case, a statement must be prepared before research activities have reached a stage of investment or commitment to implementation likely to determine subsequent development or restrict later alternatives. Statements on technology research and development programs should include an analysis not only of alternative forms of the same technology that might reduce any adverse environmental impacts but also of alternative technologies that would serve the same function as the technology under consideration. Efforts should be made to involve other Federal agencies and interested groups with relevant expertise in the preparation of such statements because the impacts and alternatives to be considered are likely to be less well defined than in other types of statements.

(e) In accordance with the policy of the Act and Executive Order 11514 agencies have a responsibility to develop procedures to insure the fullest practicable provision of timely public information and understanding of Federal plans and programs with environmental impact in order to obtain the views of interested parties. In furtherance of this policy, agency procedures should include an appropriate early notice system for informing the public of the decision to prepare a draft environmental statement on proposed administrative actions (and for soliciting comments that may be helpful in preparing the statement) as soon as is practicable after the decision to prepare the statement is made. In this connection, agencies should: (1) maintain a list of administrative actions for which environmental statements are being prepared; (2) revise the list at regular intervals specified in the agency's procedures developed pursuant to § 1500.3(a) of these guidelines (but not less than quarterly) and transmit each such revision to the Council; and (3) make the list available for public inspection on request. The Council will periodically publish such lists in the FEDERAL REGISTER. If an agency decides that an environmental statement is not necessary for a proposed action (i) which the agency has identified pursuant to § 1500.6(c)(4)(ii) as normally requiring preparation of a statement, (ii) which is similar to actions for which the agency has prepared a significant number of statements, (iii) which the agency has previously announced would be the subject of a statement, or (iv), for which the agency has made a negative determination in response to a request from

the Council pursuant to § 1500.11(f), the agency shall prepare a publicly available record briefly setting forth the agency's decision and the reasons for that determination. Lists of such negative determinations, and any evaluations made pursuant to § 1500.6 which conclude that preparation of a statement is not yet timely, shall be prepared and made available in the same manner as provided in this subsection for lists of statements under preparation.

§ 1500.7 Preparing draft environmental statements; public hearings.

(a) Each environmental impact statement shall be prepared and circulated in draft form for comment in accordance with the provisions of these guidelines. The draft statement must fulfill and satisfy to the fullest extent possible at the time the draft is prepared the requirements established for final statements by section 102(2)(C). (Where an agency has an established practice of declining to favor an alternative until public comments on a proposed action have been received, the draft environmental statement may indicate that two or more alternatives are under consideration.) Comments received shall be carefully evaluated and considered in the decision process. A final statement with substantive comments attached shall then be issued and circulated in accordance with applicable provisions of §§ 1500.10, 1500.11, or 1500.12. It is important that draft environmental statements be prepared and circulated for comment and furnished to the Council as early as possible in the agency review process in order to permit agency decisionmakers and outside reviewers to give meaningful consideration to the environmental issues involved. In particular, agencies should keep in mind that such statements are to serve as the means of assessing the environmental impact of proposed agency actions, rather than as a justification for decisions already made. This means that draft statements on administrative actions should be prepared and circulated for comment prior to the first significant point of decision in the agency review process. For major categories of agency action, this point should be identified in the procedures issued pursuant to § 1500.3(a). For major categories of projects involving an applicant and identified pursuant to § 1500.6 (c)(c)(ii) as normally requiring the preparation of a statement, agencies should include in their procedures provisions limiting actions which an applicant is permitted to take prior to completion

24

and review of the final statement with respect to his application.

(b) Where more than one agency (1) directly sponsors an action, or is directly involved in an action through funding, licenses, or permits, or (2) is involved in a group of actions directly related to each other because of their functional interdependence and geographical proximity, consideration should be given to preparing one statement for all the Federal actions involved (see § 1500.6(d)(1)). Agencies in such cases should consider the possibility of joint preparation of a statement by all agencies concerned, or designation of a single "lead agency" to assume supervisory responsibility for preparation of the statement. Where a lead agency prepares the statement, the other agencies involved should provide assistance with respect to their areas of jurisdiction and expertise. In either case, the statement should contain an environmental assessment of the full range of Federal actions involved, should reflect the views of all participating agencies, and should be prepared before major or irreversible actions have been taken by any of the participating agencies. Factors relevant in determining an appropriate lead agency include the time sequence in which the agencies become involved, the magnitude of their respective involvement, and their relative expertise with respect to the project's environmental effects. As necessary, the Council will assist in resolving questions of responsibility for statement preparation in the case of multi-agency actions. Federal Regional Councils, agencies and the public are encouraged to bring to the attention of the Council and other relevant agencies appropriate situations where a geographic or regionally focused statement would be desirable because of the cumulative environmental effects likely to result from multi-agency actions in the area.

(c) Where an agency relies on an applicant to submit initial environmental information, the agency should assist the applicant by outlining the types of information required. In all cases, the agency should make its own evaluation of the environmental issues and take responsibility for the scope and content of draft and final environmental statements.

(d) Agency procedures developed pursuant to § 1500.3(a) of these guidelines should indicate as explicitly as possible those types of agency decisions or actions which utilize hearings as part of the normal agency review process, either as a result of statutory requirement or agency practice. To the fullest extent possible, all such hearings shall include consideration of the environmental aspects of the proposed action. Agency procedures shall also specifically include provision for public hearings on major actions with environmental impact, whenever appropriate, and for providing the public with relevant information, including information on alternative courses of action. In deciding whether a public hearing is appropriate, an agency should consider: (1) The magnitude of the proposal in terms of economic costs, the geographic area involved, and the uniqueness or size of commitment of the resources involved; (2) the degree of interest in the proposal, as evidenced by requests from the public and from Federal, State and local authorities that a hearing be held; (3) the complexity of the issue and the likelihood that information will be presented at the hearing which will be of assistance to the agency in fulfilling its responsibilities under the Act; and (4) the extent to which public involvement already has been achieved through other means, such as earlier public hearings, meetings with citizen representatives, and/or written comments on the proposed action. Agencies should make any draft environmental statements to be issued available to the public at least fifteen (15) days prior to the time of such hearings.

§ 1500.8 Content of environmental statements.

(a) The following points are to be covered:

(1) A description of the proposed action, a statement of its purposes, and a description of the environment affected, including information, summary technical data, and maps and diagrams where relevant, adequate to permit an assessment of potential environmental impact by commenting agencies and the public. Highly technical and specialized analyses and data should be avoided in the body of the draft impact statement. Such materials should be attached as appendices or footnoted with adequate bibliographic references. The statement should also succinctly describe the environment of the area affected as it exists prior to a proposed action, including other Federal activities in the area affected by the proposed action which are related to the proposed action. The interrelationships and cumulative environmental impacts of the proposed action and other related Federal projects shall be presented in the statement. The amount of detail provided in such descriptions should be commensurate with the extent and expected impact of the

action, and with the amount of information required at the particular level of decisionmaking (planning, feasibility, design, etc.). In order to ensure accurate descriptions and environmental assessments, site visits should be made where feasible. Agencies should also take care to identify, as appropriate, population and growth characteristics of the affected area and any population and growth assumptions used to justify the project or program or to determine secondary population and growth impacts resulting from the proposed action and its alternatives (see paragraph (a)(1)(3)(ii), of this section). In discussing these population aspects, agencies should give consideration to using the rates of growth in the region of the project contained in the projection compiled for the Water Resources Council by the Bureau of Economic Analysis of the Department of Commerce and the Economic Research Service of the Department of Agriculture (the "OBERS" projection). In any event it is essential that the sources of data used to identify, quantify or evaluate any and all environmental consequences be expressly noted.

(2) The relationship of the proposed action to land use plans, policies, and controls for the affected area. This requires a discussion of how the proposed action may conform or conflict with the objectives and specific terms of approved or proposed Federal, State, and local land use plans, policies, and controls, if any, for the area affected including those developed in response to the Clean Air Act or the Federal Water Pollution Control Act Amendments of 1972. Where a conflict or inconsistency exists, the statement should describe the extent to which the agency has reconciled its proposed action with the plan, policy or control, and the reasons why the agency has decided to proceed notwithstanding the absence of full reconciliation.

(3) The probable impact of the proposed action on the environment.

(i) This requires agencies to assess the positive and negative effects of the proposed action as it affects both the national and international environment. The attention given to different environmental factors will vary according to the nature, scale, and location of proposed actions. Among factors to consider should be the potential effect of the action on such aspects of the environment as those listed in Appendix II of these guidelines. Primary attention should be given in the statement to discussing those factors most evidehtly impacted by the proposed action.

(ii) Secondary or indirect, as well as primary or direct, consequences for the environment should be included in the analysis. Many major Federal actions, in particular those that involve the construction or licensing of infrastructure investments (e.g., highways, airports, sewer systems, water resource projects, etc.), stimulate or induce secondary effects in the form of associated investments and changed patterns of social and economic activities. Such secondary effects, through their impacts on existing community facilities and activities, through inducing new facilities and activities, or through changes in natural conditions, may often be even more substantial than the primary effects of the original action itself. For example, the effects of the proposed action on population and growth may be among the more significant secondary effects. Such population and growth impacts should be estimated if expected to be significant (using data identified as indicated in § 1500.8(a)(1)) and an assessment made of the effect of any possible change in population patterns or growth upon the resource base, including land use, water, and public services, of the area in question.

(4) Alternatives to the proposed action, including, where relevant, those not within the existing authority of the responsible agency. (Section 102(2)(D) of the Act requires the responsible agency to "study, develop, and describe appropriate alternatives to recommended courses of action in any proposal which involves unresolved conflicts concerning alternative uses of available resources"). A rigorous exploration and objective evaluation of the environmental impacts of all reasonable alternative actions, particularly those that might enhance environmental quality or avoid some or all of the adverse environmental effects, is essential. Sufficient analysis of such alternatives and their environmental benefits, costs and risks should accompany the proposed action through the agency review process in order not to foreclose prematurely options which might enhance environmental quality or have less detrimental effects. Examples of such alternatives include: the alternative of taking no action or of postponing action pending further study; alternatives requiring actions of a significantly different nature which would provide similar benefits with different environmental impacts (e.g., nonstructural alternatives to flood control programs, or mass transit alternatives to highway construction); alternatives related to different designs

26

or details of the proposed action which would present different environmental impacts (e.g., cooling ponds vs. cooling towers for a power plant or alternatives that will significantly conserve energy); alternative measures to provide for compensation of fish and wildlife losses, including the acquisition of land, waters, and interests therein. In each case, the analysis should be sufficiently detailed to reveal the agency's comparative evaluation of the environmental benefits, costs and risks of the proposed action and each reasonable impact statement already contains such an analysis, its treatment of alternatives may be incorporated provided that such treatment is current and relevant to the precise purpose of the proposed action.

(5.) Any probable adverse environmental effects which cannot be avoided (such as water or air pollution, undesirable land use patterns, damage to life systems, urban congestion, threats to health or other consequences adverse to the environmental goals set out in section 101 (b) of the Act). This should be a brief section summarizing in one place those effects discussed in paragraph (a)(3) of this section that are adverse and unavoidable under the proposed action. Included for purposes of contrast should be a clear statement of how other avoidable adverse effects discussed in paragraph (a)(2) of this section will be mitigated.

(6) The relationship between local short-term uses of man's environment and the maintenance and enhancement of long-term productivity. This section should contain a brief discussion of the extent to which the proposed action involves tradeoffs between short-term environmental gains at the expense of long-term losses, or vice versa, and a discussion of the extent to which the proposed action forecloses future options. In this context short-term and long-term do not refer to any fixed time periods, but should be viewed in terms of the environmentally significant consequences of the proposed action.

(7) Any irreversible and irretrievable commitments of resources that would be involved in the proposed action should it be implemented. This requires the agency to identify from its survey of unavoidable impacts in paragraph (a)(5) of this section the extent to which the action irreversibly curtails the range of potential uses of the environment. Agencies should avoid construing the term "resources" to mean only the labor and materials devoted to an action. "Resources" also means the natural and cultural resources committed to loss or destruction by the action.

(8) An indication of what other interests and considerations of Federal policy are thought to offset the adverse environmental effects of the proposed action identified pursuant to paragraphs (a)(3) and (5) of this section. The statement should also indicate the extent to which these stated countervailing benefits could be realized by following reasonable alternatives to the proposed action (as identified in paragraph (a)(4) of this section) that would avoid some or all of the adverse environmental effects. In this connection, agencies that prepare cost-benefit analyses of proposed actions should attach such analyses, or summaries thereof, to the environmental impact statement, and should clearly indicate the extent to which environmental costs have not been reflected in such analyses.

(b) In developing the above points agencies should make every effort to convey the required information succinctly in a form easily understood, both by members of the public and by public decisionmakers, giving attention to the substance of the information conveyed rather than to the particular form, or length, or detail of the statement. Each of the above points, for example, need not always occupy a distinct section of the statement if it is otherwise adequately covered in discussing the impact of the proposed action and its alternatives—which items should normally be the focus of the statement. Draft statements should indicate at appropriate points in the text any underlying studies, reports, and other information obtained and considered by the agency in preparing the statement including any cost-benefit analyses prepared by the agency, and reports of consulting agencies under the Fish and Wildlife Coordination Act, 16 U.S.C. 661 et seq., and the National Historic Preservation Act of 1966, 16 U.S.C. 470 et seq., where such consultation has taken place. In the case of documents not likely to be easily accessible (such as internal studies or reports), the agency should indicate how such information may be obtained. If such information is attached to the statement, care should be taken to ensure that the statement remains an essentially self-contained instrument, capable of being understood by the reader without the need for undue cross reference.

(c) Each environmental statement should be prepared in accordance with the precept in section 102(2)(A) of the Act that all agencies of the Federal Government "utilize a systematic, interdisciplinary approach which will insure the integrated use of the natural and social sciences and the environmental design arts in planning and decisionmaking which may have an impact on man's environment." Agencies should attempt to have relevant disciplines represented on their own staffs; where this is not feasible they should make appropriate use of relevant Federal, State, and local agencies or the professional services of universities and outside consultants. The interdisciplinary approach should not be limited to the preparation of the environmental impact statement, but should also be used in the early planning stages of the proposed action. Early application of such an approach should help assure a systematic evaluation of reasonable alternative courses of action and their potential social, economic, and environmental consequences.

(d) Appendix I prescribes the form of the summary sheet which should accompany each draft and final environmental statement.

§ 1500.9 Review of draft environmental statements by Federal, Federal-State, State, and local agencies and by the public.

(a) *Federal agency review.* (1) *In general.* A Federal agency considering an action requiring an environmental statement should consult with, and (on the basis of a draft environmental statement for which the agency takes responsibility) obtain the comment on the environmental impact of the action of Federal and Federal-State agencies with jurisdiction by law or special expertise with respect to any environmental impact involved. These Federal and Federal-State agencies and their relevant areas of expertise include those identified in Appendices II and III to these guidelines. It is recommended that the listed departments and agencies establish contact points, which may be regional offices, for providing comments on the environmental statements. The requirement in section 102(2)(C) to obtain comment from Federal agencies having jurisdiction or special expertise is in addition to any specific statutory obligation of any Federal agency to coordinate or consult with any other Federal or State agency. Agencies should, for example, be alert to consultation requirements of the Fish and Wildlife Coordination Act, 16 U.S.C. 661 et seq., and the National Historic Preservation Act of 1966, 16 U.S.C. 470 et seq. To the extent possible, statements or findings concerning environmental impact required by other statutes, such as section 4(f) of the Department of Transportation Act of 1966, 49 U.S.C. 1653(f), or section 106 of the National Historic Preservation Act of 1966, should be combined with compliance with the environmental impact statement requirements of section 102(2)(C) of the Act to yield a single document which meets all applicable requirements. The Advisory Council on Historic Preservation, the Department of Transportation, and the Department of the Interior, in consultation with the Council, will issue any necessary supplementing instructions for furnishing information or findings not forthcoming under the environmental impact statement process.

(b) *EPA review.* Section 309 of the Clean Air Act, as amended (42 U.S.C. § 1857h–7), provides that the Administrator of the Environmental Protection Agency shall comment in writing on the environmental impact of any matter relating to his duties and responsibilities, and shall refer to the Council any matter that the Administrator determines is unsatisfactory from the standpoint of public health or welfare or environmental quality. Accordingly, wherever an agency action related to air or water quality, noise abatement and control, pesticide regulation, solid waste disposal, generally applicable environmental radiation criteria and standards, or other provision of the authority of the Administrator is involved, Federal agencies are required to submit such proposed actions and their environmental impact statements, if such have been prepared, to the Administrator for review and comment in writing. In all cases where EPA determines that proposed agency action is environmentally unsatisfactory, or where EPA determines that an environmental statement is so inadequate that such a determination cannot be made, EPA shall publish its determination and notify the Council as soon as practicable. The Administrator's comments shall constitute his comments for the purposes of both section 309 of the Clean Air Act and section 102(2)(C) of the National Environmental Policy Act.

(c) State and local review. Office of Management and Budget Circular No. A–95 (Revised) through its system of State and areawide clearinghouses provides a means for securnig the views of

28

State and local environmental agencies, which can assist in the preparation and review of environmental impact statements. Current instructions for obtaining the views of such agencies are contained in the joint OMB–CEQ memorandum attached to these guidelines as Appendix IV. A current listing of clearinghouses is issued periodically by the Office of Management and Budget.

(d) *Public review:* The procedures established by these guidelines are designed to encourage public participation in the impact statement process at the earliest possible time. Agency procedures should make provision for facilitating the comment of public and private organizations and individuals by announcing the availability of draft environmental statements and by making copies available to organizations and individuals that request an opportunity to comment. Agencies should devise methods for publicizing the existence of draft statements, for example, by publication of notices in local newspapers or by maintaining a list of groups, including relevant conservation commissions, known to be interested in the agency's activities and directly notifying such groups of the existence of a draft statement, or sending them a copy, as soon as it has been prepared. A copy of the draft statement should in all cases be sent to any applicant whose project is the subject of the statement. Materials to be made available to the public shall be provided without charge to the extent practicable, or at a fee which is not more than the actual cost of reproducing copies required to be sent to other Federal agencies, including the Council.

(e) *Responsibilities of commenting entities.* (1) Agencies and members of the public submitting comments on proposed actions on the basis of draft environmental statements should endeavor to make their comments as specific, substantive, and factual as possible without undue attention to matters of form in the impact statement. Although the comments need not conform to any particular format, it would assist agencies reviewing comments if the comments were organized in a manner consistent with the structure of the draft statement. Emphasis should be placed on the assessment of the environmental impacts of the proposed action, and the acceptability of those impacts on the quality of the environment, particularly as contrasted with the impacts of reasonable alternatives to the action. Commenting entities may recommend modifications to the proposed action and/or new alternatives

that will enhance environmental quality and avoid or minimize adverse environmental impacts.

(2) Commenting agencies should indicate whether any of their projects not identified in the draft statement are sufficiently advanced in planning and related environmentally to the proposed action so that a discussion of the environmental interrelationships should be included in the final statement (see § 1500.8(a)(1)). The Council is available to assist agencies in making such determinations.

(3) Agencies and members of the public should indicate in their comments the nature of any monitoring of the environmental effects of the proposed project that appears particularly appropriate. Such monitoring may be necessary during the construction, startup, or operation phases of the project. Agencies with special expertise with respect to the environmental impacts involved are encouraged to assist the sponsoring agency in the establishment and operation of appropriate environmental monitoring.

(f) Agencies seeking comment shall establish time limits of not less than forty-five (45) days for reply, after which it may be presumed, unless the agency or party consulted requests a specified extension of time, that the agency or party consulted has no comment to make. Agencies seeking comment should endeavor to comply with requests for extensions of time of up to fifteen (15) days. In determining an appropriate period for comment, agencies should consider the magnitude and complexity of the statement and the extent of citizen interest in the proposed action.

§ 1500.10 **Preparation and circulation of final environmental statements.**

(a) Agencies should make every effort to discover and discuss all major points of view on the environmental effects of the proposed action and its alternatives in the draft statement itself. However, where opposing professional views and responsible opinion have been overlooked in the draft statement and are brought to the agency's attention through the commenting process, the agency should review the environmental effects of the action in light of those views and should make a meaningful reference in the final statement to the existence of any responsible opposing view not adequately discussed in the draft statement, indicating the agency's response to the issues raised. All substantive comments received on the draft (or summaries thereof where response has been exceptionally voluminous) should be attached to the final statement, whether or not each such comment is thought to merit individual discussion by the agency in the text of the statement.

(b) Copies of final statements, with comments attached, shall be sent to all Federal, State, and local agencies and private organizations that made substantive comments on the draft statement and to individuals who requested a copy of the final statement, as well as any applicant whose project is the subject of the statement. Copies of final statements shall in all cases be sent to the Environmental Protection Agency to assist it in carrying out its responsibilities under section 309 of the Clean Air Act. Where the number of comments on a draft statement is such that distribution of the final statement to all commenting entities appears impracticable, the agency shall consult with the Council concerning alternative arrangements for distribution of the statement.

§ 1500.11 Transmittal of statements to the Council; minimum periods for review; requests by the Council.

(a) As soon as they have been prepared, ten (10) copies of draft environmental statements, five (5) copies of all comments made thereon (to be forwarded to the Council by the entity making comment at the time comment is forwarded to the responsible agency), and ten (10) copies of the final text of environmental statements (together with the substance of all comments received by the responsible agency from Federal, State, and local agencies and from private organizations and individuals) shall be supplied to the Council. This will serve to meet the statutory requirement to make environmental statements available to the President. At the same time that copies of draft and final statements are sent to the Council, copies should also be sent to relevant commenting entities as set forth in §§ 1500.9 and 1500.10(b) of these guidelines.

(b) To the maximum extent practicable no administrative action subject to section 102(2) (C) is to be taken sooner than ninety (90) days after a draft environmental statement has been circulated for comment, furnished to the Council and, except where advance public disclosure will result in significantly increased costs of procurement to the Government, made available to the public pursuant to these guidelines; neither should such administrative action be taken sooner than thirty (30) days after the final text of an environmental state-

ment (together with comments) has been made available to the Council, commenting agencies, and the public. In all cases, agencies should allot a sufficient review period for the final statement so as to comply with the statutory requirement that the "statement and the comments and views of appropriate Federal, State, and local agencies * * * accompany the proposal through the existing agency review processes." If the final text of an environmental statement is filed within ninety (90) days after a draft statement has been circulated for comment, furnished to the Council and made public pursuant to this section of these guidelines, the minimum thirty (30) day period and the ninety (90) day period may run concurrently to the extent that they overlap. An agency may at any time supplement or amend a draft or final environmental statement, particularly when substantial changes are made in the proposed action, or significant new information becomes available concerning its environmental aspects. In such cases the agency should consult with the Council with respect to the possible need for or desirability of recirculation of the statement for the appropriate period.

(c) The Council will publish weekly in the FEDERAL REGISTER lists of environmental statements received during the preceding week that are available for public comment. The date of publication of such lists shall be the date from which the minimum periods for review and advance availability of statements shall be calculated.

(d) The Council's publication of notice of the availability of statements is in addition to the agency's responsibility, as described in § 1500.9(d) of these guidelines, to insure the fullest practicable provision of timely public information concerning the existence and availability of environmental statements. The agency responsible for the environmental statement is also responsible for making the statement, the comments received, and any underlying documents available to the public pursuant to the provisions of the Freedom of Information Act (5 U.S.C., 552), without regard to the exclusion of intra- or interagency memoranda when such memoranda transmit comments of Federal agencies on the environmental impact of the proposed action pursuant to § 1500.9 of these guidelines. Agency procedures prepared pursuant to § 1500.3(a) of these guidelines shall implement these public information requirements and shall include arrangements for availability of environmental statements and comments at the head and appropriate regional offices of the responsible agency and at appropriate State and areawide clearinghouses unless the Governor of the State involved designates to the Council some other point for receipt of this information. Notice of such designation of an alternate point for receipt of this information will be included in the Office of Management and Budget listing of clearinghouses referred to in § 1500.9(c).

(e) Where emergency circumstances make it necessary to take an action with significant environmental impact without observing the provisions of these guidelines concerning minimum periods for agency review and advance availability of environmental statements, the Federal agency proposing to take the action should consult with the Council about alternative arrangements. Similarly where there are overriding considerations of expense to the Government or impaired program effectiveness, the responsible agency should consult with the Council concerning appropriate modifications of the minimum periods.

(f) In order to assist the Council in fulfilling its responsibilities under the Act and under Executive Order 11514, all agencies shall (as required by section 102(2)(H) of the Act and section 3(i) of Executive Order 11514) be responsive to requests by the Council for reports and other information dealing with issues arising in connection with the implementation of the Act. In particular, agencies shall be responsive to a request by the Council for the preparation and circulation of an environmental statement, unless the agency determines that such a statement is not required, in which case the agency shall prepare an environmental assessment and a publicly available record briefly setting forth the reasons for its determination. In no case, however, shall the Council's silence or failure to comment or request preparation, modification, or recirculation of an environmental statement or to take other action with respect to an environmental statement be construed as bearing in any way on the question of the legal requirement for or the adequacy of such statement under the Act.

§ 1500.12 Legislative actions.

(a) The Council and the Office of Management and Budget will cooperate in giving guidance as needed to assist agencies in identifying legislative items believed to have environmental significance. Agencies should prepare impact statements prior to submission of their legislative proposals to the Office of Management and Budget. In this regard, agencies should identify types of repetitive legislation requiring environmental impact statements (such as certain types of bills affecting transportation policy or annual construction authorizations).

(b) With respect to recommendations or reports on proposals for legislation to which section 102(2)(C) applies, the final text of the environmental statement and comments thereon should be available to the Congress and to the public for consideration in connection with the proposed legislation or report. In cases where the scheduling of congressional hearings on recommendations or reports on proposals for legislation which the Federal agency has forwarded to the Congress does not allow adequate time for the completion of a final text of an environmental statement (together with comments); a draft environmental statement may be furnished to the Congress and made available to the public pending transmittal of the comments as received and the final text.

§ 1500.13 Application of section 102 (2)(C) procedure to existing projects and programs.

Agencies have an obligation to reassess ongoing projects and programs in order to avoid or minimize adverse environmental effects. The section 102(2)(C) procedure shall be applied to further major Federal actions having a significant effect on the environment even though they arise from projects or programs initiated prior to enactment of the Act on January 1, 1970. While the status of the work and degree of completion may be considered in determining whether to proceed with the project, it is essential that the environmental impacts of proceeding are reassessed pursuant to the Act's policies and procedures and, if the project or program is continued, that further incremental major actions be shaped so as to enhance and restore environmental quality as well as to avoid or minimize adverse environmental consequences. It is also important in further action that account be taken of environmental consequences not fully evaluated at the outset of the project or program.

§ 1500.14 Supplementary guidelines; evaluation of procedures.

(a) The Council after examining environmental statements and agency procedures with respect to such statements will issue such supplements to these guidelines as are necessary.

31

(b) Agencies will continue to assess their experience in the implementation of the section 102(2)(C) provisions of the Act and in conforming with these guidelines and report thereon to the Council by June 30, 1974. Such reports should include an identification of the problem areas and suggestions for revision or clarification of these guidelines to achieve effective coordination of views on environmental aspects (and alternatives, where appropriate) of proposed actions without imposing unproductive administrative procedures. Such reports shall also indicate what progress the agency has made in developing substantive criteria and guidance for making environmental assessments as required by § 1500.6(c) of this directive and by section 102(2)(B) of the Act.

Effective date. The revisions of these guidelines shall apply to all draft and final impact statements filed with the Council after January 28, 1974.

RUSSELL E. TRAIN,
Chairman.

APPENDIX I—SUMMARY TO ACCOMPANY DRAFT AND FINAL STATEMENTS

(Check one) ( ) Draft. ( ) Final Environmental Statement.

Name of responsible Federal agency (with name of operating division where appropriate). Name, address, and telephone number of individual at the agency who can be contacted for additional information about the proposed action or the statement.

1. Name of action (Check one) ( ) Administrative Action. ( ) Legislative Action.
2. Brief description of action and its purpose. Indicate what States (and counties) particularly affected, and what other proposed Federal actions in the area, if any, are discussed in the statement.
3. Summary of environmental impacts and adverse environmental effects.
4. Summary of major alternatives considered.
5. (For draft statements) List all Federal, State, and local agencies and other parties from which comments have been requested. (For final statements) List all Federal, State, and local agencies and other parties from which written comments have been received.
6. Date draft statement (and final environmental statement, if one has been issued) made available to the Council and the public.

APPENDIX II—AREAS OF ENVIRONMENTAL IMPACT AND FEDERAL AGENCIES AND FEDERAL STATE AGENCIES [1] WITH JURISDICTION BY LAW OR SPECIAL EXPERTISE TO COMMENT THEREON [2]

AIR

Air Quality

Department of Agriculture—
Forest Service (effects on vegetation)

Atomic Energy Commission (radioactive substances)
Department of Health, Education, and Welfare
Environmental Protection Agency
Department of the Interior—
Bureau of Mines (fossil and gaseous fuel combustion)
Bureau of Sport Fisheries and Wildlife (effect on wildlife)
Bureau of Outdoor Recreation (effects on recreation)
Bureau of Land Management (public lands)
Bureau of Indian Affairs (Indian lands)
National Aeronautics and Space Administration (remote sensing, aircraft emissions)
Department of Transportation—
Assistant Secretary for Systems Development and Technology (auto emissions)
Coast Guard (vessel emissions)
Federal Aviation Administration (aircraft emissions)

Weather Modification

Department of Agriculture—
Forest Service
Department of Commerce—
National Oceanic and Atmospheric Administration
Department of Defense—
Department of the Air Force
Department of the Interior
Bureau of Reclamation

WATER RESOURCES COUNCIL

WATER

Water Quality

Department of Agriculture—
Soil Conservation Service
Forest Service
Atomic Energy Commission (radioactive substances)
Department of the Interior—
Bureau of Reclamation
Bureau of Land Management (public lands)
Bureau of Indian Affairs (Indian lands)
Bureau of Sports Fisheries and Wildlife
Bureau of Outdoor Recreation
Geological Survey
Office of Saline Water
Environmental Protection Agency
Department of Health, Education, and Welfare

---

[1] River Basin Commissions (Delaware, Great Lakes, Missouri, New England, Ohio, Pacific Northwest, Souris-Red-Rainy, Susquehanna, Upper Mississippi) and similar Federal-State agencies should be consulted on actions affecting the environment of their specific geographic jurisdictions.

[2] In all cases where a proposed action will have significant international environmental effects, the Department of State should be consulted, and should be sent a copy of any draft and final impact statement which covers such action.

Department of Defense—
Army Corps of Engineers
Department of the Navy (ship pollution control)
National Aeronautics and Space Administration (remote sensing)
Department of Transportation—
Coast Guard (oil spills, ship sanitation)
Department of Commerce—
National Oceanic and Atmospheric Administration
Water Resources Council
River Basin Commissions (as geographically appropriate)

Marine Pollution, Commercial Fishery Conservation, and Shellfish Sanitation

Department of Commerce—
National Oceanic and Atmospheric Administration
Department of Defense—
Army Corps of Engineers
Office of the Oceanographer of the Navy
Department of Health, Education, and Welfare
Department of the Interior—
Bureau of Sport Fisheries and Wildlife
Bureau of Outdoor Recreation
Bureau of Land Management (outer continental shelf)
Geological Survey (outer continental shelf)
Department of Transportation—
Coast Guard
Environmental Protection Agency
National Aeronautics and Space Administration (remote sensing)
Water Resources Council
River Basin Commissions (as geographically appropriate)

Waterway Regulation and Stream Modification

Department of Agriculture—
Soil Conservation Service
Department of Defense—
Army Corps of Engineers
Department of the Interior—
Bureau of Reclamation
Bureau of Sport Fisheries and Wildlife
Bureau of Outdoor Recreation
Geological Survey
Department of Transportation—
Coast Guard
Environmental Protection Agency
National Aeronautics and Space Administration (remote sensing)
Water Resources Council
River Basin Commissions (as geographically appropriate)

FISH AND WILDLIFE

Department of Agriculture—
Forest Service
Soil Conservation Service
Department of Commerce—
National Oceanic and Atmospheric Administration (marine species)
Department of the Interior—
Bureau of Sport Fisheries and Wildlife
Bureau of Land Management
Bureau of Outdoor Recreation
Environmental Protection Agency

SOLID WASTE

Atomic Energy Commission (radioactive waste)
Department of Defense—
Army Corps of Engineers
Department of Health, Education, and Welfare
Department of the Interior—
Bureau of Mines (mineral waste, mine acid waste, municipal solid waste, recycling)
Bureau of Land Management (public lands)
Bureau of Indian Affairs (Indian lands)
Geological Survey (geologic and hydrologic effects)
Office of Saline Water (demineralization)
Department of Transportation—
Coast Guard (ship sanitation)
Environmental Protection Agency
River Basin Commissions (as geographically appropriate)
Water Resources Council

NOISE

Department of Commerce—
National Bureau of Standards
Department of Health, Education, and Welfare
Department of Housing and Urban Development (land use and building materials aspects)
Department of Labor—
Occupational Safety and Health Administration
Department of Transportation—
Assistant Secretary for Systems Development and Technology
Federal Aviation Administration, Office of Noise Abatement
Environmental Protection Agency
National Aeronautics and Space Administration

RADIATION

Atomic Energy Commission
Department of Commerce—
National Bureau of Standards
Department of Health, Education, and Welfare
Department of the Interior—
Bureau of Mines (uranium mines)
Mining Enforcement and Safety Administration (uranium mines)
Environmental Protection Agency

HAZARDOUS SUBSTANCES

Toxic Materials

Atomic Energy Commission (radioactive substances)
Department of Agriculture—
Agricultural Research Service
Consumer and Marketing Service
Department of Commerce—
National Oceanic and Atmospheric Administration
Department of Defense
Department of Health, Education, and Welfare
Environmental Protection Agency

Food Additives and Contamination of Foodstuffs

Department of Agriculture—
Consumer and Marketing Service (meat and poultry products)
Department of Health, Education, and Welfare
Environmental Protection Agency

Pesticides

Department of Agriculture—
Agricultural Research Service (biological controls, food and fiber production)
Consumer and Marketing Service
Forest Service
Department of Commerce—
National Oceanic and Atmospheric Administration
Department of Health, Education, and Welfare
Department of the Interior—
Bureau of Sport Fisheries and Wildlife (fish and wildlife effects)
Bureau of Land Management (public lands)
Bureau of Indian Affairs (Indian lands)
Bureau of Reclamation (irrigated lands)
Environmental Protection Agency

Transportation and Handling of Hazardous Materials

Atomic Energy Commission (radioactive substances)
Department of Commerce—
Maritime Administration
National Oceanic and Atmospheric Administration (effects on marine life and the coastal zone)
Department of Defense—
Armed Services Explosive Safety Board
Army Corps of Engineers (navigable waterways)
Department of Transportation—
Federal Highway Administration, Bureau of Motor Carrier Safety
Coast Guard
Federal Railroad Administration
Federal Aviation Administration
Assistant Secretary for Systems Development and Technology
Office of Hazardous Materials
Office of Pipeline Safety
Environmental Protection Agency

ENERGY SUPPLY AND NATURAL RESOURCES DEVELOPMENT

Electric Energy Development, Generation, and Transmission, and Use

Atomic Energy Commission (nuclear)
Department of Agriculture—
Rural Electrification Administration (rural areas)
Department of Defense—
Army Corps of Engineers (hydro)
Department of Health, Education, and Welfare (radiation effects)
Department of Housing and Urban Development (urban areas)
Department of the Interior—
Bureau of Indian Affairs (Indian lands)
Bureau of Land Management (public lands)

Bureau of Reclamation
Power Marketing Administrations
Geological Survey
Bureau of Sport Fisheries and Wildlife
Bureau of Outdoor Recreation
National Park Service
Environmental Protection Agency
Federal Power Commission (hydro, transmission, and supply)
River Basin Commissions (as geographically appropriate)
Tennessee Valley Authority
Water Resources Council

Petroleum Development, Extraction, Refining, Transport, and Use

Department of the Interior—
Office of Oil and Gas
Bureau of Mines
Geological Survey
Bureau of Land Management (public lands and outer continental shelf)
Bureau of Indian Affairs (Indian lands)
Bureau of Sport Fisheries and Wildlife (effects on fish and wildlife)
Bureau of Outdoor Recreation
National Park Service
Department of Transportation (Transport and Pipeline Safety)
Environmental Protection Agency
Interstate Commerce Commission

Natural Gas Development, Production, Transmission, and Use

Department of Housing and Urban Development (urban areas)
Department of the Interior—
Office of Oil and Gas
Geological Survey
Bureau of Mines
Bureau of Land Management (public lands)
Bureau of Indian Affairs (Indian lands)
Bureau of Sport Fisheries and Wildlife
Bureau of Outdoor Recreation
National Park Service
Department of Transportation (transport and safety)
Environmental Protection Agency
Federal Power Commission (production, transmission, and supply)
Interstate Commerce Commission

Coal and Minerals Development, Mining, Conversion, Processing, Transport, and Use

Appalachian Regional Commission
Department of Agriculture—
Forest Service
Department of Commerce
Department of the Interior—
Office of Coal Research
Mining Enforcement and Safety Administration
Bureau of Mines
Geological Survey
Bureau of Indian Affairs (Indian lands)
Bureau of Land Management (public lands)
Bureau of Sport Fisheries and Wildlife
Bureau of Outdoor Recreation
National Park Service

Department of Labor—
  Occupational Safety and Health Administration
Department of Transportation
Environmental Protection Agency
Interstate Commerce Commission
Tennessee Valley Authority

Renewable Resource Development, Production, Management, Harvest, Transport, and Use

Department of Agriculture—
  Forest Service
  Soil Conservation Service
Department of Commerce
Department of Housing and Urban Development (building materials)
Department of the Interior—
  Geological Survey
  Bureau of Land Management (public lands)
  Bureau of Indian Affairs (Indian lands)
  Bureau of Sport Fisheries and Wildlife ·
  Bureau of Outdoor Recreation
  National Park Service
Department of Transportation
Environmental Protection Agency
Interstate Commerce Commission (freight rates)

Energy and Natural Resources Conservation

Department of Agriculture—
  Forest Service
  Soil Conservation Service
Department of Commerce—
  National Bureau of Standards (energy efficiency)
Department of Housing and Urban Development—
  Federal Housing Administration (housing standards)
Department of the Interior—
  Office of Energy Conservation
  Bureau of Mines
  Bureau of Reclamation
  Geological Survey
  Power Marketing Administration
Department of Transportation
Environmental Protection Agency
Federal Power Commission
General Services Administration (design and operation of buildings)
Tennessee Valley Authority

LAND USE AND MANAGEMENT

Land Use Changes, Planning and Regulation of Land Development

Department of Agriculture—
  Forest Service (forest lands)
  Agricultural Research Service (agricultural lands)
Department of Housing and Urban Development
Department of the Interior—
  Office of Land Use and Water Planning
  Bureau of Land Management (public la
  Bureau of Land Management (public lands)
  Bureau of Indian Affairs (Indian lands)
  Bureau of Sport Fisheries and Wildlife (wildlife refuges)

Bureau of Outdoor Recreation (recreation lands)
National Park Service (NPS units)
Department of Transportation
Environmental Protection Agency (pollution effects)
National Aeronautics and Space Administration (remote sensing)
River Basins Commissions (as geographically appropriate).

Public Land Management

Department of Agriculture—
  Forest Service (forests)
Department of Defense
Department of the Interior—
  Bureau of Land Management
  Bureau of Indian Affairs (Indian lands)
  Bureau of Sport Fisheries and Wildlife (wildlife refuges)
  Bureau of Outdoor Recreation (recreation lands)
  National Park Service (NPS units)
Federal Power Commission (project lands)
General Services Administration
National Aeronautics and Space Administration (remote sensing)
Tennessee Valley Authority (project lands)

PROTECTION OF ENVIRONMENTALLY CRITICAL AREAS—FLOODPLAINS, WETLANDS, BEACHES AND DUNES, UNSTABLE SOILS, STEEP SLOPES, AQUIFER RECHARGE AREAS, ETC.

Department of Agriculture—
  Agricultural Stabilization and Conservation Service
  Soil Conservation Service
  Forest Service
Department of Commerce—
  National Oceanic and Atmospheric Administration (coastal areas)
Department of Defense—
  Army Corps of Engineers
Department of Housing and Urban Development (urban and floodplain areas)
Department of the Interior—
  Office of Land Use and Water Planning
  Bureau of Outdoor Recreation
  Bureau of Reclamation
  Bureau of Sport Fisheries and Wildlife
  Bureau of Land Management
  Geological Survey
Environmental Protection Agency (pollution effects)
National Aeronautics and Space Administration (remote sensing)
River Basins Commissions (as geographically appropriate)
Water Resources Council

LAND USE IN COASTAL AREAS

Department of Agriculture—
  Forest Service
  Soil Conservation Service (soil stability, hydrology)
Department of Commerce—
  National Oceanic and Atmospheric Administration (impact on marine life and coastal zone management)
Department of Defense—
  Army Corps of Engineers (beaches, dredg and fill permits, Refuse Act permits)
Department of Housing and Urban Development (urban areas)

Department of the Interior—
Office of Land Use and Water Planning
Bureau of Sport Fisheries and Wildlife
National Park Service
Geological Survey
Bureau of Outdoor Recreation
Bureau of Land Management (public lands)
Department of Transportation—
Coast Guard (bridges, navigation)
Environmental Protection Agency (pollution effects)
National Aeronautics and Space Administration (remote sensing)

REDEVELOPMENT AND CONSTRUCTION IN BUILT-UP AREAS

Department of Commerce—
Economic Development Administration (designated areas)
Department of Housing and Urban Development
Department of the Interior—
Office of Land Use and Water Planning
Department of Transportation
Environmental Protection Agency
General Services Administration
Office of Economic Opportunity

DENSITY AND CONGESTION MITIGATION

Department of Health, Education, and Welfare
Department of Housing and Urban Development
Department of the Interior—
Office of Land Use and Water Planning
Bureau of Outdoor Recreation
Department of Transportation
Environmental Protection Agency

NEIGHBORHOOD CHARACTER AND CONTINUITY

Department of Health, Education, and Welfare
Department of Housing and Urban Development
National Endowment for the Arts
Office of Economic Opportunity

IMPACTS ON LOW-INCOME POPULATIONS

Department of Commerce—
Economic Development Administration (designated areas)
Department of Health, Education, and Welfare
Department of Housing and Urban Development
Office of Economic Opportunity

HISTORIC, ARCHITECTURAL, AND ARCHEOLOGICAL PRESERVATION

Advisory Council on Historic Preservation
Department of Housing and Urban Development
Department of the Interior—
National Park Service
Bureau of Land Management (public lands)
Bureau of Indian Affairs (Indian lands)
General Services Administration
National Endowment for the Arts

SOIL AND PLANT CONSERVATION AND HYDROLOGY

Department of Agriculture—
Soil Conservation Service
Agricultural Service
Forest Service
Department of Commerce—
National Oceanic and Atmospheric Administration
Department of Defense—
Army Corps of Engineers (dredging, aquatic plants)
Department of Health, Education, and Welfare
Department of the Interior—
Bureau of Land Management
Bureau of Sport Fisheries and Wildlife
Geological Survey
Bureau of Reclamation
Environmental Protection Agency
National Aeronautics and Space Administration (remote sensing)
River Basin Commissions (as geographically appropriate)
Water Resources Council

OUTDOOR RECREATION

Department of Agriculture—
Forest Service
Soil Conservation Service
Department of Defense—
Army Corps of Engineers
Department of Housing and Urban Development (urban areas)
Department of the Interior—
Bureau of Land Management
National Park Service
Bureau of Outdoor Recreation
Bureau of Sport Fisheries and Wildlife
Bureau of Indian Affairs
Environmental Protection Agency
National Aeronautics and Space Administration (remote sensing)
River Basin Commissions (as geographically appropriate)
Water Resources Council

APPENDIX III—OFFICES WITHIN FEDERAL AGENCIES AND FEDERAL-STATE AGENCIES FOR INFORMATION REGARDING THE AGENCIES' NEPA ACTIVITIES AND FOR RECEIVING OTHER AGENCIES' IMPACT STATEMENTS FOR WHICH COMMENTS ARE REQUESTED

ADVISORY COUNCIL ON HISTORIC PRESERVATION

Office of Architectural and Environmental Preservation, Advisory Council on Historic Preservation, Suite 430, 1522 K Street, N.W., Washington, D.C. 20005 254–3974

DEPARTMENT OF AGRICULTURE

Office of the Secretary, Attn: Coordinator Environmental Quality Activities, U.S. Department of Agriculture, Washington, D.C. 20250 447–3965

---

[1] Requests for comments or information from individual units of the Department of Agriculture, e.g., Soil Conservation Service, Forest Service, etc. should be sent to the Office of the Secretary, Department of Agriculture, at the address given above.

APPALACHIAN REGIONAL COMMISSION

Office of the Alternate Federal Co-Chairman, Appalachian Regional Commission, 1666 Connecticut Avenue, N.W., Washington, D.C. 20235 967–4103

DEPARTMENT OF THE ARMY (CORPS OF ENGINEERS)

Executive Director of Civil Works, Office of the Chief of Engineers, U.S. Army Corps of Engineers, Washington, D.C. 20314 693–7168

• ATOMIC ENERGY COMMISSION

For nonregulatory matters: Office of Assistant General Manager for Biomedical and Environmental Research and Safety Programs, Atomic Energy Commission, Washington, D.C. 20545 973–3208

For regulatory matters: Office of the Assistant Director for Environmental Projects, Atomic Energy Commission, Washington, D.C. 20545 973–7531

DEPARTMENT OF COMMERCE

Office of the Deputy Assistant Secretary for Environmental Affairs, U.S. Department of Commerce, Washington, D.C. 20230 967–4335

DEPARTMENT OF DEFENSE

Office of the Assistant Secretary for Defense (Health and Environment), U.S. Department of Defense, Room 3E172, The Pentagon, Washington, D.C. 20301 697–2111

DELAWARE RIVER BASIN COMMISSION

Office of the Secretary, Delaware River Basin Commission, Post Office Box 360, Trenton, N.J. 08603 (609) 883–9500

ENVIRONMENTAL PROTECTION AGENCY [2]

Director, Office of Federal Activities, Environmental Protection Agency, 401 M Street, S.W., Washington, D.C. 20460 755–0777

---

[2] Contact the Office of Federal Activities for environmental statements concerning legislation, regulations, national program proposals or other major policy issues.

For all other EPA consultation, contact the Regional Administrator in whose area the

proposed action (e.g., highway or water resource construction projects) will take place. The Regional Administrators will coordinate the EPA review. Addresses of the Regional Administrators, and the areas covered by their regions are as follows:

Regional Administrator, I,
U.S. Environmental Protection Agency
Room 2303, John F. Kennedy
Federal Bldg., Boston, Mass. 02203,
(617) 223–7210

Connecticut, Maine, Massachusetts, New Hampshire, Rhode Island, Vermont

Regional Administrator, II,
U.S. Environmental Protection Agency
Room 908, 26 Federal Plaza
New York, New York 10007
(212) 264–2525

New Jersey, New York, Puerto Rico, Virgin Islands

Regional Administrator, III,
U.S. Environmental Protection Agency
Curtis Bldg., 6th & Walnut Sts.
Philadelphia, Pa. 19106
(215) 597–9801

Delaware, Maryland, Pennsylvania, Virginia, West Virginia, District of Columbia

Regional Administrator, IV,
U.S. Environmental Protection Agency
1421 Peachtree Street
N.E., Atlanta, Ga. 30309
(404) 526–5727

Alabama, Florida, Georgia, Kentucky Mississippi, North Carolina, South Carolina, Tennessee

Regional Administrator V,
U.S. Environmental Protection Agency
1 N. Wacker Drive
Chicago, Illinois 60606
(312) 353–5250

Illinois, Indiana, Michigan, Minnesota, Ohio, Wisconsin

Regional Administrator VI,
U.S. Environmental Protection Agency
1600 Patterson Street
Suite 1100
Dallas, Texas 75201
(214) 749–1962

Arkansas, Louisiana, New Mexico, Texas, Oklahoma

Regional Administrator VII,
U.S. Environmental Protection Agency
1735 Baltimore Avenue
Kansas City, Missouri 64108
(816) 374–5493

Iowa, Kansas, Missouri, Nebraska

Commission's Advisor on Environmental Quality, Federal Power Commission, 825 N. Capitol Street, N.E., Washington, D.C. 20426 386-6084

GENERAL SERVICES ADMINISTRATION

Office of Environmental Affairs, Office of the Deputy Administrator for Special Projects, General Services Administration, Washington, D.C. 20405 343-4161

Office of the Chairman, Great Lakes Basin Commission, 3475 Plymouth Road, P.O. Box 999, Ann Arbor, Michigan 48105 (313) 769-7431

DEPARTMENT OF HEALTH, EDUCATION AND WELFARE [3]

Office of Environmental Affairs, Office of the Assistant Secretary for Administration and Management, Department of Health, Education and Welfare, Washington, D.C. 20202 963-4456

Regional Administrator VIII,
U.S. Environmental Protection Agency
Suite 900, Lincoln Tower
1860 Lincoln Street
Denver, Colorado 80203
(303) 837-3895

Colorado, Montana, North Dakota, South Dakota, Utah, Wyoming

Regional Administrator IX,
U.S. Environmental Protection Agency
100 California Street
San Francisco, California 94111
(415) 556-2320

Arizona, California, Hawaii, Nevada, American Samoa, Guam, Trust Territories of Pacific Islands, Wake Island

Regional Administrator X,
U.S. Environmental Protection Agency
1200 Sixth Avenue
Seattle, Washington 98101
(206) 442-1220

Alaska, Idaho, Oregon, Washington

[3] Contact the Office of Environmental Affairs for information on HEW's environmental statements concerning legislation, regulations, national program proposals or other major policy issues, and for all requests for HEW comment on impact statements of other agencies.

For information with respect to HEW actions occurring within the jurisdiction of the Departments' Regional Directors, contact the appropriate Regional Environmental Officer:

Region I:
    Regional Environmental Officer
    U.S. Department of Health, Education and Welfare
    Room 2007B
    John F. Kennedy Center
    Boston, Massachusetts 02203 (617) 223-6837
Region II:
    Regional Environmental Officer
    U.S. Department of Health, Education and Welfare
    Federal Building
    26 Federal Plaza
    New York, New York 10007 (212) 264-1308
Region III:
    Regional Environmental Officer
    U.S. Department of Health, Education and Welfare
    P.O. Box 13716
    Philadelphia, Pennsylvania 19101 (215) 597-6498
Region IV:
    Regional Environmental Officer
    U.S. Department of Health, Education and Welfare
    Room 404
    50 Seventh Street, N.E.
    Atlanta, Georgia 30323 (404) 526-5817

Region V:
    Regional Environmental Officer
    U.S. Department of Health, Education and Welfare
    Room 712, New Post Office Building
    433 West Van Buren Street
    Chicago, Illinois 60607 (312) 353-1644
Region VI:
    Regional Environmental Officer
    U.S. Department of Health, Education and Welfare
    1114 Commerce Street
    Dallas, Texas 75202 (214) 749-2236
Region VII:
    Regional Environmental Officer
    U.S. Department of Health, Education and Welfare
    601 East 12th Street
    Kansas City, Missouri 64106 (816) 374-3584
Region VIII:
    Regional Environmental Officer
    U.S. Department of Health, Education and Welfare
    9017 Federal Building
    19th and Stout Streets
    Denver, Colorado 80202 (303) 837-4178
Region IX:
    Regional Environmental Officer
    U.S. Department of Health, Education and Welfare
    50 Fulton Street
    San Francisco, California 94102 (415) 556-1970
Region X:
    Regional Environmental Officer
    U.S. Department of Health, Education and Welfare
    Arcade Plaza Building
    1321 Second Street
    Seattle, Washington 98101 (206) 442-0490

DEPARTMENT OF HOUSING AND URBAN DEVELOPMENT [6]

Director, Office of Community and Environmental Standards, Department of Housing and Urban Development, Room 7206, Washington, D.C. 20410
755-5980

DEPARTMENT OF THE INTERIOR [5]

Director, Office of Environmental Project Review, Department of the Interior, Interior Building, Washington, D.C. 20240 343-3891

INTERSTATE COMMERCE COMMISSION

Office of Proceedings, Interstate Commerce, Commission, Washington, D.C. 20423
343-61C

DEPARTMENT OF LABOR

Assistant Secretary for Occupational Safety and Health, Department of Labor, Washington, D.C. 20210
961-3405

MISSOURI RIVER BASINS COMMISSION

Office of the Chairman, Missouri River Basins Commission, 10050 Regency Circle, Omaha, Nebraska 68114
(402) 397-5714

NATIONAL AERONAUTICS AND SPACE ADMINISTRATION

Office of the Comptroller, National Aeronautics and Space Administration, Washington, D.C. 20546
755-8440

NATIONAL CAPITAL PLANNING COMMISSION

Office of Environmental Affairs, Office of the Executive Director, National Capital Planning Commission, Washington, D.C. 20576
382-7200

NATIONAL ENDOWMENT FOR THE ARTS

Office of Architecture and Environmental Arts Program, National Endowment for the Arts, Washington, D.C. 20506
382-5765

NEW ENGLAND RIVER BASINS COMMISSION

Office of the Chairman, New England River Basins Commission, 55 Court Street, Boston, Mass. 02108
(617) 223-6244

OFFICE OF ECONOMIC OPPORTUNITY

Office of the Director, Office of Economic Opportunity, 1200 19th Street, N.W., Washington, D.C. 20506
254-6000

---

[6] Contact the Director with regard to environmental impacts of legislation, policy statements, program regulations and procedures, and precedent-making project decisions. For all other HUD consultation, contact the HUD Regional Administrator in whose jurisdiction the project lies, as follows:

Regional Administrator I,
Environmental Clearance Officer
U.S. Department of Housing and Urban Development
Room 405, John F. Kennedy Federal Building
Boston, Mass. 02203 (617) 223-4066

Regional Administrator II,
Environmental Clearance Officer
U.S. Department of Housing and Urban Development
26 Federal Plaza
New York, New York 10007 (212) 264-8068

Regional Administrator III,
Environmental Clearance Officer
U.S. Department of Housing and Urban Development
Curtis Building, Sixth and Walnut Street
Philadelphia, Pennsylvania 19106 (215) 597-2560

Regional Administrator IV,
Environmental Clearance Officer
U.S. Department of Housing and Urban Development
Peachtree-Seventh Building
Atlanta, Georgia 30323 (404) 526-5585

Regional Administrator V,
Environmental Clearance Officer
U.S. Department of Housing and Urban Development
360 North Michigan Avenue
Chicago, Illinois 60601 (312) 353-5680

Regional Administrator VI,
Environmental Clearance Officer
U.S. Department of Housing and Urban Development
Federal Office Building, 819 Taylor Street
Fort Worth, Texas 76102 (817) 334-2867

Regional Administrator VII,
Environmental Clearance Officer
U.S. Department of Housing and Urban Development
911 Walnut Street
Kansas City, Missouri 64106 (816) 374-2661

Regional Administrator VIII,
Environmental Clearance Officer
U.S. Department of Housing and Urban Development
Samsonite Building, 1051 South Broadway
Denver, Colorado 80209 (303) 837-4061

Regional Administrator IX,
Environmental Clearance Officer
U.S. Department of Housing and Urban Development
450 Golden Gate Avenue, Post Office Box 36003
San Francisco, California 94102 (415) 556-4752

Regional Administrator X,
Environmental Clearance Officer
U.S. Department of Housing and Urban Development
Room 226, Arcade Plaza Building
Seattle, Washington 98101 (206) 583-5415

[5] Requests for comments or information from individual units of the Department of the Interior should be sent to the Office of Environmental Project Review at the address given above.

OHIO RIVER BASIN COMMISSION

Office of the Chairman, Ohio River Basin Commission, 36 East 4th Street, Suite 208–20, Cincinnati, Ohio 45202 (513) 684–3831

PACIFIC NORTHWEST RIVER BASINS COMMISSION

Office of the Chairman, Pacific Northwest River Basins Commission, 1 Columbia River, Vancouver, Washington 98660 (206) 695–3606

SOURIS-RED-RAINY RIVER BASINS COMMISSION

Office of the Chairman, Souris-Red-Rainy River Basins Commission, Suite 6, Professional Building, Holiday Mall, Moorhead, Minnesota 56560 (701) 237–5227

DEPARTMENT OF STATE

Office of the Special Assistant to the Secretary for Environmental Affairs, Department of State, Washington, D.C. 20520 632–7964

SUSQUEHANNA RIVER BASIN COMMISSION

Office of the Executive Director, Susquehanna River Basin Commission, 5012 Lenker Street, Mechanicsburg, Pa. 17055 (717) 737–0501

TENNESSEE VALLEY AUTHORITY

Office of the Director of Environmental Research and Development, Tennessee Valley Authority, 720 Edney Building, Chattanooga, Tennessee 37401 (615) 755–2002

DEPARTMENT OF TRANSPORTATION

Director, Office of Environmental Quality, Office of the Assistant Secretary for Environment, Safety, and Consumer Affairs, Department of Transportation, Washington, D.C. 20590 426–4357

Contact the Office of Environmental Quality, Department of Transportation, for information on DOT's environmental statements concerning legislation, regulations, national program proposals, or other major policy issues.

For information regarding the Department of Transportation's other environmental statements, contact the national office for the appropriate administration:

U.S. Coast Guard

Office of Marine Environment and Systems, U.S. Coast Guard, 400 7th Street, S.W., Washington, D.C. 20590, 426–2007

Federal Aviation Administration

Office of Environmental Quality, Federal Aviation Administration, 800 Independence Avenue, S.W., Washington, D.C. 20591, 426–8406

Federal Highway Administration

Office of Environmental Policy, Federal Highway Administration, 400 7th Street S.W., Washington, D.C. 20590, 426–0351

Federal Railroad Administration

Office of Policy and Plans, Federal Railroad Administration, 400 7th Street, S.W., Washington, D.C. 20590, 426–1567

Urban Mass Transportation Administration

Office of Program Operations, Urban Mass Transportation Administration, 400 7th Street, S.W., Washington, D.C. 20590, 426–4020

For other administration's not listed above, contact the Office of Environmental Quality, Department of Transportation, at the address given above.

For comments on other agencies' environmental statements, contact the appropriate administration's regional office. If more than one administration within the Department of Transportation is to be requested to comment, contact the Secretarial Representative in the appropriate Regional Office for coordination of the Department's comments:

SECRETARIAL REPRESENTATIVE

Region I Secretarial Representative, U.S. Department of Transportation, Transportation Systems Center, 55 Broadway, Cambridge, Massachusetts 02142 (617) 494–2709

Region II Secretarial Representative, U.S. Department of Transportation, 26 Federal Plaza, Room 1811, New York, New York 10007 (212) 264–2672

Region III Secretarial Representative, U.S. Department of Transportation, Mall Building, Suite 1214, 325 Chestnut Street, Philadelphia, Pennsylvania 19106 (215) 597–0407

Region IV Secretarial Representative, U.S. Department of Transportation, Suite 515, 1720 Peachtree Rd., N.W. Atlanta, Georgia 30309 (404) 526–3738

Region V Secretarial Representative, U.S. Department of Transportation, 17th Floor, 300 S. Wacker Drive, Chicago, Illinois 60606 (312) 353–4000

Region V Secretarial Representative, U.S. Department of Transportation, 9–C–18 Federal Center, 1100 Commerce Street, Dallas, Texas 75202 (214) 749–1851

Region VII Secretarial Representative, U.S. Department of Transportation, 601 E. 12th Street, Room 634, Kansas City, Missouri 64106 (816) 374–2761

Region VIII Secretarial Representative, U.S. Department of Transportation, Prudential Plaza, Suite 1822, 1050 17th Street, Denver, Colorado 80225 (303) 837–3242

Region IX Secretarial Representative, U.S. Department of Transportation, 450 Golden Gate Avenue, Box 36133, San Francisco, California 94102 (415) 556–5961

Region X Secretarial Representative, U.S. Department of Transportation, 1321 Second Avenue, Room 507, Seattle, Washington 98101 (206) 442–0590

FEDERAL AVIATION ADMINISTRATION

New England Region, Office of the Regional Director, Federal Aviation Administration, 154 Middlesex Street, Burlington, Massachusetts 01803 (617) 272–2350

Office of Assistant Secretary for Administration, Department of the Treasury, Washington, D.C. 20220 964–5391

UPPER MISSISSIPPI RIVER BASIN COMMISSION

Office of the Chairman, Upper Mississippi River Basin Commission, Federal Office Building, Fort Snelling, Twin Cities, Minnesota 55111 (612) 725–4690

Eastern Region, Office of the Regional Director, Federal Aviation Administration, Federal Building, JFK International Airport, Jamaica, New York 11430 (212) 995–3333

Southern Region, Office of the Regional Director, Federal Aviation Administration, P.O. Box 20636, Atlanta, Georgia 30320 (404) 526–7222

Great Lakes Region, Office of the Regional Director, Federal Aviation Administration, 2300 East Devon, Des Plaines, Illinois 60018 (312) 694–4500

Southwest Region, Office of the Regional Director, Federal Aviation Administration, P.O. Box 1689, Fort Worth, Texas 76101 (817) 624–4911

Central Region, Office of the Regional Director, Federal Aviation Administration, 601 E. 12th Street, Kansas City, Missouri 64106 (816) 374–5626

Rocky Mountain Region, Office of the Regional Director, Federal Aviation Administration, Park Hill Station, P.O. Box 7213, Denver, Colorado 80207 (303) 837–3646

Western Region, Office of the Regional Director, Federal Aviation Administration, P.O. Box 92007, WorldWay Postal Center, Los Angeles, California 90009 (213) 536–6427

Northwest Region, Office of the Regional Director, Federal Aviation Administration, FAA Building, Boeing Field, Seattle, Washington 98108 (206) 767–2780

FEDERAL HIGHWAY ADMINISTRATION

Region 1, Regional Administrator, Federal Highway Administration, 4 Normanskill Boulevard, Delmar, New York 12054 (518) 472–6476

Region 3, Regional Administrator, Federal Highway Administration, Room 1621, George H. Fallon Federal Office Building, 31 Hopkins Plaza, Baltimore, Maryland 21201 (301) 962–2361

Region 4, Regional Administrator, Federal Highway Administration, Suite 200, 1720 Peachtree Road, N.W., Atlanta, Georgia 30309 (404) 526–5078

Region 5, Regional Administrator, Federal Highway Administration, Dixie Highway, Homewood, Illinois 60430 (312) 799–6300

Region 6, Regional Administrator, Federal Highway Administration, 819 Taylor Street, Fort Worth, Texas 76102 (817) 334–3232

Region 7, Regional Administrator, Federal Highway Administration, P.O. Box 7186, Country Club Station, Kansas City, Missouri 64113 (816) 361–7563

Region 8, Regional Administrator, Federal Highway Administration, Room 242, Building 40, Denver Federal Center, Denver. Colorado 80225

Office of the Associate Director, Water Resources Council, 2120 L Street, N.W., Suite 800, Washington, D.C. 20037 254–6442

APPENDIX IV—STATE AND LOCAL AGENCY REVIEW OF IMPACT STATEMENTS

1. OMB Circular No. A–95 through its system of clearinghouses provides a means for securing the views of State and local environ-

Region 9, Regional Administrator, Federal Highway Administration, 450 Golden Gate Avenue, Box 36096, San Francisco, California 94102 (415) 556–3895

Region 10, Regional Administrator, Federal Highway Administration, Room 412, Mohawk Building, 222 S.W. Morrison Street, Portland, Oregon 97204 (503) 221–2065

URBAN MASS TRANSPORTATION ADMINISTRATION

Region I, Office of the UMTA Representative, Urban Mass Transportation Administration, Transportation Systems Center, Technology Building, Room 277, 55 Broadway, Boston, Massachusetts 02142 (617) 494–2055

Region II, Office of the UMTA Representative, Urban Mass Transportation Administration, 26 Federal Plaza, Suite 1809, New York, New York 10007 (212) 264–8162

Region III, Office of the UMTA Representative, Urban Mass Transportation Administration, Mall Building, Suite 1214, 325 Chestnut Street, Philadelphia, Pennsylvania 19106 (215) 597–0407

Region IV, Office of UMTA Representative, Urban Mass Transportation Administration, 1720 Peachtree Road, Northwest, Suite 501, Atlanta, Georgia 30309 (404) 526–3948

Region V, Office of the UMTA Representative, Urban Mass Transportation Administration, 300 South Wacker Drive, Suite 700, Chicago, Illinois 60606 (312) 353–6005

Region VI, Office of the UMTA Represenative, Urban Mass Transportation Administration, Federal Center, Suite 9E24, 1100 Commerce Street, Dallas, Texas 75202 (214) 749–7322

Region VII, Office of the UMTA Representative, Urban Mass Transportation Administration, c/o FAA Management Systems Division, Room 1564D, 601 East 12th Street, Kansas City, Missouri 64106 (816) 374–5567

Region VIII, Office of the UMTA Representative, Urban Mass Transportation Administration, Prudential Plaza, Suite 1822, 1050 17th Street, Denver, Colorado 80202 (303) 837–3242

Region IX, Office of the UMTA Representative, Urban Mass Transportation Administration, 450 Golden Gate Avenue, Box 36125, San Francisco, California 94102 (415) 556–2884

Region X, Office of the UMTA Representative, Urban Mass Transportation Administration, 1321 Second Avenue, Suite 5079, Seattle, Washington (206) 442–0590

mental agencies, which can assist in the preparation of impact statements. Under A-95, review of the proposed project in the case of federally assisted projects (Part I of A-95) generally takes place prior to the preparation of the impact statement. Therefore, comments on the environmental effects of the proposed project that are secured during this stage of the A-95 process represent inputs to the environmental impact statement.

2. In the case of direct Federal development (Part II of A-95), Federal agencies are required to consult with clearinghouses at the earliest practicable time in the planning of the project or activity. Where such consultation occurs prior to completion of the draft impact statement, comments relating to the environmental effects of the proposed action would also represent inputs to the environmental impact statement.

3. In either case, whatever comments are made on environmental effects of proposed Federal or federally assisted projects by clearinghouses, or by State and local environmental agencies through clearinghouses, in the course of the A-95 review should be attached to the draft impact statement when it is circulated for review. Copies of the statement should be sent to the agencies making such comments. Whether those agencies then elect to comment again on the basis of the draft impact statement is a matter to be left to the discretion of the commenting agency depending on its resources, the significance of the project, and the extent to which its earlier comments were considered in preparing the draft statement.

4. The clearinghouses may also be used, by mutual agreement, for securing reviews of the draft environmental impact statement. However, the Federal agency may wish to deal directly with appropriate State or local agencies in the review of impact statements because the clearinghouses may be unwilling or unable to handle this phase of the process. In some cases, the Governor may have designated a specific agency, other than the clearinghouse, for securing reviews of impact statements. In any case, the clearinghouses should be sent copies of the impact statement.

5. To aid clearinghouses in coordinating State and local comments, draft statements should include copies of State and local agency comments made earlier under the A-95 process and should indicate on the summary sheet those other agencies from which comments have been requested, as specified in Appendix I of the CEQ Guidelines.

ENVIRONMENTAL IMPACT STATEMENTS

Gilbert F. White

NO Federal legislation of recent years bears greater potential significance for the management of environment in the United States than does Section 102 of the National Environmental Policy Act of 1969. And no other legislation inspires a more sober recognition of the risk and uncertainty attaching to current efforts to assess the effects of manipulating soil, minerals, water, air, vegetation, transport, and land use. In the tradition of earlier attempts to specify the impacts of human interventions in interacting hydrological, biological, and social systems, the environmental impact statements required by Section 102 confront noble aspiration with seedy and incomplete performance.

Quite aside from the new opportunities provided individual citizens to enter into assessment of projects for environmental change, the preparation of impact statements demands scientific contributions of three sorts, and may stimulate a new kind of interdisciplinary collaboration. A similar, less formal development is taking place on the international scene, but will not be discussed here.

THE ENVIRONMENTAL POLICY ACT OF 1969. The act which was signed into law on January 1, 1970 (P. L. 91-190, 42USCSS 4321-47), set forth certain general aims of Federal activity in the environmental field, established the Council on Environmental Quality, and instructed all Federal agencies to include as part of future reports or recommendations on action significantly affecting the quality of the human environment an impact statement. Section 102(2) (C) defines the impact statement as follows:

Sec. 102. The Congress authorizes and directs that, to the fullest extent possible: (1) the policies, regulations, and public laws of the United States shall be interpreted and administered in accordance with the policies set forth in this Act, and (2) all agencies of the Federal Government shall—

(A) utilize a systematic, interdisciplinary approach which will insure the integrated use of the natural and social sciences and the environmental design arts in planning and in decision-making which may have an impact on man's environment;

(B) identify 'and develop methods and procedures, in consultation with the Council on Environmental Quality established by title II of this Act, which will insure that presently unquantified environmental amenities and values may be given appropriate consideration in decision-making along with economic and technical considerations;

(C) include in every recommendation or report on proposals for legislation and other major Federal actions significantly affecting the quality of the human environment, a detailed statement by the responsible official on—

(i) the environmental impact of the proposed action,

(ii) any adverse environmental effects which cannot be avoided should the proposal be implemented,

(iii) alternatives to the proposed action,

(iv) the relationship between local short-term uses of man's environment and the maintenance and enhancement of long-term productivity, and

(v) any irreversible and irretrievable commitments of resources which would be involved in the proposed action should it be implemented.

Prior to making any detailed statement, the responsible Federal official shall consult with and obtain the comments of any Federal agency which has jurisdiction by law or special expertise with respect to any environmental impact involved. Copies of such statements and the comments and views of the appropriate Federal, State, and local agencies, which are authorized to develop and enforce environmental standards, shall be made available to the President, the Council on Environmental Quality and to the public as provided by section 552 of title 5, United States Code, and shall accompany the proposal through the existing agency review processes;

(D) study, develop, and describe appropriate alternatives to recommended courses of action in any proposal which involves unresolved conflicts concerning alternative uses of available resources;

(E) recognize the worldwide and long-range character of environmental problems and, where consistent with the foreign policy of the United States, lend appropriate support to initiatives, resolutions, and programs designed to maximize international cooperation in anticipating and preventing a decline in the quality of mankind's world environment;

(F) make available to States, counties, municipalities, institutions, and individuals, advice and information useful to restoring, maintaining, and enhancing the quality of the environment;

(G) initiate and utilize ecological information in the planning and development of resource-oriented projects; and

(H) assist the Council on Environmental Quality established by title II of this Act.

PROFESSIONAL GEOGRAPHER, Vol. 35, No. 4, pp. 302-309.

Before submitting a final statement the authorized official is obliged to solicit the comments on a draft statement from other Federal agencies having responsibility or knowledge of any relevant environmental effects, and from any State and local agencies involved in developing and enforcing environmental standards. These comments then become a part of the statement. The final version is submitted to the President, the Council, and the public.

Under authority of Executive Order 11514, interim guidelines for the preparation of statements were published by the Council on May 12, 1970. (1) These left to each individual agency the decision as to how best it could prepare the required statements, but specified that draft statements should be circulated for comment within 45 days. After half a year of experience, the Council consulted with the interested agencies, and issued in January, 1971 a proposed revision of the Guidelines. These were reviewed again, and on April 23, 1971 a new set was published. (2) Under the current guidelines, draft statements, other than legislation, must be available to the public 90 days before initiating action, and the final statement 30 days before action. The two periods can run concurrently.

Although the statement is presented to the President, the Council and the public, no formal action is required from them. Likewise, no comment from reviewing agencies has any effect upon the legal authority of the sponsoring agency to proceed. Strictly speaking, a Federal agency authorized by the Congress to carry out a particular project could prepare a statement, receive unfavorable comments from all reviewers, note these comments in its final report, and go ahead with the project exactly as first proposed. Neither the President nor the Council could stop the project under authority of the National Environmental Policy Act. The President might exercise other executive authorities to do so.

Thus, the effect of the Act is to require the agencies to specify the likely impacts of their proposed projects, to obtain the comments of other interested agencies, to make public their own findings and the comments of others, and to expose themselves to critical review of both findings and method. Enough time is provided for individuals, groups, or agencies opposed to a project to gather their forces quickly and make their views known to whatever Congressional or executive units may have legal responsibility for undertaking the project. It is too early to judge the full consequences of the procedure now being followed: there have been no searching studies published of what is happening, and the process itself is still so new that adjustments are made rapidly as it unfolds. However, some insight into the process may be gained from reviewing two major interpretations of policy and from evidence as to statements submitted and legal action generated.

THE CALVERT CLIFFS DECISION. A crucial aspect of any environmental impact statement is what information in what detail the responsible agency is obliged to submit for review. If this is left solely to the discretion of the agency, important components may be foreclosed from report or discussion. The Atomic Energy Commission's first procedure for preparing statements on nuclear power plants proposed for licensing excluded non-radiological environmental questions, accepted the water quality standards adopted by State regulatory agencies, and permitted hearing boards to omit consideration of environmental factors not identified by staff or other persons.

When a citizen's group contested these rules as applied to the proposed Calvert Cliffs nuclear plant in Maryland, the procedure was overthrown by the United States Court of Appeals for the District of Columbia on July 23, 1971. The court directed the AEC to draw up a revised set of rules which would fully reflect the intent of NEPA. All agencies thereby were put on notice that their procedures were subject to discerning judicial review, and all interested citizens were alerted to the possibility of obtaining remedy from an agency rule which seemed inadequate in terms of the purposes of the Act.

THE AGRICULTURE-ENVIRONMENTAL AND CONSUMER PROTECTION PROGRAMS APPROPRIATIONS FOR FISCAL YEAR 1972. The day preceding the Calvert Cliffs decision, the conference committee for the Agricul-

44

ture-Environmental and Consumer Protection Programs Appropriations bill, Fiscal Year 1972, reported out an amendment which greatly expanded the operations under Section 102(2)(C). *(3)* The Congressional committees had become aware of the fact that unfavorable environmental impact statements might deter action on projects which promised economic benefits to the areas concerned. The basic and deep conflict over social feasibility of environmental manipulation had become apparent.

Out of the discussions came a directive that:

> in addition to the environmental effects of an action, all required reports from departments, agencies, or persons shall also include information, as prepared by the agency having responsibility for administration of the program, project, or activity involved, on the effect on the economy, including employment, unemployment, and other economic impacts.

This provision is a two-edged sword. It requires that description of environmental impacts be accompanied by indications of the related effects upon the economy, and thereby counteracts the rhetorical weight of printing out such impacts without taking account of the gains expected from the project. At the same time, it opens the door to more searching examination of the full economic implications of the projects than might be encompassed by conventional benefit-cost analysis. While champions of environmental quality now are obliged to consider the economic justification for the projects under review, they also are given an opportunity to appraise the economic consequences in a new framework. In this connection, it should be recalled that the Section 102 type of statement builds upon the experience of 35 years with Federal review of water management projects.

THIRTY-FIVE YEARS OF WATER RESOURCES PROJECT REVIEW. Perhaps the first substantial attempt to promote a statement of prospective environmental impact for Federal projects occurred in 1936 when, in response to a report from the Subcommittee on Drainage Problems and Programs of the Natural Resources Committee, President Roosevelt required all Federal agencies involved in land drainage and water storage projects to report impending programs to the Committee. *(4)* Agencies were to be informed in advance of prospective work and given an opportunity to make critical comments to the construction agency. The new scheme was intended to avoid the kind of difficulty that had arisen when water storage projects were undertaken without consideration of public health or fishery aspects or when land drainage was financed from Federal sources without considering the likely effects on wildlife propagation. The 1936 executive memorandum brought conflicts over water projects into the open but at a stage when they were so near initiation that it usually was too late to induce a significant change in plans.

To cope with that situation, steps were taken to provide for review before projects reached the stage of authorization or appropriation of funds. Executive Order 9384 in 1940 required all Federal agencies to submit to the Executive Office of the President a copy of any proposed report on water resource and land improvement projects in advance of transmittal to Congress. The report then was circulated to interested Federal agencies and in the light of those comments, a statement was attached as to whether or not the proposal was in accord with the program of the President. The effort here was to encourage agencies to consider and review proposals by others in advance of being brought into the Congressional arena. The operations of that Executive Order inevitably were hindered by the difficulty which agencies had in preparing comments. Unless they had time and personnel for study of the project in question they could not give careful reviews. If they entered the scene when the originating agency had spent years in reaching its conclusions they could not readily catch up in suggesting different judgments. The review of proposed reports was a helpful step, but led to more explicit arrangements for collaboration in the survey work. A series of authorizing acts and Federal inter-agency committees beginning in 1943 made provision for interested agencies to join in the actual surveys long before completed reports were circulated for review.

These procedures were enforced and extended by the operations of the Water Resource Council created under the Water Planning Act of 1965. There, the arrangements for consultation among Federal agencies and state agencies were developed, and interstate river basin commissions were authorized. Earlier, a most energetic attempt to consider the full social and environmental impacts of a major project had been made by the Bureau of Reclamation under the leadership of a geographer, Harland H. Barrows, in the 1940's after the start of construction of the Grand Coulee project in the Columbia Basin. This was the first time that a coordinated set of investigations by Federal, State, and local agencies concerned with the impacts of a major project had been initiated. Centering on 27 separate problems and bringing to bear the resources of all the interested Federal and State agencies, the Columbia Basin joint investigations became the basis for planning auxiliary activities associated with the Grand Coulee Dam. *(5)* But this venture, however imaginative, was not replicated in subsequent Federal water resources works and more than 20 years passed before serious attention again was given to initiating such analysis at the inception of project studies.

All of these efforts at coordination of diverse interests before an environmental change was initiated were focused on water and related land projects. Water management has been a step ahead of land, mineral, and transport management in terms of institutional provisions for coordination and of definition of standards for evaluation. Yet, when NEPA was enacted water projects were included with all other types of environmental change, and they subsequently drew as much unfavorable appraisal as any other type of project.

LESSONS FROM WATER PROJECT REVIEW. The experience with coordinated review of water projects may have at least two lessons for those who participate in preparing or reviewing Section 102 statements. The first is that within a few years after the Federal and State agencies became deeply involved in critical review of each other's projects they worked out accommodations that obscured or submerged the major points of difference among them. The Department of Agriculture stopped laboring the surplus crop aspects of Bureau of Reclamation projects to bring new land under cultivation. The Soil Conservation Service and the Corps of Engineers divided upstream-downstream sections of drainage

basins between them and rarely objected to what the other was doing. Organizations within the Federal structure strive to reduce conflict situations and work out agreements and coalitions—some tacit and some formal—to avoid open confrontation. It seems likely that similar forms of accommodation are taking shape under the Section 102 procedures and that the newer agencies, such as the Environmental Protection Agency, are slower to forge such understandings.

The second lesson from the water review experience is that when agencies were expected to offer evaluations of impacts for which it was difficult or immediately impossible to offer precise measurement they tended to fasten onto simplified and generalized methods. Thus, when faced with the need to assign values to the recreational use of a new reservoir they adopted a universal figure for the dollar value of one user-day and were slow to apply more sophisticated measures. As soon as agreement has been reached on a valuation measure or a method of analysis there is strong resistance to retain it. To the extent that a somewhat similar process is at work in the review of environmental impact statements we may expect that the methods now being developed and tried will settle before long into a conventional mode.

THE FIRST TWO YEARS OF NEPA. Very little is known about the coalitions and accommodations that are taking shape. More is known about the methods being tried. A good deal of precise information is available as to types of projects, the agencies submitting statements, the length of the statements, and the judicial actions growing out of them.

As of June 1, 1972 the Council had received 2933 statements of which 1552 were final statements. These were prepared by 30 Federal agencies, with 73 percent coming from two agencies, the Department of Transportation and the Army Corps of Engineers. An additional 10 percent of the reports were filed by the Department of Agriculture, the Department of the Interior, and the Atomic Energy Commission. Using the classification made by the Council, 49 percent of the reports deal with roads (including roads through parks), 14 percent with watershed protection and flood control, 8 percent with airports, 6 percent with navigation, and 5 percent with power generation of all types.

Brief descriptions of final statements and draft statements are reported in the *102 Monitor.* (6)

The length of the usual statement runs from 10 to 60 pages. Some cover several hundred pages, including the comments from reviewing agencies. The Alaska Pipeline statement, with its six volumes, probably holds the record for length in recent months.

The consequences of the environmental impact system are still impossible to assess with care; the time is too short, the evidence is skimpy, and the institutional adjustments are changing too rapidly. There is some reason to doubt that it can be maintained for long without drastic overhauling. It conceivably could continue in its present mode; it could continue with major shifts in procedures and interpretations; it could be frozen by a moratorium; and it could undergo legislative revision. Whatever happens, the next few years are likely to be a time of hardening or change that will shape the course of events for a long time to come.

ACTION IN THE COURTS. Because NEPA required statements on specified topics it provided a basis upon which any citizen or group could seek judicial action to require a statement where one had not been prepared or to review a statement believed to fail to meet prescribed standards. Thereby, a new era in judicial management of environmental activities in the United States was opened. No longer was it necessary for a party to show injury in order to seek remedy in the courts: any alleged violation of NEPA became grounds for stopping a project until the regulations had been met. (7)

By the end of 1971 more than 47 separate actions had been taken in U.S. district courts or appeals courts to restrain Federal agencies in some fashion. Most of these cases related to failure to file 102 statements for projects which the agencies regarded as not qualifying because they were already under construction or else did not have significant impacts. (8) The question of whether or not industries which were issued permits by the Corps of Engineers to discharge waste under the Refuse Disposal Act are obliged to submit impact statements is moot.

The integrity of research related to environmental impact statements is threatened by two unique features of the current wave of advocacy. One is the strong temptation, enforced by the level of enthusiasm for environmental action shared by many in the academic fraternity, to emphasize investigations that will support pending or prospective advocacy of positions against development. A second is the expectation that much action on the statements will take place in the public arena. To that extent, there will be temptation for investigators to choose topics, select materials, and present findings with an eye to the rhetorical demands of the forum.

However, these influences need not warp the quality of the ensuing research. They can heighten the investigator's concern to select topics that are of pressing social significance, to collaborate with people involved, and to present findings in usable form. As with most risks, the special pressures attendant upon public agitation carry the possibility of both gain and detriment.

THE PERFECT STATEMENT. It should be clear to all who study environmental systems that there can be no fully satisfactory statement complying with the instructions in Section 102. The perfect statement requires two elements inevitably lacking:

1) A complete description of the likely biological, physical and economic impacts of the proposed work, and

2) A complete description of the impacts of all practicable alternatives to the proposed work.

The first is unattainable at this time because we lack knowledge of important parts of most of the systems which would be disturbed. We understand certain processes, such as the effect of a dam upon sediment storage in the reservoir, sufficiently well to be able to predict that impact. We can predict certain events without fully understanding all the processes involved, as with the effect of thermal pollution on fresh water organisms. For a far greater number of phenomena neither understanding nor predictive skill is sufficiently strong to permit confident forecasts of what will happen.

Any impact statement is hedged explicitly or implicitly by reservations and doubts. The law expects compliance only with what is reasonable, and so the preparation of a statement becomes a matter of scientific judgment as to what degree of confidence or doubt is reasonable in the current state of knowledge. In the absence of rigorous review, the impact statement could become a new genre of scientific fiction that would submerge bureaucratic decisions in an avalanche of obfuscating paper.

The description of all practicable alternatives is no less complicated. In recent years there have been frequent appeals for canvassing the full range of possible actions to meet agreed social goals, particularly in the case of water management. (9) There are few precedents for such analysis: it goes against the grain of most agency structures and it usually involves working across disciplinary boundaries. The prevailing mood of the "quick technological fix" discourages exploration of alternatives. If water pollution threatens, the tendency is to concentrate on diluting the waste or on treating the waste; agencies are less likely to consider ways of preventing the waste. The same kind of bias is rampant in meeting housing needs, health care and urban transport. We experiment with analytical methods permitting genuine comparisons of alternatives.

Were it practicable to quantify all of the impacts of all the alternatives, a third deficiency would prevent us from producing a perfect impact statement. This is the difficulty of attaching weights to the numerous impacts in order to permit social evaluation. Such evaluation requires agreement on social aims and on the value system to be used in assessing the effects of a given action in achieving those aims. A great deal of the sense of crisis and controversy associated with environmental matters during the past decade are related to differences in value systems: when a community group contests an interstate highway it may be challenging most of all the values placed on rapid movement by higher income users.

These three difficulties are apparent whenever environmental studies are undertaken. The Section 102 procedures now encourage an explicit statement as how near or how far the agency is from reasonable answers. In dealing with them scientists can approach the impact statement as concerned citizens or can adopt either or both of two professional stances. They can make professional research contributions, and, as teachers, can affect the grounds for citizen judgment and responsibility.

THE SCIENTIST AS CITIZEN. Regardless of his professional competence, the scientist may feel an obligation to ask the same questions about an environmental impact statement as might any concerned citizen. These include: Are all significant impacts noted? Are the impacts described accurately and thoroughly? Are they assigned suitable social values? From a critical reading of the impact statement against whatever background knowledge he may possess the citizen may reasonably offer judgments as to the adequacy of the statement, needed professional advice and desirable public or judicial action.

PROFESSIONAL CONTRIBUTIONS. There are at least three ways in which geographic modes of thought may be expected to strengthen environmental impact statements.

1. The most obvious contribution is in *research which specifies process or relationships within a natural or social system affected by a project*. In this sense, any investigation yielding such findings provides grist for the mill of those who prepare the statements. The relation of timber-cutting practices to wildlife patterns, the relation of highway location to cultural diffusion; any such findings are of basic significance. They are part of the research enterprise, and the special obligation attaching to them is to see that they get into the hands of the agencies which should use them. However, it may be expected that as scientists become more aware of the deficiencies in present knowledge of certain aspects of systems affected they will divert more effort in those directions. Public review of impact statements may point out embarrassing gaps and suggest new research priorities.

An immediate need is for systematic project postaudits. One of the remarkable aspects of natural resource management is that immense stocks of money and time are expended upon preparation of plans while pitifully small amounts are spent on finding what actually happened after the plans were adopted. A principal reason for this is that the processes involved are so poorly understood and the methodology for such studies is so weak that solid conclusions are hard to come by. Efforts in that direction may nevertheless be highly rewarding when new projects are proposed. (10)

2. Inasmuch as the *methods of preparing formal impact statements* are still taking shape, it is especially important to give critical attention to them. It would be comforting if we could point to exemplary regional geographic studies as yielding all that is needed in intelligible form. We cannot do so because they generally lack precision and systematic scope in identifying impacts.

As already noted, the ideal statement would describe each perturbation in each system affected. The International Biological Program biome studies are the first genuinely comprehensive attempts to do so. A recent canvass of a highly restricted ecosystem under severe human modification—man-made lakes—reveals how complicated this can be. (11) It is not yet practicable to trace out all the impacts of a new reservoir on atmospheric, biological, and social systems, and, lacking these, the investigator may be content with reporting the gaps. Attempts may be made to predict effects through regression and similar techniques. Another method is to draw up matrices of actions and anticipated effects, assigning qualitative or roughly quantitative measures to each.

Experiments with the latter device have yielded some of the more interesting methodologies in recent months. (12) An interdisciplinary review of the Ames Reservoir on the Skunk River in Iowa, using a matrix framework, is underway by scientists at Iowa State University, the University of Iowa and the State Water Resources Institute. There is a rapidly growing literature on problems of technological assessment, and much of this touches on environmental effects. (13) Geographers are involved in estimating highway impacts, the impacts of power generation, and a variety of other projects. We should regard these studies as beginnings rather than ends, and seek to improve them or to devise less faulty alternatives.

3. A third type of contribution has to do with *methods of placing social valuations on those impacts that are identified and measured.* Frequently the descriptive analysis is mixed up with evaluation and this is to be expected, but the processes are different. It is possible to measure a change in soil productivity or lung cancer morbidity or the time consumed in the journey to work. Assigning social value to these quantities for purposes of comparison and choice is especially troublesome.

Beyond the more conventional forms of benefit-cost analysis and cost-effectiveness appraisal lie other opportunities for social accounting. These include efforts to assess group responses to threats to the habitat or sense of well-being, and to measure preferences in risk-taking. Honest investigators recognize that there are many impacts about which they are largely ignorant, and that responsible citizens and administrators must act for or against a project in the face of uncertainty. How do they weigh that uncertainty?

All of these contributions inevitably involve multidisciplinary analysis, whether by one individual correlating his work with that of others, or by teams of workers. To use teams in a genuinely constructive and creative fashion is itself an extremely trying task, and calls for further social invention. However, it has the compensation of exposing each discipline's findings to the critical appraisal of workers from neighboring fields.

Other types of contributions may be imagined. What is important here is to recognize that the initiation of a system of environmental impact statements has placed a more explicit and searching demand upon scientific analysis of environmental management than generally has prevailed in the past. New administrative, citizen, judicial, and scientific responses are taking shape. If experience with water management teaches us about the social processes at work, the next few years are likely to see a revision and hardening of procedures and investigative methods for dealing with proposed manipulations of environment.

(1) 35 Federal Register 7391–7393.

(2) 36 Federal Register 7724–7729.

(3) U.S. Congress, 92nd, 1st Session, House of Representatives, *Report No. 92–376* (July 22, 1971).

(4) U.S. National Resources Committee, Special Subcommittee of the Water Resources Committee, *Drainage Policy and Projects* (Washington, D. C.: U.S. Government Printing Office, 1936).

(5) U.S. Bureau of Reclamation, *Columbia Basin Joint Investigations,* separate volumes (Washington, D. C.: U.S. Government Printing Office, 1942–1945).

(6) Copies of the draft and final impact statements may be inspected at the document rooms of the originating agencies. They may be purchased from the National Technical Information Service, U.S. Department of Commerce, Springfield, Virginia 22151 (paper copies sell for $3.00 per statement, unless exceeding 300 pages in length, in which case $6.00; microfiche sells for $0.95) and from the Environment Law Institute, 1346 Connecticut Avenue, N. W., Washington, D. C. 20036 (paper copies designated by an ELR order sell for $0.10 per page). The *102 Monitor* lists all statements with NTIS and ELR numbers, and may be ordered from the U.S. Government Printing Office for an annual subscription of $6.00.

(7) Joseph L. Sax, *Defending the Environment* (New York: Alfred Knopf, 1970).

(8) *102 Monitor,* Vol. 1, No. 12 (1972).

(9) National Academy of Sciences—National Research Council, Committee on Water, *Alternatives in Water Management,* NAS-NRC Publication 1408 (Washington, D. C.: U.S. Government Printing Office, 1966), and National Academy of Sciences—National Research Council, Committee on Water, *Water and Choice in the Colorado Basin,* NAS-NRC Publication 1689 (Washington, D. C.: U.S. Government Printing Office, 1968).

(10) George Macinko, "The Columbia Basin Project: Expectation, Realization, Implications," *Geographical Review,* Vol. 53 (1963), pp. 185–199, and John Chadwick Day, *Managing the Lower Rio Grande: An Experience in International River Development,* University of Chicago, Department of Geography Research Paper No. 125 (1970).

(11) Scientific Committee on Problems of the Environment, *Man-Made Lakes as Modified Ecosystems* (Rome: International Council of Scientific Unions, 1972).

(12) Luna Leopold et al., *A Procedure for Evaluating Environmental Impact,* U.S. Geological Survey Circular 645 (Washington, D. C.: U.S. Government Printing Office, 1971); Ira L. Whitman et al., *Final Report on Design of an Environmental Evaluation System to the Bureau of Reclamation* (Columbus: Battelle, 1971); and Institute for Technology and Society, *Proceedings of the Symposium on Environmental Assessment of Resources Development* (Sacramento: Sacramento State College, 1971).

(13) National Academy of Engineering, *A Study of Technology Assessment,* Report of the Committee on Public Engineering Policy (Washington: NAE, 1969), and Mitre Corporation, *A Technology Assessment Methodology,* Five Volumes (Washington: The Mitre Corporation, 1971).

National Environmental Policy Act: How Well Is It Working?

—ROBERT GILLETTE

In a moment of jubilation, shortly after Congress passed the National Environmental Policy Act (NEPA), which he coauthored in 1969, Senator Henry M. Jackson acclaimed the new law as the "most important and far-reaching conservation measure ever enacted." It will be some time, of course, before anyone can fairly judge whether the law actually has lived up to Senator Jackson's description. But at the 2-year mark, NEPA has clearly established itself as one of the most controversial environmental measures of all time—one whose repercussions have rattled virtually every department and bureau of the federal government in a remarkably short time.

The law has two major features. One establishes the President's three-man Council on Environmental Quality (CEQ), which is partly responsible for encouraging the government to comply with NEPA and partly for advising the President on environmental affairs. The other feature is a broad statement of policy to the effect that government should seek to enhance the environment "by all practical means" consistent with other national policies, and that every citizen should help. What lends muscle to the lofty intentions of NEPA is an "action-forcing" provision that requires government administrators to prepare detailed statements of the environmental effects of any major action they propose, and to study all practical alternatives.

This "action" proviso is at the focal point of the controversy over NEPA and has led to efforts by some agencies to seek legislative exemptions from the law. These efforts, and the court rulings that led to them, were described in an article last week; this article deals with NEPA's more pervasive day-to-day effects on the government.

Is NEPA, in fact, producing useful results? The law's success, to a great extent, is in the eye of the beholder. Unquestionably, the law has given both community and national environmental groups a substantial new access to the courts, and, in turn, their litigation has given NEPA a forceful clout that it might never have had otherwise. The most visible offspring of this symbiotic union has been a series of federal court rulings that have dealt some stunning setbacks to major programs of the Atomic Energy Commission (AEC), the Department of the Interior, and even the Environmental Protection Agency —all of which inspires one environmental lawyer in Washington to call NEPA "the great equalizer."

Like the pistol of the same name, NEPA has also engendered a certain

SCIENCE, April, 1972, Vol. 176, pp. 146-148.

51

amount of ill-will, particularly among congressmen from districts where public works have been held up for court-ordered environmental reviews, as well as among a growing number of government administrators whose programs have been paralyzed by similar court rulings. Several observers of the new law's evolution detect a strong undercurrent of resentment toward NEPA among such mid-level officials, who often seem to regard it as less of an instrument of enforcement than as a weapon of malicious harassment.

So far, the highest government official to say so publicly is John A. Carver, Jr., a Democratic appointee to the Federal Power Commission (FPC). In a recent speech to a petroleum industry group, Carver said that "NEPA has minimal impact in any substantive way," and that, while it may be a laudable expression of policy, "its sole observable function has been that of furnishing a weapon of delay to those who would use it for that purpose."

Carver's remarks, however, obscure the fact that judicial rulings and consequent delays of pipelines, power plants, and dams have been based on what the courts found to be cursory, slanted, or otherwise inadequate environmental impact statements. Delays and the agencies' reactions to them also have tended to obscure a number of less sensational but nonetheless positive side effects of NEPA which—in the long run—may prove to be a more accurate and lasting measure of the law's worth than delays imposed by litigation.

The law and its requirement of impact statements has forced, perhaps not obviously, nearly every agency—over 40 in all—to conduct a sometimes agonizing reappraisal of the way it performs its business and the way its business affects the environment. As a direct result of NEPA, the federal government this year will spend thousands of man-hours and perhaps $20 million that it never spent before to anticipate the adverse effects of pest-control programs, military installations, highways, and numerous other major and minor public works worth billions of dollars.

All this activity has imposed an unfamiliar burden of introspection and public exposure on federal agencies, in addition to masses of new paperwork and considerable overtime labor. This process has also produced an unprecedented flood of information about the environmental effects of government activities and their underlying rationale.

Among others, Russell E. Train, the chairman of the CEQ, believes that NEPA has opened some important cracks in executive secrecy in that it forces government administrators to articulate the reasoning behind their activities—and to solicit and respond to comments from both the public and other agencies—before taking any major action.

Still, there is no clear evidence that government officials are using this new information to a significant extent in their day-to-day decisions. It would be excessive to say that thousands of impact statements are piling up uselessly on the desks of obdurate bureaucrats; one can in fact find instances in which NEPA studies have prompted changes in a project, not the least of which is the trans-Alaska pipeline. But, on the other hand, such examples are hard to come by, and those that do exist are often complicated by overtones of judicial duress or the threat of it. It is important to note at his point that nothing in the law gives anyone veto power over any project or decision; nor is there any language which says explicitly that an agency must *use* an impact statement once it has gone to the trouble of writing one. Environmental groups hope the courts will eventually make that interpretation of the law, but so far the courts have not.

On balance, it seems as if federal agencies are still much more intent on meeting the letter of the law than on voluntarily adopting its spirit. As Robert Cahn, a member of the CEQ, puts it, "NEPA has been a very effective tool for arousing and informing the public, but it is not yet an effective tool in the decision-making process. . . . Perhaps it's too much to expect this kind of revolutionary measure to work as fast as we'd hoped, and for agencies to cancel or modify projects as a result of it this soon."

In the past 2 years, more than 4000 environmental impact statements have poured into the CEQ's small quarters near the White House. Six employees screen them for poorly done or otherwise remarkable statements, although the CEQ tries to avoid commenting on them individually; that is the job of the various agencies and it is the council's intent to make the process as self-operable as possible.

The volume of statements is deceiving in a way, since roughly half of them are brief and rather perfunctory documents concerning small highway projects and new airport construction financed through the Department of Transportation. (DOT is the leader in numbers but not quality. The Department of Housing and Urban Development and the FPC also rank near the bottom of the quality scale. Although impact statements are generally improving in sophistication and thoroughness, many, CEQ sources say, still amount to little more than post facto justifications of decisions already made.)

Each month's accumulation of statements is listed and summarized in a publication from the CEQ, the *102 Monitor,* named after section 102 of NEPA which requires them. The latest selection begins with a 48-page discussion from the Department of Agriculture on its annual fire ant spraying program and ends with a 13-page document from the DOT concerning the repaving of 4.4 miles of roadway in Lafayette County, Wisconsin. Although most of the 200 statements in between run no more than 100 pages, there are exceptions: The final impact statement on the trans-Alaska pipeline, released late last month, fills nine volumes and weighs 18 pounds. Interior Secretary Rogers C. B. Morton describes this weighty compilation as the most thorough examination of environmental effects that "any work of man has ever had." In any case it is one of the longest and, from all appearances, a great improvement over the first try— a 200-page paper so poor that even the Army Corps of Engineers found itself complaining about it last year.

As might be expected, such a massive new occupation as the writing of impact statements has brought with it some difficult learning experiences and even some organizational changes in a number of departments and bureaus. Each of more than 40 agencies has had to compose complex guidelines for writing its statements, and then has had to train hundreds of professional and clerical employees to use the guidelines. Some agencies, like the AEC, have had to start from scratch a second time, after a federal court ruling, in effect, invalidated the first set.

Throughout the Executive Branch the advent of NEPA has also fostered the appearance of new offices of environmental affairs and improved the fortunes of old ones, as agency heads have come to recognize that a deftly written impact statement can make all the difference between smooth sailing for a program and complete paralysis. Now, hardly a federal agency is without an environmental office, and those that lack one have not escaped NEPA's grasp entirely. The Securities and Exchange Commission, for example, requires corporate stock prospectuses to disclose a company's expenditures for meeting pollution control regulations and to own up to environmental lawsuits hanging over it.

Rough estimates of what complying with NEPA has cost the government in manpower and dollars are impressive but nonetheless small compared with overall budgets and employment. The AEC, for example, has 200 employees doing nothing but writing its own impact statements and reviewing scores of them from other agencies. (Any given statement generates anywhere from 5 to 35 sets of comments from sister agencies.) Atomic Energy Commission chairman James R. Schlesinger estimates that this effort will cost the commission about $6 million in fiscal 1973, or less than 1 percent of the AEC budget.

The Agriculture Department estimates that impact studies and statements for the Forest Service, pesticide programs, flood-control projects, and a wide assortment of other projects will cost $2 million this year. The Interior Department predicts an outlay of $8 million and the diversion of 400 to 600 man-years to NEPA activities. An added expense for the Interior Department is a new computer system to keep track of hundreds of NEPA documents circulating through its Washington headquarters and field offices scattered across the country.

There is a widespread feeling in Washington, and not just among environmentalists, that all this prodigious labor must have had a salutory effect on the federal bureaucracy, that it has been or will be something of a consciousness-raising experience. As Russell Train told a recent Senate hearing, the result of the mandatory analyses and the interagency consultations "can only be more informed decision-making." Despite some complaints about the assiduousness with which the courts have been enforcing NEPA, Interior Secretary Morton and AEC Chairman Schlesinger have voiced similar thoughts. Roger Cramton, the chairman of an obscure but elite group called the Administrative Conference of the United States, an efficiency-promoting arm of the Executive Branch, predicts that the initial anger and resentment that mid-level bureaucrats have felt toward NEPA will give way to "an institutional viewpoint more sympathetic to environmental, as opposed to purely programmatic, values."

"Admittedly this is largely a prediction rather than an accomplished fact," Cramton adds; and he goes on to warn that it's entirely possible that NEPA may give rise to a new form of "bureaucratic gamesmanship," in which an agency's expertise is used to shape impact reports to fit preconceived decisions rather than the other way around. Representative John Dingell (D–Mich.) the other coauthor of NEPA, worries about this possibility too. The law's requirements, he said in a recent speech, are often complied with grudgingly, "behind a facade of false enthusiasm," and a risk exists that the law may do no more than spawn a race of adept memo artists "totally lacking in vision and concerned only with robotlike compliance. . . :"

Such fears are not without substance. In actuality, the main objective of most agencies appears to be one of writing defensible impact statements while minimizing changes and consequent delays in their work—most of which was under way when NEPA became law.

There is some feeling at the CEQ that the machinery for producing NEPA reports, while becoming larger and more adept, has not begun to mesh satisfactorily with the machinery for making decisions. Added support for this view comes from an investigation by the Government Accounting Office of seven agencies' activities under NEPA. The study, made at Representative Dingell's request, has concentrated almost exclusively on procedural details for preparing statements, but some of the GAO investigators nevertheless came away with the personal impression that the law's identifiable effects on agency decisions have been less than monumental. "NEPA is more than just a papermill," one GAO man said, "but one concern is that impact studies are not being done soon enough to really affect the decision process. Agencies tend to wait until after it's decided that a power plant or a highway is needed, and after the site is selected, before thinking about the impact."

The CEQ has tried to compile a list of exemplary accomplishments under NEPA, but so far the list is conspicuously short. For one, the CEQ justifiably credits itself with convincing President Nixon to kill the Cross-Florida barge canal, and after all, NEPA created the council, which the President initially had thought unnecessary. As another example, the Interior Department says that NEPA studies have led it to tighten design requirements for the trans-Alaska pipeline, and that if the line is built it will be less detrimental to the Alaskan tundra than it might have been before.

Further inquiries reveal some evidence that NEPA has forced federal highway authorities to pay more attention to known prehistoric Indian sites rather than blithely paving them over because they were not officially listed in the Federal Register. The Interior Department's Bureau of Reclamation can also proudly claim that it will dig a borrow pit for gravel behind a small earthen dam in southeastern Idaho as a result of NEPA studies, rather than in front, where the pit would remain as a visible scar on the landscape for decades. (This has by no means become standard practice, however. Nor has the need for the dam itself been seriously questioned.) Further, in the Department of Agriculture, the annual acreage to be sprayed for gypsy moths this year has been sharply reduced, partly, but only partly, as a result of reappraisals forced by NEPA.

This is a very hard thing to document," Train concludes. The problem, he explains, is that one never hears about the decisions that aren't made or about projects that were modified early in the game as a result of NEPA studies. Precisely why is unclear. It may be that government administrators are reluctant to admit where they had gone astray and that a nettlesome law has shown them the light. To some observers however, the notion of unsung environmental heroes in the depths of federal agencies seems implausible. At any event, modesty of this sort is an unfamiliar virtue.

Certainly NEPA has had some beneficial spinoff that weighs heavily against its drawbacks. The public exposure it provides to formerly closed administrative procedures represents an important new restraint on executive arrogance. In creating the CEQ, the law placed a vigorous, though not always successful, advocate for environmental interests within the sanctum of the White House.

But before the law goes much further toward lifting the scales from the eyes of the builders and diggers in the federal government, the courts will probably have to take a second bold step in reading NEPA's lofty language —and require that agency administrators make a reasonable showing that their decisions do in fact take account of all the new environmental information that it generates.

National Environmental Policy Act:
Signs of Backlash Are Evident

It is as much the duty of government to render prompt justice against itself, in favor of citizens, as it is to administer the same between individuals.—ABRAHAM LINCOLN

Robert Gillette

It's a rare occasion when Congress produces a piece of legislation that measures up to the lofty purpose of governmental self-control that Lincoln had in mind. Having done so, the chances are great that Congress will soon break out in a rash of second thoughts once the practical difficulties of enforcing self-control hit home.

This, at least, would seem to be the main lesson to be drawn from a bitter fight currently shaping up in Washington over the future of the 2-year-old National Environmental Policy Act (NEPA), a law that President Nixon symbolically chose to sign as his first official act of the new decade and one that his chief environmental adviser, Russell E. Train, has called "one of the most significant policy reforms in recent history."

History notwithstanding, the signs of a backlash against NEPA are becoming evident. A few high government officials like John A. Carver, Jr., a member of the Federal Power Commission (FPC), consider it a "paper monster . . . of great potential harm" and suggest that perhaps "Congress should take another look." And federal agencies, ranging from the Atomic Energy Commission (AEC) to the Department of Transportation, are pressing for new legislation to grant them special dispensations from NEPA's burdensome requirement of preparing environmental impact statements for major government actions.

For the most part, these proposed dispensations have a narrow intent—not so much to emasculate NEPA as to circumvent some particularly troublesome court rulings under it. Such judicial short-circuits may help relieve the pressures from agencies and industries that are building against the law. However, a number of conservation leaders in Washington fear that the restiveness they sense now may intensify into a movement to repeal the law once the election is safely past.

NEPA has two fundamental and apparently irritating purposes: to open to public view a major new source of information about the way in which the government's activities affect the environment and, in so doing, to goad the whole federal establishment into adopting a more sympathetic attitude toward a fragile biosphere.

SCIENCE, April, 1972, Vol. 176, pp. 30-33.

56

As federal legislation goes, NEPA is brief and not very complicated. In rather sweeping though scarcely controversial terms it sets forth a general policy that the government shall, among other things, "assure for all Americans safe, healthful, productive, and esthetically and culturally pleasing surroundings." NEPA's principal means for accomplishing this—and the sorest point of the current controversy—is the requirement that government agencies prepare environmental impact statements for every "major" action, which includes a description of the probable adverse effects and a discussion of alternatives.

Some of the discontent toward NEPA springs from the uncomfortable burden of paperwork and soul-searching it has imposed on federal bureaucrats.

The most immediate source of anxiety, however, is the enthusiasm and rigor with which federal courts have been interpreting NEPA. This is the law that environmental groups invoked to stop the $3-billion trans-Alaska pipeline in 1970 and the $400-million Tennessee-Tombigbee Waterway last year. Court rulings under NEPA have delayed the operation of a half a dozen nuclear power plants and have tied the Atomic Energy Commission up in such a tangle of paperwork that, according to chairman James R. Schlesinger, the AEC has been unable to complete a single licensing action since last summer.

Less well known, though no less infuriating to the executive branch, was a court decision in January that forced the Interior Department to postpone its plans to sell oil and gas leases on tracts of Gulf Coast waters covering an area half the size of Rhode Island. The Treasury Department was counting on $400 million in revenues from this sale to offset the fiscal 1972 deficit, but now will have to wait at least until fiscal 1973. NEPA is also the law that let two obscure Cleveland lawyers throw a monkey wrench in the Nixon Administration's elaborate scheme to control water pollution by issuing discharge permits to industry. In each instance these nettlesome setbacks have resulted from federal court rulings in which one or more judges agreed that a federal agency—whether by reason of simple misunderstanding or out of pure intransigence—had failed to comply fully with NEPA procedures in assessing the impact of various projects.

A Swarm of Suits

Altogether, district and appeals courts have handed down more than 160 decisions under NEPA, with new rulings being tallied at the rate of about one a week. This frenetic rate of activity results partly from environmental groups' quick recognition of the law as a versatile tool for calling the government to account for its activities, partly from a strong inclination of the courts to uphold the private citizen's standing to sue the government under NEPA, and partly because the law is new and its language rather vague.

As one U.S. District judge has said, NEPA is "a relatively new statute, so broad, yet opaque, that it will take longer than usual to comprehend fully its import."

By and large, though, most of the 160 rulings have added to a fabric of precedent around the law without stopping government projects. Russell E. Train, the chairman of the President's Council on Environmental Quality (CEQ), which NEPA established, estimates that no more than 15 percent of the litigation so far has led to delays in federal projects. Moreover, Train points out, the role of the courts has generally been "the traditional one of ensuring that governmental process prescribed by statute is working correctly. . . ."

Thus most of the cases so far have revolved around such questions as who must comply with NEPA (the answer is just about every federal agency); whether NEPA applies to projects begun before the law was passed (yes, if major decisions are still to be made); and whether an agency can pass off someone else's description of a project's impact as its own (no).

In light of some of the repercussions, though, the seeming simplicity of these questions and answers is deceiving. A number of agency heads, among them the AEC's James Schlesinger, complain that NEPA contains no hint of guidance for handling the special problems that might have been expected to arise during the present "transition period" when the law is still new and many of the projects it affects were already under way when the law was passed Schlesinger also thinks that the courts have put too much emphasis on fine details of procedure in preparing impact statements while ignoring the urgency of the projects themselves.

Similarly, FPC chairman John Nassikas asserts that by stopping the Alaskan pipeline and the Gulf Coast offshore drilling projects the courts may exacerbate shortages of low-sulfur fossil fuels. He also contends that power shortages may occur this summer in the East and Midwest unless at least one of the blockaded nuclear power plants is allowed to run and unless as many as 45 other fossil-fueled and nuclear plants can obtain federal water discharge permits this spring.

Environmentalists, on the other hand,

say that the overwhelming majority of delays in operating new power plants result not from their litigation but from construction and labor problems and that, in any case, administrative solutions can be found for troublesome court rulings and that no legislative relief is necessary. These views have some support within the Administration and among many, though not all, of NEPA's congressional backers.

Nevertheless, dark intimations of electric power shortages and the lingering sting of the citizens' suit that stopped the water pollution permit program have been enough to nurture a significant backlash against NEPA.

The roots of reaction against the law can be traced most directly to the controversial "Calvert Cliffs" ruling against the Atomic Energy Commission last summer (*Science*, 27 August). The suit, brought in part by the Sierra Club, accused the AEC of failing to consider fully the effects on the Chesapeake Bay of hot water discharged from a new nuclear power plant at Calvert Cliffs, Maryland. The AEC countered that it was sufficient to take the word of a state agency or the Environmental Protection Agency (EPA) that effluents would be within federal limits. A three-judge appeals court—denouncing the AEC for making a "mockery" of NEPA— ruled that, in every licensing action, the AEC must determine for itself the impact of a plant's effluents, then weigh these environmental "costs" against the plant's presumed benefits. In so doing, the AEC would not foreclose the possibility that it might have to apply even stricter standards in special circumstances.

Against the wishes of the utility industry and some members of the Joint Committee on Atomic Energy—which remains "promotion-minded," even if the AEC no longer is—the AEC decided not to appeal the Calvert Cliffs ruling. Instead, it set out to draw up rigorous new guidelines for writing its impact statements and then began composing these reports, some more than 300 pages long, for more than 100 nuclear reactors and fuel facilities. While all this may yet result in more stringent controls of thermal pollution, the immediate upshot was to mire the commission's severely understaffed regulatory branch in a deep bog of paperwork and to bring licensing activities to a virtual halt.

To make matters worse, the AEC then struck on the idea of issuing "interim" operating licenses to nuclear plants for low-power test runs before the new impact statements were finished, only to have this plan abruptly scotched by a suit brought by the Izaak Walton League and the Attorney General of Illinois against the issuance of such a license to Commonwealth Edison's new Quad Cities plants 1 and 2 near Chicago. The suit contended that thermal discharges from the two reactors might interfere with reproduction in two major species of fish in the Mississippi River. The reactors are still idle, although the FPC says they're "urgently" needed to fatten power reserves in the Midwest this summer.

Bills to Skirt NEPA

The AEC appealed the Quad Cities decision, but, under pressure from the joint committee and the FPC, it is also pushing legislation to circumvent this ruling as well as the Calvert Cliffs decision. Two bills before the joint committee—one from Representative Craig Hosmer (R–Calif.) and a more modest one from the AEC—would allow the AEC to issue its interim licenses after all. Both the agency and the committee apparently will continue to press these bills in Congress, even though plaintiffs in the Quad Cities case have since dropped their suit in exchange for a promise from the utility to build a $20 million closed-circuit water-cooling system for the contested plant.

A second effort to shield the AEC from NEPA emanates from Senator Howard H. Baker (R–Tenn.), who has tacked an amendment onto the Senate water pollution control bill (S. 2770) that would, in Baker's words, "throw out Calvert Cliffs." As a number of leading environmentalists read it, the amendment, which appears in similar form in the House version of the bill, would allow the AEC to revert to its former practice of ignoring a case-by-case balancing of pollution costs against benefits that the court found so essential. Baker insists that environmentalists are simply reading too much between the lines.

Still another end run around the courts concerns a NEPA suit brought last December against the Administration's water pollution permit program by two Cleveland lawyers, Jerome S. Kalur and Donald W. Large. Among his findings in the suit, U.S. District Judge Aubrey E. Robinson left the clear impression that at least some of the 25,000 permit applications now pending before the Army Corps of Engineers and the EPA (which share responsibility for the program) would have to be accompanied by impact statements, no matter how time-consuming the writing of them might be. The EPA now assumes that most of the 25,000 permits would require statements, and the mere thought of all that paperwork has paralyzed the program since December. (Most of these permits apply to major industrial outfalls.) In fact, there is a large body of opinion in Washington that the EPA has taken an overly gloomy view of its predicament.

Environmental groups, as well as congressmen like Representative Henry P. Reuss (D–Wis.), who in large part fathered the permit program, suggest that the court could be satisfied and the workload greatly reduced by writing one impact statement per major watershed, or one per major aggregation of discharge pipes, or one for the entire program. The White House, however, is spurning such administrative solutions as these and has opted instead for a quick legislative remedy —which probably will take the form of a bill to exempt the permit program from NEPA.

This decision runs counter to a view held widely within the Administration as well as by the environmental movement, that no agency should be exempt from NEPA and that having to justify the reasoning behind its pollution control programs (though not its individual enforcement actions) might be a very useful exercise for the EPA. Even the Interior Department seems to think so. Secretary Rogers C. B. Morton was to have testified to this effect in Senate hearings on NEPA last month, but the page of his testimony containing these views was removed at the last minute at the request of the CEQ and the White House Office of Management and Budget. The CEQ chairman, Russell Train, says that he supports circumvention of court rulings under NEPA as a means of dealing with "temporary, transitional problems."

To be sure, none of these proposed dispensations directly alters NEPA, and it would probably be rash at this point to take them as evidence of a coherent movement to cripple the law. But what worries environmentalists, as well as NEPA's two main authors,

Senator Henry Jackson (D–Wash.) and Representative John Dingell (D–Mich.), is that a feeding frenzy may develop among federal agencies once a few loopholes have been opened in the law.

The Department of Transportation, for instance, is anxious to relieve itself of the burden of impact-statement writing for highway projects and would prefer to let state highway agencies do the work instead. And FPC chairman Nassikas has hinted that he may seek to protect his commission's licensing activities from NEPA. The aggregate effect of such exemptions, one staff aide for Representative Dingell insists, is to weaken the law. "You get enough of them on the books and you'll just wall NEPA off from reality."

Strategic Retreat

Despite this prospect, the environmental movement is in a poor position to protect what has turned out to be its most versatile tool of law. Financial problems and ideological splits have weakened the environmental lobby in recent months, and late last month the movement took a sound drubbing in a fruitless attempt to insert strengthening amendments in the House water pollution bill. Their confidence apparently shaken, Dingell and Jackson have opted for a strategic retreat. Jackson has prepared an amendment to NEPA that would allow the President to exempt individual projects from the law for a limited time, and Dingell has his own bill to allow interim licenses for nuclear plants. It would expire, however, in July 1973.

As a Dingell aide puts it, "A self-sealing loophole is preferable to having the wolves gnawing chunks out of the law." But the wolves may have the last word after all if the John Carver's have their way.

THE SUPREME COURT AND MICKEY MOUSE

Jeanne Nienaber

Not so very long ago conflicts over land in the wild west were settled irreverently, often by means of a shootout in which the resolution was quick, if not just or civilized. Today, such conflicts are settled by a usually lengthy process of bargaining and adjudication wherein the aggrieved party eventually brings his case before the courts of the land. After five years of dispute one such case, popularly known as the Mineral King case, made it to the Supreme Court and was heard last fall. Civilized, yes; quick, no.

In some respects it is a confusing battle. It was dubbed the "Mom vs. Apple Pie" dispute by one of the weekly news magazines because of the difficulty in distinguishing the good guys from the bad. No one in this struggle for terrain, for the right to dictate the fate of a small alpine valley located in the California high Sierras, wears a white hat. It is a drama depicted in shades of grey.

Who are the protagonists? Curiously enough, the struggle is between some popular and widely respected groups in American society, the most famous of which is that captor of the juvenile American imagination, Walt Disney Productions. Standing behind the Disney company's plans to develop Mineral King Valley into a high-density, year-round recreational resort are four federal land-managing agencies. Arrayed against them, and waving the ecology banner, are outraged conservationists. They are led by the Sierra Club, perhaps the most strident conservation organization around today. Their opposition to this and other developments which would drastically change the nature of the area in question recalls to mind earlier critiques of industrial society. The conservationists are thus the new Romantics of the twentieth century.

Formally entitled "Sierra Club v. Morton, et al.," it is the membership of the Sierra Club which claimed in the courts to be the aggrieved party. They brought suit against officials of the U.S. Forest Service, the National Park Service, and the Departments of Agriculture and the Interior for making plans for the construction, by Disney, of the multimillion dollar recreational resort. Obviously a complicated case, the outcome will surely be considered a landmark decision in the history of environmental law if only because the highest court in the land chose

AMERICAN FORESTS, July, 1972, pp. 29-41.

to hear it.

The Supreme Court heard the case in November of 1971. Five months later, on April 19, 1972, the Court issued its decision. In a 4-3 opinion, the justices decided that the Sierra Club did not have sufficient standing to sue. It was a major setback for the conservation organization which had purposefully set out to enlarge the public's right to sue the federal government. While a number of substantive issues are involved in the Mineral King case, it was apparent during the oral presentation last November that the case would probably be decided on the issue of standing. Questions by the justices dealt not so much with the merits of the case as with the justification the Club could give concerning right to sue.

They failed to convince a majority of the Court that their status as a membership organization with a special interest in the conservation and sound maintenance of the national parks, game refuges, and forests of the country gave them sufficient standing to sue on behalf of the general public. In writing the majority opinion, Justice Potter Stewart declared that "The Sierra Club failed to allege that it or its members would be affected in any of their activities or pastimes by the Disney development. Nowhere in the pleadings or affidavits did the Club state that its members use Mineral King for any purpose, much less that they use it in any way that would be significantly affected by the proposed actions of the respondents."

Of course, individual Sierra Club members do in fact use the Mineral King area, and their activities would be affected by the Disney development. The Court knew that as well

as does the Sierra Club. But the Club desired a test case on the standing issue, and so argued that the organization's concern about the environment gives it the right to sue on its own behalf. No other plaintiffs—no individual or party directly affected by the project—were included in the suit. The Court chose not to accept the Club's argument, noting that "broadening the categories of injury that may be alleged in support of standing is a different matter from abandoning the requirement that the party seeking review must have himself suffered an injury."

Justice Blackmun dissented from this opinion on the grounds that the Mineral King case was not an ordinary suit, but posed serious and fundamental environmental questions. In effect, he argued that the Sierra Club should have been given standing, in order that the case could be heard on its merits. Justice William O. Douglas, known to be a strong supporter of conservation values, also dissented. In his minority opinion, he offers a rather creative and innovative solution for the standing issue: That we need to fashion a federal rule that allows environmental issues to be litigated before federal agencies or courts in the name of the inanimate object about to be "despoiled, defaced, or invaded by roads and bulldozers and where injury is the subject of public outrage." Environmental objects like rivers, lakes, groves of trees, air, and so on would thus have the same legal status as do corporations and ships.

From the viewpoint of those who would want to see the Mineral King area left undeveloped, it was unfortunate that the Sierra Club, in its argument before the Court last November, did not present a very strong or compelling discussion of the standing issue, but chose, rather, to focus on the merits of the case.

The effect of this decision on the Sierra Club in particular and the environmental movement in general, is only speculative at this point. It is clear, however, that the conservationists did not win any new legal rights as they hoped to in this case. The Supreme Court chose instead to adhere to the traditional notion of standing, which does not allow a group or individual the right to sue solely to protect "the public interest." In spite of the fact that the majority opinion against the Club was cushioned by sympathetic statements in support of environmental values, the decision can not be construed as a victory for conservationists.

What is most likely is that conservationists may begin to reassess the tactics they have employed in recent years, tactics which have heavily depended upon the use of litigation. This most recent setback may actually have been expected, to some degree. For, in a recent Sierra Club bulletin, the editorial cautions against an excessive reliance on litigation as a means of resolving environmental conflicts, and suggests that conservation groups need to start thinking more in terms of "political action." This includes grass roots mobilization and education, renewed efforts at dialogue with federal, state, and local bureaucracies, and lobbying in Congress and in State legislatures. These activities have been somewhat neglected in recent years, as conservationists have flooded the courts with environmental lawsuits. In the Mineral King decision, it is as though the majority of the Supreme Court were saying as much.

The foundation of the conflict is over what constitutes the public interest in the area of land-use policy. Widely opposed values and opinions clashed head-on in the Mineral King dispute, and it was clear that there exists no agreed-upon definition of the public good as it pertains to land-use decisions. Is building a $35 million recreational complex in the high Sierras, on federal land, a better or more reasonable alternative than leaving the valley in its seminatural state, for the use of summer campers and backpackers? The Forest Service, on whose land the Disney corporation has a contract to build, answers with a firm "yes." Their administrative superior, the Agriculture Department, concurs. The National Park Service and their overseer, the Department of the Interior, which are involved to the extent that an access road into Mineral King traverses the adjoining national park, answer with a somewhat less enthusiastic affirmative. Naturally the Sierra Club responds with a vehement "no".

Though all four federal agencies were named in the Sierra Club's suit, the principal battle was with the Forest Service. They initiated plans for the development. All construction, except for part of an access road, would take place on national forest land. In the suit the Sierra Club contended that the Forest Service and the Department of Agriculture (which agreed to the plans) exceeded the limits of their authority in granting such a permit to Disney. Legal technicalities are involved, but what it boils down to is a question of size. The Sierra Club claimed that no administrative statute gives the Forest Service the right to lease more than eighty acres to a concessionaire for the purpose of recreational development. The Mineral King complex would involve thousands of acres. But, the Forest Service maintains, the letter of the law has not been violated. The so-called eighty acre limitation dates from a 1915 law passed by the U.S. Congress and amended in 1956 which states that the Forest Service may lease up to eighty acres to a concessionaire, for a duration of thirty years. As demand for bigger and better recreation developments grew, the agency responded by combining various types of permits so as to enable the concessionaire to construct the necessary facilities: lodges, ski runs, hiking trails, parking facilities, and so on. The more "permanent" structures are thus built within the boundaries of the eighty acres while the presumably more expendable amenities, such as parking lots and ski runs, are normally leased to the concessionaire via what the agency calls a "terminable permit" These may involve hundreds or even thousands of additional acres.

There are precedents for this action. The Mineral King plans, and the manner in which they have been administered, are not unique. Scores of ski areas, including some of the most popular in the United States, happen to be located on national forest land and also happen to cover a great deal more than eighty acres. The Forest Service was of course alarmed that a ruling against their practice of combining permits would make all these areas illegal, resulting in their closure and a very frustrated skiing population. Whether this practice is an instance of bureaucratic sleight-of-hand or whether the acreage statute is outmoded and needs to be brought into the 1970's is still an unresolved issue. What is needed now is a Congressional review of the practice.

The magnitude of the proposed development was the Sierra Club's principal objection. But there were others. So, they included the National Park Service and the Interior Department in their law suit for allowing the construction of an access road through national park land. By so allowing, the Club maintained that they violated one of their own statutes which holds that no rights-of-way shall be approved through a national park which will be used for "non-park purposes." The controversy revolved around conflicting interpretations as to what the primary purpose of the access road would be: Shall it be used as a scenic roadway through Sequoia National Park, or is its real intention one of providing access to the Disney development on national forest land? A slippery question, indeed.

Incidentally, it was only with great reluctance that the Park Service and the Interior Department agreed to the upgrading of the access road through their park. For approximately a year former Secretary of the Interior Stewart Udall found himself at loggerheads with former Secretary of Agriculture Orville Freeman. Udall was not at all pleased with the Mineral King project, particularly when it involved park terrain, and he publicly said so. His position was that the time had long since come when land-managing agencies should be innovative in terms of transportation problems, and so he requested that the Forest Service do studies of alternative transportation systems and routes into Mineral King. This the Forest Service did, but found that the financial cost of train transport into the Valley would be prohibitive. The dispute was eventually resolved late in 1967 by former President Johnson's trouble-shooter agency, the Bureau of the Budget. Secretary Udall's objections were overriden by officials in the Budget Bureau who mediated the conflict.

When the Forest Service first announced its plans for Mineral King in March of 1965, the Sierra Club rather promptly objected. The organization's head office in San Francisco wrote to the agency's San Francisco regional office requesting that they postpone making an award on the project. They felt that the agency had not sufficiently studied the area to determine its suitability for a recreational development of considerable magnitude. The Club was concerned about the ecology of the area, the threat to wildlife. They also complained that the Forest Service hadn't adequately solicited public opinion (i.e., theirs) regarding the project.

In retrospect, these criticisms of the agency's decision-making procedures were well-founded. The agency itself acknowledged that they had put the cart before the horse, and only after having decided to develop Mineral King for recreational purposes did they seriously begin to study the area. They had made this decision as they had made countless others, in an era when there was very little public interest in environmental matters. It was made more or less unilaterally, and independent of public participation. They believed,

however, that they were responding to public demand for more winter recreation areas. They of course did not foresee the public awakening that was to occur a few years hence, and it was their misfortune to be caught in the midst of the Ecology Movement with a project that drew criticism from so many quarters, both within government and without. Back in 1964 and 1965, when they planned the project, few people knew or cared what the Forest Service was doing.

There was the Sierra Club, however, and its objections. The agency listened to them but nevertheless decided to go ahead with its plans and the contract award. One reason for this was that they had been trying to get development of Mineral King off the ground since the late 1940's, when the agency first initiated a "winter sports investigation" of the area. They tried, in 1949, to interest private developers in the project but no one came forward. The difficulties of winter access into Mineral King were then financially prohibitive and so the Forest Service shelved the project for more than twenty years. Incidentally, at that time, the Sierra Club knew about the project and was on record as favoring a limited ski development in the Valley.

Another reason for proceeding with the project involved increased public demand for outdoor recreation in California. In particular, the demand for skiing was growing. Residents trapped in urban and suburban sprawls were looking to the national parks and forest for places to get away from it all. Use of the public lands was estimated to be growing at a rate of six to ten percent per year. The Forest Service responded to these pressures by casting around for suitable winter sports sites on its terrain. Among others, they selected Mineral King. For while it is hardly a stone's throw from either of the State's two metropolitan areas, Los Angeles and San Francisco, the automobile orientation of Californians is well known. A drive of some 250 miles appeared not an unreasonable distance for the ski enthusiast to travel.

Moreover, the agency was reasonably confident that private money in the form of interested concessionaires would now be forthcoming. Walt Disney himself had already contacted the Forest Service to express his interest in a joint ski development and, unknown to the agency, his corporation had already begun buying up the privately-owned developable land adjacent to Mineral King. Another prospective developer suggested that there might be a solution to the access road problem at this time; it turned out that the State of California agreed to pick up the tab for the cost of upgrading the road. Three months after the Forest Service announced its plans for Mineral King, former Governor Edmund G. Brown announced the inclusion of the formerly county-owned "Mineral King road" in the State's highway plan. Two of the top contenders for the Mineral King award were immediately credited with having done some effective lobbying in Sacramento.

Six proposals in all were submitted on the Mineral King project. After a lengthy period of evaluation, Walt Disney's proposal was selected and, in 1966, he was given an initial three-year planning contract.

It was an impressive and ambitious project which the Disney corporation submitted. The initial financial investment was estimated to be approximately $35 million. The plans included: an alpine village modeled after European ski resorts, an underground parking lot, a monorail system to take visitors from their cars to the village, lodges accommodating 7,000 people per night, restaurants with a seating capacity of 2,200, a chapel, an ice-skating rink, a ski school and ski developments geared for 11,000 skiers per hour, a souvenir shop, heliport, theater, stables, riding trails, and, in their own words, "a unique swimming pool built to look and feel exactly like the 'storied old swimming hole . . .'" The Disney corporation also reserved the names "Mineral King Airways" and "Mineral King Stagecoach Lines" with the State of California with the obvious intent of providing intrastate public transportation to their development.

If such a project sounds like a Bacchanalian Garden of Eden to some, it sent shudders down the spines of many conservationists. They envisioned a Sierran Disneyland where elves, Bambi-like creatures, and hordes of transfixed visitors gambol around in a carefully constructed and controlled fantasy land. Even if such a vision of things to come was exaggerated, the development was obviously not going to be consistent with the credo of conservationists: "In wildness is the preservation of the world." Led by the Sierra Club, they prepared for battle. They took on not only the federal government's land-managing agencies, but one of the country's principal cultural institutions, Disney and his World.

The Sierra Club, however, clashed head-on with the Forest Service's determination to see the project through. The agency was unwilling to abandon their plans after having already overcome innumerable obstacles standing in the way of the Mineral King development. In response to the conservationists' objections, they scaled down Disney's original projections of size, hoping thereby that they could appease some of the opposition. Unfortunately no agreement was reached between the Sierra Club and the Forest Service. Claims of intransigence were hurled back and forth, both sides complaining that the other was being unyielding. Relations between the two became increasingly strained and finally, in 1969, the conservationists turned to the courts as their last resort. No further bargaining was thereafter possible on this issue, and the Club's use of litigation in this instance tended to have a negative spill-over effect on subsequent disagreements. In environmental disputes, as in so many other social and political conflicts, adjudication became the ultimate non-violent weapon.

There exists a core issue in virtually all of the recent conflicts over the environment. It is illustrated by this case, in which the two opposed points of view, preservation versus development, became almost irreconcilable. There is presently very little middle-ground on which to meet. Conservationists have taken the lead in telling the country that the system has pushed development far enough, that the natural world is already altered far beyond what is reasonable or healthy, and that limits have to be set to our transforming Nature into Artifice. Their questioning of basic values and their near-militancy confound politicians and administrators who are accustomed to practicing the arts of accommodation and compromise in land-use policy.

They are on the defensive and in the minority. Since it is impossible to stop all development everywhere, the tactic has been to select certain test cases and to push for precedent-setting victories. There have been a few. Given a sufficient number of these, either in the courts or through newly-enacted legislation, they hope to reverse our persistent and thoroughgoing mania for "progress".

Though both sides might deny it, the importance of Mineral King is only partly due to its intrinsic value. While beautiful, it is not a Grand Canyon or a Yosemite and if developed the loss of this area of semi-wilderness to the nation's well-being would not be fatal. A much more serious loss, for instance, will be that of a significant part of the Alaskan wilderness and wildlife to the pipeline. Yet Mineral King has symbolic importance. To the Forest Service, it is intended to serve as a "model" development for future recreational projects. To the Sierra Club, the Valley served as a vehicle to test both the issue of standing and to question the limits of administrative autonomy in the field of land-use policy. Both sides, the Sierra Club and the Forest Service, are standing firm. There are principles, prejudices, and commitments involved.

From the agency's standpoint, the argument in favor of developing places like Mineral King is based primarily on the supply-demand equation. There aren't enough recreation facilities to go around, particularly in a state such as California where the population is both large and mobile. Also, among the recreation-consuming public, so the argument goes, there is greater demand for developed recreation sites than there is for undeveloped, or wilderness, areas. Statistics are cited by the Forest Service. In California, roughly ten percent of the total national forest land is classified as wilderness, while less than one percent is developed for ski and other winter-related sports. If anything, the agency claims, the imbalance is presently in favor of wilderness enthusiasts.

Consequently, exasperation with the Sierra Club over the Mineral King case tends to run high within the agency. They feel the Club is being obstinate and uncompromising, and that they are pushing only their own "narrow" interests regardless of what a majority of Californians prefer. The conservationists are thus frequently charged with being elitists, which, in the context of the American political tradition, is a serious charge indeed. Such an accusation has caused the ruin of many politicians and movements.

But if the Forest Service is exasperated with the Sierra Club, the feeling is mutual. The latter organization vociferously objects to what it perceives as a pernicious tendency within the agency: the transformation from preserver and protector of the environment to the exploiter. Spokesmen for the Club explain that some time during the 1950's the Forest Service switched from a "custodial" to a "managerial" philosophy of land management. Traditional roles and practices were modified. No longer did the agency see its function in terms of protecting the national forests, but they became the actual, and active, entrepreneurs of that land. Use of the forests intensified, and the agency increasingly

became geared towards an ethic of production and consumption. It is an ethic which, incidentally, can include recreation as a commodity as easily as it includes the harvesting and sale of timber. Rather than a policy of preservation and protection, the Sierra Club claims, the Forest Service was catering to users by a "come one, come all" philosophy.

Criticism such as this, however, is not confined to the practices and policies of the U.S. Forest Service. There exists a pervasive trend in this society in which numerous socio-economic factors dovetail to produce a most unfortunate result. That, to conservationists, is the alienation of man from nature. Rather than leave the Mineral King Valley, for instance, in its present state, where hikers and picnickers now enjoy a day or two away from smog, concrete, and congestion, the impetus is towards turning it into another urban environment. If the trend persists, and conservationists are alarmed that it will, they see the not-too-distant end result as one of ecological disaster and spiritual ruin. The values taught by nature and by wilderness will be completely lost.

They are, of course, fighting an uphill battle. The country has become urbanized, technology is entrenched, material comforts are as much desired out in the sticks as they are in the cities and suburbs. Americans have embraced, for the most part, a set of values inconsistent with the wilderness ethic. They choose, by way of recreation, the comfortable path. Our federal land managers whom the Sierra Club sued are only responding to those preferences. And private developers are

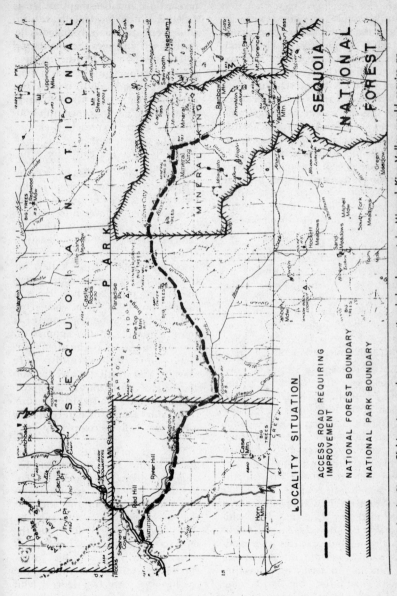

LOCALITY SITUATION

	ACCESS ROAD REQUIRING IMPROVEMENT
	NATIONAL FOREST BOUNDARY
	NATIONAL PARK BOUNDARY

Basis for the Sierra Club's suit was that a recreational development in Mineral King Valley would require an access road through neighboring Sequoia National Park and heavy traffic might damage the ecology of the area

69

simply capitalizing on and encouraging this situation. It is not a new story.

In November of 1970, a few weeks before the snow came, before the dirt road became impassable, and before Mineral King was locked away for its winter hibernation, I spent a day up there, alone with the Valley. I hiked its trails, drank from its clear streams, watched its mountains change shape and color as the sun passed overhead. I did not encounter a single other human being, happily, the entire day. I sang out loud, unselfconsciously, and rested beneath the branches of a young fir tree. I was alone, but never lonely. I do not remember a day, since then, quite as well spent. And I wonder now how my experience in the Valley will contrast with that of the thousands of visitors who will come to the Disney development.

There is something to be said for leaving a place like Mineral King free from the works of men. But it is a difficult gospel to preach. It almost has to be experienced. And that, naturally, is what the battle for Mineral King is about.

Environmental Law (II): A Strategic Weapon Against Degradation?

Luther J. Carter

In any assessment of achievements in the new field of environmental law, perhaps the largest success that can be claimed is that many government officials are being held more accountable than ever before for their decisions. Environmental lawyers are, in effect, helping to open up the system, and by more than just a crack. A few patently undesirable government policies, such as that allowing general use of DDT, have been abandoned because somebody went to court. But the more common result of environmental lawsuits has been to bring delay in the starting of various programs and public works projects, giving citizens and elected officials an eleventh-hour chance to take a second look. Furthermore, in such matters as off-shore oil and gas leases or the development of power or water projects, the courts are now not only demanding disclosure of the rationale behind the undertaking but also a reexamination of that rationale in terms of more rigorously assessed benefits and alternatives.

These results, most of which have come within the last 5 years, have been brought about in no small part by a relatively small number of public interest lawyers. At this point, one wonders whether in the future environmental law will lead to still deeper consequences. The answer may depend to a great extent upon how much discretion the legislative branch—itself not irreproachable in representing the public interest—is willing to allow judges in reviewing the performance of large, complex, and often intransigent bureaucracies.

In an earlier article, the Environmental Defense Fund (EDF) was treated as a signal example of a public interest group practicing environmental law, and, in EDF's case, emphasizing collaboration between lawyers and scientists. Taken altogether, environmental lawyers seem to represent a young elite of the American bar--most are under 35, and many have received high academic honors. Besides the attorneys with EDF, there are those with a number of other groups that are practicing environmental law either exclusively or as a significant part of a more general public interest·practice.

One such group is the Sierra Club's Legal Defense Fund (LDF), based in San Francisco (with a branch in Denver) and led by James W. Moorman, a North Carolinian and 1962 graduate of the Duke University School of Law. In August 1969 Moorman, as a staff attorney at the newly created Center for Law and Social Policy in Washington, became one of the first, if not

SCIENCE, March 1973, Vol. 179, pp. 1310-1312, 1350.

71

the first, full-time environmental lawyer. It has been characteristic of the
public interest law groups to call on
one another for help, and, as it happened, EDF asked Moorman to represent it in litigation aimed at banning
DDT. Also, EDF, together with the
Wilderness Society and Friends of the
Earth, had Moorman represent them in
a suit to stop construction of the trans-
Alaska pipeline.

EPA on Its Mettle

The DDT ban declared recently by
the Environmental Protection Agency
was a matter of administrative discretion, but the fact is that, as the result
of court rulings obtained by Moorman
for EDF, the agency was on its mettle
to show that it had taken careful account of the harm done by this chemical to fish and wildlife and of its carcinogenic effect on experimental animals. Also, the recent decision by the
U.S. Circuit Court of Appeals for the
District of Columbia continuing (at
least temporarily) the injunction against
construction of the pipeline was only
the latest development in the suit initiated by Moorman on behalf of EDF
and the other plaintiffs.

The Sierra Club has been bringing
and participating in lawsuits since the
mid-1960's, but the LDF was not established as a separate entity until 1971.
The LDF has only four staff attorneys,
yet this group carries on a large volume of litigation, drawing upon its
sizable list of volunteer attorneys to
handle many of its cases. The LDF
represents the Sierra Club, and other
public interest clients, in cases involving
the public lands, such as the ones over
timber management in the Tongass National Forest in Alaska and over the proposed Disney recreational development
in Mineral King Valley. It also handles
cases concerned with problems such as
air pollution and other threats to rural
and urban environments—for instance,
the proposed new Los Angeles international airport. The LDF is supported by

the Sierra Club Foundation, some individual contributors, and by the Ford
Foundation, with about one-fifth of the
LDF budget coming from the latter
source.

While Ford Foundation support has
been important to the LDF and to
EDF, it has been the mainstay of several other groups requiring special mention. One of these is the Center for
Law and Social Policy, which, with a
legal staff of 13, remains one of the
largest public interest law groups. About
a third of the center's cases pertain to
environmental law, the most noted being the Alaska pipeline case, in which
staff attorney Dennis M. Flannery is
now chief counsel.

A second group begun and supported
largely by Ford Foundation money is
the Natural Resources Defense Council
(NRDC), with 12 regular staff attorneys, two staff scientists, and offices
in New York City, Washington, and
Palo Alto. The idea for NRDC originated with a few students in the Yale
Law School class of 1969. Even before
they had their degrees, they were approaching the Ford Foundation, and,
somewhat to their surprise, the officials
there were interested, although the
question whether to enter so potentially
controversial a field seems to have
caused them much agonizing.

J. G. Speth, Jr., a member of this
group and now a NRDC attorney in
Washington, recalls that one thing that
seemed really to give the Ford Foundation officials pause was the fact that
these budding environmental lawyers
lacked a board of directors. "Go
forth and get a board, we were told,"
Speth says. It turned out that some
well-known people associated with the
Scenic Hudson Preservation Conference, such as David Sive, Mrs. Louis
Auchincloss, James Marshall, and
Stephen P. Duggan, were looking for
a staff to undertake a broad, continuing
program in environmental law.

"So this little marriage took place
and in 1970 we got the Ford grant,"

Speth says, adding that, besides the Scenic Hudson people who joined the NRDC board, there were people such as Charles (*Greening of America*) Reich of Yale, René J. Dubos of Rockefeller University, George Woodwell of the Brookhaven National Laboratory, and Joshua Lederberg of Stanford. (Laurance Rockefeller and John B. Oakes, an editor of the New York *Times,* later joined the board.) Once the NRDC staff, which had ability but little experience, learned its way around the courthouse, it began making an imprint—court rulings in a few important NRDC cases I shall come to in a moment.

Still another organization that has depended largely on Ford Foundation support is the Environmental Law Institute, publisher of the *Environmental Law Reporter,* which comments upon as well as reports important court rulings. The *Reporter* has helped environmental lawyers keep up with their fast-developing field, and one of its articles is credited with providing the theory used in at least one major precedent-setting decision. The Environmental Law Institute does not litigate. The basic purpose of the institute—which, incidentally, currently has under way a National Science Foundation–supported study of federal environmental law—is to take a comprehensive view of the field and help its development conceptually. It is typical of the environmental law fraternity, where almost everyone seems to know (or at least know of) everybody else, that Frederick R. Anderson, Jr., editor in chief of the *Reporter,* is a hometown friend of James Moorman and that he and EDF's William Butler were friends at Oxford, where they both were Marshall Scholars.

Altogether, full-time public interest attorneys doing a significant amount of environmental law work number not more than about 60, counting the staffs of the previously mentioned groups, plus lawyers with groups such as two other Ford Foundation–supported

organizations in the West, the Center for Law in the Public Interest in Los Angeles and Public Interest Advocates, Inc., in San Francisco, and those with Businessmen and Professional People for the Public Interest in Chicago, and with several Washington groups, including Ralph Nader's Center for Responsive Law, the firm of Berlin, Roisman, and Kessler, and the environmental law unit with the National Wildlife Federation.

(Financially, most of the public interest law groups are largely dependent on foundation support and whatever money they can scrape up from wealthy contributors. The Ford Foundation has said that it will continue its support for the public interest law groups for about 5 more years. After that, what? The merger of some groups with closely allied interests—for instance, EDF, NRDC, and LDF—is one possibility, in that overhead and the high cost of large-scale fund solicitation could be shared. This might be unnecessary, however, if the courts would begin routinely allowing recovery of attorney's fees from defendants in those cases where the public interest law groups prevail. The favorable ruling on fee recovery in *La Raza Unida v. Volpe,* a San Francisco Bay area highway case decided in 1971, is regarded as an encouraging precedent.)

NEPA Effectively Used

In surveying the field of environmental law, one must ask: Are the public interest lawyers really proving effective in an overall way, or are they simply dashing about fighting fires? To look first at the positive side of the matter, it is clear that the National Environmental Policy Act of 1969 (NEPA), requiring environmental impact statements for federally supported and regulated activities, is being effectively used to force government agencies and some corporate interests to rethink many of their policies and programs. Court challenges under NEPA

73

have, for one thing, often served to intensify public interest in the matters in dispute.

Given the political potency of the oil industry, the conservation groups would have had no chance of stopping construction of the trans-Alaska pipeline had they not gone to court. Because they did go, and were able to invoke NEPA, they have made the Nixon Administration, the oil companies, and the public think in a more sophisticated manner about alternatives, such as the possibility of a pipeline across Canada (*Science*, 9 March). Also, by pressing for and eventually obtaining an injunction against further construction of the Cross Florida Barge Canal, environmentalists influenced the White House in its decision to terminate (*Science*, 29 January 1971) this Corps of Engineers project, which was regarded dubiously even by the Secretary of the Army's office.

For a company faced with frustrating delays in carrying out its plans, time can be big money, and the environmental lawyers have in some cases taken advantage of this to bring about negotiations in the public interest. A good illustration is the settlement reached in the case involving the $150-million facility to be built at Cove Point on Chesapeake Bay by the Columbia LNG Corporation, which will be importing liquefied natural gas from Algeria. The Sierra Club and the Maryland Conservation Council brought suit against the company's initial plan, which was to acquire a 1100-acre bay-side site and build a pipeline on a pier extending a mile out into the bay. The suit was dropped, however, after the company agreed to lay the pipeline under water and dedicate 600 acres to open space through scenic easements, with a mile of beach to be leased to the state for $1 per year. Several state and federal agencies had responsibilities in the matter, but it remained for the environmental groups to defend the bay environment.

The Cove Point settlement points up the fact that by no means is all of the effective work in environmental law done inside the courtroom. The public interest lawyers often seek to influence decisions through discussions with government officials and through participation in formal administrative proceedings.

Yet, significant though the achievements of environmental law have been, it is not clear whether environmental litigation will turn out to be a strategic weapon in the war against environmental deterioration or one useful mainly for tactical aims. Thus far, relatively few projects or policies deemed environmentally destructive have been definitely stopped or overturned. And most of the preliminary injunctions granted by courts under NEPA probably will be dissolved once the judges have become satisfied that adequate environmental impact statements are in hand. The courts have been moving, little by little, to define the obligations which government agencies have, under NEPA and other statutes, but no one yet knows how meaningful those rulings will be for the long term.

NEPA has been commonly regarded, even by its original congressional sponsor (Senator Henry M. Jackson of Washington), as a statute mandating systematic analysis of environmental impact and full public disclosure, but not one establishing substantive standards by which a proposed project or policy may be declared unlawful. Under this interpretation, once an agency has complied with NEPA's procedural requirements, its final decisions cannot be challenged, except under the usual rule that administrative decisions cannot be arbitrary. This interpretation now appears to have been modified but not overturned.

In *Calvert Cliffs Coordinating Committee v. Atomic Energy Commission*, the U.S. Circuit Court of Appeals for the District of Columbia held that agencies must make a "finely tuned and 'systematic' balancing analysis" in resolving conflict among environmental, economic, and social values. This ruling would seem to establish a subtle but possibly significant new standard for judging whether an agency's decision-making has been arbitrary or not. (Anthony Z. Roisman, of Berlin, Roisman, and Kessler, was chief counsel for the plaintiffs in this important precedent-setting case.)

The *Calvert Cliffs* ruling was in fact cited in the opinion last November by the Eighth Circuit Court of Appeals in the Cossatot River case, involving a challenge by EDF against a Corps of Engineers dam project in Arkansas. In an immediate sense, EDF came out a loser, for the court held that the Corps had complied with NEPA and that construction of the dam should not be stopped. But, to EDF's satisfaction, the court did emphasize that NEPA prescribes a policy—for example, among the several stated objectives of the act, there is one calling for an environment "support[ing] diversity and variety of individual choice"—as well as a procedure. The intent of NEPA, the court indicated, is not to fill government archives with futile impact studies.

Also, a 1971 ruling by the Circuit Court of Appeals for the District of Columbia in *NRDC v. Morton*, substantially upheld NRDC's contention that the Department of the Interior's impact statement on a scheduled (but later canceled) sale of 80 oil and gas leases on the Gulf of Mexico continental shelf was inadequate. NRDC had argued that a wide range of alternatives to the sale—varying from increases in oil imports to the gasification of coal and the development of solar energy—should have been thoroughly discussed. The court agreed, at least with respect to alternatives possible in the near future.

A February ruling by a federal district judge in another NRDC suit—this one opposing a small watershed (or stream channelization) project on Chicod Creek in North Carolina—was also encouraging to environmentalists. The judge, in part citing *Calvert Cliffs*, continued to enjoin construction of the project, finding that the impact statement failed to consider a number of pertinent factors, including the *cumulative* impact of such relatively small undertakings on the regional environment. Another ruling counted as significant by environmentalists was the recent one by a district judge in the case brought by the Sierra Club against the Trinity River project in Texas. There, the judge held, among other things, that the Corps of Engineers' benefit-cost analysis procedures were deficient because environmentally related benefits were counted while environmentally related "costs" were ignored.

Nonetheless, instances where the federal courts block a project or policy on its merits are expected to be rare, and many environmental lawyers want Congress to declare that each person is "entitled by right" to a quality environment and to establish a few basic criteria by which the courts can determine when that right is being infringed. A bill to accomplish this has been pending for a year or so in the Senate Commerce Committee's subcommittee on the environment which is chaired by Senator Philip A. Hart of Michigan.

As now written, the Hart bill would allow the courts to enjoin any activity, private or governmental, if the "environmental and economic costs . . . exceed the benefits" or if the purpose of the activity can be achieved in a more environmentally acceptable and no less socially beneficial manner. Private activities in compliance with standards and permits issued under the federal air and water pollution control acts would not be subject to these tests. *But* policies and decisions of all federal agencies, including the Environmental Protection Agency (EPA), would be subject to the tests insofar as they are discretionary and not arrived at through compliance with specific congressional directives. (The "citizens suit" provisions of the existing air and water pollution acts apply largely to enforcement of policies and regulations that are *nondiscretionary*.)

The Hart bill is similar in thrust to the Michigan Environmental Protection Act of 1970 and to measures enacted in Connecticut, Minnesota, and Massachusetts. It is strong stuff and it will face strong opposition, with, in all likelihood, Senator Jackson and Senator Edmund S. Muskie of Maine, the fathers of NEPA and EPA, respectively, probably among its foes, which already include Nixon Administration officials. At this point the groups that have gone on record in favor of the bill are principally environmental law and conservation organizations, although the measure has been endorsed by a few groups such as the Americans for Democratic Action, the League of Women Voters, and the Federation of American Scientists.

If enacted, the Hart bill would, in effect, represent an extension of the public trust doctrine, making the use of all resources (not merely submerged tidal lands) subject to a test in the public interest to be administered by either state or federal courts. Beyond doubt, environmentalists will be taking a risk if judges are allowed to second-guess the legislative and executive branches on the merits of environmental issues. As some recent opinions show, some judges exude the sentiments of a Thoreau while others think more like the manager of a copper smelter.

Yet the opinions of most judges are appealable, and Congress itself can set limits on judicial discretion. What Congress cannot do is to legislate comprehensively on all of the nation's important environmental questions. The whole vast problem of land use regulation is, for example, one in which the Congress probably will not legislate in any but the broadest fashion. But Congress cannot safely leave those problems on which it does not legislate in a detailed way to the largely unchecked discretion of federal and state bureaucracies. If a fail-safe is to be found to protect environmental values, it may have to be the judiciary, coaxed by a new breed of environmental attorneys.

SECTION II

SOME CULTURAL BACKGROUND

Social Benefit versus Technological Risk

What is our society willing to pay for safety?

Chauncey Starr

The evaluation of technical approaches to solving societal problems customarily involves consideration of the relationship between potential technical performance and the required investment of societal resources. Although such performance-versus-cost relationships are clearly useful for choosing between alternative solutions, they do not by themselves determine how much technology a society can justifiably purchase. This latter determination requires, additionally, knowledge of the relationship between social benefit and justified social cost. The two relationships may then be used jointly to determine the optimum investment of societal resources in a technological approach to a social need.

Technological analyses for disclosing the relationship between expected performance and monetary costs are a traditional part of all engineering planning and design. The inclusion in such studies of *all* societal costs (indirect as well as direct) is less customary, and obviously makes the analysis more difficult and less definitive. Analyses of social value as a function of technical performance are not only uncommon but are rarely quantitative. Yet we know that implicit in every nonarbitrary national decision on the use of technology is a trade-off of societal benefits and societal costs.

In this article I offer an approach for establishing a quantitative measure of benefit relative to cost for an important element in our spectrum of social values—specifically, for accidental deaths arising from technological developments in public use. The analysis is based on two assumptions. The first is that historical national accident records are adequate for revealing consistent patterns of fatalities in the public use of technology. (That this may not always be so is evidenced by the paucity of data relating to the effects of environmental pollution.) The second assumption is that such historically revealed social preferences and costs are sufficiently enduring to permit their use for predictive purposes.

In the absence of economic or sociological theory which might give better results, this empirical approach provides some interesting insights into accepted social values relative to personal risk. Because this methodology is based on historical data, it does not serve to distinguish what is "best" for society from what is "traditionally acceptable."

SCIENCE, September 1969, Vol. 165, pp. 1232-1238.

Maximum Benefit at Minimum Cost

The broad societal benefits of advances in technology exceed the associated costs sufficiently to make technological growth inexorable. Shef's socioeconomic study (1) has indicated that technological growth has been generally exponential in this century, doubling every 20 years in nations having advanced technology. Such technological growth has apparently stimulated a parallel growth in socioeconomic benefits and a slower associated growth in social costs.

The conventional socioeconomic benefits—health, education, income—are presumably indicative of an improvement in the "quality of life." The cost of this socioeconomic progress shows up in all the negative indicators of our society—urban and environmental problems, technological unemployment, poor physical and mental health, and so on. If we understood quantitatively the causal relationships between specific technological developments and societal values, both positive and negative, we might deliberately guide and regulate technological developments so as to achieve maximum social benefit at minimum social cost. Unfortunately, we have not as yet developed such a predictive system analysis. As a result, our society historically has arrived at acceptable balances of technological benefit and social cost empirically—by trial, error, and subsequent corrective steps.

In advanced societies today, this historical empirical approach creates an increasingly critical situation, for two basic reasons. The first is the well-known difficulty in changing a technical subsystem of our society once it has been woven into the economic, political, and cultural structures. For example, many of our environmental-pollution problems have known engineering solutions, but the problems of economic readjustment, political jurisdiction, and social behavior loom very large. It will take many decades to put into effect the technical solutions we know today. To give a specific illustration, the pollution of our water resources could be completely avoided by means of engineering systems now available, but public interest in making the economic and political adjustments needed for applying these techniques is very limited. It has been facetiously suggested that, as a means of motivating the public, every community and industry should be required to place its water intake downstream from its outfall.

In order to minimize these difficulties, it would be desirable to try out new developments in the smallest social groups that would permit adequate assessment. This is a common practice in market-testing a new product or in field-testing a new drug. In both these cases, however, the experiment is completely under the control of a single company or agency, and the test information can be fed back to the controlling group in a time that is short relative to the anticipated commercial lifetime of the product. This makes it possible to achieve essentially optimum use of the product in an acceptably short time. Unfortunately, this is rarely the case with new technologies. Engineering developments involving new technology are likely to appear in many places simultaneously and to become deeply integrated into the systems of our society before their impact is evident or measurable.

This brings us to the second reason for the increasing severity of the problem of obtaining maximum benefits at minimum costs. It has often been stated that the time required from the conception of a technical idea to its first application in society has been drastically shortened by modern engineering organization and management. In fact, the history of technology does not support this conclusion. The bulk of the evidence indicates that the time from conception to first application (or demonstration) has been roughly unchanged by modern management, and depends chiefly on the complexity of the development.

However, what *has* been reduced substantially in the past century is the time from first use to widespread integration into our social system. The techniques for *societal diffusion* of a new technology and its subsequent exploitation are now highly developed. Our ability to organize resources of money, men, and materials to focus on new technological programs has reduced the diffusion-exploitation time by roughly an order of magnitude in the past century.

Thus, we now face a general situation in which widespread use of a new technological development may occur before its social impact can be properly assessed, and before any empirical adjustment of the benefit-versus-cost relation is obviously indicated.

It has been clear for some time that predictive technological assessments are a pressing societal need. However, even if such assessments become available, obtaining maximum social benefit at minimum cost also requires the establishment of a relative value system for the basic parameters in our objective of improved "quality of life." The empirical approach implicitly involved an intuitive societal balancing of such values. A predictive analytical approach will require an explicit scale of relative social values.

For example, if technological assessment of a new development predicts an increased per capita annual income of

x percent but also predicts an associated accident probability of y fatalities annually per million population, then how are these to be compared in their effect on the "quality of life"? Because the penalties or risks to the public arising from a new development can be reduced by applying constraints, there will usually be a functional relationship (or trade-off) between utility and risk, the x and y of our example.

There are many historical illustrations of such trade-off relationships that were empirically determined. For example, automobile and airplane safety have been continuously weighed by society against economic costs and operating performance. In these and other cases, the real trade-off process is actually one of dynamic adjustment with the behavior of many portions of our social systems out of phase, due to the many separate "time constants" involved. Readily available historical data on accidents and health, for a variety of public activities, provide an enticing stepping-stone to quantitative evaluation of this particular type of social cost. The social benefits arising from some of these activities can be roughly determined. On the assumption that in such historical situations a socially acceptable and essentially optimum trade-off of values has been achieved, we could say that any generalizations developed might then be used for predictive purposes. This approach could give a rough answer to the seemingly simple question "How safe is safe enough?"

The pertinence of this question to all of us, and particularly to governmental regulatory agencies, is obvious. Hopefully, a functional answer might provide a basis for establishing performance "design objectives" for the safety of the public.

Voluntary and Involuntary Activities

Societal activities fall into two general categories—those in which the individual participates on a "voluntary" basis and those in which the participation is "involuntary," imposed by the society in which the individual lives. The process of empirical optimization of benefits and costs is fundamentally similar in the two cases—namely, a reversible exploration of available options—but the time required for empirical adjustments (the time constants of the system) and the criteria for optimization are quite different in the two situations.

In the case of "voluntary" activities, the individual uses his own value system to evaluate his experiences. Although his eventual trade-off may not be consciously or analytically determined, or based upon objective knowledge, it nevertheless is likely to represent, for that individual, a crude optimization appropriate to his value system. For example, an urban dweller may move to the suburbs because of a lower crime rate and better schools, at the cost of more time spent traveling on highways and a higher probability of accidents. If, subsequently, the traffic density increases, he may decide that the penalties are too great and move back to the city. Such an individual optimization process can be comparatively rapid (because the feedback of experience to the individual is rapid), so the statistical pattern for a large social group may be an important "real-time" indicator of societal trade-offs and values.

"Involuntary" activities differ in that the criteria and options are determined not by the individuals affected but by a controlling body. Such control may be in the hands of a government agency, a political entity, a leadership group, an assembly of authorities or "opinion-makers," or a combination of such bodies. Because of the complexity of large societies, only the con-

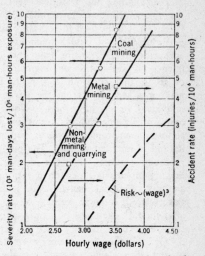

Fig. 1. Mining accident rates plotted relative to incentive.

trol group is likely to be fully aware of all the criteria and options involved in their decision process. Further, the time required for feedback of the experience that results from the controlling decisions is likely to be very long. The feedback of cumulative individual experiences into societal communication channels (usually political or economic) is a slow process, as is the process of altering the planning of the control group. We have many examples of such "involuntary" activities, war being perhaps the most extreme case of the operational separation of the decision-making group from those most affected. Thus, the real-time pattern of societal trade-offs on "involuntary" activities must be considered in terms of the particular dynamics of approach to an acceptable balance of

81

social values and costs. The historical trends in such activities may therefore be more significant indicators of social acceptability than the existent trade-offs are.

In examining the historical benefit-risk relationships for "involuntary" activities, it is important to recognize the perturbing role of public psychological acceptance of risk arising from the influence of authorities or dogma. Because in this situation the decision-making is separated from the affected individual, society has generally clothed many of its controlling groups in an almost impenetrable mantle of authority and of imputed wisdom. The public generally assumes that the decision-making process is based on a rational analysis of social benefit and social risk. While it often is, we have all seen after-the-fact examples of irrationality. It is important to omit such "witch-doctor" situations in selecting examples of optimized "involuntary" activities, because in fact these situations typify only the initial stages of exploration of options.

Quantitative Correlations

With this description of the problem, and the associated caveats, we are in a position to discuss the quantitative correlations. For the sake of simplicity in this initial study, I have taken as a measure of the physical risk to the individual the fatalities (deaths) associated with each activity. Although it might be useful to include all injuries (which are 100 to 1000 times as numerous as deaths), the difficulty in obtaining data and the unequal significance of varying disabilities would introduce inconvenient complexity for this study. So the risk measure used here is the statistical probability of

fatalities per hour of exposure of th individual to the activity considered.

The hour-of-exposure unit was chos en because it was deemed more closel related to the individual's intuitiv process in choosing an activity than year of exposure would be, and gav substantially similar results. Anothe possible alternative, the risk per activ ity, involved a comparison of too man dissimilar units of measure; thus, i comparing the risk for various mode of transportation, one could use ris per hour, per mile, or per trip. As thi study was directed toward exploring methodology for determining social ac ceptance of risk, rather than the safes mode of transportation for a particula trip, the simplest common unit—tha of risk per exposure hour—was chose

The social benefit derived from eac activity was converted into a dolla equivalent, as a measure of integrate value to the individual. This is perhap the most uncertain aspect of the co relations because it reduced the "qua ity-of-life" benefits of an activity to a overly simplistic measure. Nevertheles the correlations seemed useful, and n better measure was available. In th case of the "voluntary" activities, th amount of money spent on the activit by the average involved individual wa assumed proportional to its benefit him. In the case of the "involuntary" a tivities, the contribution of the activit to the individual's annual income (or th equivalent) was assumed proportion to its benefit. This assumption roughly constant relationship betwee benefits and monies, for each class activities, is clearly an approximatio However, because we are dealing i orders of magnitude, the distortior likely to be introduced by this appro imation are relatively small.

In the case of transportation mode the benefits were equated with the su

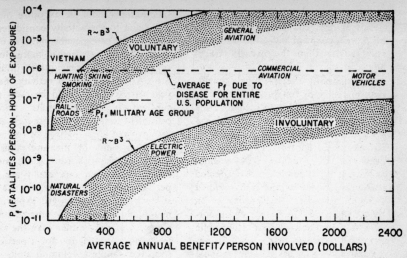

Fig. 2. Risk (R) plotted relative to benefit (B) for various kinds of voluntary and involuntary exposure.

of the monetary cost to the passenger and the value of the time saved by that particular mode relative to a slower, competitive mode. Thus, airplanes were compared with automobiles, and automobiles were compared with public transportation or walking. Benefits of public transportation were equated with their cost. In all cases, the benefits were assessed on an annual dollar basis because this seemed to be most relevant to the individual's intuitive process. For example, most luxury sports require an investment and upkeep only partially dependent upon usage. The associated risks, of course, exist only during the hours of exposure.

Probably the use of electricity provides the best example of the analysis of an "involuntary" activity. In this case the fatalities include those arising from electrocution, electrically caused fires, the operation of power plants, and the mining of the required fossil fuel. The benefits were estimated from a United Nations study of the relation-

ship between energy consumption and national income; the energy fraction associated wtih electric power was used. The contributions of the home use of electric power to our "quality of life"—more subtle than the contributions of electricity in industry—are omitted. The availability of refrigeration has certainly improved our national health and the quality of dining. The electric light has certainly provided great flexibility in patterns of living, and television is a positive element. Perhaps, however, the gross-income measure used in the study is sufficient for present purposes.

Information on acceptance of "voluntary" risk by individuals as a function of income benefits is not easily available, although we know that such a relationship must exist. Of particular interest, therefore, is the special case of miners exposed to high occupational risks. In Fig. 1, the accident rate and the severity rate of mining injuries are plotted against the hourly wage (*2, 3*).

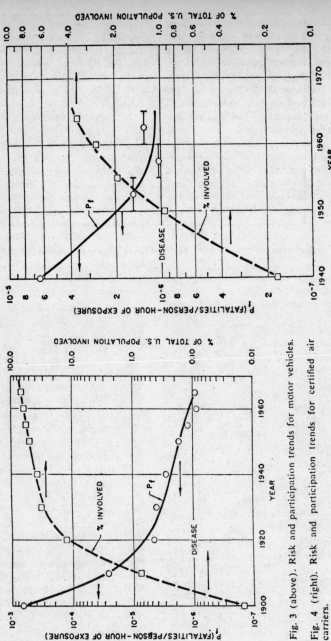

Fig. 3 (above). Risk and participation trends for motor vehicles.

Fig. 4 (right). Risk and participation trends for certified air carriers.

The acceptance of individual risk is an exponential function of the wage, and can be roughly approximated by a third-power relationship in this range. If this relationship has validity, it may mean that several "quality of life" parameters (perhaps health, living essentials, and recreation) are each partly influenced by any increase in available personal resources, and that thus the increased acceptance of risk is exponentially motivated. The extent to which this relationship is "voluntary" for the miners is not obvious, but the subject is interesting nevertheless.

Risk Comparisons

The results for the societal activities studied, both "voluntary" and "involuntary," are assembled in Fig. 2. (For details of the risk-benefit analysis, see the appendix.) Also shown in Fig. 2 is the third-power relationship between risk and benefit characteristic of Fig. 1. For comparison, the average risk of death from accident and from disease is shown. Because the average number of fatalities from accidents is only about one-tenth the number from disease, their inclusion is not significant.

Several major features of the benefit-risk relations are apparent, the most obvious being the difference by several orders of magnitude in society's willingness to accept "voluntary" and "involuntary" risk. As one would expect, we are loathe to let others do unto us what we happily do to ourselves.

The rate of death from disease appears to play, psychologically, a yardstick role in determining the acceptability of risk on a voluntary basis. The risk of death in most sporting activities is surprisingly close to the risk of death from disease—almost as though, in sports, the individual's subconscious computer adjusted his courage and made him take risks associated with a fatality level equaling but not exceeding the statistical mortality due to involuntary exposure to disease. Perhaps this defines the demarcation between boldness and foolhardiness.

In Fig. 2 the statistic for the Vietnam war is shown because it raises an interesting point. It is only slightly above the average for risk of death from disease. Assuming that some long-range societal benefit was anticipated from this war, we find that the related risk, as seen by society as a whole, is not substantially different from the average nonmilitary risk from disease. However, for individuals in the military-service age group (age 20 to 30), the risk of death in Vietnam is about ten times the normal mortality rate (death from accidents or disease). Hence the population as a whole and those directly exposed see this matter from different perspectives. The disease risk pertinent to the average age of the involved group probably would provide the basis for a more meaningful comparison than the risk pertinent to the national average age does. Use of the figure for the single group would complicate these simple comparisons, but that figure might be more significant as a yardstick.

The risks associated with general aviation, commercial aviation, and travel by motor vehicle deserve special comment. The latter originated as a "voluntary" sport, but in the past half-century the motor vehicle has become an essential utility. General aviation is still a highly voluntary activity. Commercial aviation is partly voluntary and partly essential and, additionally, is subject to government administration as a transportation utility.

Travel by motor vehicle has now reached a benefit-risk balance, as shown

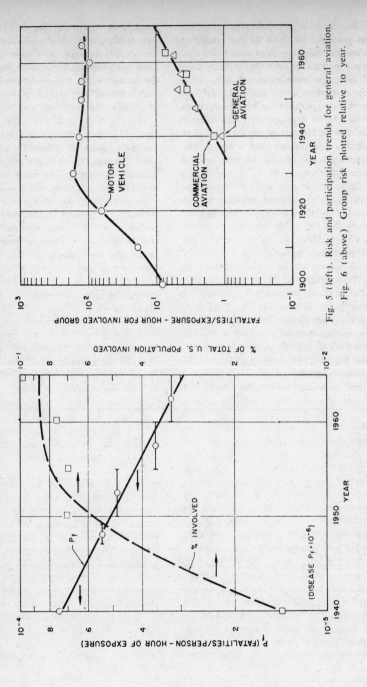

Fig. 5 (left). Risk and participation trends for general aviation.
Fig. 6 (above) Group risk plotted relative to year.

in Fig. 3. It is interesting to note that the present risk level is only slightly below the basic level of risk from disease. In view of the high percentage of the population involved, this probably represents a true societal judgment on the acceptability of risk in relation to benefit. It also appears from Fig. 3 that future reductions in the risk level will be slow in coming, even if the historical trend of improvement can be maintained (4).

Commercial aviation has barely approached a risk level comparable to that set by disease. The trend is similar to that for motor vehicles, as shown in Fig. 4. However, the percentage of the population participating is now only 1/20 that for motor vehicles. Increased public participation in commercial aviation will undoubtedly increase the pressure to reduce the risk, because, for the general population, the benefits are much less than those associated with motor vehicles. Commercial aviation has not yet reached the point of optimum benefit-risk trade-off (5).

For general aviation the trends are similar, as shown in Fig. 5. Here the risk levels are so high (20 times the risk from disease) that this activity must properly be considered to be in the category of adventuresome sport. However, the rate of risk is decreasing so rapidly that eventually the risk for general aviation may be little higher than that for commercial aviation. Since the percentage of the population involved is very small, it appears that the present average risk levels are acceptable to only a limited group (6).

The similarity of the trends in Figs. 3–5 may be the basis for another hypothesis, as follows: the acceptable risk is inversely related to the number of people participating in an activity.

The product of the risk and the percentage of the population involved in each of the activities of Figs. 3–5 is plotted in Fig. 6. This graph represents the historical trend of total fatalities per hour of exposure of the population involved (7). The leveling off of motor-vehicle risk at about 100 fatalities per hour of exposure of the partici-

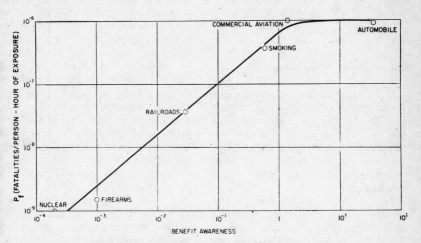

Fig. 7. Accepted risk plotted relative to benefit awareness (see text).

pating population may be significant. Because most of the U.S. population is involved, this rate of fatalities may have sufficient public visibility to set a level of social acceptability. It is interesting, and disconcerting, to note that the trend of fatalities in aviation, both commercial and general, is uniformly upward.

Public Awareness

Finally, I attempted to relate these risk data to a crude measure of public awareness of the associated social benefits (see Fig. 7). The "benefit awareness" was arbitrarily defined as the product of the relative level of advertising, the square of the percentage of population involved in the activity, and the relative usefulness (or importance) of the activity to the individual (8). Perhaps these assumptions are too crude, but Fig. 7 does support the reasonable position that advertising the benefits of an activity increases public acceptance of a greater level of risk. This, of course could subtly produce a fictitious benefit-risk ratio—as may be the case for smoking.

Atomic Power Plant Safety

I recognize the uncertainty inherent in the quantitative approach discussed here, but the trends and magnitudes may nevertheless be of sufficient validity to warrant their use in determining national "design objectives" for technological activities. How would this be done?

Let us consider as an example the introduction of nuclear power plants as a principal source of electric power. This is an especially good example because the technology has been primar-

ily nurtured, guided, and regulated by the government, with industry undertaking the engineering development and the diffusion into public use. The government specifically maintains responsibility for public safety. Further, the engineering of nuclear plants permits continuous reduction of the probability of accidents, at a substantial increase in cost. Thus, the trade-off of utility and potential risk can be made quantitative.

Moreover, in the case of the nuclear power plant the historical empirical approach to achieving an optimum benefit-risk trade-off is not pragmatically feasible. All such plants are now so safe that it may be 30 years or longer before meaningful risk experience will be accumulated. By that time, many plants of varied design will be in existence, and the empirical accident data may not be applicable to those being built. So a very real need exists now to establish "design objectives" on a predictive-performance basis.

Let us first arbitrarily assume that nuclear power plants should be as safe as coal-burning plants, so as not to increase public risk. Figure 2 indicates that the total risk to society from electric power is about 2×10^{-9} fatality per person per hour of exposure. Fossil fuel plants contribute about 1/5 of this risk, or about 4 deaths per million population per year. In a modern society a million people may require a million kilowatts of power, and this is about the size of most new power stations. So, we now have a target risk limit of 4 deaths per year per million-kilowatt power station (9).

Technical studies of the consequences of hypothetical extreme (and unlikely) nuclear power plant catastrophes, which would disperse radioactivity into populated areas, have indicated that abou

10 lethal cancers per million population might result (10). On this basis, we calculate that such a power plant might statistically have one such accident every 3 years and still meet the risk limit set. However, such a catastrophe would completely destroy a major portion of the nuclear section of the plant and either require complete dismantling or years of costly reconstruction. Because power companies expect plants to last about 30 years, the economic consequences of a catastrophe every few years would be completely unacceptable. In fact, the operating companies would not accept one such failure, on a statistical basis, during the normal lifetime of the plant.

It is likely that, in order to meet the economic performance requirements of the power companies, a catastrophe rate of less than 1 in about 100 plant-years would be needed. This would be a public risk of 10 deaths per 100 plant-years, or 0.1 death per year per million population. So the economic investment criteria of the nuclear plant user—the power company—would probably set a risk level 1/200 the present socially accepted risk associated with electric power, or 1/40 the present risk associated with coal-burning plants.

An obvious design question is this: Can a nuclear power plant be engineered with a predicted performance of less than 1 catastrophic failure in 100 plant-years of operation? I believe the answer is yes, but that is a subject for a different occasion. The principal point is that the issue of public safety can be focused on a tangible, quantitative, engineering design objective.

This example reveals a public safety consideration which may apply to many other activities: The economic require-ment for the protection of major capital investments may often be a more demanding safety constraint than social acceptability.

Conclusion

The application of this approach to other areas of public responsibility is self-evident. It provides a useful methodology for answering the question "How safe is safe enough?" Further, although this study is only exploratory, it reveals several interesting points. (i) The indications are that the public is willing to accept "voluntary" risks roughly 1000 times greater than "involuntary" risks. (ii) The statistical risk of death from disease appears to be a psychological yardstick for establishing the level of acceptability of other risks. (iii) The acceptability of risk appears to be crudely proportional to the third power of the benefits (real or imagined). (iv) The social acceptance of risk is directly influenced by public awareness of the benefits of an activity, as determined by advertising, usefulness, and the number of people participating. (v) In a sample application of these criteria to atomic power plant safety, it appears that an engineering design objective determined by economic criteria would result in a design-target risk level very much lower than the present socially accepted risk for electric power plants.

Perhaps of greatest interest is the fact that this methodology for revealing existing social preferences and values may be a means of providing the insight on social benefit relative to cost that is so necessary for judicious national decisions on new technological developments.

Appendix: Details of
Risk-Benefit Analysis

Motor-vehicle travel. The calculation of motor-vehicle fatalities per exposure hour per year is based on the number of registered cars, an assumed 1½ persons per car, and an assumed 400 hours per year of average car use [data from *3* and *11*]. The figure for annual benefit for motor-vehicle travel is based on the sum of costs for gasoline, maintenance, insurance, and car payments and on the value of the time savings per person. It is assumed that use of an automobile allows a person to save 1 hour per working day and that a person's time is worth $5 per hour.

Travel by air route carrier. The estimate of passenger fatalities per passenger-hour of exposure for certified air route carriers is based on the annual number of passenger fatalities listed in the *FAA Statistical Handbook of Aviation* (see *12*) and the number of passenger-hours per year. The latter number is estimated from the average number of seats per plane, the seat load factor, the number of revenue miles flown per year, and the average plane speed (data from *3*). The benefit for travel by certified air route carrier is based on the average annual air fare per passenger-mile and on the value of the time saved as a result of air travel. The cost per passenger is estimated from the average rate per passenger-mile (data from *3*), the revenue miles flown per year (data from *12*), the annual number of passenger boardings for 1967 (132×10^6, according to the United Air Lines News Bureau), and the assumption of 12 boardings per passenger.

General aviation. The number of fatalities per passenger-hour for general aviation is a function of the number of annual fatalities, the number of plane hours flown per year, and the average number of passengers per plane (estimated from the ratio of fatalities to fatal crashes) (data from *12*). It is assumed that in 1967 the cash outlay for initial expenditures and maintenance costs for general aviation was 1.5×10^9. The benefit is expressed in terms of annual cash outlay per person, and the estimate is based on the number of passenger-hours per year and the assumption that the average person flies 20 hours, or 4000 miles, annually. The value of the time saved is based on the assumption that a person's time is

worth $10 per hour and that he saves 60 hours per year through traveling the 4000 miles by air instead of by automobile at 50 miles per hour.

Railroad travel. The estimate of railroad passenger fatalities per exposure hour per year is based on annual passenger fatalities and passenger-miles and an assumed average train speed of 50 miles per hour (data from *11*). The passenger benefit for railroads is based on figures for revenue and passenger-miles for commuters and noncommuters given in *The Yearbook of Railroad Facts* (Association of American Railroads, 1968). It is assumed that the average commuter travels 20 miles per workday by rail and that the average noncommuter travels 1000 miles per year by rail.

Skiing. The estimate for skiing fatalities per exposure hour is based on information obtained from the National Ski Patrol for the 1967–68 southern California ski season: 1 fatality, 17 days of skiing. 16,500 skiers per day, and 5 hours of skiing per skier per day. The estimate of benefit for skiing is based on the average number of days of skiing per year per person and the average cost of a typical ski trip [data from "The Skier Market in Northeast North America," *U.S. Dep. Commerce Publ.* (1965)]. In addition, it is assumed that a skier spends an average of $25 per year on equipment.

Hunting. The estimate of the risk in hunting is based on an assumed value of 10 hours' exposure per hunting day, the annual number of hunting fatalities, the number of hunters, and the average number of hunting days per year [data from *11* and from "National Survey of Fishing and Hunting," *U.S. Fish Wildlife Serv. Publ.* (1965)]. The average annual expenditure per hunter was $82.54 in 1965 (data from *3*).

Smoking. The estimate of the risk from smoking is based on the ratio for the mortality of smokers relative to nonsmokers, the rates of fatalities from heart disease and cancer for the general population, and the assumption that the risk is continuous [data from the *Summary of the Report of the Surgeon General's Advisory Committee on Smoking and Health* (Government Printing Office, Washington, D.C., 1964)]. The annual intangible benefit to the cigarette smoker is calculated from the American Cancer Society's estimate that 30 percent of the population smokes cigarettes, from the number of cigarettes smoked per year (see *3*), and from the assumed retail cost of $0.015 per cigarette.

Vietnam. The estimate of the risk associated with the Vietnam war is based on the assumption that 500,000 men are exposed there annually to the risk of death and that the fatality rate is 10,000 men per year. The benefit for Vietnam is calculated on the assumption that the entire U.S. population benefits intangibly from the annual Vietnam expenditure of $30 × 10⁹.

Electric power. The estimate of the risk associated with the use of electric power is based on the number of deaths from electric current; the number of deaths from fires caused by electricity; the number of deaths that occur in coal mining, weighted by the percentage of total coal production used to produce electricity; and the number of deaths attributable to air pollution from fossil fuel stations [data from *3* and *11* and from *Nuclear Safety* *5*, 325 (1964)]. It is assumed that the entire U.S. population is exposed for 8760 hours per year to the risk associated with electric power. The estimate for the benefit is based on the assumption that there is a direct correlation between per capita gross national product and commercial energy consumption for the nations of the world [data from Briggs, *Technology and Economic Development* (Knopf, New York, 1963)]. It is further assumed that 35 percent of the energy consumed in the U.S. is used to produce electricity.

Natural disasters. The risk associated with natural disasters was computed for U.S. floods (2.5×10^{-10} fatality per person-hour of exposure), tornadoes in the Midwest (2.46×10^{-10} fatality), major U.S. storms (0.8×10^{-10} fatality), and California earthquakes (1.9×10^{-10} fatality) (data from *11*). The value for flood risk is based on the assumption that everyone in the U.S. is exposed to the danger 24 hours per day. No benefit figure was assigned in the case of natural disasters.

Disease and accidents. The average risk in the U.S. due to disease and accidents is computed from data given in *Vital Statistics of the U.S.* (Government Printing Office, Washington, D.C., 1967).

References and Notes

1. A. L. Shef, "Socio-economic attributes of our technological society," paper presented before the IEEE (Institute of Electrical and Electronics Engineers) Wescon Conference, Los Angeles, August 1968.
2. *Minerals Yearbook* (Government Printing Office, Washington, D.C., 1966).
3. *U.S. Statistical Abstract* (Government Printing Office, Washington, D.C., 1967).
4. The procedure outlined in the appendix was used in calculating the risk associated with motor-vehicle travel. In order to calculate exposure hours for various years, it was assumed that the average annual driving time per car increased linearly from 50 hours in 1900 to 400 hours in 1960 and thereafter. The percentage of people involved is based on the U.S. population, the number of registered cars, and the assumed value of 1.5 people per car.
5. The procedure outlined in the appendix was used in calculating the risk associated with, and the number of people who fly in, certified air route carriers for 1967. For a given year, the number of people who fly is estimated from the total number of passenger boardings and the assumption that the average passenger makes six round trips per year (data from *3*).
6. The method of calculating risk for general aviation is outlined in the appendix. For a given year, the percentage of people involved is defined by the number of active aircraft (see *3*); the number of people per plane, as defined by the ratio of fatalities to fatal crashes; and the population of the U.S.
7. Group risk per exposure hour for the involved group is defined as the number of fatalities per person-hour of exposure multiplied by the number of people who participate in the activity. The group population and the risk for motor vehicles, certified air route carriers, and general aviation can be obtained from Figs. 3–5.
8. In calculating "benefit awareness" it is assumed that the public's awareness of an activity is a function of *A*, the amount of money spent on advertising; *P*, the number of people who take part in the activity; and *U*, the utility value of the activity to the person involved. *A* is based on the amount of money spent by a particular industry in advertising its product, normalized with respect to the food and food products industry, which is the leading advertiser in the U.S.
9. In comparing nuclear and fossil fuel power stations, the risks associated with the plant effluents and mining of the fuel should be included in each case. The fatalities associated with coal mining are about ¼ the total attributable to fossil fuel plants. As the tonnage of uranium ore required for an equivalent nuclear plant is less than the coal tonnage by more than an order of magnitude, the nuclear plant problem primarily involves hazard from effluent.

10. This number is my estimate for maximum fatalities from an extreme catastrophe resulting from malfunction of a typical power reactor. For a methodology for making this calculation, see F. R. Farmer, "Siting criteria—a new approach," paper presented at the International Atomic Energy Agency Symposium in Vienna, April 1967. Application of Farmer's method to a fast breeder power plant in a modern building gives a prediction of fatalities less than this assumed limit by one or two orders of magnitude.

11. "Accident Facts," *Nat. Safety Counc. Publ.* (1967).

12. *FAA Statistical Handbook of Aviation* (Government Printing Office, Washington, D.C., 1965).

How Should We Treat Environment?

University organization presently permits only
piecemeal consideration of environmental problems.

F. Kenneth Hare

I was asked this question recently by
a group at a major American university, and I have spent a long time
pondering it. What should be the scope
of environmental studies? How should
they be organized? What is the relation
between the political interest in environment and the things that make sense on
the campus? I believe that we can answer these questions only if we are
willing to poke hard at the university's
cherished myths, and that we shall
not make any sense politically until
we have sorted ourselves out. The
climate of the times demands that we
do make political sense.

I had read an illuminating study of
the political implications of concern for
the environment (1), and in August I
had the chance of listening to a dis-
course Caldwell gave privately (2). Although silent during the discussion that
followed, I responded next day with
an open letter to Caldwell's host, C. P.
Runge, who has allowed me to amplify
this letter into an article for wider
circulation. I am not the first person
to be set in motion by Caldwell's
clarity and realism. In spite of his involvement in congressional affairs he
looks at the question as I think all
academics must—as one that we cannot
ignore.

I will look mainly at the question
of environmental studies in large, struc-
turally complex universities like those
spread widely over the Middle West.
We all know the conservative quality of
such places, where nothing can easily
be done for either the first or the last
time. The status quo is defended in
depth by the vested interests of a large
number of able people. Among these
interests are those of the traditional
departments and the largely analytical
disciplines they profess. Also strong are
the numerous special institutes and
centers that have gotten started in spite
of the resistance of the departments.
When we propose to start up a broad-
spectrum, synthesizing effort like environmental studies we run full tilt into
all these vested interests.

We also bang ourselves against the
clan spirit of the traditional faculty
groupings. Humanists, social scientists,
natural scientists, and professionals like
lawyers and engineers may fight like
cats within the clan, but they close
ranks and hitch up their kilts when
someone questions their loyalties. Environmental studies have to involve
many of these clans, which are not
used to combining in the way required.
If we suggest, as I do, that some of
them—notably the humanists—may be

SCIENCE, January, 1970, Vol. 167, pp. 352-355.

93

utterly trans' rmed by such combinations, we alarm the timid and anger the Tories among them.

But the greatest hazard in our path is inherent in Lyndon Johnson's acid query "Therefore, what?," which he is said to have thrown at a group of professors who had just briefed him on the Middle Eastern situation. The political interest in the environment demands proposals for *action*—on all time scales, from the immediate assault on pollution problems and other festering sores of today, to the long-term reconstruction of society in a better relation with environment. At present we are not equipped to make such proposals. We are not action-oriented, and on every campus there is a deadweight of opinion that regards action-oriented programs as hostile to the academic life.

In many ways this fear is justified. Being action-oriented, getting ourselves involved in planning society's future, and mending its present broken bones, does indeed threaten the selfish individualism and pursuit of our own **private thing that we call academic freedom.** If we take on the job outlined by Caldwell, we must have a lot more institutional discipline. If the university as a whole adopts social goals of this kind, we must accept a greater degree of common directed action—of teamwork—than we are used to in most faculties. Doctors and engineers do this all the time. It will be in the humanities and social science areas where the shock will be most felt, because these are the chief homes of the lone wolf (*3*).

I must also stress the incompetence of the established disciplines to tackle many of society's real problems. What we mean by a discipline is an agreed, tested body of method—usually analytical—that we bring to bear on problems of our own choosing. The essence of our thinking is that we cannot tackle problems that do not fit the competence of our own discipline. It is true that we constantly try to enlarge that competence. Confronted with a new problem, we spare no effort to improve our methods. But if we do not succeed, we do not tackle the problem, and we tend to condemn colleagues who try.

Public policy—such as environmental control and design policies—can never insulate itself in this way. It has to face the real problems as they present themselves in all their complexity, and policy makers have to act on highly inadequate preparation and incomplete evidence. Policy-making is a crude process in which synthesis or just guesswork precedes accurate analysis. Moreover, it is nearly always broad spectrum in character, because no important social problem is ever simple and none ever lies fully within the competence of a single academic discipline. Even such questions as monetary and fiscal policy contain large components outside economics. We therefore arrive at the pessimistic conclusions that (i) the existing departmental and disciplinary structure of the university is out of kilter with the needs of action-oriented, policy-directed programs, and that (ii) we do not yet know how to adapt ourselves to this sort of challenge. We shall have to change, in fact, without knowing how to start.

What change, and how do we bring it off?

Our usual response is to say, "We are dealing with an interdisciplinary problem"; or, like the American Water Resources Association, "a multidisciplinary problem." In the past 20 years North American universities have said this many thousands of times. The result has been the proliferation of institutes, centers, programs, and so forth, dedicated to some problem, usually dominated by an individual with an idea, and legitimized by a committee. Most of these ventures have a short life, and most fail to survive the departure of the dominant individual. We can easily see that the step toward environmental studies is another and very ambitious move of this kind, and we must stop to ask ourselves the larger question—how do we create a more stable kind of interdisciplinary organism? *(4)*.

The answer, I suggest, is that the study of problems such as we have been discussing is not simply interdisciplinary in the sense that it involves several of the old disciplines. Instead it demands a new kind of discipline, basically synthesizing in method. I am sure that the university will have to answer more and more calls to solve social problems, and that, if we do not answer these calls, we shall be bypassed by the creation of new kinds of institutions more flexible and realistic in outlook. I conclude that we must learn to develop these new disciplines of synthesis, and make them as rigorous as the older analytical disciplines. I can hear the scoffers scoffing—but, if we do not tackle this, we shall deserve to be counted out. By all means let us encourage interdisciplinary ventures— but in the hope that they will indeed become disciplines of the new kind.

I am aware that this is a gross oversimplification. No discipline is ever wholly analytic or wholly synthetic. None is completely logical and consistent in its methods. It is clear nonetheless that chemistry and physics are quite different from geography and history. The first two characteristically isolate phenomena and study them as exactly as they can under close experimental control; the second two take the world as it comes—or as it came— and necessarily deal with a complex of things and events. As a geographer I have recently been feeling, ironically, that the tide of events is turning my way. My colleagues and I have been trying for a century to deal with a problem that is now announced as new —the study of man in his environmental setting.

There are, that is to say, a few of the broad disciplines already, and there are moves toward more. Systems thinking is popular, and the jargon of systems analysis even more so. Among many of the new social quantifiers the word "synthesis" is regarded with contempt: "multivariate analysis" sounds better. I suggest that the past century was the era in which we achieved great things by dissecting reality so that we could look at its fine texture; and that is how most of our existing disciplines got going. The next century will be that in which we learn to cope intellectually with complexes of things, and especially with those that make up the environment of man.

Organization

Turning now to organization, I agree with Caldwell and others who say that success in environmental studies depends on the will to do it rather than on specific structural changes. What such ventures need are dedicated charismatic leaders, well known and respected on the campus, who will set out to create this will. I do not think that a massive before-the-fact recasting of the academic façade will achieve anything, and, unless you are in a very untypical university, it will engender factional opposition. So why not proceed informally?

If you decide to take the plunge, I suggest you gather round you all the like-minded members of the university you can find. Do not call yourselves a committee—be like the most successful scientific society I know, the Friends of the Pleistocene, which I believe has no officers, no journal, no headquarters, no subscription—but lots of members and solid achievement. The group or cabal (a term I favor) ought to point to its own most galvanic member and say, "You are it!" And he in turn ought to be trusted to go to Washington to fight for funds, having first got the pledges he needs from those willing to help. If you succeed and in 2 or 3 years have begun to get solid results, it ought to be easier to persuade other groups on the campus to join in.

Scope

And finally, the question of scope. This is difficult, because without even trying you can relate nearly everything to the theme "man and environment." The scope of an academic program in environmental studies has to be broad enough to catch the imagination of faculty and students, but narrow enough to avoid differences. It also has to be clearly related to social goals, for reasons of conscience as well as fundraising.

At the outset I make the distinction between (i) short-term correction of technological errors, broadly "pollution control," and (ii) long-term design and control of the environment. The first is often summarized as "environmental quality," though this is a misnomer. I object also to the notion of "restoring the quality," because we should have to go too far back in time to do it—at least to the Neolithic.

The short-term problem of pollution control is as far as present-day public concern goes, except for certain farsighted men in and out—mostly out—of the universities. The Tukey Report of 1965 (5) defines this problem concisely; the report admits that Western industrial societies have made a mess of their own home, partly because human beings are just messy, but also because of the overconfident use of technological aids such as pesticides, the profligate overuse of resources like water, and the burning of fossil fuels. This has messed up America, and threatens to mess up the world. The report makes 104 sweeping recommendations for action, adding that this is an incomplete list, and publishes valuable appendices that offer the most authoritative review of the pollution problem. Hardly any of the recommendations have been acted upon, though they have had some effect on government practices.

It is quite clear that many of the problems defined by the authors of the Tukey report can be tackled by the universities. They stress the need for graduates trained in the necessary skills and fired with a concern for environmental restoration. Many of the specific recommendations touch on the need for the universities to undertake research and research-training in the field. It is also clear that the large modern university can be and already is involved in tackling the ad hoc problems enumerated in the report.

I do not, however, believe that a major university can sweepingly alter its work and outlook by adopting such a negative theme as the correction of past error. Something altogether more exciting and far reaching is needed. I look for this in the idea that in future we shall increasingly control and design our environment. We live in an era

96

when we can extend our horizons for such control from the walls of our house to the ends of the earth. It will take time, but I have no doubt that we can and must convert this planet, not into a spaceship, which it already is, but into a safer and more comfortable home for our whole species and for the other living things with whom we coexist—and without whom, of course, we could neither eat nor breathe.

Boulding has argued that economics and ecology must come together; otherwise ecology is only bird-watching and egg-snatching, and economics continues to be dismal (6). We have to earn our living by seeing to it that the rest of the living world can survive, too.

If we take this long-term, exalted view, how do we define environment? From a man's-eye view we can perceive these possibilities: (i) The natural environment, which means the physical-biotic world outside society, and our interactions with it. This view supposes that it is feasible to separate our handi-work from that of nature. It is the view that President Johnson took when he established the Environmental Science Services Administration. In his message he spoke of a unified treatment of the natural environment (7). It is also the logic behind the creation in 1965 of Britain's Natural Environment Research Council, though I can testify as a founding member of that body that it took my colleagues a good while before they would have admitted, by majority vote, that a unified treatment of the environment was a useful exercise (8). (ii) The social environment, which arises from the obvious fact that each of us has to survive in a matrix of our fellow men, and that each society must coexist with surrounding societies. In practice for most of us this means the problems of the Western city, with its nightmare inade-

quacies. On a world scale it must also mean the tensions of rural India and Pakistan, the Red Guards of Maoist China, and the tribal strife of some African countries. Nearly all the deep-seated political problems of the world reside here. It is often argued that a major function of environmental design must be to reduce these tensions—as, for example, in the rebuilding of city centers. (iii) The built environment, which recognizes that man-made structures provide the actual home of both working and sleeping mankind, and in the richer societies that it also accommodates his play, his higher culture (whatever that may mean), and his vulgarities. Geographers have long talked about the cultural landscape, meaning that the built element in environment extends to the countryside. Landscape architects have a similar concern. (iv) Finally, there is the total environment, which pops up in the more exalted literature, and which seems to mean (i) + (ii) + (iii). The trouble with such concepts is that the thing environed gets so mixed up with the environment that they become rather fuzzy.

I am not sure that we ought not to add to this list the spatial or geographic environment, in which (i), (ii), and (iii) occur intermixed, but are sufficiently spread out to be manageable. Certainly the environment of the ecologically minded geographer is a rather different thing from the sum of the components of the natural environment.

In many universities that have launched environmental studies, there is only provision to look after the natural environment, and the grouping consists of various interested parties in the physical and biological sciences, sometimes with the geographers thrown in. In others, the entire enterprise is given a strongly ecological twist. In still others the emphasis is upon planning, and the prime movers are architects. The number of open options is large, but one rarely finds a case where a university has committed itself deeply to a broadly based curriculum. In all cases known to me these are new universities—Wisconsin at Green Bay, East Anglia (U.K.), and Waterloo (Ontario), for example. In these places, environmental studies have been elevated to a par with arts, science, and the other traditional faculties. This is easy when the world seems young.

I assume that in major, highly evolved centers, where the great strength lies in the diversity of research skills and in the numbers of first-rate thinkers in the relevant disciplines, the starting point should be in research and graduate training. The enterprise's sponsors ought to start out by saying something like the following:

1) The university considers that the study of man's environment, natural, social, built, and complex, presents a splendid focus for future academic development. It not only touches on a life-and-death problem for the supporting society, but opens up new lines of intellectual experiment that ought to keep us busy for a generation or more.

2) The framework of a unified program of environmental studies is ecological in the largest sense. It is made up of the links that in the real world connect a man's work and play with the people that surround him, his society with neighboring societies, and human society at large with the rest of the natural world. These links allow flows of energy and mass between domains, the kind of thing that some ecologists deal with in the ecology of biota. They also represent, for those connecting man with man directly, links in some kind of intellectual domain; if I were as obscure as Teilhard, I would call these the strands of the noosphere. And finally, and in concrete terms, the links represent, for civilized as well as barbarous societies, lines along which some of man's most important institutions must operate. We have achieved the proper outlook for environmental studies when and if we can see, or to want to see, these links in a unified ecological framework.

3) We have to admit that our viewpoint is that of Western industrialized society, and that we shall be working out our program in the light of that society's past mistakes and assumptions for its own future. This implies (i) that the Western value system is of direct concern to us, and that humanists ought to be deeply involved in environmental studies; and (ii) that we must not make the mistake of assuming that other societies have similar relations with environment, nor should they be expected to have Westernized ambitions for the future. Rather, in fact, the reverse. It should be a major objective of those involved in environmental studies to alter the Western outlook on such questions. We shall solve our environmental problems only by deepseated changes in society itself.

4) Given that we achieve this altered outlook, it still seems likely that Western society will become even more completely urbanized in the future. It is hence necessary that the social sciences and psychology play a major role in environmental studies. The field of urban and regional planning is equally central, though I share Boulding's feeling that much of what we have done in these areas is well-meant error (9). I think it is clear, nevertheless, that we shall increasingly try to deliberately design and build our future environment:

and the core of our program should be a painstaking attempt to create a better atmosphere for such conscious creation.

5) Putting environmental theory into practice means political action, and the evolution of institutions to cope with the new ideas and requirements. Hence we can not hope to succeed without political scientists like Caldwell, institutions like Resources for the Future and the Conservation Foundation, and concerned public figures.

All this adds up to the fact that a really positive and successful program of environmental studies ought to involve a large part of the university, and it ought to spread downward until it contributes heavily to the undergraduate curriculum and influences what is done in the schools.

References and Notes

1. L. K. Caldwell, in *Future Environments of North America*, F. F. Darling and J. P. Milton, Eds. (Natural History Press, New York, 1969), pp. 648-671.
2. I owe a debt to C. P. Runge, and to C. A. Engman, R. Bryson, and V. R. Potter (Univ. of Wisconsin) for many discussions of this subject, and for permission to publish this article.
3. At least one graduate dean, on hearing me express this view, says that engineers are as troublesome as the rest of us!
4. I realized this point only after discussion with Bryson and Potter. See also V. R. Potter, *Land Econ.* 38(1), 1 (1962).
5. J. W. Tukey, chairman, and Environmental Panel, President's Science Advisory Committee, report, *Restoring the Quality of Our Environment* (White House, Washington, D.C., 1965).
6. K. E. Boulding, in *Future Environments of North America*, F. F. Darling and J. P. Milton, Eds. (Natural History Press, New York, 1966), pp. 225-234.
7. L. B. Johnson, letter of transmittal to the Congress, on Reorganization Plan No. 2, 1965, the United States Weather Bureau. See *Bull. Amer. Meteorol. Soc.* 46, 457 (1965).
8. I compared the two bodies in F. K. Hare, *Geography* 51(2), 99 (1966).
9. K. E. Boulding, in *Future Environments of North America*, F. F. Darling and J. P. Milton, Eds. (Natural History Press, New York, 1966), pp. 291-292.

Man and His Environment

Economic factors are more important than population growth in threatening the quality of American life.

Ansley J. Coale

The way our economy is organized is an essential cause, if not *the* essential cause, of air and water pollution, and of the ugly and sometimes destructive accumulation of trash. I believe it is also an important element in such dangerous human ecological interventions as changes in the biosphere resulting from the wholesale use of inorganic fertilizers, of the accumulation in various dangerous places such as the fatty tissue of fish and birds and mammals of incredibly stable insecticides. We can properly attribute such adverse effects to a combination of a high level of economic activity and the use of harmful technological practices that are inconsistent with such a high level.

The economist would say that harmful practices have occurred because of a disregard of what he would call *externalities*. An externality is defined as a consequence (good or bad) that does not enter the calculations of gain or loss by the person who undertakes an economic activity. It is typically a cost (or a benefit) of an activity that accrues to someone else. A fence erected in a suburban neighborhood for privacy also affords a measure of privacy to the neighbor—a cost or a benefit depending on how he feels about privacy versus keeping track of what goes on next door. Air pollution created by an industrial plant is a classic case of an externality; the operator of a factory producing noxious smoke imposes costs on everyone downwind, and pays none of these costs himself—they do not affect his balance sheet at all. This, I believe, is the basic economic factor that has a degrading effect on the environment: we have in general permitted economic activities without assessing the operator for their adverse effects. There has been no attempt to evaluate—and to charge for—externalities. As Boulding says, we pay people for the goods they produce, but do not make them pay for the bads.

To put the same point more simply: environmental deterioration has arisen to a large extent because we have treated pure air, pure water, and the disposal of waste as if they were free. They cannot be treated as free in a modern, urban, industrial society.

There are a number of different kinds of policies that would prevent, or at least reduce, the harmful side effects of some of our economic activities, either by preventing or reducing the volume of the harmful activity, or by inducing a change in technique. Other policies might involve curative rather than preventive steps, such as cleaning up trash along the highways, if we cannot prevent people from de-

SCIENCE, October, 1970, Vol. 170, pp. 132-136.

positing it there.

Among the possibilities are steps that would make externalities internal. An example that I find appealing, although it is perhaps not widely practical, is to require users of flowing water to take in the water downstream of their operation and discharge it upstream. A more general measure is to require the recycling of air or water used in industrial processes, rather than permitting the free use of fresh water and clean air, combined with the unmonitored discharge of exhaust products.

Public authorities can charge for unfavorable external effects by imposing a tax on operations that are harmful to the environment. The purpose of such taxes is to reduce the volume of adverse effects by inducing a shift in technique or by reducing the volume of production by causing a rise in price. Also, the tax receipts could be used to pay for mitigating the effect. An example of a desirable tax is one imposed to minimize the use of disposable cans and bottles for soft drinks and beer. Not long ago the majority of manufacturers produced these commodities in containers that were to be returned. The producer offered a modest price for returning bottles as an inducement. It has proven cheaper to use disposable glass bottles and cans; recently aluminum cans have rapidly increased in popularity, substituting a container that lasts indefinitely for the tin cans that would sooner or later rust away. Everyone is familiar with the resultant clutter on beaches, in parks, and along the highways. If a tax of 10 cents per unit were imposed on each disposable container, it would clearly be cheaper to go back to returnables. If some manufacturers found it advantageous to pay the 10-cent tax, the receipts could be used to pay for cleaning up highways and beaches.

Another approach that would induce people to give up economic activities with harmful effects on others is to make individuals and corporations financially liable for any damage caused by their operations. The resultant litigation would be an unwarranted windfall for lawyers, but financial liability might be a very potent factor in reducing pollution.

There is general agreement that our knowledge of what affects the environment is wholly inadequate. Because of inadequate monitoring and measurement, we do not know what is happening to the atmosphere or the biosphere; we need research to keep track of what is going on as well as to develop the techniques that will produce the goods we want with fewer of the bads we do not want.

An Economist's Review of Resource Exhaustion

One of the questions most frequently raised about the environmental effects of modern life is the rapid and rising rate of extraction of raw materials. Are we running out of resources?

I would first like to note that the distinction between renewable and nonrenewable resources is not a clear one. There are, of course, instances of nonrenewable resources in the form of concentrated sources of energy, such as the fossil fuels. These are reservoirs of reduced carbon embodying radiant energy from the sun that accumulated over many thousands of years. When these fuels are used, the energy that is released is to a large extent radiated into space, and we have no way of reclaiming it. The geological processes that are constantly renewing the fossil deposits of carbon are so slow compared to the rate at which we are burning the fuels that the designation "nonrenewable" is appropriate.

On the other hand, when we think of our resources of such useful materials as the metallic elements of iron, copper, nickel, lead, and so forth, we should realize that spaceship Earth has the same amount of each element as it had a million years ago, and will have the same amount a million years from now. All we do with these resources is to move them around. The energy we use is lost, but the minerals we find useful are still with us. It does not pay to recycle these minerals (that is to use them repeatedly by reclaiming scrap) because the deposits of minerals in the ground or in the ocean are still such a cheap source. It must be noted that the mining of fresh ore is cheaper than the use of scrap in part because miners are not charged for their "externalities." If harmful by-products of mining could not be discharged into streams, if mine tailings were regulated, and erosion-producing or even unesthetic practices forbidden, minerals would be more expensive and recycling more attractive. In the production of any metallic element, the easier sources are exploited first. As mining gets more difficult, the ore gets more expensive, and recycling becomes more nearly competitive. It seems wholly probable that the technology of recycling will be improved.

The surprising fact is that raw materials are not at the moment very costly, and moreover their cost relative to the cost of finished goods has not been increasing. The gross national product in the United States is more than $4500 per capita and the raw materials component per capita is less than $100. The price of raw materials relative to the price of finished goods is no higher now than at the beginning of the century, and if we were running out of raw materials, they would surely be rising in relative expensiveness. A prominent exception is saw lumber, which is substantially more expensive relative to the cost of finished wooden products than it used to be.

The reason that the future of our resource situation always seems so bleak and the past seems quite comfortable is that we can readily construct a plausible sounding estimate of the future demand for a particular raw material, but cannot form such a plausible picture of the future supply. To estimate the future demand, we need merely note the recent trends in the per capita consumption of whatever it is we are concerned about, utilize whatever plausible projection of population we are prepared to accept, multiply the two together and project an astonishingly high rate of usage 50 years in the future. If this demand does not seem overwhelming, we need only make a projection 100 years in the future. What we cannot so readily foresee is the discovery of new sources and of new techniques of extraction, and, in particular, the substitution of other raw materials or the substitution of other industrial processes which change the demand away from the raw material we are considering. Hence it can always be made to appear that in the future we are going to run out of any given material, but that at present we never have.

It is possible to set plausible limits to the stores of fossil fuels that we are likely to discover, and with the very rapid rise in the use of these fuels they will surely become more expensive in some not too distant time. It should be noted, however, that we will not suddenly "run out" of fossil fuels. Long before the last drop of oil is used, oil will have become much more expensive. If gasoline were $5 or $10 a gallon, we would utilize it much more sparingly, with small economical automobile engines, or perhaps the substitution of some non-petroleum-based fuel altogether. In fact, the principal user of our petroleum deposits may be the petrochemical industries. I have given this special attention to fossil fuels because there is no substitute in prospect for such fuels in small mobile units such as automobiles. On the other hand, the supply of overall energy seems to pose no problem. There seems to be ample fissionable material to supply rising energy needs for many centuries, if breeding reactors are perfected. If fusion proves a practical source, the supply of energy can properly be considered limitless.

Another aspect of the relation of the United States economy to resources that is much publicized today is the fact that we are consuming such a large fraction of the current annual extraction of raw materials in the world. A much quoted figure is that 6 percent of the world's population is using 30 percent of the resources. It is concluded from figures such as these that we are robbing the low-income countries of the world of the basis of their future prosperity—that we are using up not only our resources, but theirs as well. Most economists would find this a very erroneous picture of the effect of our demand for the raw materials extracted in the less developed parts of the world. The spokesmen for the less developed countries themselves constantly complain about the adverse terms of trade that they face on world markets. The principal source of their concern is the low price of raw materials and the high price of finished goods. The most effective forms of assistance that the developed countries (including the United States) give to the less developed countries are the

purchases they make from the less developed countries in international trade. A developing country needs receipts from exports in order to finance the purchase of the things they need for economic development. For example, in order to industrialize, a nonindustrialized country must for a long time purchase capital equipment from more advanced countries, and the funds for such purchases come from exports—principally of raw materials. Economists in the developing countries feel that the demand for raw materials is inadequate. Perhaps the most important adverse effect of slowing down the growth of the gross national product in the United States would be that it would diminish the demand for primary products that we would otherwise import from the less developed countries. After all, if a developing country wants to retain its raw materials at home, it can always place an embargo on their export. However, it would be a policy very damaging to economic progress of that very country.

Note that the effect of our high demand for raw materials is a different matter from the desirability of the domestic control of mineral resources within the developing countries. Selling oil on the world market provides immense economic advantages to a developing country. Whether foreign interests should be represented in the extraction of raw materials is another question.

Population Growth in the United States

I shall begin a discussion of population with a brief description of recent, current, and future population trends in the United States. Our population today is a little over 200 million, having increased by slightly more than

50 percent since 1940. I think it is likely to increase by nearly 50 percent again in the 30 years before the end of the century.

This rate of increase cannot continue long. If it endured throughout the next century, the population would reach a billion shortly before the year 2100. Within six or seven more centuries we would reach one person per square foot of land area in the United States, and after about 1500 years our descendants would outweigh the earth if they continued to increase by 50 percent every 30 years. We can even calculate that, at that rate of increase, our descendants would, in a few thousand years, form a sphere of flesh whose radius would, neglecting relativity, expand at the velocity of light.

Every demographer knows that we cannot continue a positive rate of increase indefinitely. The inexorable arithmetic of compound interest leads us to absurd conditions within a calculable period of time. Logically we must, and in fact we will, have a rate of growth very close to zero in the long run. The average rate of increase of mankind from the inception of the species until the present is zero to many decimal places. If we agree that 10,000 years from now we can have no more than one person per square foot, and that the population of the world will at a minimum exceed that of Richmond, Virginia, we can say that the average annual growth of population will be within one per thousand of zero.

The only questions about attaining a zero rate of increase for any population is when and how such a rate is attained. A zero rate of increase implies a balance between the average birth and death rates, so the choice of how to attain a zero rate of increase is a choice between low birth and death rates that are approximately equal. The

average growth rate very near to zero during mankind's past history has been attained with high birth and death rates—with an average duration of life that until recently was no more than 30 or 35 years. I have no difficulty in deciding that I would prefer a zero rate of growth with low rather than high birth and death rates, or with an average duration of life in excess of 70 years, as has been achieved in all of the more advanced countries of the world, rather than the life that is "nasty, brutish, and short." The remaining question then is *when* should our population growth level off.

A popular answer today is "immediately." In fact a zero rate of increase in the United States starting immediately is not feasible and I believe not desirable. The reason is the age composition of the population that our past history of birth and death rates has left to us. We have an especially young population now because of the postwar baby boom. One consequence is that our death rate is much lower than it would be in a population that had long had low fertility. That is, because our population is young, a high proportion of it is concentrated in ages where the risk of mortality is small. Therefore, if we were to attain a zero growth rate immediately, it would be necessary to cut the birth rate about in half. For the next 15 or 20 years, women would have to bear children at a rate that would produce only a little over one child per completed family. At the end of that time we would have a very peculiar age distribution with a great shortage of young people. The attendant social and economic disruptions represent too large a cost to pay for the advantages that we might derive from reducing growth to zero right away.

In fact, a more reasonable goal

would be to reduce fertility as soon as possible to a level where couples produced just enough children to insure that each generation exactly replaced itself. If this goal (early attainment of fertility at a replacement level) were reached immediately, our population would increase 35 to 40 percent before it stabilized. The reason that fertility at the mere replacement level would produce such a large increase in population is again the age distribution we have today. There are many more people today under 20 than 20 to 40, and when the relatively numerous children have moved into the childbearing ages, they will greatly outnumber the persons now at those ages, and when the current population under age 20 moves into the old ages, they will be far more numerous than the people now at the old ages. Thus to move the population to replacement would be to insure approximately that the number of children under 20 will be about the same as it is today, but that the number above that age will be substantially higher. The net effect is the increase of 35 to 40 percent mentioned just above. It is the built-in growth in our age composition that led me to state earlier that I think an increase in the order of 50 percent of the U.S. population is not unlikely.

A sensible choice in reducing our growth rate to zero then is between early or late attainment of fertility at the replacement level. Is there any reason that we should not attempt to attain a fertility at replacement as soon as possible? My own opinion is that an early move in that direction is desirable, but for the sake of completeness, I must point out that there is a non-negligible cost associated with attaining a stationary population—the population that will exist with fertility at

replacement after the age distribution left over from the past has worked out its transitory consequences.

A stationary population with the mortality levels that we have already attained has a much older age distribution than any the United States has ever experienced. It has more people over 60 than under 15, and half the population would be over 37 rather than over 27, as is the case today. It would be an age distribution much like that of a health resort.

Moreover, if we view the age pyramid in the conventional way, with the number of males and females being drawn out as in the branches of a Christmas tree (age representing altitude of the tree) the pyramid for the stationary population is virtually vertical until age 50 because of the small number of deaths under the favorable mortality conditions we have attained. In contrast, the age distribution of the United States to date has always tapered more or less sharply with increasing age. The stationary population with its vertical sides would no longer conform in age composition to the shape of the social structure—to the pyramid of privilege and responsibility. In a growing population, the age pyramid does conform, so there is a rough consonance of shape between diminishing numbers at higher ages and the smaller number of high positions relative to low positions. In a stationary population there would no longer be a reasonable expectation of advancement as a person moves through life. I have indicated that sooner or later we must have a stationary population, so that sooner or later we must adjust to such an age composition. I am pointing to this disadvantage to show that there is a choice between moving more gradually to a stationary population at the expense of a larger ultimate population size in order to continue to enjoy for a longer time the more desirable age distribution of a growing population.

Connection between
Population and Pollution

The connection between the current growth in our population and the deterioration of our environment of which we have all become aware is largely an indirect one. The problem has arisen because we are permitting the production of bads (pollution, or negative externalities) along with goods. There seems little doubt that the rapid increase in the production of goods has been responsible for the rapid increase in the production of bads, since we have made no effective effort to prevent the latter from accompanying the former. But per capita increase in production has been more important than population growth. It has been calculated that if we were to duplicate the total production of electricity in the United States in 1940 in a population enjoying the 1969 per capita usage of energy, the population could be only 25 million rather than 132 million people there were in 1940. Population has increased by 50 percent, but per capita use of electricity has been multiplied several times. A similar statement can even be made about the crowding of our national parks. The population has increased by about 50 percent in the last 30 years—attendance in national parks has increased by more than 400 percent.

A wealthy industrial urban population of 100 million persons would have most of the pollution problems we do. In fact, Sydney, Australia, has problems of air and water pollution and of traffic jams, even though the total population of Australia is about 12 million in an area 80 percent as big as the United States. Australia is actually more urbanized than the United States, in spite of its relatively small population and large overall area.

If we have the will and intelligence to devise and apply proper policies, we can improve our environment and can do so either with the current population of 200 million, or with the population that we will probably have in another 50 years of 300 million. On the other hand, if we ignore environmental problems and continue to treat pure air and water and the disposal of trash as if they were free, and if we pay no attention to the effects of the techniques that we employ upon the balance of nature, we will be in trouble whether our population grows or not. There is no doubt that slower population growth would make it easier to improve our environment, but not much easier.

Policies That Would Affect
the Growth of Population

We must, at some time, achieve a zero rate of population, and the balance should surely be achieved at low birth and death rates rather than at high rates. If, as at present, only about 5 percent of women remain single at the end of the childbearing span, and if 96 percent of women survive to the mean age of childbearing, and if finally the sex ratio at birth remains about 105 males for every 100 females, married couples must have an average of about 2.25 children to replace themselves. What kinds of policies might be designed to assure such a level of fertility or, more generally, to produce the fertility level that is at the moment socially desirable?

I begin with a set of policies that are consistent with general democratic and humanitarian principles, although a minority of the population would oppose them on religious grounds. These are policies that would, through education and the provision of clinical services, try to make it possible for every conception to be the result of a deliberate choice, and for every choice to be an informed one, based on an adequate knowledge of the consequences of bearing different numbers of children at different times. A component of such a set of policies would be the development of more effective means of contraception to reduce the number of accidental pregnancies occurring to couples who are trying to avoid conception. These are policies that call for a substantial government role and I think that an effective government program in these areas is already overdue. I personally believe that education in the consequences of childbearing and in the techniques of avoiding pregnancy, combined with the provision of contraceptive services, should be supplemented by the provision of safe and skillful abortion upon request. It is clear that the public consensus in favor of abortion is not nearly as clear-cut as that in favor of contraception, and I know that the extent and the strength of the moral objection to induced abortion is much greater. Nevertheless, I am persuaded by experience in Japan and eastern Europe that the advantages of abortion provided under good medical auspices to cause the early termination of unwanted pregnancies are very important to the women affected, as is evident in the fact that when medically safe abortion has been made available at low cost, the number of abortions has initially been as great or greater than the number of live births. Later there is a typical tendency for women to resort to contraception rather than repeated abortions.

The reason I favor abortion is that such a high proportion of births that occur today are unwanted, and because a large number of desperate pregnant women (probably more than a half a million annually) resort to clandestine abortions today, with high rates of serious complications. In contrast, early abortion, under skilled medical auspices, is less dangerous than tonsillectomy, and substantially less dangerous than carrying a child to full term.

In recent years the number of births that were unwanted in the United States constituted about 20 percent of the total (an unwanted birth was defined as one in which the woman said that conception occurred either as a result of a failure of contraception or in the absence of contraception but without the intent to become pregnant as soon as possible, when at the time the conception occurred the husband or wife or both did not want another child then or later). The rate at which women are having children today would lead to a completed family size of slightly under three children. If all unwanted births were eliminated, the number of children born per married woman would be about 2.4 or 2.5 on average. This is very little above replacement, and when allowance is made for the likely possibility that women understated the proportion of births that were unwanted, it is probable that the elimination of unwanted births would bring a fertility at or below replacement.

If it is true that the elimination of unwanted pregnancies would reduce fertility very nearly to replacement, it must be conceded that this outcome is fortuitous. It is highly unlikely that over a substantial period of time the free choice by each couple of the number of children they want would lead exactly to the socially desirable level of fertility. The erratic behavior of fertility in America and in other advanced industrialized countries in the last 30 or 40 years is ample evidence that when fertility is voluntarily controlled, the level of fertility is subject to major fluctuations, and I see no logical reason to expect that on average people would voluntarily choose a number of children that would keep the long-run average a little above two per couple. In other words, we must acknowledge the probable necessity of instituting policies that would influence the number of children people want. However, there is no need for haste in formulating such policy, since, as I have indicated, improved contraceptive services combined with a liberal provision of abortion would probably move our fertility at present quite close to replacement, and a gradual increase in population during the next generation would not be a major addition to the problems we already face.

Policies intended to affect people's preferences for children should be designed within the framework of our democratic traditions. They should be designed, for example, to encourage diversity and permit freedom of choice. An average of 2.25 children does not require that 75 percent of couples have two children and 25 percent three, although that would produce the desired average. Another possibility is a nearly even division of family size among zero, one-, two-, three-, four-, and five-child families. The ideal policy would affect the decision at the margin and not try to impose a uniform pattern on all. I do not think that people who prefer to have more than the average number of children should be subject to ridicule or abuse.

It is particularly difficult to frame acceptable policies influencing the number of children that people want. While it is still true that so many large families result from unwanted pregnancies, the unwanted child that is the most recent birth in a large family already faces many deprivations. The psychological disadvantages of the unwanted child cause some of our most serious social problems. In addition to these psychological disadvantages, the unwanted child in a large impoverished family faces an inadequate diet, much below average chances for schooling, and generally inferior opportunities. I hardly think it a wise or humane policy to handicap him further by imposing a financial burden on his parents as a result of his birth.

When unwanted births have become negligible in number, we could imagine trying to design a policy in which the couple is asked to pay some part of the "externalities" that an additional birth imposes on society. In the meantime, I suggest as a desirable supplement to better contraception and free access to abortion the extension of more nearly equal opportunities in education and employment for women, so that activities outside of the home become a more powerful competitor to a larger family. We should start now devoting careful attention to formulation of policies in this area—policies that could increase fertility when it fell too low as well as policies to induce people to want fewer children.

Some aspects of the deterioration of our environment appear to be critical and call for prompt action. We need to start now to frame and apply actions that would arrest the careless destruction of the world in which we live. We also need policies to reduce promptly the incidence of unwanted births. In the long run we shall also need ways to influence the number of births people want. To design policies consistent with our most cherished social and political values will not be easy, and it is fortunate that there is no valid reason for hasty action.

American Institutions and Ecological Ideals

Scientific and literary views of our expansionary life-style are converging.

Leo Marx

Anyone familiar with the work of the classic American writers (I am thinking of men like Cooper, Emerson, Thoreau, Melville, Whitman, and Mark Twain) is likely to have developed an interest in what we recently have learned to call ecology. One of the first things we associate with each of the writers just named is a distinctive, vividly particularized setting (or landscape) inseparable from the writer's conception of man. Partly because of the special geographic and political circumstances of American experience, and partly because they were influenced by the romantic vision of man's relations with nature, all of the writers mentioned possessed a heightened sense of place. Yet words like *place, landscape,* or *setting* scarcely can do justice to the significance these writers imparted to external nature in their work. They took for granted a thorough and delicate interpenetration of consciousness and environment. In fact it now seems evident that these gifted writers had begun, more than a century ago, to measure the quality of American life against something like an ecological ideal.

The ideal I have in mind, quite simply, is the maintenance of a healthy life-enhancing interaction between man and the environment. This is layman's language for the proposition that every organism, in order to avoid extinction or expulsion from its ecosystem, must conform to certain minimal requirements of that system. What makes the concept of the ecosystem difficult to grasp, admittedly, is the fact that the boundaries between systems are always somewhat indistinct, and our technology is making them less distinct all the time. Since an ecosystem includes not only all living organisms (plants and animals) but also the inorganic (physical and chemical) components of the environment, it has become extremely difficult, in the thermonuclear age, to verify even the relatively limited autonomy of local or regional systems. If a decision taken in Moscow or Washington can effect a catastrophic change in the chemical composition of the entire biosphere, then the idea of a San Francisco, or Bay Area, or California, or even North American ecosystem loses much of its clarity and force. Similar difficulties arise when we contemplate the global rate of human population growth. All this is only to say that, on ecological grounds, the case for world government is beyond

SCIENCE, November, 1970, Vol. 170, pp. 945-952

argument. Meanwhile, we have no choice but to use the nation-states as political instruments for coping with the rapid deterioration of the physical world we inhabit.

The chief question before us, then, is this: What are the prospects, given the character of America's dominant institutions, for the fulfillment of this ecological ideal? But first, what is the significance of the current "environmental crusade"? Why should we be skeptical about its efficacy? How shall we account for the curious response of the scientific community? To answer these questions I will attempt to characterize certain of our key institutions from an ecological perspective. I want to suggest the striking convergence of the scientific and the literary criticism of our national life-style. In conclusion I will suggest a few responses to the ecological crisis indicated by that scientific-literary critique.

Limits of Conservationist Thought

In this country, until recently, ecological thinking has been obscured by the more popular, if limited, conservationist viewpoint. Because our government seldom accorded protection of the environment a high priority, much of the responsibility for keeping that end in view fell upon a few voluntary organizations known as the "conservation movement." From the beginning the movement attracted people with enough time and money to enjoy the outdoor life: sportsmen, naturalists (both amateur and professional), and of course property owners anxious to protect the sanctity of their rural or wilderness retreats. As a result, the conservationist cause came to be identified with the special interests of a few

private citizens. It seldom, if ever, has been made to seem pertinent to the welfare of the poor, the nonwhite population, or, for that matter, the great majority of urban Americans. The environment that mattered most to conservationists was the environment beyond the city limits. Witness the names of such leading organizations as the Sierra Club, the National Wildlife Federation, the Audubon Society, and the Izaac Walton League. In the view of many conservationists nature is a world that exists apart from, and for the benefit of, mankind.

The ecological perspective is quite different. Its philosophic root is the secular idea that man (including his works—the secondary, or man-made, environment) is wholly and ineluctably embedded in the tissue of natural process. The interconnections are delicate, infinitely complex, never to be severed. If this organic (or holistic) view of nature has not been popular, it is partly because it calls into question many presuppositions of our culture. Even today an excessive interest in this idea of nature carries, as it did in Emerson's and in Jefferson's time, a strong hint of irregularity and possible subversion. (Nowadays it is associated with the antibourgeois defense of the environment expounded by the long-haired "cop-outs" of the youth movement.) Partly in order to counteract these dangerously idealistic notions, American conservationists often have made a point of seeming hardheaded, which is to say, "realistic" or practical. When their aims have been incorporated in national political programs, notably during the administrations of the two Roosevelts, the emphasis has been upon the efficient use of resources under the supervision of well-trained technicians (1). Whatever the achievements of such programs, as implemented by the admirable if narrowly defined work of such agencies as the National Park Service, the U.S. Forest Service, or the Soil Conservation Service, they did not raise the kinds of questions about our overall capacity for survival that are brought into view by ecology. In this sense, conservationist thought is pragmatic and meliorist in tenor, whereas ecology is, in the purest meaning of the word, radical.

The relative popularity of the conservation movement helps to explain why troubled scientists, many of whom foresaw the scope and gravity of the environmental crisis a long while ago, have had such a difficult time arousing their countrymen. As early as 1864 George Perkins Marsh, sometimes said to be the father of American ecology, warned that the earth was "fast becoming an unfit home for its noblest inhabitant," and that unless men changed their ways it would be reduced "to such a condition of impoverished productiveness, of shattered surface, of climatic excess, as to threaten the depravation, barbarism, and perhaps even extinction of the species" (2). No one was listening to Marsh in 1864, and some 80 years later, according to a distinguished naturalist who tried to convey a similar warning, most Americans still were not listening. "It is amazing," wrote Fairfield Osborn in 1948 (3, p. 194), "how far one has to travel to find a person, even among the widely informed, who is aware of the processes of mounting destruction that we are inflicting upon our life sources."

The Environment Crusade, circa 1969

But that was 1948, and, as we all know, the situation now is wholly changed. Toward the end of the 1960's there was a sudden upsurge of public interest in the subject. The devastation of the environment and the threat of overpopulation became too obvious to be ignored. A sense of anxiety close to panic seized many people, including politicians and leaders of the communications industry. The mass media began to spread the alarm. Television gave prime coverage to a series of relatively minor yet visually sensational ecological disasters. Once again, as in the coverage of the Vietnam War, the close-up power of the medium was demonstrated. The sight of lovely beaches covered with crude oil, hundreds of dead and dying birds trapped in the viscous stuff, had an incalculable effect upon a mass audience. After years of indifference, the press suddenly decided that the jeremiads of naturalists might be important news, and a whole new vocabulary (*environment, ecology, balance of nature, population explosion*, and so on) entered common speech. Meanwhile, the language of reputable scientists was escalating to a pitch of excitement comparable with that of the most fervent young radicals. Barry Commoner, for example, gave a widely reported speech describing the deadly pollution of California water reserves as a result of the excessive use of nitrates as fertilizer. This method of increasing agricultural productivity, he said, is so disruptive of the chemical balance of soil and water that within a generation it could poison irreparably the water supply of the whole area. The *New York Times* ran the story under the headline: "Ecologist Sees U.S. on Suicidal Course" (4). But it was the demographers and population biologists, worried about behavior even less susceptible to regulatory action, who used the most portentous rhetoric. "We must realize that unless we are extremely lucky," Paul Ehrlich told an audience in the summer of 1969, "everybody will disappear in a cloud of blue steam in 20 years" (5).

To a layman who assumes that responsible scientists choose their words with care, this kind of talk is bewildering. How seriously should he take it? He realizes, of course, that he has no way, on his own, to evaluate the factual or scientific basis for these fearful predictions. But the scientific community, to which he naturally turns, is not much help. While most scientists calmly go about their business, activists like Commoner and Ehrlich dominate the headlines. (One could cite the almost equally gloomy forecasts of Harrison Brown, George Wald, René Dubos, and a dozen other distinguished scholars.) When Anthony Lewis asked a "leading European biologist" the same question—how seriously should one take this idea of the imminent extinction of the race?—the scholar smiled, Lewis reports, and said, "I suppose we have between 35 and 100 years before the end of life on earth" (6). No—what is bewildering is the disparity between words and action, between the all-too-credible prophecy of disaster and the response—or rather the nonresponse—of the organized scientific community. From a layman's viewpoint, the professional scientific organizations would seem to have an obligation here—where nothing less than human survival is in question—either to endorse or to correct the pronouncements of their distinguished colleagues. If a large number of scientists do indeed endorse the judgment of the more vociferous ecologists, then the inescapable question is: What are they doing about it? Why do they hesitate to use the concerted prestige and force

of their profession to effect radical changes in national policy and behavior? How is it that most scientists, in the face of this awful knowledge, if indeed it is knowledge, are able to carry on business more or less as usual? One might have expected them to raise their voices, activate their professional organizations, petition the Congress, send delegations to the President, and speak out to the people and the government. Why, in short, are they not mounting a campaign of education and political action?

Why Are Most Scientists Undisturbed?

The most plausible answer seems to be that many scientists, like many of their fellow citizens, are ready to believe that such a campaign already has begun. And if, indeed, one accepts the version of political reality disseminated by the communications industry, they are correct: the campaign *has* begun. By the summer of 1969 it had become evident that the media were preparing to give the ecological crisis the kind of saturation treatment accorded the civil rights movement in the early 1960's and the anti-Vietnam War protest after that. (Observers made this comparison from the beginning.) Much of the tone and substance of the campaign was set by the advertising business. Thus, a leading teen-age magazine, *Seventeen*, took a full-page ad in the *New York Times* to announce, beneath a picture of a handsome collegiate couple strolling meditatively through autumn leaves, "The environment crusade emphasizes the fervent concerns of the young with our nation's 'quality of life.' Their voices impel us to act now on the mushrooming problems of conservation and ecology" (7). A more skeptical voice might impel us to think about the Madison Avenue strategists who had recognized a direct new path into the lucrative youth market. The "crusade," as they envisaged it, was to be a bland, well-mannered, clean-up campaign, conducted in the spirit of an adolescent love affair and nicely timed to deflect student attention from the disruptive political issues of the 1960's. A national survey of college students confirmed this hope. "Environment May Eclipse Vietnam as College Issue," the makers of the survey reported, and one young man's comment seemed to sum up their findings: "A lot of people are becoming disenchanted with the antiwar movement," he said. "People who are frustrated and disillusioned are starting to turn to ecology" (8). On New Year's Day 1970, the President of the United States joined the crusade. Adapting the doomsday rhetoric of the environmentalists to his own purposes, he announced that "the nineteen-seventies absolutely must be the years when America pays its debt to the past by reclaiming the purity of its air, its waters and our living environment. It is literally now or never" (9).

Under the circumstances, it is understandable that most scientists, like most other people (except for the disaffected minority of college students), have been largely unresponsive to the alarmist rhetoric of the more panicky environmentalists. The campaign to save the environment no longer seems to need their help. Not only have the media been awakened, and with them a large segment of the population, but the President himself, along with many government officials, has been enlisted in the cause. On 10 February 1970, President Nixon sent a special message to the Congress outlining a comprehensive 37-point program of action against pollution. Is it any wonder that the mood at recent meetings of conservationists has become almost cheerful—as if the movement, at long last, really had begun to move? After all, the grim forecasts of the ecologists necessarily have been couched in conditional language, thus: *If* California farmers continue their excessive use of nitrates, *then* the water supply will be irreparably poisoned. But now that the facts have been revealed, and with so much government activity in prospect, may we not assume that disaster will be averted? There is no need, therefore, to take the alarmists seriously—which is only to say that most scientists still have confidence in the capacity of our political leaders, and of our institutions, to cope with the crisis.

But is that confidence warranted by the current "crusade"? Many observers have noted that the President's message was strong in visionary language and weak in substance. He recommended no significant increase in funds needed to implement the program. Coming from a politician with a well-known respect for strategies based on advertising and public relations, this high-sounding talk should make us wary. Is it designed to protect the environment or to assuage anxiety or to distract the antiwar movement or to provide the cohesive force necessary for national unity behind the Republican administration? How can we distinguish the illusion of activity fostered by the media—and the President—from auguries of genuine action? On this score, the frequently invoked parallel of the civil rights and the antiwar movements should give us pause. For, while each succeeded in focusing attention upon a dangerous situation, it is doubtful whether either got us very far along toward the elimination of the danger. At first each movement won spectacular victories, but now, in retrospect, they too look more like ideological than substantive gains. In many ways the situation of blacks in America is more desperate in 1970 than it was in 1960. Similarly, the war in Southeast Asia, far from having been stopped by the peace movement, now threatens to encompass other countries and to continue indefinitely. This is not to imply that the strenuous efforts to end the war or to eradicate racism have been bootless. Some day the whole picture may well look quite different; we may look back on the 1960's as the time when a generation was prepared for a vital transformation of American society.

Nevertheless, scientists would do well to contemplate the example of these recent protest movements. They would be compelled to recognize, for one thing, that, while public awareness may be indispensable for effecting changes in national policy, it hardly guarantees results. In retrospect, indeed, the whole tenor of the civil rights and antiwar campaigns now seems much too optimistic. Neither program took sufficient account of the deeply entrenched, institutionalized character of the collective behavior it aimed to change. If leaders of the campaign to save the environment were to make the same kind of error, it would not be surprising. A certain innocent trust in the efficacy of words, propaganda, and rational persuasion always has characterized the conservation movement in this country. Besides, there is a popular notion that ecological problems are in essence technological, not political, and therefore easier to solve than the problems of racism, war, or imperialism. To indicate why this view

is a mistaken one, why in fact it would be folly to discount the urgency of the environmental crisis on these grounds, I now want to consider the fitness of certain dominant American institutions for the fulfillment of the ecological ideal.

The Dynamism of America

Seen from an ecological perspective, a salient characteristic of American society is its astonishing dynamism. Ever since the first European settlements were established on the Atlantic seaboard, our history has been one of virtually uninterrupted expansion. How many decades, if any, have there been since 1607 when this society failed to expand its population, territory, and economic power? When foreigners speak of Americanization they invariably have in mind this dynamic, expansionary, unrestrained behavior. "No sooner do you set foot upon American ground," wrote de Tocqueville, "than you are stunned by a kind of tumult; a confused clamor is heard on every side, and a thousand simultaneous voices demand the satisfaction of their social wants. Everything is in motion around you. . . " (10). To be sure, a majority of these clamorous people were of European origin, and their most effective instrument for the transformation of the wilderness—their science and technology—was a product of Western culture. But the unspoiled terrain of North America gave European dynamism a peculiar effervescence. The seemingly unlimited natural resources and the relative absence of cultural or institutional restraints made possible what surely has been the fastest-developing, most mobile, most relentlessly innovative society in world history.

114

By now that dynamism inheres in every aspect of our lives, from the dominant national ethos to the structure of our economic institutions down to the deportment of individuals.

The ideological counterpart to the nation's physical expansion has been its celebration of quantity. What has been valued most in American popular culture is growth, development, size (bigness), and—by extension—change, novelty, innovation, wealth, and power. This tendency was noted a long while ago, especially by foreign travelers, but only recently have historians begun to appreciate the special contribution of Christianity to this quantitative, expansionary ethos. The crux here is the aggressive, man-centered attitude toward the environment fostered by Judeo-Christian thought: everything in nature, living or inorganic, exists to serve man. For only man can hope (by joining God) to transcend nature. According to one historian of science, Lynn White (11), the dynamic thrust of Western science and technology derives in large measure from this Christian emphasis, unique among the great world religions, upon the separation of man from nature.

But one need not endorse White's entire argument to recognize that Americans, from the beginning, found in the Bible a divine sanction for their violent assault upon the physical environment. To the Puritans of New England, the New World landscape was Satan's territory, a hideous wilderness inhabited by the unredeemed and fit chiefly for conquest. What moral precept could have served their purpose better than the Lord's injunction to be fruitful and multiply and subdue the earth and exercise dominion over every living creature? Then, too, the millennial cast of evangelical protestantism

made even more dramatic the notion that this earth, and everything upon it, is an expendable support system for man's voyage to eternity. Later, as industrialization gained momentum, the emphasis shifted from the idea of nature as the devil's country to the idea of nature as commodity. When the millennial hope was secularized, and salvation was replaced by the goal of economic and social progress, it became possible to quantify the rate of human improvement. In our time this quantifying bent reached its logical end with the enshrinement of the gross national product—one all-encompassing index of the state of the union itself.

Perhaps the most striking thing about this expansionary ethos, from an ecological viewpoint, has been its capacity to supplant a whole range of commonsense notions about man's relations with nature which are recognized by some preliterate peoples and are implicit in the behavior of certain animal species. These include the ideas that natural resources are exhaustible, that the unchecked growth of a species will eventually lead to its extinction, and that other organisms may have a claim to life worthy of respect.

The Expansionary System

The record of American business, incomparably successful according to quantitative economic measures like the gross national product, also looks quite different when viewed from an ecological perspective. Whereas the environmental ideal I have been discussing affirms the need for each organism to observe limits set by its ecosystem, the whole thrust of industrial capitalism has been in the opposite direction: it has placed the highest premium upon ingenious methods for circumventing those limits. After comparing the treatment that various nations have accorded their respective portions of the earth, Fairfield Osborn said this of the United States (3, p. 175): "The story of our nation in the last century as regards the use of forests, grasslands, wildlife and water sources is the most violent and the most destructive in the long history of civilization." If that estimate is just, a large part of the credit must be given to an economic system unmatched in calling forth man's profit-making energies. By the same token, it is a system that does pitifully little to encourage or reward those constraints necessary for the long-term ecological well-being of society. Consider, for example, the fate of prime agricultural lands on the borders of our burgeoning cities. What happens when a landowner is offered a small fortune by a developer? What agency protects the public interest from the irretrievable loss of topsoil that requires centuries to produce? Who sees to it that housing, factories, highways, and shopping centers are situated on the far more plentiful sites where nothing edible ever will grow? The answer is that no such agencies exist, and the market principle is allowed to rule. Since World War II approximately one-fifth of California's invaluable farm land has been lost in this way. Here, as in many cases of air and water pollution, the dominant motive of our business system—private profit—leads to the violation of ecological standards.

Early in the industrial era one might reasonably have expected, as Thorstein Veblen did, that the scientific and technological professions, with their strong bent toward rationality and efficiency, **would help to control the ravening economic appetites whetted by America's** natural abundance. Veblen assumed that well-trained technicians, engineers, and scientists would be repelled by the wastefulness of the business system. He therefore looked to them for leadership in shaping alternatives to a culture obsessed with "conspicuous consumption." But, so far, that leadership has not appeared. On the contrary, this new technical elite, with its commitment to highly specialized, value-free research, has enthusiastically placed its skill in the service of business and military enterprise. This is one reason, incidentally, why today's rebellious young are unimpressed by the claim that the higher learning entails a commitment to rationality. They see our best-educated, most "rational" elite serving what strikes them as a higher irrationality. So far from providing a counterforce to the business system, the scientific and technological professions in fact have strengthened the ideology of American corporate capitalism, including its large armaments sector, by bringing to it their high-minded faith in the benign consequences of the most rapidly accelerating rate of technological innovation attainable.

But not only are we collectively committed, as a nation, to the idea of continuing growth; each subordinate unit of the society holds itself to a similar standard of success. Each state, city, village, and neighborhood; each corporation, independent merchant, and voluntary organization; each ethnic group, family, and child—each person —should, ideally speaking, strive for growth. Translated into ecological terms, this popular measure of success—becoming bigger, richer, more powerful—means gaining control over more and more of the available resources. When resources were thought to be inexhaustible, as they were thought to be throughout most of our national history, the release of these unbounded entrepreneurial energies was considered an aspect of individual liberation. And so it was, at least for large segments of the population. But today, when that assumption no longer makes sense, those energies are still being generated. It is as if a miniaturized version of the nation's expansionary ethos had been implanted in every citizen—not excluding the technicians and scientists. And when we consider the extremes to which the specialization of function has been carried in the sciences, **each expert working his own minuscule sector of the knowledge industry, it is easier to account for the unresponsiveness of the scientific community to the urgent warnings of alarmed ecologists. If most scientists and engineers seem not to be listening, much less acting, it is because these highly skilled men are so busy doing what every good American is supposed to do.**

On the other hand, it is not surprising that a clever novelist like Norman Mailer (*12*), or a popular interpreter of science like Rachel Carson (*13*), or an imaginative medical researcher like Alan Gregg (*14*) each found it illuminating in recent years to compare the unchecked growth of American society, with all the resulting disorder, to the haphazard spread of cancer cells in a living organism. There is nothing new, of course, about the analogy between the social order and the human body; the conceit has a long history in literature. Since the early 1960's, however, Mailer has been invoking the more specific idea of America as a carcinogenic environment. Like any good poetic figure, this one has a basis in fact. Not only does it call to mind the radioactive

matter we have deposited in the earth and the sea, or the work of such allegedly cancer-producing enterprises as the tobacco and automobile industries, or the effects of some of the new drugs administered by doctors in recent years, but, even more subtly, it reminds us of the parallel between cancer and our expansionary national ethos, which, like a powerful ideological hormone, stimulates the reckless, uncontrolled growth of each cell in the social organism.

In the interests of historical accuracy and comprehensiveness, needless to say, all of these sweeping generalizations would have to be extensively qualified. The record is rich in accounts of determined, troubled Americans who have criticized and actively resisted the nation's expansionary abandon. A large part of our governmental apparatus was created in order to keep these acquisitive, self-aggrandizing energies within tolerable limits. And of course the full story would acknowledge the obvious benefits, especially the individual freedom and prosperity, many Americans owe to the very dynamism that now threatens our survival. But in this brief compass my aim is to emphasize that conception of man's relation to nature which, so far as we can trace its consequences, issued in the *dominant* forms of national behavior. And that is a largely one-sided story. It is a story, moreover, to which our classic American writers, to their inestimable credit, have borne eloquent witness. If there is a single native institution which has consistently criticized American life from a vantage like that of ecology, it is the institution of letters.

America's Pastoral Literature

A notable fact about imaginative

literature in America, when viewed from an ecological perspective, is the number of our most admired works written in obedience to a pastoral impulse (15). By "pastoral impulse" I mean the urge, in the face of society's increasing power and complexity, to retreat in the direction of nature. The most obvious form taken by this withdrawal from the world of established institutions is a movement in space. The writer or narrator describes, or a character enacts, a move away from a relatively sophisticated to a simpler, more "natural" environment. Whether this new setting is an unspoiled wilderness, like Cooper's forests and plains, Melville's remote Pacific, Faulkner's Big Woods, or Hemingway's Africa, or whether it is as tame as Emerson's New England village common, Thoreau's Walden Pond, or Robert Frost's pasture, its significance derives from the plain fact that it is "closer" to nature: it is a landscape that bears fewer marks of human intervention.

This symbolic action, which reenacts the initial transit of Europeans to North America, may be understood in several ways, and no one of them can do it justice. To begin with, there is an undeniable element of escapism about this familiar, perhaps universal, desire to get away from the imperatives of a complicated social life. No one has conveyed this feeling with greater economy or simplicity than Robert Frost in the first line of his poem "Directive": "Back out of all this now too much for us." Needless to say, if our literary pastoralism lent expression only to this escapist impulse, we would be compelled to call it self-indulgent, puerile, or regressive.

But fortunately this is not the case. In most American pastorals the movement toward nature also may be under-stood as a serious criticism, explicit or implied, of the established social order. It calls into question a society dominated by a mechanistic system of value, keyed to perfecting the routine means of existence, yet oblivious to its meaning and purpose. We recall Thoreau's description, early in *Walden*, of the lives of quiet desperation led by his Concord neighbors, or the first pages of Melville's *Moby-Dick*, with Ishmael's account of his moods of suicidal depression as he contemplates the meaningless work required of the inhabitants of Manhattan Island. At one time this critical attitude toward the workaday life was commonly dismissed as aristocratic or elitist. We said that it could speak only for a leisure class for whom deprivation was no problem. But today, in a society with the technological capacity to supply everyone with an adequate standard of living, that objection has lost most of its force. The necessary conditions for giving a decent livelihood to every citizen no longer include harder work, increased productivity, or endless technological innovation. But of course such an egalitarian economic program would entail a more equitable distribution of wealth, and the substitution of economic sufficiency for the goal of an endlessly "rising" standard of living. The mere fact that such possibilities exist explains why our literary pastorals, which blur distinctions between the economic, moral, and esthetic flaws of society, now seem more cogent. In the 19th century, many pastoralists, like today's radical ecologists, saw the system as potentially destructive in its innermost essence. Their dominant figure for industrial society, with its patent confusion about ends and means, was the social machine. Our economy is the kind of system, said Thoreau, where men become the tools of their tools.

Of course, there is nothing particularly American about this pessimistic literary response to industrialism. Since the romantic movement it has been a dominant theme of all Western literature. Most gifted writers have expended a large share of their energy in an effort to discover—or, more precisely, to imagine—alternatives to the way of life that emerged with the industrial revolution. The difference is that in Europe there was a range of other possible lifestyles which had no counterpart in this country. There were enclaves of pre-industrial culture (provincial, esthetic, religious, aristocratic) which retained their vitality long after the bourgeois revolutions, and there also was a new, revolutionary, urban working class. This difference, along with the presence in America of a vast, rich, unspoiled landscape, helps to explain the exceptionally strong hold of the pastoral motive upon the native imagination. If our writers conceived of life from something like an ecological perspective, it is largely because of their heightened sensitivity to the unspoiled environment, and man's relation to it, as the basis for an alternative to the established social order.

What, then, can we learn about possible alternatives from our pastoral literature? The difficulty here lies in the improbability which surrounds the affirmative content of the pastoral retreat. In the typical American fable the high point of the withdrawal toward nature is an idyllic interlude which gains a large measure of its significance from the sharp contrast with the everyday, "real," world. This is an evanescent moment of peace and contentment when the writer (or narrator, or protagonist) enjoys a sense of integration with the surrounding environment that approaches ecstatic fulfill-

ment. It is often a kind of visionary experience, couched in a language of such intense, extreme, even mystical feeling that it is difficult for many readers (though not, significantly, for adherents of today's youth culture) to take it seriously. But it is important to keep in view some of the reasons for this literary extravagance. In a commercial, optimistic, self-satisfied culture, it was not easy for writers to make an alternate mode of experience credible. Their problem was to endow an ideal vision—some would call it utopian—with enough sensual authenticity to carry readers beyond the usual, conventionally accepted limits of commonsense reality. Nevertheless, the pastoral interlude, rightly understood, does have a bearing upon the choices open to a postindustrial society. It must be taken, not as representing a program to be copied, but as a symbolic action which embodies values, attitudes, modes of thought and feeling alternative to those which characterize the dynamic, expansionary life-style of modern America.

The focus of our literary pastoralism, accordingly, is upon a contrast between two environments representing virtually all aspects of man's relation to nature. In place of the aggressive thrust of 19th-century capitalism, the pastoral interlude exemplifies a far more restrained, accommodating kind of behavior. The chief goal is not, as Alexander Hamilton argued it was, to enhance the nation's corporate wealth and power; rather it is the Jeffersonian "pursuit of happiness." In economic terms, then, pastoralism entails a distinction between a commitment to unending growth and the concept of material sufficiency. The aim of the pastoral economy is *enough*—enough production and consumption to insure a decent quality of life. Jefferson's dislike of industrialization was based on this standard; he was bent on the subordination of quantitative to qualitative "standards of living."

From a psychological viewpoint, the pastoral retreat affirmed the possibility of maintaining man's mental equilibrium by renewed emphasis upon his inner needs. The psychic equivalent of the balance of nature (in effect the balance of *human* nature) is a more or less equal capacity to cope with external and internal sources of anxiety. In a less-developed landscape, according to these fables, behavior can be more free, spontaneous, authentic—in a word, more natural. The natural in psychic experience refers to activities of mind which are inborn or somehow primary. Whether we call them intuitive, unconscious, or preconscious, the significant fact is that they do not have to be learned or deliberately acquired. By contrast, then, the expansionary society is figured forth as dangerously imbalanced on the side of those rational faculties conducive to the manipulation of the physical environment. We think of Melville's Ahab, in whom the specialization of function induces a peculiar kind of power-obsessed, if technically competent, mentality. "My means are sane," he says, "my motive and my object mad."

This suspicion of the technical, highly trained intellect comports with the emphasis in our pastoral literature upon those aspects of life that are common to all men. Whereas the industrial society encourages and rewards the habit of mind which analyzes, separates, categorizes, and makes distinctions, the felicity enjoyed during the pastoral interlude is a tacit tribute to the opposite habit. This kind of pleasure derives from the connection-making, analogiz-

ing, poetic imagination—one that aspires to a unified conception of reality. At the highest or metaphysical level of abstraction, then, romantic pastoralism is holistic. During the more intense pastoral interludes, an awareness of the entire environment, extending to the outer reaches of the cosmos, affects the perception of each separate thing, idea, event. In place of the technologically efficient but limited concept of nature as a body of discrete manipulatable objects, our pastoral literature presents an organic conception of man's relation to his environment.

A Convergence of Insights

What I am trying to suggest is the striking convergence of the literary and the ecological views of America's dominant institutions. Our literature contains a deep intuition of the gathering environmental crisis and its causes. To be sure, the matter-of-fact idiom of scientific ecology may not be poetic or inspiring. Instead of conveying Wordsworthian impulses from the vernal wood, it reports the rate at which monoxide poisoning is killing the trees. Nevertheless, the findings of ecologists confirm the indictment of the self-aggrandizing way of life that our leading writers have been building up for almost two centuries. In essence it is an indictment of the destructive, power-oriented uses to which we put scientific and technological knowledge. The philosophic source of this dangerous behavior is an arrogant conception of man, and above all of human consciousness, as wholly unique—as an entity distinct from, and potentially independent of, the rest of nature.

As for the alternative implied by the pastoral retreat, it also anticipates cer-

...in insights of ecology. Throughout ...is body of imaginative writing, the ...rn toward nature is represented as a ...eans of gaining access to governing ...alues, meanings, and purposes. In the ...ast, to be sure, many readers found ...e escapist, sentimental overtones of ...is motive embarrassing. As a teacher, ... can testify that, until recently, many ...ragmatically inclined students were ...ut off by the obscurely metaphysical, ...ccultish notions surrounding the idea ...f harmony with nature. It lacked ...pecificity. But now all that is chang-...g. The current environmental crisis ...as in a sense put a literal, factual, ...ften quantifiable base under this poetic ...lea. Nature as a transmitter of signals ...nd a dictator of choices now is pres-...nt to us in the quite literal sense that ...e imbalance of an ecosystem, when ...cientifically understood, defines certain ...recise limits to human behavior. We ...re told, for example, that if we con-...nue contaminating Lake Michigan at ...e present rate, the lake will be "dead" ... roughly 10 years. Shall we save the ...ke or continue allowing the cities and ...dustries which pollute it to reduce ...xpenses and increase profits? As such ...hoices become more frequent, man's ...elations with nature will in effect be ...en to set the limits of various eco-...omic, social, and political practices. ...nd the concept of harmonious rela-...ons between man and the physical en-...ironment, instead of seeming to be a ...ague projection of human wishes, ...ust come to be respected as a neces-...ary, realistic, limiting goal. This con-...ergence of literary and scientific in-...ght reinforces the naturalistic idea ...at man, to paraphrase Melville, must ...ventually lower his conceit of attain-...ble felicity, locating it not in power ...r transcendence but in a prior need ... sustain life itself.

A Proposal and Some Conclusions

Assuming that this sketch of America's dominant institutions as seen from a pastoral-ecological vantage is not grossly inaccurate, what inferences can we draw from it? What bearing does it have upon our current effort to cope with the deterioration of the environment? What special significance does it have for concerned scientists and technologists? I shall draw several conclusions, beginning with a specific recommendation for action by the American Association for the Advancement of Science.

First, then, let me propose that the Association establish a panel of the best qualified scientists, representing as many as possible of the disciplines involved, to serve as a national review board for ecological information. This board would take the responsibility for locating and defining the crucial problems (presumably it would recruit special task forces for specific assignments) and make public recommendations whenever feasible. To be sure, some scientists will be doing a similar job for the government, but, if an informed electorate is to evaluate the government's program, it must have an independent source of knowledge. One probable objection is that scientists often disagree, and feel reluctant to disagree in public. But is this a healthy condition for a democracy? Perhaps the time has come to lift the dangerous veil of omniscience from the world of science and technology. If the experts cannot agree, let them issue minority reports. If our survival is at stake, we should be allowed to know what the problems and the choices are. The point here is not that we laymen look to scientists for *the* answer, or that we expect them to save us. But we do ask for their active involvement in solving problems about which they are the best-informed citizens. Not only should such a topflight panel of scientists be set up on a national basis, but—perhaps more important—similar committees should be set up to help make the best scientific judgment available to the citizens of every state, city, and local community.

But there will also be those who object on the ground that an organization as august as the American Association for the Advancement of Science must not be drawn into politics. The answer, of course, is that American scientists and technologists are now and have always been involved in politics. A profession whose members place their services at the disposal of the government, the military, and the private corporations can hardly claim immunity now. Scientific and technological knowledge unavoidably is used for political purposes. But it also is a national resource. The real question in a democratic society, therefore, is whether that knowledge can be made as available to ordinary voters as it is to those, like the Department of Defense or General Electric, who can most easily buy it. If scientists are worried about becoming partisans, then their best defense is to speak with their own disinterested public voice. To allow the burden of alerting and educating the people to fall upon a few volunteers is a scandal. Scientists, as represented by their professional organizations, have a responsibility to make sure that their skills are used to fulfill as well as to violate the ecological ideal. And who knows? If things get bad enough, the scientific community may take steps to discourage its members from serving the violators.

There is another, perhaps more compelling, reason why scientists and technologists, as an organized professional group, must become more actively involved. It was scientists, after all, who first sounded the alarm. What action we take as a society *and how quickly we take it* depend in large measure upon the credibility of the alarmist. Who is to say, if organized science does not, which alarms we should take seriously? What group has anything like the competence of scientists and technologists to evaluate the evidence? Or, to put it negatively, what group can do more, by mere complacency and inaction, to insure an inadequate response to the environmental crisis?

It is a well-known fact that Americans hold the scientific profession in the highest esteem. So long as most scientists go about their business as usual, so long as they seem unperturbed by the urgent appeals of their own colleagues, it is likely that most laymen including our political representatives will remain skeptical.

The arguments for the more active involvement of the scientific community in public debate illustrate the all-encompassing and essentially political character of the environmental crisis. If the literary-ecological perspective affords an accurate view, we must eventually take into account the deep-seated institutional causes of our distress. No cosmetic program, no clean-up-the-landscape activity, no degree of protection for the wilderness, no antipollution laws can be more than the mere beginning. Of course such measures are worthwhile, but in undertaking them we should acknowledge their superficiality. The devastation of the environment is at bottom a result of the kind of society we have built and the kind of people we are. It follows, therefore, that environmentalists should join forces, wherever common aims can be found, with other groups concerned to change basic institutions. To arrest the deterioration of the environment it will be necessary to control many of the same forces which have prevented us from ending the war in Indochina or giving justice to black Americans. In other words, it will be necessary for ecologists to determine where the destructive power of our society lies and how to cope with it. Knowledge of that kind, needless to say, is political. But then it seems obvious, on reflection, that the study of human ecology will be incomplete until it incorporates a sophisticated mode of political analysis.

Meanwhile, it would be folly, given the character of American institutions, to discount the urgency of our situation either on the ground that technology will provide the solutions or on the ground that countermeasures are proposed. We cannot rely on technology because the essential problem is not technological. It inheres in all of the ways in which this dynamic society generates and uses its power. It calls into question the controlling purposes of all the major institutions which actually determine the nation's impact upon the environment: the great business corporations, the military establishment, the universities, the scientific and technological elites. and the exhilarating expansionary ethos by which we all live. Throughout our brief history, a passion for personal and collective aggrandizement has been the American way. One can only guess at

the extent to which forebodings of ecological doom have contributed to the revulsion that so many intelligent young people feel these days for the idea of "success" as a kind of limitless ingestion. In any case, most of the talk about the environmental crisis that turns on the word *pollution*, as if we face a cosmic-scale problem of sanitation, is grossly misleading. What confronts us is an extreme imbalance between society's hunger—the rapidly growing sum of human wants—and the limited capacities of the earth.

References and Notes

1. S. P. Hays, *Conservation and the Gospel of Efficiency* (Harvard Univ. Press, Cambridge, Mass., 1959).
2. *Man and Nature*, David Lowenthal, Ed. (Harvard Univ. Press, Cambridge, Mass., 1965), p. 43.
3. F. Osborn, *Our Plundered Planet* (Little, Brown, Boston, 1948).
4. *New York Times* (19 Nov. 1969).
5. *Ibid.* (6 Aug. 1969).
6. *Ibid.* (15 Dec. 1969).
7. *Ibid.* (5 Dec. 1969).
8. *Ibid.* (30 Nov. 1969).
9. *Ibid.* (2 Jan. 1969).
10. A. de Tocqueville, *Democracy in America*, Phillips Bradley, Ed. (Knopf, New York, new ed., 1946), vol. 1, p. 249.
11. L. White, Jr., *Science* 155, 1203 (1967).
12. N. Mailer, *Cannibals and Christians* (Dial, New York, 1966).
13. R. Carson, *Silent Spring* (Houghton Mifflin, Boston, 1962).
14. A. Gregg, *Science* 121, 681 (1955).
15. L. Marx, *The Machine in the Garden; Technology and the Pastoral Ideal in America* (Oxford Univ. Press, New York, 1964).
16. For comment and criticism I thank my Amherst colleagues L. Brower, B. DeMott, J. Epstein, R. Fink, A. Guttmann, W. Hexter, G. Kateb, R. Snellgrove, W. Taubman, and J. W. Ward; I also thank W. Berthoff, D. Lowenthal, J. Marx, B. McKie, and N. Podhoretz.

123

Ethics and Population Limitation

What ethical norms should be brought to bear in controlling population growth?

Daniel Callahan

Throughout its history, the human species has been preoccupied with the conquest of nature and the control of death. Human beings have struggled to survive, as individuals, families, tribes, communities, and nations. Procreation has been an essential part of survival. Food could not have been grown, families sustained, individuals supported, or industry developed without an unceasing supply of new human beings. The result was the assigning of a high value to fertility. It was thought good to have children: good for the children themselves, for the parents, for the society, and for the species. While it may always have been granted that extenuating circumstances could create temporary contraindications to childbearing, the premise on which the value was based endured intact. There remained a presumptive right of individual procreation, a right thought to sustain the high value ascribed to the outcome: more human beings.

That the premise may now have to be changed, the value shifted, can only seem confounding. As Erik Erikson has emphasized, it is a risky venture to play with the "fire of creation," especially when the playing has implications for almost every aspect of individual and collective life (1). The

reasons for doing so would have to be grave. Yet excessive population growth presents such reasons—it poses critical dangers to the future of the species, the ecosystem, individual liberty and welfare, and the structure of social life. These hazards are serious enough to warrant a reexamination and, ultimately, a revision of the traditional value of unrestricted procreation and increase in population.

The main question is the way in which the revision is to proceed. If the old premise—the unlimited right of and need for procreation—is to be rejected or amended, what alternative premises are available? By what morally legitimate social and political processes, and in light of what values, are the possible alternatives to be evaluated and action taken? These are ethical questions, bearing on what is taken to constitute the good life, the range and source of human rights and obligations, the requirements of human justice and welfare. If the ethical problems of population limitation could be reduced to one overriding issue, matters would be simplified. They cannot. Procreation is so fundamental a human activity, so wide-ranging in its personal and social impact, that controlling it poses a wide range of ethical issues. My aim here is primarily to

SCIENCE, February, 1972, Vol. 175, pp. 487-494.

see what some of the different ethical issues are, to determine how an approach to them might be structured, and to propose some solutions.

With a subject so ill-defined as "ethics and population limitation," very little by way of common agreement can be taken for granted. One needs to start at the "beginning," with some basic assertions.

Facts and Values

There would be no concern about population limitation if there did not exist evidence that excessive population growth jeopardizes present and future welfare. Yet the way the evidence is evaluated will be the result of the values and interests brought to bear on the data. Every definition of the "population problem" or of "excessive population growth" will be value-laden, expressive of the ethical orientations of those who do the defining. While everyone might agree that widespread starvation and malnutrition are bad, not everyone will agree that crowding, widespread urbanization, and a loss of primitive forest areas are equally bad. Human beings differ in their assessments of relative good and evil. To say that excessive population growth is bad is to imply that some other state of population growth would be good or better—for example, an "optimum level of population." But as the demographic discussion of an optimum has made clear, so many variables come into play that it may be possible to do no more than specify a direction: "the desirability of a lower *rate* [italics added] of growth" (2).

If the ways in which the population problem is defined will reflect value orientations, these same definitions will have direct implications for the ways in which the ethical issues are posed. An apocalyptic reading of the demographic data and projections can, not surprisingly, lead to coercive proposals. Desperate problems are seen to require desperate and otherwise distasteful solutions (3). Moreover, how the problem is defined, and how the different values perceived to be at stake are weighted, will have direct implications for the priority given to population problems in relation to other social problems. People might well agree that population growth is a serious issue, but they might (and often do) say that other issues are comparatively more serious (4). If low priority is given to population problems, this is likely to affect the perception of the ethical issues at stake.

Why Ethical Questions Arise

Excessive population growth raises ethical questions because it threatens existing or desired human values and ideas of what is good. In addition, all or some of the possible solutions to the problem have the potential for creating difficult ethical dilemmas. The decision to act or not to act in the face of the threats is an ethical decision. It is a way of affirming where the human good lies and the kinds of obligations individuals and societies have toward themselves and others. A choice in favor of action will, however, mean the weighing of different options, and most of the available options present ethical dilemmas.

In making ethical choices, decisions will need to be made on (i) the human good and values that need to be served or promoted—the ends; (ii) the range of methods and actions consistent and coherent with those ends—the means; and (iii) the procedure and rationale to be used in trying to decide both upon ends and means and upon their relation to each other in specific situations—the ethical criteria for decision-making. A failure to determine the ends, both ultimate and proximate, can make it difficult or impossible to choose the appropriate means. A failure to determine the range of possible means can make it difficult to serve the ends. A failure to specify or articulate the ethical criteria for decision-making can lead to capricious or self-serving choices, as well as to the placing of obstacles in the way of a rational resolution of ethical conflicts.

In the case of ethics and the population problem, both the possibilities and the limitations of ethics become apparent. In the face of a variety of proposals to solve the population problem, some of them highly coercive, a sensitivity to the ethical issues and some greater rigor in dealing with them is imperative. The most fundamental matters of human life and welfare are at stake. Yet because of the complexity of the problem, including its variability from one nation or geographical region to the next, few hard and fast rules can be laid down about what to do in a given place at a given time.

Still, since some choices must be made (and not to choose is to make a choice as well), the practical ethical task will be that of deciding upon the available options. While I will focus on some of the proposed options for reducing birthrates, they are not the only ones possible. Ralph Potter has discussed some others (5).

It has generally been assumed that policy must be primarily, if not exclusively, concerned with bringing about a decline in the rate of population increase through a reduction in the birthrate. But there are other choices. It is generally considered desirable but impossible to increase resources at a sufficient pace and through an adequate duration to preserve the present level of living for all within an expanding population. It is generally considered possible but undesirable to omit the requirement that all persons have access to that which is necessary for a good life. There is still the option of redefining what is to be considered necessary for a good life or of foregoing some things necessary for a good life in order to obtain an equitable distribution in a society that preserves the autonomy of parents to determine the size of their families.

A useful way of posing the issue practically is to envision the ethical options ranked on a preferential scale, from the most desirable to the least desirable. For working purposes, I will adopt as my own the formulation of Kenneth E. Boulding: "A moral, or ethical, proposition is a statement about a rank order of preferences among alternatives, which is intended to apply to more than one person" (6). Ethics enters at that point when the preferences are postulated to have a value that transcends individual tastes or inclinations. Implicitly or explicitly, a decision among alternatives becomes an ethical one when it is claimed that one or another alternative *ought* to be chosen—not just by me, but by others as well. This is where ethics differs from tastes or personal likings, which, by definition, imply nonobligatory preferences that are applicable to no more than one person (even if the tastes are shared).

General Ethical Issues

I will assume at the outset that there is a problem of excessive population rowth, a problem serious for the world as a whole (with a 2 percent annual growth rate), grave for many developing nations (where the growth rate approaches 3 percent per annum), and possibly harmful for the developed nations as well (with an average 1 percent growth rate). The threats posed by excessive population growth are numerous: economic, environmental, agricultural, political, and socio-psychological. There is considerable agreement that something must be done to meet these threats. For the purpose of ethical analysis, the first question to be asked is, "In trying to meet these threats, what human ends are we seeking to serve?" Two kinds of human ends can be distinguished—proximate and ultimate.

Among the important proximate ends being sought in attempts to reduce birthrates in the developing countries are a raising of literacy rates, a reduction in dependency ratios, the elimination of starvation and malnutrition, more rapid economic development, and an improvement in health and welfare services; among these ends in the developed countries are a maintenance or improvement of the quality of life, the protection of nonrenewable resources, and the control of environmental pollution. For most purposes, it will be sufficient to cite goals of this sort. But for ethical purposes, it is critical to consider not just proximate, but ultimate ends as well. For it is legitimate to ask of the specified proximate ends what ultimate human ends they are meant to serve. Why is it important to raise literacy rates? Why is it necessary to protect nonrenewable resources? Why ought the elimination of starvation and malnutrition to be sought? For the most part, these are questions that need not be asked or that require no elaborate answers. The ethical importance of such questions is that they force us to confront the goals of human life. Unless these goals are confronted at some point, ethics cannot start or finish.

Philosophically, solving the population problem can be viewed as determining at the outset what final values should be pursued. The reason, presumably, that a reduction in illiteracy rates is sought is that it is thought valuable for human beings to possess the means of achieving knowledge. The elimination of starvation and malnutrition is sought because of the self-evident fact that human beings must eat to survive. The preservation of nonrenewable resources is necessary in order that human life may continue through future generations. There is little argument about the validity of these propositions, because they all presuppose some important human values: knowledge, life, and survival of the species, for instance. Historically, philosophers have attempted to specify what, in the sense of "the good," human beings essentially seek. What do they, in the end, finally value? The historical list of values is long: life, pleasure, happiness, knowledge, freedom, justice, and self-expression, among others.

This is not the place to enter into a discussion of all of these values and the philosophical history of attempts to specify and rank them. Suffice it to say that three values have had a predominant role, at least in the West: freedom, justice, and security-survival. Many of the major ethical dilemmas posed by the need for population limitation can be reduced to ranking and interpreting these three values. Freedom is prized because it is a condition for self-determination and the achievement of knowledge. Justice, particularly distributive justice, is prized because it entails equality of treatment and opportunity and an equitable access to those resources and opportunities necessary for human development. Security-survival is prized because it constitutes a fundamental ground for all human activities.

Excessive population growth poses ethical dilemmas because it forces us to weight and rank these values in trying to find solutions. How much procreative freedom, if any, should be given up in order to insure the security-survival of a nation or a community? How much security-survival can be risked in order to promote distributive justice? How much procreative freedom can be tolerated if it jeopardizes distributive justice?

Ethical dilemmas might be minimized if there were a fixed agreement on the way the three values ought to be ranked. One could say that freedom is so supreme a value that both justice and security-survival should be sacrificed to maintain it. But there are inherent difficulties in taking such a position. It is easily possible to imagine situations in which a failure to give due weight to the other values could result in an undermining of the possibility of freedom itself. If people cannot survive at the physical level, it becomes impossible for them to exercise freedom of choice, procreative or otherwise. If the freedom of some is unjustly achieved at the expense of the freedom of others, then the overall benefits of freedom are not maximized. If security-survival were given the place of supremacy, situations could arise in which this value was used to justify the suppression of freedom or the perpetuation of social injustice. In that case, those suppressed might well ask, "Why live if one cannot have freedom and justice?"

For all of these reasons it is difficult and perhaps unwise to specify a fixed and abstract rank order of preference among the three values. In some circumstances, each can enter a valid claim against the others. In the end, at the level of abstractions, one is forced to say that all three values are critical; none can permanently be set aside.

The Primacy of Freedom

In the area of family planning and population limitation, a number of national and international declarations have given primacy to individual freedom. The Declaration of the 1968 United Nations International Conference on Human Rights is representative (7, 8): ". . . couples have a basic human right to decide freely and responsibly on the number and spacing of their children and a right to adequate education and information in this respect." While this primacy of individual freedom has been challenged (9), it retains its position, serving as the ethical and political foundation of both domestic and foreign family planning and population policies. Accordingly, it will be argued here that (i) the burden of proof for proposals to limit freedom of choice (whether on the grounds of justice or security-survival) rests with those who make the proposals, but that (ii) this burden can, under specified conditions, be discharged if it can be shown that a limitation of freedom of choice in the name of justice or security-survival would tend to maximize human welfare and human values. This is only to say that, while the present international rank order of preference gives individual freedom primacy, it is possible to imagine circumstances that would require a revision of the ranking.

One way of approaching the normative issues of ranking preferences in population limitation programs and proposals is by locating the key ethical actors, those who can be said to have obligations. Three groups of actors can be identified: individuals (persons, couples, families), the officers and agents of voluntary (private-external) organizations, and the government officials responsible for population and family planning programs. I will limit my discussion here to individuals and governments. What are the ethical obligations of each of the actors? What is the right or correct course of conduct for them? I will approach these questions by first trying to define some general rights and obligations for each set of actors and then by offering some suggested resolutions of a number of specific issues.

I begin with individuals (persons, couples, families) because, in the ranking of values, individual freedom of choice has been accorded primacy by some international forums—and it is individuals who procreate. What are the rights and obligations of individuals with regard to procreation?

Individuals have the right voluntarily to control their own fertility in accordance with their personal preferences and convictions (7, p. 15). This right logically extends to a choice of methods to achieve the desired control and the right to the fullest possible knowledge of available methods and their consequences (medical, social, economic, and demographic, among others).

Individuals are obligated to care for the needs and respect the rights of their existing children (intellectual, emotional, and physical); in their deci-sion to have a child (or another child), they must determine if they will be able to care for the needs and respect the rights of the child-to-be. Since individuals are obliged to respect the rights of others, they are obliged to act in such a way that these rights are not jeopardized. In determining family size, this means that they must exercise their own freedom of choice in such a way that they do not curtail the freedom of others. They are obliged, in short, to respect the requirements of the common good in their exercise of free choice (10). The source of these obligations is the rights of others.

The role of governments in promoting the welfare of their citizens has long been recognized. It is only fairly recently, however, that governments have taken a leading role in an antinatalist control of fertility (11). This has come about by the establishment, in a number of countries, of national family planning programs and national population policies. While many countries still do not have such policies, few international objections have been raised against the right of nations to develop them. So far, most government population policies have rested upon and been justified in terms of an extension of freedom of choice. Increasingly, though, it is being recognized that, since demographic trends can significantly affect national welfare, it is within the right of nations to adopt policies designed to reduce birthrates and slow population growth.

A preliminary question must, therefore, be asked. Is there any special reason to presume or suspect that governmental intervention in the area of individual procreation and national fertility patterns raises problems which, in *kind*, are significantly different from other kinds of interventions? To put the question another way, can the ethicopolitical problems that arise in this area be handled by historical and traditional principles of political ethics, or must an entirely new ethic be devised?

I can see no special reason to think that the formation of interventionist, antinatalist, national population policies poses any unique *theoretical* difficulties. To be sure, the perceived need to reduce population growth is historically new; there exists no developed political or ethicopolitical tradition dealing with this specific problem. Yet the principle of governmental intervention in procreation-related behavior has a long historical precedent: in earlier, pronatalist population policies, in the legal regulation of marriage, and in laws designed to regulate sexual behavior. It seems a safe generalization to say that governments have felt (and generally have been given) as much right to intervene in this area as in any other where individual and collective welfare appears to be at stake. That new forms of intervention may seem to be called for or may be proposed (that is, in an anti- rather than pronatalist direction) does not mean that a new ethical or political principle is at issue. At least, no such principle is immediately evident.

Yet, if it is possible to agree that no new principles are involved, it is still possible to argue that a further extension of an old principle—the right of government intervention into procreation-related behavior—would be wrong. Indeed, it is a historical irony that, after a long international struggle to establish individuals' freedom of choice in controlling their own fertility, that freedom should immediately be challenged in the name of the population crisis. Irony or not, there is no cause to be surprised by such a course of events. The history of human liberty is studded with instances in which, for a variety of reasons, it has been possible to say that liberty is a vital human good and yet that, for the sake of other goods, restriction of liberty seems required. A classical argument for the need of a government is that a formal and public apparatus is necessary to regulate the exercise of individual liberty for the sake of the common good.

In any case, the premise of my discussion will be that governments have as much right to intervene in procreation-related behavior as in other areas of behavior affecting the general welfare. This right extends to the control of fertility in general and to the control of individual fertility in particular. The critical issue is the way in which this right is to be exercised—its conditions and limits—and that issue can only be approached by first noting some general issues bearing on the restriction of individual freedom of choice by governments.

Governments have the right to take those steps necessary to insure the preservation and promotion of the common good—the protection and advancement of the right to life, liberty, and property. The maintenance of an orderly and just political and legal system, the maintenance of internal and external security, and an equitable distribution of goods and resources are also encompassed within its rights. Its obligations are to act in the interests of the people, to observe human rights, to respect national values and traditions, and to guarantee justice and equality. Since excessive population growth can touch upon all of these elements of national life, responses to population problems will encompass both the rights and the obligations of governments. However, governmental acts should represent collective national decisions and be subject to a number of stipulations.

I now recapitulate the points made so far and summarize some propositions, which I then use to suggest solutions to some specific ethical issues.

1) General moral rules: (i) individuals have the right to freedom of procreative choice, and they have the obligation to respect the freedom of others and the requirements of the common good; (ii) governments have the right to take those steps necessary to secure a maximization of freedom, justice, and security-survival, and they have the obligation to act in such a way that freedom and justice are protected and security-survival enhanced.

2) Criteria for ethical decision-making: (i) one (individual, government, organization) is obliged to act in such a way that the fundamental values of freedom, justice, and security-survival are respected; (ii) in cases of conflict, one is obliged to act in such a way that any limitation of one or more of the three fundamental values—a making of exceptions to the rules concerning these values—continues to respect the values and can be justified by the promise of increasing the balance of good over evil.

3) Rank order of preference: (i) those choices of action that ought to be preferred are those that accord primacy to freedom of choice; (ii) if conditions appear to require a limitation of freedom, this should be done in such a way that the direct and indirect harmful consequences are minimized and the chosen means of limitation are just—the less the harm, the higher the ranking.

Some Specific Ethical Issues

Since it has already been contended that individual freedom of choice has primacy, the ethical issues to be specified here will concentrate on those posed for governments. This focus will, in any event, serve to test the limits of individual freedom.

Faced with an excessive population growth, a variety of courses are open to governments. They can do nothing at all. They can institute, develop, or expand voluntary family planning programs. They can attempt to implement proposals that go "beyond family planning" (12).

Would it be right for governments to go beyond family planning if excessive population growth could be shown to be a grave problem? This question conceals a great range of issues. Who would decide if governments have this right? Of all the possible ways of going beyond family planning, which could be most easily justified and which would be the hardest to justify? To what extent would the problem have to be shown to be grave? As a general proposition, it is possible ethically to say that governments would have the right to go beyond family planning. The obligation of governments to protect fundamental values could require that they set aside the primacy of individual freedom in order to protect justice and security-survival. But everything would depend on the way they proposed to do so.

Would it be right for governments to establish involuntary fertility controls? These might include (if technically feasible) the use of a mass "fertility control agent," the licensing of the right to have children, compulsory temporary or permanent steriliza-

131

tion, or compulsory abortion (12). Proposals of this kind have been put forth primarily as "last resort" methods, often in the context that human survival may be at stake. "Compulsory control of family size is an unpalatable idea to many," the Ehrlichs have written, "but the alternatives may be much more horrifying . . . human survival seems certain to require population control programs. . . ." (3, p. 256). Their own suggestion is manifestly coercive: "If . . . relatively uncoercive laws should fail to bring the birthrate under control, laws could be written that would make the bearing of a third child illegal and that would require an abortion to terminate all such pregnancies" (3, p. 274).

That last suggestion requires examination. Let us assume for the moment that the scientific case has been made that survival itself is at stake and that the administrative and enforcement problems admit of a solution. Even so, some basic ethical issues would remain. "No one," the United Nations has declared, "shall be subjected to torture or to cruel, inhuman, or degrading treatment or punishment" (13, Article 5). It is hard to see how compulsory abortion, requiring governmental invasion of a woman's body, could fail to qualify as inhuman or degrading punishment. Moreover, it is difficult to see how this kind of suggestion can be said to respect in any way the values of freedom and justice. It removes free choice altogether, and in its provision for an abortion of the third child makes no room for distributive justice at all; its burden would probably fall upon the poorest and least educated. It makes security-survival the prime value, but to such an extent and in such a way that the other values are ignored altogether. But

could not one say, when survival itself is at stake, that this method would increase the balance of good over evil? The case would not be easy to make (i) because survival is not the only human value at stake; (ii) because the social consequences of such a law could be highly destructive (for example, the inevitably massive fear and anxiety about third pregnancies that would result from such a law); and (iii) because it would be almost impossible to show that this is the *only* method that would or could work to achieve the desired reduction in birthrates.

Would it be right for governments to develop "positive" incentive programs, designed to provide people with money or goods in return for a regulation of their fertility? These programs might include financial rewards for sterilization, for the use of contraceptives, for periods of nonpregnancy or nonbirth, and for family planning bonds or "responsibility prizes" (12, p. 2). In principle, incentive schemes are noncoercive; that is, people are not forced to take advantage of the incentive. Instead, the point of an incentive is to give them a choice they did not previously have.

Yet there are a number of ethical questions about incentive plans. To whom would they appeal most? Presumably, their greatest appeal would be to the poor, those who want or need the money or goods offered by an incentive program; they would hold little appeal for the affluent, who already have these things. Yet if the poor desperately need the money or goods offered by the incentive plan, it is questionable whether, in any real sense, they have a free choice. Their material needs may make the incentive seem coercive to them. Thus, if it is only or mainly the poor who would find the inducements of an incentive plan attractive, a question of distributive justice is raised. Because of their needs, the poor have less choice than the rich about accepting or rejecting the incentive; this could be seen as a form of exploitation of poverty. In sum, one can ask whether incentive schemes are or could be covertly coercive, and whether they are or could be unjust (14). If so, then while they may serve the need for security-survival, they may do so at the expense of freedom and justice.

At least three responses seem possible. First, if the need for security-survival is desperate, incentive schemes might well appear to be the lesser evil, compared with more overtly coercive alternatives. Second, the possible objections to incentive schemes could be reduced if, in addition to reducing births, they provided other benefits as well. For instance, a "family planning bond" program would provide the additional benefit of old-age security (15). Any one of the programs might be defended on the grounds that those who take advantage of it actually want to control births in any case (if this can be shown). Third, much could depend upon the size of the incentive benefits. At present, most incentive programs offer comparatively small rewards; one may doubt that they offer great dilemmas for individuals or put them in psychological straits. The objection to such programs on the grounds of coercion would become most pertinent if it can be shown that the recipients of an incentive benefit believe they have no real choice in the matter (because of their desperate poverty or the size of the benefit); so far, this does not appear to have been the case (16).

While ethical objections have been leveled at incentive programs because of some experienced corrupt practices in their implementation, this seems to raise less serious theoretical issues. Every program run by governments is subject to corruption; but there are usually ways of minimizing it (by laws and review procedures, for instance). Corruption, I would suggest, becomes a serious theoretical issue only when and if it can be shown that a government program is *inherently* likely to create a serious, inescapable, and socially damaging system of corruption. This does not appear to be the case with those incentive programs so far employed or proposed.

Would it be right for governments to institute "negative" incentive programs? These could take the form of a withdrawal of child or family allowances after a given number of children, a withdrawal of maternity benefits after a given number, or a reversal of tax benefits, to favor those with small families (12, p. 2). A number of objections to such programs have been raised. They are directly coercive in that they deprive people of free choice about how many children they will have by imposing a penalty on excess procreation; thus they do not attach primary importance to freedom of choice. They can also violate the demands of justice, especially in those cases where the burden of the penalties would fall upon those children who would lose benefits available to their siblings. And the penalties would probably be more onerous to the poor than to the rich, further increasing the injustice. Finally, from quite a different perspective, the social consequences of such programs could be most undesirable. They could, for instance, worsen the health and welfare of those mothers,

133

families, and children who would lose needed social and welfare benefits. Moreover, such programs could be patently unjust in those places where effective contraceptives do not exist (most places at present). In such cases, people would be penalized for having children whom they could not prevent with the available birth control methods.

It is possible to imagine ways of reducing the force of these objections. If the penalties were quite mild, more symbolic than actual [as Garrett Hardin has proposed (17)], the objection from the viewpoint of free choice would be less; the same would apply to the objection from the viewpoint of justice. Moreover, if the penalty system were devised in such a way that the welfare of children and families would not be harmed, the dangerous social consequences would be mitigated. Much would depend, in short, upon the actual provisions of the penalty plan and the extent to which it could minimize injustice and harmful social consequences. Nonetheless, penalty schemes raise serious ethical problems. It seems that they would be justifiable only if it could be shown that security-survival was at stake and that, in their application, they would give due respect to freedom and justice. Finally, it would have to be shown that, despite their disadvantages, they promised to increase the balance of good over evil—which would include a calculation of the harm done to freedom and justice and a weighing of other, possibly harmful, social consequences.

An additional problem should be noted. Any penalty or benefit scheme would require some method of governmental surveillance and enforcement. Penalty plans, in particular, would invite evasion—for example, hiding the birth of children to avoid the sanctions of the scheme. This likelihood would be enhanced among those who objected to the plan on moral or other grounds, or who believed that the extra children were necessary for their own welfare. One does not have to be an ideological opponent of "big government" to imagine the difficulties of trying to ferret out violators or the lengths to which some couples might go to conceal pregnancies and births. Major invasions of privacy, implemented by a system of undercover agents, informants, and the like, would probably be required to make the scheme work. To be sure, there are precedents for activities of this kind (as in the enforcement of income tax laws), but the introduction of further governmental interventions of this kind would raise serious ethical problems, creating additional strains on the relationship between the government and the people. The ethical cost of an effective penalty system would have to be a key consideration in the development of any penalty program.

Would it be right for governments to introduce antinatalist shifts in social and economic institutions? Among such shifts might be a raising of marriage ages, manipulation of the family structure away from nuclear families, and bonuses for delayed marriage (12, pp. 2–3). The premise of these proposals is that fertility patterns are influenced by the context in which choices are made and that some contexts (for example, higher female employment) are anti- rather than pronatalist. Thus, instead of intervening directly into the choices women make, these proposals would alter the environment of choice; freedom of individual choice would remain. The attractiveness of these proposals lies in

134

their noninterference with choice; they do not seem to involve coercion. But they are not without their ethical problems, at least in some circumstances. A too-heavy weighting of the environment of choice in an antinatalist direction would be tantamount to an interference with freedom of choice—even if, technically, a woman could make a free choice. In some situations, a manipulation of the institution of marriage (for example, raising the marriage age) could be unjust, especially if there exist no other social options for women.

The most serious problems, however, lie in the potential social consequences of changes in basic social institutions. What would be the long-term consequences of a radical manipulation of family structure for male-female relationships, for the welfare of children, for the family? One might say that the consequences would be good or bad, but the important point is that they would have to be weighed. Should some of them appear bad, they would then have to be justified as entailing a lesser evil than the continuation of high birthrates. If some of the changes promised to be all but irreversible once introduced, the justification would have to be all the greater. However, if the introduction of shifts in social institutions had some advantages in addition to antinatalism—for instance, greater freedom for women, a value in its own right—these could be taken as offsetting some other, possibly harmful, consequences.

Would it be right for the government of a developed nation to make the establishment of a population control program in a developing nation a condition for extending food aid (18, 19)? This would be extremely difficult to justify on ethical grounds. At the very least, it would constitute an interference in a nation's right to self-determination (20). Even more serious, it would be a direct exploitation of one nation's poverty in the interests of another nation's concept of what is good for it; and that would be unjust. Finally, I would argue that, on the basis of Article 3 of the "Universal Declaration of Human Rights" (21), a failure to provide needed food aid would be a fundamental violation of the right to life (when that aid could, without great cost to the benefactor nation, be given). The argument that such aid, without an attendant population control program, would only make the problem worse in the long run, is defective. Those already alive, and in need of food, have a right to security-survival. To willfully allow them to die, or to deprive them of the necessities of life, in the name of saving even more lives at a later date cannot be justified in the name of a greater preponderance of good over evil. There could be no guarantee that those future lives would be saved, and there would be such a violation of the rights of the living (including the right to life) that fundamental human values would be sacrificed.

Would it be right for a government to institute programs that go beyond family planning—particularly in a coercive direction—for the sake of future generations? This is a particularly difficult question, in great part because the rights of unborn generations have never been philosophically, legally, or ethically analyzed in any great depth (22). On the one hand, it is evident that the actions of one generation can have profound effects on the options available to future generations. And just as those living owe much of their own welfare to those who preceded

135

them (beginning with their parents), so, too, the living would seem to have obligations to the unborn. On the other hand, though, the living themselves do have rights—not just potential, but actual. To set aside these rights, necessary for the dignity of the living, in favor of those not yet living would, I think, be to act arbitrarily.

A general solution might, however, be suggested. While the rights of the living should take precedence over the rights of unborn generations, the living have an obligation to refrain from actions that would endanger future generations' enjoyment of the same rights that the living now enjoy. This means, for instance, that the present generation should not exhaust nonrenewable resources, irrevocably pollute the environment, or procreate to such an extent that future generations will be left with an unmanageably large number of people. All of these obligations imply a restriction of freedom. However, since the present generation does have the right to make use of natural resources and to procreate, it must be demonstrated (not just asserted) that the conduct of the present generation poses a direct threat to the rights of future generations. In a word, the present generation cannot be deprived of rights on the basis of vague speculations about the future or uncertain projections into the future.

Do governments have the right unilaterally to introduce programs that go beyond family planning? It is doubtful that they do. Article 21 of the "Universal Declaration of Human Rights" (13) asserts that "Everyone has the right to take part in the government of his country, directly or through freely chosen representatives . . . . The will of the people shall be the basis of the authority of government." There

is no evident reason that matters pertaining to fertility control should be exempt from the requirements of this right. By implication, not only measures that go beyond family planning, but family planning programs as well require the sanctions of the will of the people and the participation of the people in important decisions.

A Ranking of Preferences

The preceding list of specific issues by no means exhausts the range of possible ethical issues pertaining to governmental action; it is meant only to be illustrative of some of the major issues. Moreover, the suggested solutions are only illustrative. The complexities of specific situations could well lead to modifications of them. That is why ethical analysis can rarely ever say exactly what ought to be done in x place at y time by z people. It can suggest general guidelines only.

I want now to propose some general ethical guidelines for governmental action, ranking from the most preferable to the least preferable.

1) Given the primacy accorded freedom of choice, governments have an obligation to do everything within their power to protect, enhance, and implement freedom of choice in family planning. This means the establishment, as the first order of business, of effective voluntary family planning programs.

2) If it turns out that voluntary programs are not effective in reducing excessive population growth, then governments have the right, as the next step, to introduce programs that go beyond family planning. However, in order to justify the introduction of such programs, it must be shown that

136

voluntary methods have been adequately and fairly tried, and have nonetheless failed and promise to continue to fail. It is highly doubtful that, at present, such programs have "failed"; they have not been tried in any massive and systematic way (23).

3) In choosing among possible programs that go beyond family planning, governments must first try those which, comparatively, most repect freedom of choice (that is, are least coercive). For instance, they should try "positive" incentive programs and manipulation of social structures before resorting to "negative" incentive programs and involuntary fertility controls.

4) Further, if circumstances force a government to choose programs that are quasi- or wholly coercive, they can justify such programs if, and only if, a number of prior conditions have been met: (i) if, in the light of the primacy of free choice, a government has discharged the burden of proof necessary to justify a limitation of free choice— and the burden of proof is on the government (this burden may be discharged by a demonstration that continued unrestricted liberty poses a direct threat to distributive justice or security-survival); and (ii) if, in light of the right of citizens to take part in the government of their country, the proposed limitations on freedom promise, in the long run, to increase the options of free choice, decisions to limit freedom are collective decisions, the limitations on freedom are legally regulated and the burden falls upon all equally, and the chosen means of limitation respect human dignity, which will here be defined as respecting those rights specified in the United Nations' "Universal Declaration of Human Rights" (13). The end—even security-survival—does not justify the means

when the means violate human dignity and logically contradict the end.

As a general rule, the more coercive the proposed plan, the more stringent should be the conditions necessary to justify and regulate the coercion. In addition, one must take account of the possible social consequences of different programs, consequences over and above their impact on freedom, justice, and security-survival. Thus, if it appears that some degree of coercion is required, that policy or program should be chosen which (i) entails the least amount of coercion, (ii) limits the coercion to the fewest possible cases, (iii) is most problem-specific, (iv) allows the most room for dissent of conscience, (v) limits the coercion to the narrowest possible range of human rights, (vi) threatens human dignity least, (vii) establishes the fewest precedents for other forms of coercion, and (viii) is most quickly reversible if conditions change.

While it is true to say that social, cultural, and political life requires, and has always required, some degree of limitation of individual liberty—and thus some coercion—that precedent does not, in itself, automatically justify the introduction of new limitations (24). Every proposal for a new limitation must be justified in · its own terms—the specific form of the proposed limitation must be specifically justified. It must be proved that it represents the least possible coercion, that it minimizes injustice to the greatest extent possible, that it gives the greatest promise of enhancing security-survival, and that it has the fewest possible harmful consequences (both short- and long-term).

Freedom and Risk-Taking

The approach I have taken to the

ethics of population limitation has been cautionary. I have accepted the primacy of freedom of choice as a given not only because of its primacy in United Nations and other declarations, but also because it is a primary human value. I have suggested that the burden of proof must lie with those proposals, policies, or programs that would place the primacy elsewhere. At the same time, I have laid down numerous conditions necessary to discharge the burden of proof. Indeed, these conditions are so numerous, and the process of ethical justification so difficult, that the possibility of undertaking decisive action may seem to have been excluded. This is a reasonable concern, particularly if time is short. Is it reasonable to give the ethical advantage to freedom of choice (25)? Does this not mean that a great chance is being taken? Is it not unethical to take risks of that sort, and all the more so since others, rather than ourselves, will have to bear the burden if the risk-taking turns out disastrously? In particular, would it not be irresponsible for governments to take risks of this magnitude?

Three kinds of responses to these questions are possible. First, as mentioned, it can and has been argued that freedom of choice has not been adequately tested. The absence of a safe, effective, and inexpensive contraceptive has been one hindrance, particularly in developing countries; it is reasonable to expect that such a contraceptive will eventually be developed. The weakness of existing family planning programs (and population policies dependent upon them) has, in great part, been the result of inadequate financing, poor administration, and scanty research and survey data. These are correctable deficiencies, assuming that nations give population limitation a high priority. If they do not give population limitation a high priority, it is unlikely that more drastic population policies could be successfully introduced or implemented. Very little effort has been expended anywhere in the world to educate people and persuade them to change their procreation habits. Until a full-scale effort has been made, there are few good grounds for asserting that voluntary limitation will be ineffective.

Second, while the question of scientific-medical-technological readiness, political viability, administrative feasibility, economic capability, and assumed effectiveness of proposals that would go beyond family planning is not directly ethical in nature, it has important ethical implications. If all of these categories seem to militate against the practical possibility of instituting very strong, immediate, or effective coercive measures, then it could become irresponsible to press for or support such measures. This would especially be the case if attention were diverted away from what could be done, for example, an intensification of family planning programs.

Third, primacy has been given to freedom of choice for ethical reasons. Whether this freedom will work as a means of population limitation is a separate question. A strong indication that freedom of choice will be ineffective does not establish grounds for rejecting it. Only if it can be shown that the failure of this freedom to reduce population growth threatens other important human values, thus establishing a genuine conflict of values, would the way be open to remove it from the place of primacy. This is only another way of asserting that freedom of choice is a right, grounded in a commitment to human dignity. The concept of a "right" becomes meaningless if rights are wholly subject to tests of economic, social, or demographic utility, to be given or withheld depending upon their effectiveness in serving social goals.

In this sense, to predicate human rights at all is to take a risk. It is to assert that the respect to be accorded human beings ought not to be dependent upon majority opinion, cost-benefit analysis, social utility, governmental magnanimity, or popular opinion. While it is obviously necessary to adjudicate conflicts among rights, and often to limit one right in order to do justice to another, the pertinent calculus is that of rights, not of utility. A claim can be entered against the primacy of one right only in the name of one or more other important rights. The proper route to a limitation of rights is not directly from social facts (demographic, economic, and so on) to rights, as if these facts were enough in themselves to prove the case against a right. The proper route is from showing that the social facts threaten rights, and in what way, to showing that a limitation of one right may be necessary to safeguard or enhance other rights. To give primacy to the right of free choice is to take a risk. The justification for the risk is the high value assigned to the right, a value that transcends simply utilitarian considerations.

References and Notes

1. E. H. Erikson, *Insight and Responsibility* (Norton, New York, 1964), p. 132.
2. B. Berelson, in *Is There an Optimum Level of Population?*, S. F. Singer, Ed. (McGraw-Hill, New York, 1971), p. 305.
3. See, for instance, P. R. Ehrlich and A. H. Ehrlich, *Population, Resources, Environment Isues in Human Ecology* (Freeman, San Francisco, 1970), pp. 321-324.
4. A 1967 Gallup Poll, for example, revealed that, while 54 percent of those surveyed felt that the rate of American population growth posed a serious problem, crime, racial discrimination, and poverty were thought to be comparatively more serious social problems. J. F. Kanther, *Stud. Fam. Plann.* No. 30 (May 1968), p. 6.
5. R. B. Potter, Jr., in *Freedom, Coercion and the Life Sciences*, L. Kass and D. Callahan, Eds., in press.
6. K. E. Boulding, *Amer. Econ. Rev.* 59, 1 (March 1969).
7. *Final Act of the International Conference on Human Rights* (United Nations, New York, 1968), p. 15.
8. "Declaration on Population: The World Leaders Statement," *Stud. Fam. Plann.* No. 26 (January 1968), p. 1.
9. For instance, not only has Garrett Hardin, in response to the "The World Leaders' Statement" (8), denied the right of the family to choose family size, he has also said that "If we love the truth we must openly deny the validity of the Universal Declaration of Human Rights, even though it is promoted by the United Nations" [*Science* 162, 1246 (1968)]. How literally is one to take this statement? The declaration, after all, affirms such rights as life, liberty, dignity, equality, education, privacy, and freedom of thought. Are none of these rights valid? Or, if those rights are to remain valid, why is only the freedom to control family size to be removed from the list?
10. See A. S. Parkes, in *Biology and Ethics*, F. J. Ebling, Ed. (Academic Press, New York, 1969), pp. 109-116.
11. In general, "antinatalist" means "attitudes or policies directed toward a reduction of births," and "pronatalist" means "attitudes or policies directed toward an increase in births."
12. See B. Berelson, *Stud. Fam. Plann.* No. 38 (February 1969), p. 1.
13. "Universal Declaration of Human Rights," in *Human Rights: A Compilation of International Instruments of the United Nations* (United Nations, New York, 1967).
14. See E. Pohlman and K. G. Rao, *Licentiate* 17, 236 (1967).
15. See, for instance, R. G. Ridker, *Stud. Fam. Plann.* No. 43 (June 1969), p. 11.
16. The payments made in six different family planning programs are listed in *Incentive Payments in Family Planning Programmes* (International Planned Parenthood Federation, London, 1969), pp. 8-9.
17. G. Hardin, *Fam. Plann. Perspect.* 2, 26 (June 1970).
18. See, for example, W. H. Davis, *New Repub.* (20 June 1970), p. 19.
19. P. R. Ehrlich, *The Population Bomb* (Ballantine Books, New York, 1968), pp. 158-173.
20. See the "International Covenant on Economic, Social and Cultural Rights," Article 1, section 1, paragraph 1, in *Human Rights: A Compilation of International Instruments of the United Nations* (United Nations, New York, 1967), p. 4: "All people have the

right to self-determination. By virtue of that right they freely determine their political status and freely pursue their economic, social and cultural development."

21. "Everyone has the right to life, liberty and the security of person" (13).

22. One of the few recent discussions on the obligation to future generations is in M. P. Golding [*UCLA Law Review* 15, 457 (February 1968)].

23. See D. Nortman, in *Reports on Population/ Family Planning* (Population Council, New York, December 1969), pp. 1–48. Judith Blake is pessimistic about the possibilities of family planning programs [*J. Chronic Dis.* 18, 1181 (1965)]. See also J. Blake [*Science* 164, 522 (1969)] and the reply of O. Harkavy, F. S. Jaffe, S. M. Wishik [*ibid.* 165, 367 (1969)].

24. See E. Pohlman, *Eugen. Quart.* 13, 122 (June 1966): "The spectre of 'experts' monkeying around with such private matters as family size desires frightens many people as being too 'Big Brotherish.' But those involved in eugenics, or psychotherapy, or child psychology, or almost any aspect of family planning are constantly open to the charge of interfering in private lives, so that the charge would not be new. . . . Of course, many injustices have been done with the rationale of being 'for their own good.' But the population avalanche may be used to justify—perhaps rationalize—contemplation of large-scale attempts to manipulate family size desires, even rather stealthily." This mode of reasoning may explain how some people will think and act, but it does not constitute anything approaching an ethical justification.

25. P. R. Ehrlich (19, pp. 197-198) argues that the taking of strong steps now to curb population growth is the wiser and safer gamble than doing nothing or too little. This seems to me a reasonable enough position, up to a point. That point would come when the proposed steps would seriously endanger human dignity; an ethic of survival, at the cost of other basic human values, is not worth the cost.

26. This article is an abridgment of an "Occasional Paper" [*Ethics and Population Limitation* (Population Council, New York, 1971)] and was written while the author was a staff associate at the Population Council in 1969–70. I would particularly like to thank Bernard Berelson for his suggestions and criticisms.

Technology Assessment and Social Control

A conceptual framework proposed.

Michael S. Baram

The emerging concepts of corporate responsibility and technology assessment are, to a considerable extent, responses to problems arising from technological developments and their applications by industry and government. These problems appear in the relatively discrete sectors of consumer protection and occupational safety and in the diffuse sectors of community quality of life and the national and international environments.

Consumer Protection

As products have become more sophisticated and defects in them less easily detected by the consumer, the common-law principle of caveat emptor, "let the buyer beware" has been largely abandoned by the courts, and the principle of strict corporate liability has been frequently adopted (1). Federal and state legislation and regulatory agencies for consumer protection have multiplied with this shifting of responsibility. Nevertheless, common law, legislation, and regulation pertaining to product safety have been largely ineffective (1, p. 2):

. . . federal authority to curb hazards in consumer products is virtually non-existent . . . legislation consists of a series of isolated acts treating specific hazards in narrow product categories. . . . Despite its humanitarian adaptations to meet the challenge of product-caused injuries, the common law puts no reliable restraint upon product hazards.

As a result, Ralph Nader and other crusaders have mobilized citizens against specific technological developments embodied in hazardous products and processes—such as the Corvair and various food additives.

The 92nd Congress enacted the Consumer Product Safety Act, thereby creating an independent commission with the authority to develop mandatory safety standards for many product categories and to carry out related functions to protect consumers (2). However, regulation of automobiles, drugs, boats, foods, and other product categories is excluded and left to existing programs. The commission is expected to maintain the regulatory agency tradition of reliance on industrial testing and reports; and "Except for the availability of [commission] information and the opportunity for litigants to argue the fact of compli-

SCIENCE, May, 1973, Vol. 180, pp. 465-473.

ance or noncompliance with mandatory Government standards, the law is expected to have little effect on products liability litigation" (3). It is too early to determine whether or not the law will bring about an effective regulatory program.

Occupational Health and Safety

The incidence of harm to workers, the difficulties of employee recovery under the common law, and the inability of the judicial system to internalize such "costs" sufficiently to bring about a preventive approach by corporate management are among the factors that led to workmen's compensation laws and insurance programs (4), and agency standards for occupational hazards. The National Labor Relations Act (5), and most recently the Occupational Safety and Health Act (6) have provided frameworks for decision-making on automation and hazardous technological developments. Nevertheless, high injury rates persist in several industrial sectors (7) as old and new technology continues to create lethal environments for employees —for example, "The National Academy of Sciences reports a study showing that the life-span of radiologists is five years shorter than the national average . . ." (8, p. 13).

The introduction of new automation technology has traditionally brought about strong union opposition because of impacts on job security (9). Now, impacts on employee health provide new bases for opposition. As a result, some new, highly automated plants have been shut down—Rio Tinto's lead processing plant in the United Kingdom and General Motors' Vega plant in Lordstown, Ohio, have recently suspended operations until the economic

and the physical and mental health effects of new automation technology on employees could be determined and diminished (10).

Community Quality of Life

The impacts of industrial and government technology on health, land use, esthetics, and other aspects of community quality of life (11) have finally aroused organized citizen opposition. Government transportation and energy programs are now persistently opposed by local communities. Corporations that have traditionally provided the economic base for communities are now increasingly confronted by litigants seeking compensatory damages, restraining orders, and injunctions; by newly aggressive local officials responding to citizen complaints and invoking long-dormant police powers against noise, smoke, and other nuisances; and by state and federal officials enforcing air and water quality programs. Despite judicial reluctance to enjoin ongoing industrial activity that concurrently provides local economic benefits and environmental degradation (12), the expanding enforcement of public nuisance and pollution control laws has recently brought about a number of plant closures (13).

Nevertheless, the economic objectives of states and local communities and the fear of job losses and other dislocations that would arise from project or plant shutdowns will continue to determine the pace at which community quality of life is rehabilitated and environmental degradation controlled (14). The complex task of resource management must be undertaken by state and local governments. How else to reconcile the objectives of economic and social opportunity—

142

housing, economic development, transportation, and so on—with enhanced community quality of life—open space, recreation, esthetically pleasing surroundings, population stability? The reconciliation of such diverse objectives will not be possible until the consequences of technology can be systematically assessed, until rational siting and land use guidelines have been established, and until state and regional planning find a viable political structure.

National Environmental Quality

Ehrlich, Commoner, and other early crusaders may have been critically received, but nations are now embarking on serious, more effective pollution control programs. In the United States, the new water pollution control program has been designed to achieve use of the "best practicable" pollution control technology by 1977, the "best available" technology by 1983, and a national "no pollution discharge" goal by 1985 (15). The air quality program provides authority for federal control over new stationary sources of air pollution, over automotive emissions, and over all sources of air pollutants hazardous to human health (16). New legislation has established federal authority to limit the noise emissions of numerous corporate products (17); and laws to tighten up control over pesticides and hazardous materials have again been enacted (18).

The national commitment now authorizes control over most forms of pollution caused by technological processes, ensuring more rigorous analysis, regulation, enforcement, and citizen participation. Nevertheless, many technology-created pollution problems remain—the management and disposal of radioactive waste, toxic materials, sludge, and solid waste. In addition, new technologies such as weather modification and marine resource extraction are now being developed and experimentally applied, and they will undoubtedly create new problems and new legislation in our already "law-ridden society" (19, p. 32). The pattern is obvious and disturbing: the development of a technological advance, insistence upon its application by interest groups in industry and government, utilization, the appearance of environmental problems, legislation, regulation, and extensive litigation to control environmental impacts (20).

Assumptions

These problems of consumers, employees, communities, and nations are the results of the processes we use to develop, apply, and regulate our technology—of our methods of social control. Social control is, in turn, the result of complex interactions of underlying political, economic, and cultural forces.

What is to be done? We can continue to grapple with the problems as they crystallize, using the established and ineffective patterns of post hoc legislation, regulation, and litigation. On the other hand, we can boldly attempt to alter the underlying forces or causes, and their interactions, but this calls for information we do not have and demands an acknowledgement that the forces at work in different political systems are yielding substantially similar problems (21).

The most feasible strategy appears to be one of intervening in those decision-making processes of the public and private sectors that bring about technological applications; such intervention would take the form of introducing new frameworks for planning and decision-making. The development and use of coherent frameworks for technology assessment and utilization could meet many of the demands for corporate and governmental responsibility. Clearly, the use of such frameworks will affect the underlying social forces not directly confronted and will entail considerable reliance on established legal and regulatory procedures (22, 23).

The task of developing frameworks for technology assessment and utilization must be undertaken in full recognition of several realities.

1) Application of any such framework to a particular technological advance will yield differences in opinion and information from professionals, as well as from concerned citizens.

2) Continuing research, monitoring experiments, and changing designs will not necessarily resolve such differences, but will generally reveal the trans-scientific nature of decisions to be made about the further development and utilization of a specific technological advance: for example, the decisions will ultimately involve value-based consideration of the probable harm of the advance and the scope, magnitude, and acceptability of that harm (24).

3) Receptors—consumers, employees, and citizens generally—will find elitist decision-making and compensatory solutions to possible harmful effects inadequate, and they will actively seek to participate in the planning, design, and implementation stages of the technology application process.

4) A multiplicity of inadequate decision frameworks for technology assessment and utilization already exist and are employed by, for example, Congress, regulatory agency officials, corporate management, insurance rate-setters, courts, and organized citizen's groups.

Given this statement of the problem and these assumptions, it appears that the task is to somehow "get it all together"—to develop an understanding of how technology interacts with society and its institutions of social control; to demonstrate that citizens, corporations, and public institutions are all interrelated in specific patterns and thereby share responsibility for rational planning and decision-making; and to shape a common conceptual framework that can be readily applied by each decision-maker, in order that the different results can be compared meaningfully and used to choose knowledgeably among alternatives.

Developing a Coherent Framework

Technology is dependent upon processes that occur in four interrelated contexts: basic research, applied research, the development of prototypes for testing or experimentation, and ongoing production and utilization. Although it is difficult to pinpoint the path of any specific development, it is clear that most technology (in the form of processes, products, or techniques) in use today was brought about by the interactions of people and findings in these four contexts (25).

Within each context different levels and kinds of resources, or inputs are required—for example, manpower, funds, time, facilities, education, and materials—but large social and economic commitments and irreversible commitments of natural resources are usually made only when the development and experimentation phase is undertaken. These large commitments lend an inevitability to the technologi-

144

cal advance, because few courts and federal agencies have been willing to halt major socioeconomic commitments, irrespective of hazards to individuals or society (26).

The technology that emerges subsequently brings about social and environmental effects, or outputs—direct and indirect, primary and secondary, beneficial and detrimental, measurable and unmeasurable. Whether one uses nuclear power or the snowmobile as an example of current applications of technology, several classes of effects are apparent. These include effects on health (mental and physical, somatic and genetic), economy (individual and corporate, local and national, international), environment (pollution, disruptions of ecosystems), resources (availability of materials, land, and waters for competing uses), values (changes that are ultimately reflected in new law and policy), and sociopolitical institutions and processes (structural and substantive changes). As these and other effects are aggregated, they determine the quality of life.

We have no quantifiable information on many of these effects; nor can we accurately predict potential effects, their synergism, or the intervention of exogenous forces such as population migration or natural disasters. We do not have devices sophisticated enough to monitor and assess many of these effects, nor do we have articulated goals or indices to measure progress toward such goals (23). Decisions on goals, indices, and effects are now, and will probably always remain, transscientific.

But we have learned one thing well —that impacts and amenities which are unmeasurable or unquantifiable are nevertheless real and should be as integral to decision-making as quantifiable technical and economic consider-

ations. At the federal level, this has been clearly expressed in the National Environmental Policy Act (NEPA) of 1969 (27), which requires that "unquantified environmental amenities and values" be considered along with technological and economic or quantitative inputs to public agency decision-making on projects, permits, contracts, and other major actions when such actions are likely to result in significant environmental impacts. Agencies are now struggling with this new requirement as they develop environmental impact assessments, which are subsequently exposed to the public for review before agency action. Public response to over 3000 impact statements during the past 2 years has ranged from acquiescence, to intervention in agency proceedings, to political pressure, to extensive litigation (28).

Following this brief discussion of inputs to and outputs of the process of technological advance, a simple model can be developed which relates a specific technological development to resources (inputs) and effects (outputs) (Fig. 1).

The implementation of each program will depend on a variety of decision-makers in both public and private sectors and at varying jurisdictional levels—local, state, regional, and federal. These decision-makers function as controls on any program in essentially two ways (Fig. 2): (i) by controlling resources (for example, public and private sources of manpower and funds for research and development; land use and natural resource authorities; federal and state legislatures, whose enactments may be essential to the availability of other program resources; and educators, who determine training programs) and (ii) by controlling the detrimental effects (for example, the courts by means of prelim-

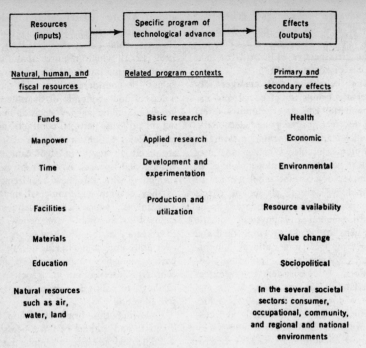

Fig. 1. Resources (inputs) and effects (outputs) of technological developments.

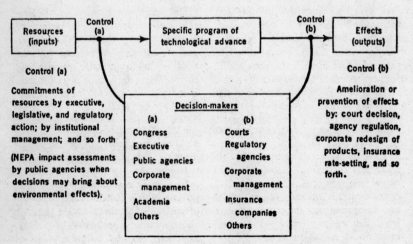

Fig. 2. Decision-makers.

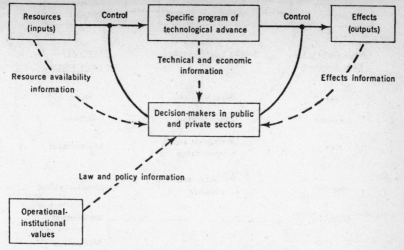

Fig. 3. Information flows to decision-makers.

inary or permanent injunctions or awards of compensatory damages; federal agencies, such as the Food and Drug Administration and the Environmental Protection Agency, and their state counterparts by engaging in standard-setting, regulation, and enforcement; and program managers, corporate management, and insurance rate-setters by bringing about program or product redesign to abate or ameliorate specific effects).

To further develop this model, some of the major influences on decision-makers who control technological developments must be determined. These influences (Fig. 3) include information on: (i) resource availability; (ii) technical and economic feasibility; (iii) actual and potential effects; and (iv) operational-institutional values, which are comprised of the common law, legislation, economic and social policy, institutional management policies, and other "given" values that have been recognized and accepted by decision-

makers as of the time any specific decision is made regarding further program development. These include diverse and often conflicting laws and policies—for example, NEPA (to foster the conservation and rational use of resources) and the oil depletion allowance (to foster rapid exploitation of resources).

To complete this general model, the social dynamics of any program of technological advance must be considered further—specifically, the responses of individual citizens and organized interest groups to perceived resource commitments and program effects (Fig. 4). These responses can be manifested through institutional procedures for changing the laws and policies that influence decision-makers—a lengthy process requiring extensive aggregation of voters or shareholders and generally undertaken in order to influence future decisions, not the particular decision that provoked the response.

Responses can also be manifested

147

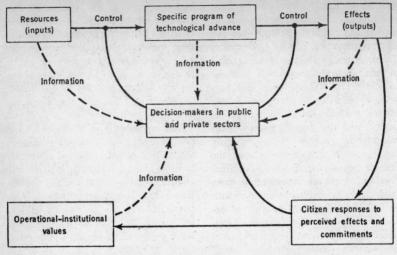

Fig. 4. Summary of influences on decision-making.

through formal, adversarial procedures to challenge decision-making—for example, injured consumers can go to court and disturbed environmentalists can intervene in agency proceedings or seek judicial review of agency decisions. Finally, a variety of informal procedures can be employed to feed back responses to decision-makers—such as demonstrations, employee absenteeism, product boycotts, consumer choice, or quasipolitical campaigns. The environmental and consumer protection movements serve as vivid examples of these new pressures on decision-makers, pressures new only in their intensity.

Citizens responding to perceived detrimental effects or resource misuse comprise a diverse group of consumers, shareholders, unions, crusaders, and citizens' organizations, ranging from those with national objectives (for example, the Sierra Club) to those with local or self-interest objectives (for example, labor unions, airport neighbors). The responses manifested through institutional, formal-adversarial, or informal procedures for exerting pressure on decision-makers may, in time, become so widespread or aggregated that they will be incorporated into the common law or form the basis for new management policy or legislation and, as such, become part of the matrix of operational-institutional values. This has already occurred to a considerable extent with regard to environmental and consumer protection responses.

Although the sector of society that responds adversely to the effects of a specific technological development does not normally constitute a democratic majority in its early stages, the issues raised by such responses deserve serious consideration, and the procedures for eliciting such responses are being strengthened by the courts and legislatures. First, the responses represent new perceptions, new "pieces of the truth" that were either unknown to, ignored, or lightly considered by decision-makers. Second, they represent market and political influence that can be magnified by use of the media. Third, although they may be ignored at first, these responses will continue to appear in various forms and may bring about delays that are more costly after a program has been started (the utilities and the Atomic Energy Commission, for example, are now finding this out as they attempt to further the nuclear power program: plant construction and operation are running more than 2 years behind schedule, with greatly increased costs, because of extensive litigation and hearings (29), which resulted from an earlier failure to consider citizens' concern about thermal and radioactive waste disposal, reactor safety, and related ecological and health issues. Fourth, such responses are based on real concerns, will often find larger public support, and eventually could result in stringent legislation or judicial findings that decision-makers would have to live with (30).

Finally, a citizenry that expresses a diversity of interests is the most effective mode of promoting the accountability of decision-makers to the full social context in which they operate. Too often, decision-makers in all institutions have failed to inform the public about the bases and risks of decisions, thereby precluding feedback of larger social issues and humanistic concerns in their effort to promote institutional or self-interest objectives (31). But the benefits of an informed and responsive public have now been adequately demonstrated. Cars will be cleaner by 1975; the Army Corps of Engineers will not continue to dam rivers and spend public funds without more rigorous analysis of impacts and needs; the Food and Drug Administration will begin informing the public of the chemical contents and quality control criteria of specific consumer products they regulate; maximum permissible exposures of workers and the public to power-plant radiation have been falling. These are some of the recent "accountability" benefits that are being derived from public pressure.

Decision-making in both public and private institutions supporting technological programs and applications is becoming more complicated and less efficient, in the institutional, short-term sense; but long-term efficiencies, in terms of larger social interests such as public health, can be expected. In more pragmatic economic and political terms, it has become increasingly apparent that it is in the long-term self-interest of decision-makers and their institutions to be open and responsive to the interests of the public. As David Rockefeller has defined the issue for the private sector (32):

The question really comes down to this: Will business leaders seize the initiative to make necessary changes and take on new responsibilities voluntarily, or will they wait until these are thrust upon them by law? Some adjustments are inevitable . . . there may have to be new laws to force consideration of the quality-of-life dimension so that more socially responsive firms will not suffer a competitive disadvantage. It is up to the businessman to make common cause with other reformers . . . to initiate necessary reforms that will make it possible for business to continue to function in a new climate as a constructive force in our society.

In the public sector, opposition to projects and the failing credibility of programs have prompted several agencies to increase citizen participation in program planning and design—beyond the environmental impact statement requirements of NEPA (33).

The model I have presented (Fig. 4)

does not provide any answers, but it can be used for several purposes: to widen the perceptions of planners, designers, and decision-makers responsibile for specific technological advances and applications; to depict the interrelationships of resources, effects, decision-makers, institutions, and citizens; to develop policy, management, or program alternatives in the corporate, congressional, and public agency sectors that support and regulate technological development and utilization; and to assess, with public participation, the impacts of technological developments before they are utilized. Above all, the model articulates an accounting system, or framework, for decision-making that is dynamic and that can be used by all of the decision-makers, irrespective of their interests. The model has also proved helpful in the development of curricula and research: by making possible the ordering and integration of diverse perspectives and events and by providing an understanding of the patterns of technological development, application, and impacts, as well as social responses to technology. This understanding extends to technology in general, as well as to developments in such specific areas as mariculture, housing, and bioengineering (34).

Reforms in Process

A number of recent legal developments can be related directly to the model, particularly to the sector designated "citizen responses to perceived effects and commitments" of technology. For citizen responses to be responsible, the flow of information to the public about effects and commitments —actual and potential—must be coherent and balanced, and it must present alternatives with their uncertainties in comparable terms. For citizen responses to be meaningful, the processes of planning, design, and decision-making must be accessible to citizens and open to their concerns.

For example, NEPA requires federal agencies to assess environmental impacts before "major actions" are taken. These actions range from the Atomic Energy Commission's approval of a construction license for a nuclear plant to be built by a utility, to the funding of increments of the highway program by the Department of Transportation, to authorization by the Department of Agriculture for the use of herbicides and pesticides. The responsibility for assessment is broad and must include full consideration of five issues (35):

1) potential environmental impacts,

2) unavoidable adverse impacts,

3) irreversible commitments of resources,

4) short-term use considerations versus long-term resource needs, and

5) alternatives to the proposed action.

Draft and final impact assessments are made available to other governmental officials and to the public for review and further development under guidelines established by the Council on Environmental Quality (36, 37). Although NEPA does not provide veto power to any official, even if the project poses real environmental hazards, the act does provide new information to the public—by exposing the extent to which environmental effects are being considered by the agency— and provides an enlarged record for judicial review of agency decisions. Obvious deficiencies in an agency's procedure, the scope of its statement, or the content of its statement will, on the basis of experience since NEPA was enacted, result in citizen intervention in agency processes, political opposition, and litigation. Many projects proposed and assessed have been delayed, and, in some cases, projects have been abandoned. Other projects have proceeded after being redesigned to ameliorate those effects on the environment that generated controversy (23, pp. 221–267).

Most projects involve applications of existing technology, but a few involve the development of new technologies—for example, the Department of Transportation's air cushion vehicle, the Atomic Energy Commission's liquid metal fast breeder reactor, cloud seeding experiments of the National Science Foundation and the National Oceanographic and Atmospheric Administration, and the use of polyvinylchloride containers, to be approved by the Internal Revenue Service, for alcoholic beverages (38).

NEPA does not expressly require consideration of social, health, or economic impacts or of secondary effects such as subsequent population migration and land development. These considerations are frequently ignored or treated in cursory fashion, even though they are integral to comprehensive assessment of project impacts and decision-making. NEPA does not impose assessment and exposure processes on industry or the private sector, but, whenever a utility, corporation, or other private institution is the applicant or intended beneficiary of federal agency funds, license, or other "major action," its proposal is subject to the NEPA process. There have been suggestions that NEPA be extended directly to the private sector, but as yet these have not been seriously considered at the federal level. However, variants of NEPA have been adopted by several states, and more states are expected to follow suit (39). Because of state and local control of land use,

state versions of NEPA have the potential for directly affecting land development activities in the private sector. This potential has been realized in California, where the state supreme court has determined that the state's Environmental Quality Act requires county boards of supervisors to conduct environmental assessments before issuing building permits for housing projects and other land developments to the private sector (40). Similar requirements may apply to the private sector in Massachusetts, where the new environmental assessment requirements are imposed on "political subdivisions" as well as on state agencies and officials (41).

Therefore, the model can be further developed by adding environmental impact assessments by public decision-makers at the point where resources are to be committed to certain types of projects that apply "old" technology, as well as to certain activities that will involve the further advance or application of new technology. Concomitantly, the flow of information to citizens has been enhanced.

The development of impact statements is a meaningless exercise unless they are actually used in decision-making (42). It is difficult to use impact statements because of the diversity and the essentially unquantifiable nature of the new factors they present—since most agency decision-making depends on quantification of technical and economic factors (37). The use of impact statements in the last stage of a project, such as the awarding of construction contracts, is deceptive. The earlier stages of planning and design may not have included assessment, thereby precluding citizen inputs at a time when more important changes in project plans and alternatives could have been accomplished. In other words, effective use of impact assessment techniques and citizen feedback can be more readily achieved in the earlier, less tangible stages of a project—precisely when most agencies prefer to plan and design without public intervention. Hopefully, litigation and subsequent judicial review will impose the NEPA framework earlier in agency processes (43).

Further difficulties with the NEPA process have become apparent. There is an inherent conflict in the requirement that the agency proponent of a project assess it and discuss alternatives. After all, the agency has already selected an alternative and has undertaken the impact assessment essentially to justify its choice. Subsequent discussion of alternatives is too often a superficial process of setting up "straw alternatives" for facile criticism. Clearly, independent review of all the alternatives, including the proposed agency action, would be desirable. However, independent review would also require the structuring of new agency procedures and independent institutions for assessment (44).

Finally, the problem of dealing with unquantifiable impacts remains. The assignment of values and weights to environmental and social amenities may either be arbitrary or intentionally designed to produce decisions that had been predetermined by agency officials.

Despite these difficulties and the numerous conflicts and increased costs that now attend agency programs, NEPA is slowly forcing wiser environmental practices, more sensitive agency bureaucracies, and more effective roles for citizens. It is possible that the NEPA process could eventually provide the basis, not for conflict in the courtroom or at agency hearings, but for negotiation in good faith between interested parties over points of dis-

pute as revealed by the environmental assessment (45). The resolution of labor-management conflicts under the National Labor Relations Board provides useful experience that should be reviewed for possible application to the NEPA context.

A major extension of NEPA practices to the assessment of new technology may have been accomplished with the passage of the Technology Assessment Act of 1972 (46). This law established within the legislative branch an Office of Technology Assessment (OTA) to ". . . provide early indications of the probable beneficial and adverse impacts of the applications of technology and to develop other coordinate information which may assist the Congress. . . ." The office is required to undertake several tasks (46, sect. 3):

1) identifying existing or probable impacts of technology or technological programs;
2) where possible, ascertaining cause and effect relationships;
3) identifying alternative technological methods of implementing specific programs;
4) identifying alternative programs for achieving requisite goals;
5) estimating and comparing the impacts of alternative methods and programs;
6) presenting findings of completed analyses to the appropriate legislative authorities;
7) identifying areas where additional research or data collection is required . . .;
8) undertaking . . . additional associated activities. . . .

Assessments to be carried out ". . . shall be made available to the initiating . . . or other appropriate committees of the Congress . . . [and] may be made available to the public . . ." (46).

The law does not distinguish between technological developments in the public agency and private sectors and presumably includes technology being developed with private funds. Although provided with the authority to subpoena witnesses, OTA ". . . shall not, itself, operate any laboratories, pilot plants, or test facilities." The broad language of the assessment requirements and the way in which assessments are used by Congress effectively preclude a substantial replication of the litigation and other conflicts that have characterized the NEPA experience.

Political conditions will inevitably determine the initiation of OTA studies and their use by congressional committees, and it appears that the public will, in general, be unable to secure judicial review to promote accountability of OTA and Congress.

The burden of formulating guidelines to describe when OTA should be called upon by Congress and prescribing procedures for providing information to the public clearly lies with the OTA board and advisory council. Above all, it appears essential that OTA develop and articulate a coherent framework for all technology assessments to be undertaken. Such a framework would prevent OTA assessments from becoming skillfully contrived, ad hoc case studies, which would be essentially closed to the introduction of important information from citizens and interest groups. OTA therefore has the additional burden of laying out a framework that will replace the multiple, partial models employed by different interests, that will promote inputs from interdisciplinary and humanistic sources, and that will clearly present, in a replicable format, the quantifiable and unquantifiable costs and benefits of new technological developments and applications.

Procedures to enhance the flow of balanced information on technological developments to the public will inevitably face the problem of information manipulation and secrecy practices (47).

The public's need for information is especially great in the field of science and technology, for the growth of specialized scientific knowledge threatens to outstrip our collective ability to control its effects on our lives.

Secrecy on the part of public agencies and the executive branch is still common practice to protect decision-making processes from public criticism, despite the 1967 Freedom of Information Act (48). However, sustained public pressures for the release of non-classified information have made such secrecy more controversial and somewhat more difficult to justify. The recent passage of the Federal Advisory Committee Act may bring about the diminution of another important form of secrecy in the public sector—agency advisory committee proceedings and recommendations, which are used in setting standards and other decision processes (49).

The common law of trade secrets is similarly invoked to protect corporate information—presumably from the competition (the common law basis for the concept) (50), but increasingly from the public and government. The Environmental Protection Agency has been unable to secure information on the quantities of polychlorinated biphenyls (PCB's) made and sold by the one American manufacturer, despite evidence that PCB's are now part of the international pollution problem (51). In other industrial technology sectors, however, congressional legislation has provided the government with access to information and procedures normally cloaked by trade secrecy. For example, section 206(c) of the Clean Air Act (16) provides that the Envi-

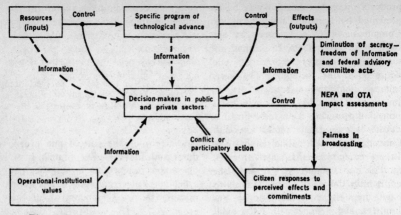

Fig. 5. Summary of influences and recent developments for decision-making.

ronmental Protection Agency may:

> . . . enter at reasonable times, any plant or other establishment of such [auto engine] manufacturer, for the purpose of conducting tests of vehicles or engines in the hands of the manufacturer or . . . to inspect . . . records, files, papers, processes, controls, and facilities used by such manufacturer in conducting tests . . . [regarding motor vehicle and engine compliance with EPA regulations].

A similar section in the 1972 Water Pollution Control Act (*15*, sect. 308) also provides the Environmental Protection Agency access to secret information held by water polluters. It appears that Congress is now aware of trade secrecy as an obstruction to pollution control and is willing to begin limiting the antisocial uses of secrecy to some extent.

Finally, trade secrecy, in its present forms, will certainly obstruct the development of meaningful "corporate social audits" that David Rockefeller and other industrial leaders have called for. Legal sanctions for corporate secrecy obviously must be challenged if

corporate responsibility and technology assessment are to be realized.

Beyond secrecy lies the problem of corporate advertising for new products and technological processes. Here, too, developments in the courts and regulatory agencies indicate that better information must be provided the public. The rapid evolution of the "Fairness Doctrine" now means that radio and television broadcast licensees must make reasonable and fair presentations of the contrasting sides of a controversial issue, once such issue has been raised (usually by advertising) on licensee broadcast time. As expressed in a recent law review note: "This obligation is incurred even at the licensee's expense if no sponsorship is available . . . [although] the licensee has discretion to determine how the contrasting sides will be presented and who will be the spokesman" (*52*, p. 109).

The doctrine has been applied by federal courts to cases of product advertising (cigarettes, large-engine automobiles, and high-test gasolines) in which it was felt that only one side of a controversial issue—the effect of such products on public health—was being presented by Federal Communications Commission (FCC) licensees in the form of advertisements. In the case of cigarettes, Banzhaff v. FCC (53), the court noted that its ruling for equal time for countercommercials or presentations promoted the first amendment policy of fostering the widest possible debate and dissemination of information on matters of public importance. In the case of commercials for automobiles and high-octane gasolines, the court noted, "When . . . the hazards to health implicit in air pollution are enlarged and aggravated by such products, then the parallel with cigarette advertising is exact . . ." (54) and ignored possible impacts on advertising and licensees as it sent the case back to the FCC for redetermination.

The idea that broadcast licensees should present balanced information on advertised but controversial technological processes or products is now a reality. Once again, the flow of information to the public, as indicated on the model (Fig. 5), is being enhanced and new corporate attitudes and advertising practices should follow. (The NEPA, OTA, secrecy, and "Fairness" developments can now be depicted on the model.)

How will this enhanced flow of information be used by citizens responding to the effects of technology? What will be the nature and forms of the resulting new pressures on decision-makers?

On the model, the broad arrow from citizens to decision-makers represents not a flow of information, but adversarial processes in courts and agency proceedings. For decision-makers to learn from an endless series of adversarial processes is a slow, costly, and painful task that benefits only lawyers.

The task facing the public sector and corporate decision-makers who are responsible for applications of technology is to transform this relationship from an adversarial one to one of joint decision-making and negotiation of differences in good faith among all interested parties—in short, to establish an ongoing dialogue and joint effort at assessing and planning the uses of technology (55). This effort will require new institutional management procedures, the development of more sophisticated assessment techniques, the articulation of assumptions by decision-makers, an opening up of project or program planning and design stages, and, ultimately, structural and substantive changes in the political system.

"Who speaks for the public?" will become a central issue—one that the federal agencies and the courts are now grappling with in the context of NEPA (56). Perhaps technology itself may provide some assistance here. Citizen-feedback technology exists, has been used experimentally, and has demonstrated a remarkable potential for both informing citizens and eliciting opinions and information useful for decision-making (57). The enhanced process orientation that could result from applications of the recommended model, improved information flow, and new citizen-feedback techniques would ensure continuing recognition in decision-making of the pervasive social impacts of technology.

Can these numerous, fragmented developments in technology and in our legal and political systems be integrated into a coherent framework for the social control of technology? It has been noted that (58, p. 729):

. . . two major intellectual developments of the 17th century occurred almost simultaneously in law and science. The first was the drive for systematic arrangements and presentation of existing knowledge into scientifically organized categories . . . the second . . . was the concern with degrees of certainty or . . . probability. . . By the end of the 17th century . . . traditional views . . . had been upset and new methods of determining truth and investigating the natural world had replaced those that had been accepted for centuries . . . there was a strong movement toward arranging both concepts and data into some rational ordering that could be easily communicated and fitted into the materials of other fields so that a universal knowledge might emerge . . . traditions of legal history and legal argumentation that assume the law's autonomous march through history are seriously in need of correction. . . .

It is now time to replicate this experience, develop a coherent framework for the social control of technology, and ensure that forthcoming processes of technology assessment and utilization will be systematic and humane.

References and Notes

1. *Final Report of National Commission on Product Safety* (Government Printing Office, Washington, D.C., 1970), pp. 73–79.
2. Public Law 92-573 (1972).
3. *U.S. Law Week.* **41** (No. 16), p. 1061 (1972).
4. See, for example, J. Sweet, in *Legal Aspects of Architecture, Engineering and the Construction Process* (West, St. Paul, Minn., 1970), sect. 30.07, pp. 634–637.
5. 29 U.S. Code 151.
6. 29 U.S. Code 651. See *Job Safety and Health Act of 1970* (Bureau of National Affairs, Washington, D.C., 1971) for collection of relevant materials.
7. D. Cordtz, *Fortune* (November 1972), p. 112.
8. As discussed by F. Grad, in *Environmental Law* (Bender, New York, 1971), pp. 1–115.
9. *Harv. Law Rev.* **84**, 1822 (1971).
10. Coverage in the media has been extensive. See the 1971 and 1972 issues of *London Observer* and *New York Times*—for example, *New York Times* (7 March 1972), p. 17.
11. *Man's Health and the Environment* (Department of Health, Education, and Welfare, Washington, D.C., 1970), pp. 97–125
12. Boomer *v.* Atlantic Cement Co., 26 New York 2nd ser. 219, 257 New Eng. 2nd ser. 870 (1970) provides a classic example of judicial caution.
13. See "Economic dislocation early warning system reports" of the Environmental Protection Agency, Washington, D.C. (mimeographed).
14. Note, for example, the numerous requests for variances from air pollution control requirements by industry and chambers of commerce that are now being processed and granted.
15. Public Law 92-500 (1972).
16. 42 U.S. Code 1857, as amended by Public Law 90-148 (1967), Public Law 91-604 (1970), and Public Law 92-157 (1971).
17. Public Law 92-574 (1972).
18. Public Law 92-516 (1972).
19. *Legal Systems for Environment Protection*, legislative study No. 4 (U.N. Food and Agriculture Organization, Rome, 1972), pp. 23–32.
20. Congressional recognition of the relationship between technological advance and environmental deterioration is expressed in Title I, Section 101(a) of Public Law 91-190 (1970).
21. C. S. Russell and H. H. Landsberg, *Science* **172**, 1307 (1971); M. I. Goldman, *Science* **170**, 37 (1970).
22. The Council on Environmental Quality has partially defined the task (*23*, p. 343): "The contemporary world is to a great extent determined by technology. . . . The scale and speed of technological change may well have outstripped the ability of our institutions to control and shape the human environment. . . . It is important to understand the emerging technologies of the future and their implications for the environment and our way of life. . . . Predicting what and how new technologies will shape the future is a difficult task. . . . Even more difficult than predicting future technological developments is assessing what the full impact of any particular technology will be. . . . Despite the difficulties of assessing technology, it is essential that it be done. . . . We must develop the institutional mechanisms capable of making technology assessments. . . ." Implicit in the council's proposal is the need for new methods to be employed in the development of assessments and the need for assurance that such assessments will indeed be used in decision-making in relevant public and private institutions.
23. Council on Environmental Quality, *Environmental Quality: Third Annual Report* (Government Printing Office, Washington, D.C., 1972).
24. A. Weinberg, *Science* **177**, 27 (1972).
25. See, for example, *Technology in Retrospect and Critical Events in Science* (National Science Foundation, Washington, D.C., 1968).
26. B. Portnoy, *Cornell Law Rev.* **55**, 861 (1970).
27. 42 U.S. Code 4321.
28. See *102 Monitor,* the monthly report of the Council on Environmental Quality, for listings of environmental impact assessments and periodic reviews of litigation related to NEPA. Also see (*23*, pp. 221–267) for a comprehensive survey of NEPA implementation.
29. No data available at this time. Statement based on conversations with professionals familiar with nuclear power program.
30. See, for example, Calvert Cliffs Coordinating Committee *v.* Atomic Energy Commission, 449 Fed. Rep., 2nd ser. 1109 (D.C. Cir. Ct. 1971).
31. As Senator Sam Ervin (D–N.C.) has said: "When the people do not know what their government is doing, those who govern are not accountable for their actions—and accountability is basic to the democratic system. By using devices of secrecy, the government attains the power to 'manage' the news and through it to

manipulate public opinion. Such power is not consonant with a nation of free men . . . and the ramifications of a growing policy of governmental secrecy is extremely dangerous to our liberty" [*The Nation* (8 November 1971), p. 456].

32. Boston *Globe* (5 May 1972), p. 17.

33. See *Congr. Rec.*, 5 October 1972, p. 517059, regarding the Corps of Engineers and *Policy and Procedure Memorandum 90-4* (Department of Transportation, Washington, D.C., 1972) regarding the federal highway program.

34. The model is being used in the presentation of "Law and the social control of science and technology" and "Legal aspects of environmental quality," two graduate courses, and in several research projects at M.I.T. by the author.

35. Public Law 91-190 (1970), sect. 102 (2) (c).

36. *Fed. Reg.* 36, 7724 (23 April 1971).

37. Council on Environmental Quality, "Memorandum for agency and general counsel liaison on NEPA matters" (mimeographed), 16 May 1972.

38. See the *102 Monitor* of the Council on Environmental Quality for abstracts of draft and final impact assessments, some of which grapple with new technological developments.

39. See *102 Monitor* 1 (No. 6), 1 (July 1971) for action by six jurisdictions. Since this review, Massachusetts has adopted its version of NEPA: Chap. 781 of Massachusetts Acts of 1972, amending Chap. 30 of Massachusetts General Laws. Connecticut is now considering similar action.

40. Friends of Mammoth *v.* Mono County, 4 Environ. Rep. Cases 1593, Calif. S. Ct. (1972).

41. Chap. 30, Massachusetts General Laws, sect. 62.

42. In Calvert Cliffs Coordinating Committee *v.* AEC (*30*), the court's ruling included discussion of the "balancing process" that agencies must undertake in project decision-making to comply fully with NEPA, in addition to procedural compliance in the development of impact assessment: "The sort of consideration of environmental values which NEPA compels is clarified in Section 102(2) (A) and (B). In general, all agencies must use a 'systematic, interdisciplinary approach' to environmental planning and evaluation 'in decision-making which may have an impact on man's environment.' In order to include all possible environmental factors in the decisional equation, agencies must 'identify and develop methods and procedures . . . which will insure that presently unquantified environmental amenities and values be given appropriate consideration in decision-making along with economic and technical considerations.' 'Environmental amenities' will often be in conflict with 'economic and technical considerations.' To 'consider' the former 'along with' the latter must involve a balancing process. In some instances environmental costs may outweigh economic and technical benefits and in other instances they may not. But NEPA mandates a rather finely tuned and 'systematic' balancing analysis in each instance."

43. See, for example, Stop H-3 Association *v.* Volpe, 4 Environ. Rep. Cases 1684 (1972), where the U.S. District Court for Hawaii held that highway project design work and further test borings be enjoined until an impact assessment has been developed and used, since such work

"would increase the stake which . . . agencies already have in the [project]" and reduce any subsequent consideration of alternatives.

44. M. Baram and G. Barney, *Technol. Rev.* 73 (No. 7), 48 (1971).

45. The "Leopold Matrix" is a useful mechanism for promoting rational discussion and systemic resolution of project impacts by the proponents and opponents of a project in a nonadversarial setting. The matrix disaggregates impacts, calls for designation of probability of magnitude and signficance of each impact, and can be completed by each of the interested parties in a project controversy. Comparative analysis of the results reveals important areas of difference of opinion and enables the parties to consider a variety of strategies for reducing these differences, such as design change or the need for concurrent projects to offset specific impacts. For example, waste water from a housing project may be one of the bases for community opposition, yet state and federal funds and programs may be available to reduce the problem. See *A Procedure for Evaluating Environmental Impact*, circular No. 645 (U.S. Geological Survey, Washington, D.C., 1971). Also see P. Bereano (unpublished manuscript, 1971) for application of the "Leopold Matrix" to technology assessment.

46. Public Law 92-484 (1972). For the text of the bill and relevant background, see U.S. Senate, Committee on Rules and Administration, subcommittee on computer services, *Office of Technology Assessment for the Congress* (92nd Congr. 2nd sess., 2 March 1972).

47. Soucie *v.* David, 2 Environ. Rep. Cases 1626 (D.C. Cir. Ct., 1971).

48. 5 U.S. Code 552.

49. Public Law 92-463 (1972) and Executive Order 11686 (1972). Also see U.S. House of Representatives, committee on Government Operations, *Advisory Committees* (92nd Congr., 2nd sess., 4 November 1971).

50. M. Baram, *Harv. Bus. Rev.* 46 (No. 6), 66 (1968).

51. *Chlorinated Hydrocarbons in the Marine Environment* (National Academy of Sciences, Washington, D.C., 1971), p. 17: "Recommendation: Removal of obstacles to public access to chemical production data. Among the causes contributing to the lack of available data on the chlorinated hydrocarbons is a legal structure that allows manufactures of a given material, when there are no more than two producers, the right to hold their production figures as privileged information.* The panel recognizes the economic rationale that deters the release of production figures by such manufacturers and understands that our government is charged by law with the protection of their proprietary interest. Indeed, we approve the principle that governmental action should not artificially affect competition. However, we also feel that there are times when it is not in the public interest for government to maintain as privileged data that are necessary for research into the state of our environment and for an assessment of its condition. In that regard, we recognize the possibility that it is not always competitive concerns alone that determine the less than candid posture assumed by industry concerning production figures. We recommend that the laws relating to the

registration of chemical substances and to the release of production figures by the Department of Commerce and the Bureau of the Census be reexamined and revised in the light of existing evidence of environmental deterioration. The protection afforded manufacturers by government is an artificial obstacle to effective environmental management, particularly with reference to the polychlorinated hydrocarbons. In view of other impediments—technological, methodological, and financial—such protection is clearly inappropriate."

* For example, the Monsanto Chemical Company has refused to release its production figures for PCB's, although requested to do so by many scientists and government officials."

52. B. Wiggins, *Natur. Resour. J.* 12 (No. 1), 108 (1972).
53. 405 Fed. Rep. 2nd ser. 1082 (1968); certiorari denied, 396 Supreme Ct. 824 (1969).
54. Frends of the Earth *v.* Federal Communications Commission, 2 Environ. Rep. Cases 1900 (D.C. Cir. Ct., 1971).
55. Of course, the achievement of a consensus is not sufficient to ensure responsible decisions: there must also be an integration of technical perspectives on long-term material and individual needs, which may have been ignored by the parties to the consensus. Such needs are usually too remote (for example, teratogenic effects) or hidden (for example, ground water depletion) to be accorded full consideration by project proponents and citizen adversaries.
56. See Sierra Club *v.* Morton, 45 Supreme Ct. 727 (1972), wherein the Supreme Court provided the latest answer to when ". . . a party has a sufficient stake in an otherwise justiciable controversy to obtain judicial resolution of that controversy. . . ." The court noted that injury other than economic harm is sufficient to bring a person within the zone of standing; that merely because an injury is widely shared by the public does not preclude an individual from asserting it as a basis for personal standing; that injury sufficient for standing can include esthetic, conservational, and recreational injury, as well as economic and health injury. But the court noted that ". . . broadening the categories of injury that may be alleged in support of standing is a different matter from abandoning the requirement that the party seeking review must have himself suffered the injury . . ." and that ". . . a party seeking review must allege facts showing that he is himself adversely affected . . ." in order to prevent litigation by those ". . . who seek to do no more than vindicate their value preferences through the judicial process."
57. T. Sheridan, "Technology for group dialogue and social choice," M.I.T. report to the National Science Foundation on grant GT-16, "Citizen feedback and opinion formulation," 1971; and D. Ducsik, N. Lemmelshtrich, M. Goldsmith, E. Jochem, "Class exercise simulating community participation in decision-making on large projects: radiation case study" (unpublished manuscript, 1972).
58. B. Shapiro, *Stanford Law Rev.* 21, 727 (1969).
59. I wish to thank Dennis W. Ducsik, a doctoral candidate in the department of civil engineering at M.I.T. who is pursuing an interdisciplinary program in environmental resource management and technology assessment, for his help as a research assistant in the project and in the development of this article. I also wish to acknowledge the support of the National Endowment for the Humanities (grant No. EO-5809-71-265).

SECTION III

SOME RESOURCES BACKGROUND

RESOURCES IN

AMERICA'S FUTURE

AT FIRST GLANCE natural resources may not seem to be as important in the U.S. economy as they used to be. The resource industries like farming, mining, logging, and other direct production of raw materials represent a steadily shrinking share of the total economy. Less than a century ago half the working population of the United States was engaged in such pursuits. Today one-tenth of the working force performs these tasks (and turns out five times as much). More and more Americans—already two-thirds of the population—live in cities or suburbs.

The country is well along in the change-over from a "products" economy to a "processing and service" economy. But this does not mean that natural resources have become less necessary. It suggests rather the magnitude and diversity of activities that now rest on the base of natural resources—manufacturing, transportation, marketing, government, education, national defense, the arts, and the many other aspects of modern society. Natural resources—land and its products like timber, crops and livestock; water; the mineral fuels; and metals and other nonfuel minerals—are still the indispensable physical stuff of which civilization is built.

RESOURCES (Resources for the Future, Inc.), June, 1963, No. 13, pp. 1-8.

For a long time the United States has used mor resource products than any other country. In 195 the President's Materials Policy Commission note with some awe that since the beginning of the Fir World War consumption of most of the fuels and othe minerals in this country alone had been greater tha total world consumption for all the preceding centuries That was eleven years ago. The national appetite fc resource materials has grown since then. And it wi keep on growing. A much larger number of people— perhaps around 330 million by the year 2000 as agains 180 million in 1960—will want an even higher averag level of living than today's: better diets, better housing more cars and consumer goods of all kinds, bette educational and cultural opportunities, more facilitie for outdoor recreation, and so on. At the same tim they will insist on a strong defense establishment, an apparently they will want to continue large-scale ex ploration of outer space and programs of assistance t less developed countries.

Can the United States over the balance of th twentieth century count on enough natural resourc supplies to sustain a rate of economic growth sufficien to fulfill all of these aspirations? That is the central question behind Resources for the Future's broad inquiry into the future domestic demand for natural resources and the goods and services derived from them, and into the prospects for meeting such requirements.

The answer is a qualified yes. With due regard to the requirements of other countries, the indications are that the American people *can* obtain the natural resources and resource products that they will need between now and the year 2000. Whether or not they *will* depends on how hard and how well they work at it.

"Neither a long view of the past, nor current trends, nor our most careful estimates of future possibilities suggest any general running out of resources in this country during the remainder of this century . . . The possibilities of using lower grades of raw material, of substituting plentiful materials for scarce ones, of getting more use out of given amounts, of importing some things from other countries, and of making multiple use of land and water resources seem to be sufficient guarantee against across-the-board shortage.

"There is, however, great likelihood of severe problems of shortage (or, as in the case of agriculture during the next decade or two, of surplus) from time to time in particular regions or segments of the economy, for particular raw materials. Deficiencies either of quantity or quality in the environmental resources of land and water undoubtedly will also occur in some instances."

THESE CONCLUSIONS, qualified as they are, relate almost entirely to the physical side of resource problems. Problems of quality, touched on only briefly in the study, are equally important and probably more difficult.

"Simply having enough oil, metals, land, and water would not spell a satisfactory life for most people. For example, there is surely enough land for urban expansion for many years to come and probably for outdoor recreation also, but the quality of it could be allowed to deteriorate to the point where it would yield unsatisfactory services. Similarly, burned-over forest land and abandoned strip mines lie ugly and useless for many years unless treated and restored. Pollution of water does not usually prevent its use, but it does make use less pleasant and more costly. The relationship of people to resources, which usually has been expressed in terms of quantity, needs to be restated for modern times to emphasize what is happening to the quality of resources."

Questions of resource quantity alone give one plenty to think about; since Malthus' time a century and a half ago, the fear that the earth's material riches will run out has preyed on people's minds. In recent years, especially since the President's Materials Policy Commission brought out its report, scarcity has been thought of more in terms of cost than of physically running out. While this refinement modifies the problem of scarcity, it is not in itself a solution. If the costs of obtaining scarce natural resource products or developing substitutes should rise significantly in relation to other costs, society would be devoting increasing shares of capital and manpower to their production; this would be a drag on the continued rise in average levels of living that is hoped for.

The estimates of possible U.S. needs for the next four decades developed in the new RFF study sug-

161

gest resource requirements of unprecedented size. The projections indicate a tripling of requirements for both energy fuels and metals by the year 2000, almost a tripling for timber, and almost a doubling for farm products and for withdrawals of fresh water. Other important uses of water, such as recreation and dilution of wastes, cannot as yet be statistically measured.

The conclusion that such amounts can be available—plus the quantities needed in the years between—depends on three assumptions: continuing gains in technology, improvements in political and social arrangements, and a reasonably free flow of world trade. Two other assumptions on which the whole system of projections rests are that there will be no large-scale war or widespread economic depression like that of the early 1930's.

Undoubtedly there are limits to particular natural resources in particular places, but this has not meant that through history resources have in any general sense become increasingly scarce in this country. The degree of economic scarcity varies not only with the intensity of demand for resource products but also with the technology of exploiting them or developing substitutes.

"The early frontier farmer, hemmed in by forests and trying to work. a field full of stones with a crude plow, was probably not impressed by superabundance of cropland. . . . The limits of economic scarcity have been pushed back in step with the growth in demand—and sometimes even faster."

The limiting factor usually is not the physical volume of any substance within the confines of the earth, but the cost of obtaining the desired materials and making them useful.

FOR EACH of the major groupings of resources the generally favorable outlook is contingent on steady improvements in technology and on keeping political and economic arrangements abreast of developments.

If crop and livestock yields do not keep rising, the projections of ample supplies of food and fiber will not be realized. Even when one assumes development of faster growing hybrid trees and better forestry practices in general, shortages of domestic timber might be a brake on economic growth without larger imports and some substitution of light metals and plastics for wood. Space needs of growing cities and highway systems and the very large expected increases in demand for outdoor recreation could cause a shortage in the total land supply unless effective programs of more intensive use or multiple use are developed.

In many instances adequate supplies of fuels and of the nonfuel minerals appear to depend on better methods of discovery and extraction, or larger imports, or both. For some metals even world supplies may become inadequate by the end of the century, so that substitution of more plentiful materials, either natural or synthetic, may have to provide the escape hatch from scarcity. For the next few decades adequacy of usable fresh water depends more on better social machinery for devising and administering broad river basin programs than on gains in technology, though both will help.

Even though recent trends are in the right direction, the required degree of technological and institutional advance cannot be expected to come about automatically. The general conclusions that point to potential adequacy of supply are projections of what can happen with appropriate public and private ac-

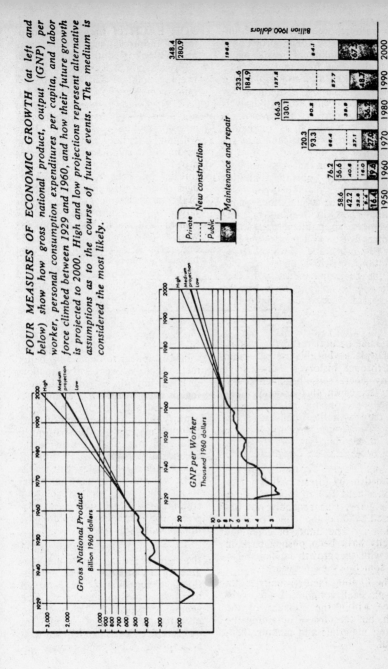

FOUR MEASURES OF ECONOMIC GROWTH (at left and below) show how gross national product, output (GNP) per worker, personal consumption expenditures per capita, and labor force climbed between 1929 and 1960, and how their future growth is projected to 2000. High and low projections represent alternative assumptions as to the course of future events. The medium is considered the most likely.

163

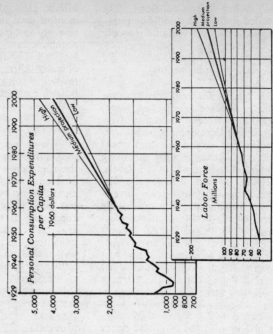

THE DOLLAR VALUE OF CONSTRUCTION is one guide to the amounts of structural materials—particularly wood, steel, and cement—that are likely to be used during the rest of this century. Projections take off from billions of 1960 dollars spent on private and public new construction and on maintenance and repair in 1950 and 1960.

Personal Consumption Expenditures per Capita

1960 dollars

High
Medium projection
Low

Labor Force

Millions

High
Medium projection
Low

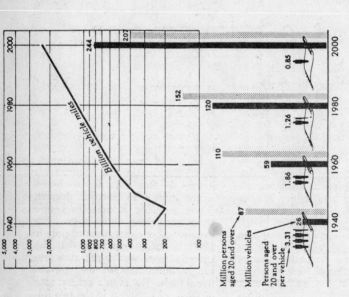

Billion vehicle miles

Million persons aged 20 and over — 67

Million vehicles

Persons aged 20 and over per vehicle — 3.31

	1940	1960	1980	2000
Billion vehicle miles			152	244
		110		207
Million vehicles	26	59	120	
Persons aged 20 and over per vehicle	3.31	1.86	1.26	0.85

IF 1930-60 TRENDS PERSIST, by the year 2000 there will be more private vehicles of one kind or another than there are people over 20 years old.

164

tion, rather than predictions. The detailed findings that indicate possible scarcity for certain resource products are not predictions either; they simply point to a need for especially vigorous action.

THE NEED for continued technological advance calls for large, varied and effective programs of research and development in science, engineering, economics, and management, backed up by a strong system of education at all levels. All this, in turn, will require discriminating but large-scale investment. Maintenance of a reasonably free flow of world trade raises questions of tariffs and other import controls and of overseas investment: How can the advantages of low-cost materials from abroad be reconciled with national security, the position of affected regions and industries in this country, and the interests of friendly nations? Needs for flexibility and innovations of public policy will be especially great in management of land and water resources—how, for instance, to take the social, economic, and legal steps that will facilitate a shift from low-value use of water in irrigation to higher-value municipal and industrial uses; or how to make sure that planning for both urban growth and larger timber output allows for recreation space and sheer natural beauty.

"We do not envision any single, monolithic Resource Policy, through the application of which all resource problems will be solved. . . . Policies, like actions, tend to come in bits and pieces, never thoroughly consistent in their direction. The real task is to make them more consistent, to fit them more to a well-conceived pattern. Clearly established general objectives and well-designed processes of policy debate and formulation, plus systematic review and evaluation, offer the best guarantee of policy improvements."

Scientific Design for a Crystal Ball

THE TERM "PROJECTION" as used by economists means a determination of what the future course of some statistical measure (annual copper production, for instance, or average income per family) would be under a certain set of starting assumptions. The assumptions, broad or narrow, daring or cautious, always determine the result. Projections never are predictions of what is actually going to happen in the wide world of reality. Yet they can be far more than theoretical exercises. It is the extensive use of projections within a comprehensive framework that has enabled three social scientists without pretensions to the gift of prophecy to undertake an appraisal of the future adequacy of natural resources in the United States.

Why choose the end of the century as a target date? A shorter span would be safer, for the uncertainties multiply as projection is extended. But it is not so useful if the aim is to uncover possible future problems in time for people to do something about them. For example, if one cast forward only to 1980 he might conclude that the United States would not run into supply difficulties for the conventional fuels. But even a general idea of what may happen in the two fol-

	1950	1960	Medium projections 1980	2000
		(Million acres)		
Cropland, including pasture[2]	478	447	443	476
Grazing land[2]	700	700	700	700
Farmland, non-producing	45	45	45	45
Commercial forest land[3]	484	484	484	484
Recreation (excluding reservoir areas and city parks)	42	44	76	134
Urban (including city parks)	17	21	32	45
Transportation	25	26	28	30
Wildlife refuge	14	15	18	20
Reservoirs	10	12	15	20
Total specified[3]	1,815	1,794	1,841	1,954
Other land (residual)	89	110	63	—50
Total land area[1]	1,904	1,904	1,904	1,904

[1] Excluding Alaska and Hawaii.

[2] All adjustments for feeding requirements are made in cropland, with grazing land held constant.

[3] Does not provide for increased acreage to meet projected commercial forest demand. As much as 300 million new acres might have to be put into forest use at this time if the timber requirements projected for 2000 were to be met entirely from domestic timber supply.

lowing decades suggests that the nation has done well not to wait until then to begin developing nuclear power and the technology for using substitute sources of liquid fuels. Many resource investment decisions that will have to be made in the next few years—decisions on multiple purpose dams, launching new conservation programs, and the like—will bear fruit for the next few decades and can best be decided in an economic perspective of forty years.

IN MAKING the projections it was necessary first of all to have a working idea of what the nation's economy and society at large might be like in the year 2000 and along the way. What would the broad picture be if current trends, as modified by already discernible patterns of change, remain in operation? By stating all the assumptions, and giving each step of the fairly complicated reasoning, this device conveys more than a general impression. Each conclusion can be checked back, and readers who disagree with any particular piece of data or interpretation may substitute their own.

The starting point of the calculations is the handful of over-all factors like population, labor force, and gross national product that generally indicate the size and shape of the national economy. Another key factor, the progress of technology, also has been considered here, affecting both productivity and patterns of consumption.

Then, within the limits of the total economy, one can begin to calculate levels of demand for the large categories of human needs and wants—food, clothing, shelter, heat and power, transportation, durable goods of all sorts, military equipment, outdoor recreation and other identifiable requirements of an advanced industrial society. Requirements for specific resources do not as a general rule enter the picture at this stage. Consumers—whether individuals or industries—usually are much more interested in the services obtained than in what particular product supplies them so long as they encounter no noticeable price penalties.

Next, and with much thought to the possibilities of substitution and technological change, these requirements for end products are translated into requirements for such resource products as agricultural raw materials, steel, lumber, textile fibers, and the like. From these, in turn, the converging demands on land, water, fuels, and other minerals are estimated. Finally, these projected demands are considered in relation to availability of supply. The estimates of future availability, though generally not as elaborately worked out as the requirements projections, rest on careful analysis of evidence now at hand on the basic resources of land, water, and minerals and the technology of getting goods and services from them. The fact that large deposits are still undiscovered adds to the uncertainties for mineral fuels and metals.

In almost all cases projections have been made at three levels— low, medium and high—not only at the final stage but in most of the preliminary stages as well, starting with population. This has been done to discover where different basic assumptions might lead in various combinations. If even the low projection of demand indicates pressure on a certain resource product, problems of adequacy are almost certain to arise. If the high projection reveals no pressure on supply it is equally likely that there is no problem. All three levels of assumption are quite within reason, but the middle levels are considered most likely. Unless specially designated, the medium projections are the only ones cited throughout this issue of *Resources*.

THE RESOURCE appraisal has been made on a comprehensive basis. The common body of assumptions and basic projections of population and GNP that underlies the whole study keeps the projections for particular consumer needs and particular resource demands consistent with the outlook for the entire economy. For instance, metals, lumber, and cement compete as structural materials; projected use of any one affects the projections for the other two. Because all goods and services compete for the consumer's dollar, only an over-all constraint on total projected expenditure can keep the sum of the parts from exceeding the whole.

All reasonably possible advances in technology have been taken into account. This is not common practice. Because of the multitude of uncertainties, many projection makers assume that there will be no technological change.

"We believe that in striving for the closest possible appreciation of the future, it is better to guess, even on slender evidence, than to ignore. A footloose speculation four decades ago about dieselization of the railroads would have yielded a better projection of future coal and oil demand than one based on the assumption that locomotives would forever carry boilers."

No major changes in future price relationships have been assumed beyond those that may be implicit in past and current consumption trends. That is, estimates of supply conditions have not been allowed to affect projections of requirements. This is obviously unrealistic, in contrast with the other major assumptions, particularly that of continued technological advance. Changes in relative cost and price surely will occur if a product becomes scarcer or more plentiful and thereby help "solve" the problem by bringing supply and demand closer together by substitutions, greater investment to increase output, or other means. This one departure from realism is deliberate. The main purpose of the whole study is to test adequacy of resource supplies, not to cover up possible future trouble spots by allowing market action to adjust them automatically.

Resources in the Next 40 Years

WHEN THE NATION'S projected demands upon resources for the rest of the century are compared with estimates of supplies that can be reasonably expected to become available, a kind of resource-by-resource balance sheet emerges. The brief summaries that follow also suggest some of the problems that may arise.

Land. Present cropland acreage (around 470 million acres) can satisfy food and fiber demand during the next forty years, with acreage surpluses likely for more than half of this period. This can be done, however, only if increasing demand is accompanied by continuing and substantial improvements in crop yields—say 100 bushels an acre for corn, about double the present average, and 35 bushels for wheat, an increase of about 50 per cent.

Urban land requirements are projected at 45 million acres by 2000, more than double the 1960 acreage; recreation at 130 million acres, more than three times the 1960 figure. Requirements for other uses of land —highways and air fields, reservoirs and watersheds, and wildlife refuges —also will rise sharply.

Projected demand for forest products by the end of the century is so much larger than the foreseeable domestic supply that at present yields something like 300 million acres would have to be added to the existing 484 million acres of commercial forest land to meet requirements. This is unreasonable; the practical alternative is more intensive management of existing commercial forest land, along with intensified efforts to find substitutes, and perhaps larger imports.

All demands for land by the year 2000, each taken separately, add up to 50 million acres more than the 1,900 million-acre total area of the 48 contiguous states. This "deficit" suggests a need for increased multiple use of land and for more intensive management in general.

Water. The nation's total demand for fresh water is expected to keep growing at a rate at least equal to that of population. Irrigation withdrawals may increase by half by the year 2000; municipal use may double and manufacturing use quadruple. There is no prospect of water shortage on a nation-wide scale.

Localized water shortages will not seriously impair continued national growth, although they may limit local economic growth. The supply estimates do not allow for any significantly large contributions to supply through technological gains. Substantial advances in desalinization have been made in recent years and more are expected. But the cost reductions now in prospect are not large enough to suggest that more than a small fraction of total demand for fresh water will be met in this way during the next four decades. Much is still to be learned of both the theory and practice of weather modification.

In the East, severe pollution of water supplies will be the main problem. The total supply is more than ample for the rest of the century for municipal, industrial, and agricultural uses; the question is how much of the total will remain fit to use, particularly for recreation.

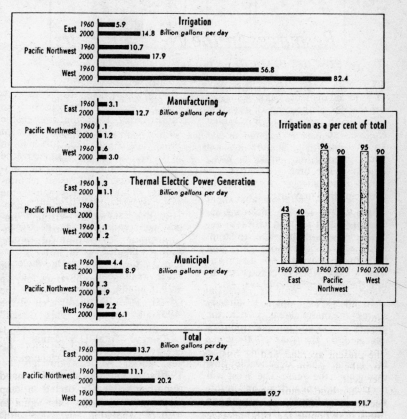

A COMPARISON OF WATER USES in three great regions of the United States, 1960 and projections for 2000. The figures represent "withdrawal depletions," which are the actual losses during use; they do not include withdrawn water that is later returned to lakes and streams.

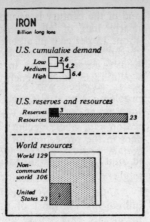

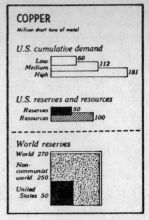

HOW U.S. DEMAND for two key metals relates to potential U.S. and world supplies during the rest of the century. The projections for cumulative demand 1960-2000 allow for a higher or a lower demand than the preferred medium. The term "reserves" applies to known ore deposits assumed to be minable with current technology and economic conditions. "Resources" includes in addition all ore that has been identified as potentially recoverable. Estimates for both reserves and resources are in terms of metal content of the ores.

A variety of pollution abatement efforts will be needed, including action of industries and cities to reduce contamination and to treat waste water more thoroughly, and additional storage to augment stream flow when necessary to dilute the concentration of wastes.

In the West, water is already scarce in many areas. With the growth of population and industry expected by the year 2000, losses from projected withdrawals will be far greater than dependable flow throughout the year. The West will need not only new dams and reservoirs, long-distance transport of water, water conservation, and perhaps desalinization, but also better allocation of water resources among competing uses. Industrial and municipal use of additional supplies of water appear to have higher eco-

nomic priority than irrigation.

In the Pacific Northwest, irrigation will remain by far the largest contributor to withdrawal depletions. The distinctive water problem of the region as a whole is fuller realization, in co-operation with Canada, of the great hydroelectric potential of the Columbia River.

Energy. Total U.S. demand for energy is expected to triple by the year 2000. At least through the 1970's, it appears that U.S. energy requirements can be met at no significant increase in real cost and with no sweeping changes in the relationship between oil, natural gas, and coal. Toward the end of the century nuclear energy is expected to become important in the generation of electricity. The proportion of all energy, regardless of source, used in the form of electricity is expected to keep on increasing.

Coal requirements are expected to increase steadily throughout the period; but coal's share in total energy use in the United States probably will continue to decline, though not so fast as in the past twenty years. Successful gasification or liquefaction of coal could slow or even reverse this trend. So could delays in the assumed rise in nuclear generation of electricity. Coal reserves are ample for a much longer period than this century.

Oil and gas requirements are projected to keep rising during the next four decades. The cumulative requirements for both fuels are so large that even assuming that the nation would import 20 per cent of the oil it uses over the forty-year period it seems doubtful that the remaining requirements can be obtained from domestic deposits even with significant technological advances in finding and recovery. Other possibilities at home or nearby are extraction of liquid petroleum from the shales of the Colorado plateau and tar sands of northern Canada, and gasification of coal into a high-Btu fuel. Farther afield, vast supplies of oil are known to exist in the Middle East, Venezuela, North Africa and elsewhere, and not unlikely to be found in parts of the world as yet only sporadically explored, and there are good possibilities for long-distance shipment of natural gas in liquid form.

Nuclear-powered production of electricity should become significant during the period after a slow start in the late '60's. By 1980, less than 5 per cent of all energy use and less than 20 per cent of all electricity generation is projected to come from nuclear reactors. The share by the end of the century is assumed to be nearly half of all electricity and about 15 per cent of all energy. Successful production of nuclear process heat reactors, for use in industry, would raise nuclear energy's share in the total.

Only 3.6 per cent of the national total in 1960, hydropower for the nation as a whole declines to 2 per cent in the projection for 2000. In certain regions, notably the Pacific Northwest, hydropower's share of total energy will remain much larger.

Nonfuel Minerals. Domestic requirements for most of the major metals are expected to grow faster than population. Steel requirements, for example, are expected to increase by 200 per cent by the year 2000; aluminum by 800 per cent; and even lead, a slow-rising metal, by 100 per cent. Patterns of consumption will continue to change. In 1960, iron and steel accounted for 90 per cent of the total volume of metals used in the United States, and aluminum for almost 6 per cent. By the year 2000 these ratios are projected to have shifted to 79 per cent and 17 per cent, respectively. It is difficult to generalize about future adequacy of minerals, for each must be examined in the light of its own situation; and even then the unsatisfactory state of reserve and resource estimates and meager knowledge of the cost implications of new technology make many judgments precarious. New advances in methods of discovery and extraction could bring in larger supplies than it now seems safe to anticipate. So could more rapid gains in knowing how to use lower grades of ore. It seems clear, however, that for many mineral materials the United States will become even more dependent upon imports than it is now.

Salient points in the outlook for

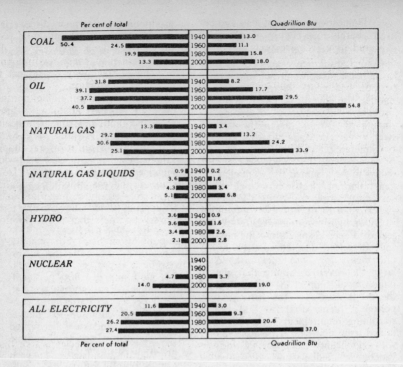

	Per cent of total		Quadrillion Btu
COAL	50.4	1940	13.0
	24.5	1960	11.1
	19.9	1980	15.8
	13.3	2000	18.0
OIL	31.8	1940	8.2
	39.1	1960	17.7
	37.2	1980	29.5
	40.5	2000	54.8
NATURAL GAS	13.3	1940	3.4
	29.2	1960	13.2
	30.6	1980	24.2
	25.1	2000	33.9
NATURAL GAS LIQUIDS	0.9	1940	0.2
	3.6	1960	1.6
	4.3	1980	3.4
	5.1	2000	6.8
HYDRO	3.6	1940	0.9
	3.6	1960	1.6
	3.4	1980	2.6
	2.1	2000	2.8
NUCLEAR		1940	
		1960	
	4.7	1980	3.7
	14.0	2000	19.0
ALL ELECTRICITY	11.6	1940	3.0
	20.5	1960	9.3
	26.2	1980	20.8
	27.4	2000	37.0

Per cent of total · Quadrillion Btu

CHANGES IN THE PATTERN OF ENERGY SOURCES. *The projections for 1980 and 2000 are compared with the record for 1940 and 1960.*

a few individual minerals are noted briefly in the paragraphs that follow.

Cumulative demands for iron and steel through the end of the century exceed currently identified domestic reserves of iron ore in this country by some 40 per cent. At present the high cost of mining the large domestic deposits of low-grade ore qualifies only a small fraction for inclusion in U.S. reserves. One may expect this fraction to increase in the coming years. World reserves of iron ore appear adequate to U.S. needs, even with due allowance for rapidly growing needs in other countries.

World-wide reserves of bauxite, at present the preferred source of aluminum, are equivalent to world-wide cumulative demand, and advancing technology makes a gradual shift to lower-grade bauxite and high-alumina clays feasible with minimal effects on cost.

U.S. reserves of copper are at or below 50 million tons, while the projected cumulative demand is 110 million tons. The non-communist world as a whole has reserves amounting to about half the needed supply. These reserves, however, are backed up by an ample reservoir of potential ore of low copper content—but not lower than is now being mined profitably in the United States. Such potential ore can be used with only gradual cost increases, if any, through the end of the century.

Domestic reserves of lead amount to barely one-eighth of projected cumulative requirements, and to about one-third for zinc. For the whole non-communist world, roughly calculated requirements exceed the estimated reserves of both lead and zinc. There is some doubt whether this picture may not be unduly affected by the poor quality of the reserve estimates.

U.S. demand for manganese, now about 1 million tons a year, is projected to triple by 2000. The United States is dependent on foreign supply. While in the non-communist world identified reserves barely exceed projected demand, there seems to be a large potential for increased production from new discoveries, slag heaps near steel mills, and possibly ocean-floor nodules; at the same time manganese requirements per ton of steel may be subject to substantial reduction.

Reserves of nonmetallic nonfuel minerals appear adequate — lime, rock and sand; salt; and potash and phosphate for fertilizer. The long-run outlook for sulfur appears hopeful mainly because of world-wide increase in sulfur recovery from sour oil and gas. Plentiful supplies of alternative source materials, such as gypsum, could alleviate any temporary tightness that might develop over the next forty years.

RIDDLES OF FUTURE THINGS

AMUSE NOT THYSELF about the Riddles of future things. Study Prophecies when they are become Histories and past hovering in their causes. Eye well things past and present, and let conjectural sagacity suffise for things to come. There is a sober Latitude for prescience in contingencies of discoverable Tempers, whereby discerning Heads see sometimes beyond their Eyes and Wise Men become Prophetical. Leave cloudy predictions to their Periods, and let appointed Seasons have the lot of their accomplishments. 'Tis too early to study such Prophecies before they have been long made, before some train of their causes have already taken Fire, laying open in part what lay obscure and before buryed unto us. For the voice of Prophecies is like that of Whispering-places: They who are near or at a little distance hear nothing, those at the farthest extremity will understand all. But a Retrograde cognition of times past, and things which have already been, is more satisfactory than a suspended Knowledge of what is yet Unexistent. And the greatest part of Time being already wrapt up in things behind us; it's now somewhat late to bait after things before us; for futurity still shortens, and time present sucks in time to come.— Sir Thomas Browne (1605-1682) *Christian Morals.*

Man-Made Climatic Changes

Man's activities have altered the climate of urbanized
areas and may affect global climate in the future.

Helmut E. Landsberg

Climate, the totality of weather conditions over a given area, is variable.
Although it is not as fickle as weather,
is fluctuates globally as well as locally
in irregular pulsations. In recent years
some people have voiced the suspicion
that human activities have altered the
global climate, in addition to having
demonstrated effects on local microclimates. There have also been a number of proposals advocating various
schemes for deliberately changing global climate, and a number of actual
small-scale experiments have been carried out. For most of the larger proposals, aside from considerations of
feasibility and cost, one can raise the
objection that a beneficial effect in one
part of the earth could well be accompanied by deterioration elsewhere, aside
from the inevitable disturbances of the
delicate ecological balances.

But the question "Has man inadvertently changed the global climate,
or is he about to do so?" is quite legitimate. It has been widely discussed publicly—unfortunately with more zeal
than insight. Like so many technical
questions fought out in the forum of
popular magazines and the daily press,
the debate has been characterized by
misunderstandings, exaggerations, and
distortions. There have been dire predictions of imminent catastrophe by
heat death, by another ice age, or by
acute oxygen deprivation. The events
foreseen in these contradictory proph-
esies will obviously not all come to pass
at the same time, if they come to pass
at all. It seems desirable to make an
attempt to sort fact from fiction and
separate substantive knowledge from
speculation.

Natural Climatic Fluctuations

In order to assess man's influence, we
must first take a look at nature's processes.

The earth's atmosphere has been in
a state of continuous slow evolution
since the formation of the planet. Because of differences in the absorptive
properties of different atmospheric constituents, the energy balance near the
surface has been undergoing parallel
evolution. Undoubtedly the greatest
event in this evolution has been the
emergence of substantial amounts of
oxygen, photosynthetically produced by
plants (1). The photochemical development of ozone in the upper atmosphere, where it forms an absorbing lay-

SCIENCE, Dec. 1970, Vol. 170, pp. 1265-1274.

er for the short-wave ultraviolet radiation and creates a warm stratum, is climatically also very important, especially for the forms of organic life now in existence. But for the heat balance of the earth, carbon dioxide (CO_2) and water vapor, with major absorption bands in the infrared, are essential constituents. They absorb a substantial amount of the dark radiation emitted by the earth's surface. The condensed or sublimated parts of the atmospheric water vapor also enter prominently into the energy balance. In the form of clouds they reflect incoming short-wave radiation from the sun, and hence play a major role in determining the planetary albedo. At night, clouds also intercept outgoing radiation and radiate it back to the earth's surface (2).

Over the past two decades Budyko (3) has gradually evolved models of the global climate, using an energy balance approach. These models incorporate, among other important factors, the incoming solar radiation, the albedo, and the outgoing radiation. Admittedly they neglect, as yet, nonlinear effects which might affect surface temperatures (4) but it seems unlikely that, over a substantial period, the nonlinear effects of the atmosphere-ocean system will change the basic results, though they may well introduce lags and superimpose rhythms. Budyko's calculations suggest that a 1.6 percent decrease in incoming radiation or a 5 or 10 percent increase in the albedo of the earth could bring about renewed major glaciation.

The theory that changes in the incoming radiation are a principal factor governing the terrestrial climate has found its major advocate in Milankovitch (5). He formulated a comprehensive mathematical model of the time variations of the earth's position in space with respect to the sun. This included the periodic fluctuations of the inclination of the earth's axis, its precession, and the eccentricity of its orbit. From these elements he calculated an insolation curve back into time and the corresponding surface temperature of the earth. He tried to correlate minima with the Pleistocene glaciations. These views have found considerable support in isotope investigations, especially of the $^{18}O/^{16}O$ ratio in marine shells (6) deposited during the Pleistocene. Lower ^{18}O amounts correspond to lower temperatures. Budyko and others (7) raise some doubts that Milankovitch's theory can explain glaciations but admit that it explains some temperature fluctuations. For the last 1700 years there is also evidence that the ^{18}O content of Greenland glacier ice is inversely correlated to a solar activity index based on auroral frequencies (8). Again, low values of ^{18}O reflect the temperature at which the precipitation that formed the firn fell.

The fluctuations of externally received energy are influenced not only by the earth's position with respect to the sun but also by changes in energy emitted by the sun. Extraterrestrial solar radiation fluctuates with respect to spectral composition, but no major changes in total intensity have yet been measured outside the atmosphere. The occurrence of such fluctuations is indicated by a large number of statistical studies (9), but ironclad proof is still lacking. Such fluctuations are of either long or short duration. They have been tied to the solar activity cycle. Inasmuch as details are yet unknown, their effect on climate is at present one factor in the observed "noise" pattern.

In the specific context of this discussion, we are not concerned with the major terrestrial influences on climate, such as orogenesis, continental drift, and pole wanderings. But other, somewhat lesser, terrestrial influences are also powerful controllers of climate. They include volcanic eruptions that bring large quantities of dust and CO_2 into the air, and natural changes of albedo such as may be caused by changes in snow and ice cover, in cloudiness, or in vegetation cover (10). The fact that we have not yet succeeded in disentangling all the cause-and-effect relations of natural climatic changes considerably complicates the analysis of possible man-made changes.

The Climatic Seesaw

It was only a relatively short time ago that instrumental records of climate first became available. Although broad-scale assessments of climate can be made from natural sources, such as tree rings (11) or pollen associations, and, in historical times, from chronicles that list crop conditions or river freezes, this is tenuous evidence. But a considerable number of instrumental observations of temperatures and precipitation are available for the period from the early 18th century to the present, at least for the Northern Hemisphere. These observations give a reasonably objective view of climatic fluctuations for the last two and a half centuries. This is, of course, the interval in which man and his activities have multiplied rapidly. These long climatic series are mostly from western Europe (12), but recently a series for the eastern seaboard of the United States has been reconstructed from all available data sources. In this series Philadelphia is used as an index location, since it is centrally located with respect to all the earlier available records (13). Figures 1 and 2 show the annual values for temperature and precipitation for a 230-year span; there are some minor gaps where the data were inadequate. These curves are characteristic of those for other regions, too. In particular they reflect the restlessness of the atmosphere. Many analysts have simply considered the variations to be quasi-random. Here I need only say that they do not reflect any pronounced one-sided trends. However, there are definite long or short intervals in which considerable one-sided departures from a mean are notable. On corresponding curves representing data for a larger area that encompasses most of the regions bordering the Atlantic, the major segments are those for the late 18th century, which was warm; the 19th century, which was cool; and the first half of the 20th century, in which there was a notable rising trend. This trend was followed by some cooling in the past 2 decades.

In the precipitation patterns, "noise" masks all trends, but we know that during a period in the middle of the last century there was considerably more precipitation than there is now. For shorter intervals, spells of drought alternate with high precipitation. Sometimes, for small areas, these can be quite spectacular. An example is the seasonal snowfall on Mount Washington, in New Hampshire; there the snowfall increased from an average of 4.5 meters in the winters of 1933–34 to 1949–50 to an annual average of 6 meters in the period 1951–52 to 1966–67 (14). Yet these values should not be taken as general climatic trends for the globe, or even for the hemisphere. Even if we take indices that integrate various climatic influences, we still cannot make categorical statements. Glacier conditions are typical in this group of indices. For example, the glaciers on the west coast of Greenland have been repeatedly surveyed since 1850. In consonance with temperature trends for lower latitudes, they showed their farthest advances in the 7th decade of the 19th century and have been retreating ever since (15). This pattern fits the temperature curves to the 1950 turning point, but, although glaciers in mostly from western Europe (12), but recently a series for the eastern seaboard of the United States has been reconstructed from all available data sources. In this series Philadelphia is used as an index location, since it is centrally located with respect to all the earlier available records (13). Figures 1 and 2 show the annual values for temperature and precipitation for a 230-year span; there are some minor gaps where the data were inadequate. These curves are characteristic of those for other regions, too. In particular they reflect the restlessness of the atmosphere. Many analysts have simply considered the variations to be quasi-random. Here I need only say that they do not reflect any pronounced one-sided trends. However, there are definite long or short intervals in which considerable one-sided departures from a mean are notable. On corresponding curves representing data for a larger area that encompasses most of the regions bordering the Atlantic, the major segments are those for the late 18th century, which was warm; the 19th century, which was cool; and the first half of the 20th century, in which there was a notable rising trend. This trend was followed by some cooling in the past 2 decades.

In the precipitation patterns, "noise" masks all trends, but we know that during a period in the middle of the last century there was considerably more precipitation than there is now. For shorter intervals, spells of drought alternate with high precipitation. Sometimes, for small areas, these can be quite spectacular. An example is the seasonal snowfall on Mount Washington, in New Hampshire; there the snowfall increased from an average of 4.5 meters in the winters of 1933–34 to 1949–50 to an annual average of 6 meters in the period 1951–52 to 1966–67 (14). Yet these values should not be taken as general climatic trends for the globe, or even for the hemisphere. Even if we take indices that integrate various climatic influences, we still cannot make categorical statements. Glacier conditions are typical in this group of indices. For example, the glaciers on the west coast of Greenland have been repeatedly surveyed since 1850. In consonance with temperature trends for lower latitudes, they showed their farthest advances in the 7th decade of the 19th century and have been retreating ever since (15). This pattern fits the temperature curves to the 1950 turning point, but, although glaciers in some regions of the world have been advancing since then, this is by no means true of all glaciers. The question of whether these changes reflect (i) relatively short-term temperature fluctuations, or (ii) alterations in the alimenting precipitation, or (iii) a combination of these two factors remains unanswered.

Many of the shorter fluctuations are likely to be only an expression of atmospheric interaction with the oceans. Even if external or terrestrial impulses affect the energy budget and cause an initial change in atmospheric circulation, notable lag and feedback mechanisms involving the oceans produce pulsations which, in turn, affect the atmosphere (*16*). The oceans have a very large thermal inertia, and their horizontal motions and vertical exchanges are slow. Namias (*17*) has investigated many of the fluctuations of a few years' duration. He concluded, for example, that drought conditions on the in the 1960's were directly affected by the prevailing wind system- and by sea-surface temperatures in the vicinity but that the real dominant factor was a wind-system change in the North Pacific. Such teleconnections (relations among conditions in distant parts of the globe) complicate interpretations of local or even regional data tremendously. The worldwide effect of changes in the Pacific wind system is obvious from Namias's estimate that accelerations and decelerations cause large-scale breaks in the regime of sea-surface temperatures. These seem to occur in sequences of approximately 5 years and may cause temperature changes of 0.5°C over the whole North Pacific. Namias estimates that this can cause differences of 8×10^{18} grams in the annual amounts of water evaporated from the surface. The consequences for worldwide cloud and rain formation are evident. It is against this background that we have to weigh climatic changes allegedly wrought by man.

Carbon Dioxide

The fact that the atmospheric gases play an important role in the energy budget of the earth was recognized early. Fourier, and then Pouillet and Tyndall, first expressed the idea that these gases acted as a "greenhouse" (*18*). After the spectrally selective absorption of gases was recognized, their role as climatic controls became a subject of wide debate. The capability of CO_2 to intercept long-wave radiation emitted by the earth was put forward as a convenient explanation for climatic changes. Arrhenius (*19*) made the first quantitative estimates of the magnitude of the effect, which he mainly attributed to fluctuating volcanic activity, although he also mentioned the burning of coal as a minor source of CO_2. The possibility that man-made CO_2 could be an important factor in the earth's heat balance was not seriously considered until Callendar (*20*), in 1938, showed evidence of a gradual increase in CO_2 concentration in the earth's atmosphere. But it was Plass (*21*) who initiated the modern debate on the subject, based on his detailed study of the CO_2 absorption spectrum. The crucial question is, How much has CO_2 increased as a result of the burning of fossil fuels? It is quite difficult to ascertain even the mean amount of CO_2 in the surface layers of the atmosphere, especially near vegetation. There are large diurnal and annual variations. Various agriculturists have reported concentrations ranging from 210 to 500 parts per million. The daily amplitudes during the growing season are about 70 parts per million (*22*). Nearly all early measurements were made in environments where such fluctuations took place. This, together with the lack of precision of the measurements, means that our baseline—atmospheric CO_2 concentrations prior to the spectacular rise in fossil fuel consumption of this century—is very shaky. Only since the International Geophysical Year have there been some regularly operating measuring points in polar regions and on high mountains and reliable data from the oceans which give some firm information on the actual increase (*23*).

The best present estimate places the increase in atmospheric CO_2 since

1860 at 10 to 15 percent. This is hardly a spectacular change, but the rate of increase has been rising, and various bold extrapolations have been made into the 21st century. Much depends on the sinks for CO_2 which at present are not completely known. At present concentrations, atmospheric O_2 and CO_2 stay in approximate equilibrium, through the photosynthetic process in plants. It is estimated that 150×10^9 tons of CO_2 per year are used in photosynthesis (24). A corresponding amount is returned to the atmosphere by decay, unless the total volume of plant material increases (25). This volume is one of the unknowns in the estimates of CO_2 balance. Perhaps satellite sensors can give some bulk information on that point in the future. The oceans are a major sink for CO_2. The equilibrium with the bicarbonates dissolved in seawater determines the amount of CO_2 in the atmosphere. In the exchange between atmosphere and ocean, the temperature of the surface water enters as a factor. More CO_2 is absorbed at lower surface-water temperatures than at higher temperatures. I have already pointed out the fact that surface-water temperatures fluctuate over long or short intervals; most of these ups and downs are governed by the wind conditions. The interchange of the cold deep water and the warm surface water through downward mixing and upwelling, in itself an exceedingly irregular process, controls, therefore, much of the CO_2 exchange (26). Also, the recently suggested role of an enzyme in the ocean that facilitates absorption of CO_2 has yet to be explored. Hence it is quite difficult to make long-range estimates of how much atmospheric CO_2 will disappear in the oceanic sink. Most extrapolators assume essentially a constant rate of removal. Even the remaining question of how much the earth's temperature will change with a sharp increase in the CO_2 content of the atmosphere cannot be unambiguously answered. The answer depends on other variables, such as atmospheric humidity and cloudiness. But the calculations have been made on the basis of various assumptions. The model most widely used is that of Manabe and Wetherald (27). They calculate, for example, that, with the present value for average cloudi-

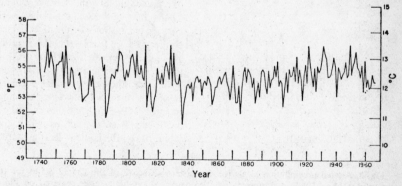

Fig. 1. Annual temperatures for the eastern seaboard of the United States for the period 1738 to 1967—a representative, reconstructed synthetic series centered on Philadelphia.

179

ness, an increase of atmospheric CO_2 from 300 to 600 parts per million would lead to an increase of 2°C in the mean temperature of the earth at the surface. At the same time the lower stratosphere would cool by 15°C. At the present rate of accumulation of CO_2 in the atmosphere, this doubling of the CO_2 would take about 400 years. The envisaged 2°C rise can hardly be called cataclysmic. There have been such worldwide changes within historical times. Any change attributable to the rise in CO_2 in the last century has certainly been submerged in the climatic "noise." Besides, our estimates of CO_2 production by natural causes, such as volcanic exhalations and organic decay, are very inaccurate; hence the ratio of these natural effects to anthropogenic effects remains to be established.

Dust

The influence on climate of suspended dust in the atmosphere was first recognized in relation to volcanic erup-tions. Observations of solar radiation at the earth's surface following the spectacular eruption of Krakatoa in 1883 showed measurable attenuation. The particles stayed in the atmosphere for 5 years (28). There was also some suspicion that summers in the Northern Hemisphere were cooler after the erup-tion. The inadequacy and unevenness of the observations make this conclu-sion somewhat doubtful. The main ex-ponent of the hypothesis that volcanic dust is a major controller of terrestrial climate was W. J. Humphreys (29). In recent years the injection into the atmo-sphere of a large amount of dust by an eruption of Mount Agung has renewed interest in the subject, not only because of the spectacular sunsets but also be-cause there appears to have been a cool-ing trend since (30). The Mount Agung eruption was followed, in the 1960's, by at least three others from which volcanic constituents reached strato-spheric levels: those of Mount Taal, in 1965; Mount Mayon, in 1968; and Fernandina, in 1968. Not only did small dust particles reach the strato-sphere but it seems likely that gaseous

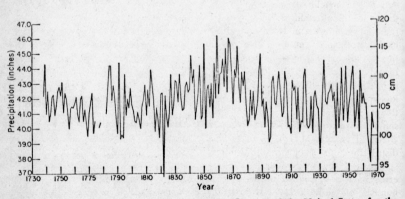

Fig. 2. Annual precipitation totals for the eastern seaboard of the United States for the period 1738 to 1967—a representative, reconstructed synthetic series centered on Phila-delphia.

constituents reaching these levels caused the formation of ammonium sulfate particles through chemical and photochemical reactions (*31*). The elimination of small particulates from the stratosphere is relatively slow, and some backscattering of solar radiation is likely to occur.

As yet man cannot compete in dust production with the major volcanic eruptions, but he is making a good try. However, most of his solid products that get into the atmosphere stay near the ground, where they are fairly rapidly eliminated by fallout and washout. Yet there is some evidence that there has been some increase in the atmospheric content of particles less than 10^{-4} centimeter in diameter (*32*). The question is simply, What is the effect of the man-made aerosol? There is general agreement that it depletes the direct solar radiation and increases radiation from the sky. Measurements of the former clearly show a gradual increase in turbidity (*33*), and the same increase in turbidity has been documented by observations from the top of Mauna Loa, which is above the level of local contamination (*34*). From these observations the conclusion has been drawn that the attentuation of direct solar radiation is, in part at least, caused by backscattering of incoming solar radiation to space. This is equivalent to an increase in the earth's albedo and hence is being interpreted as a cause of heat loss and lowered temperatures (*35*). But things are never that categorical and simple in the atmosphere. The optical effects of an aerosol depend on its size distribution, its height in the atmosphere, and its absorptivity. These properties have been studied in detail by a number of authors (*36*). It is quite clear that most man-made particulates stay close to the ground. Temperature

inversions attend to that. And there is no evidence that they penetrate the stratosphere in any large quantities, especially since the ban, by most of the nuclear powers, of nuclear testing in the atmosphere. The optical analyses show, first of all, that the backscatter of the particles is outweighed at least 9 to 1 by forward scattering. Besides, there is a notable absorption of radiation by the aerosol. This absorption applies not only to the incoming but also to the outgoing terrestrial radiation. The effectiveness of this interception depends greatly on the overlapping effect of the water vapor of the atmosphere. Yet the net effect of the man-made particulates seems to be that they lead to heating of the atmospheric layer in which they abound. This is usually the stratum hugging the ground. All evidence points to temperature rises in this layer, the opposite of the popular interpretations of the dust effect. The aerosol and its fallout have other, perhaps much more far-reaching, effects, which I discuss below. Suffice it to say, here, that man-made dust has not yet had an effect on global climate beyond the "noise" level. Its effect is puny as compared with that of volcanic eruptions, whose dust reaches the high stratosphere, where its optical effect, also, can be appreciable. No documented case has been made for the view that dust storms from deserts or blowing soil have had more than local or regional effects.

Dust that has settled may have a more important effect than dust in suspension. Dust fallen on snow and ice surfaces radically changes the albedo and can lead to melting (*37*). Davitaya (*38*) has shown that the glaciers of the high Caucasus have an increased dust content which parallels the development of industry in eastern Europe.

Up until 1920 the dust content of the glacier was about 10 milligrams per liter. In the 1950's this content increased more than 20-fold, to 235 milligrams per liter. So long as the dust stays near the surface, it should have an appreciable effect on the heat balance of the glacier. There is fairly good evidence, based on tracers such as lead, that dusts from human activities have penetrated the polar regions. Conceivably they might change the albedo of the ice, cause melting, and thus pave the way for a rather radical climatic change—and for a notable rise in sea level. There has been some speculation along this line (39), but, while these dusts have affected microclimates, there is no evidence of their having had, so far, any measurable influence on the earth's climate. The possibility of deliberately causing changes in albedo by spreading dust on the arctic sea ice has figured prominently in discussions of artificial modification of climate. This seems technologically feasible (40). The consequences for the mosaic of climates in the lower latitudes have not yet been assessed. Present computer models of world climate and the general circulation are far too crude to permit assessment in the detail necessary for ecological judgments.

All of the foregoing discussion applies to the large-scale problems of global climate. On that scale the natural influences definitely have the upper hand. Although monitoring and vigilance is indicated, the evidence for man's effects on global climate is flimsy at best. This does not apply to the local scale, as we shall presently see.

Extraurban Effects

For nearly two centuries it has been said that man has affected the rural climates simply by changing vast areas from forest to agricultural lands. In fact, Thomas Jefferson suggested repetitive climatic surveys to measure the effects of this change in land use in the virgin area of the United States (41). Geiger has succinctly stated that man is the greatest destroyer of natural microclimates (42). The changeover from forest to field locally changes the heat balance. This leads to greater temperature extremes at the soil surface and to altered heat flux into and out of the soil. Cultivation may even accentuate this. Perhaps most drastically changed is the low-level wind speed profile because of the radical alteration in aerodynamic roughness. This change leads to increased evaporation and, occasionally, to wind erosion. One might note here that man has reversed to some extent the detrimental climatic effects of deforestation in agricultural sectors, by planting hedges and shelter belts of trees. Special tactics have been developed to reduce evaporation, collect snow, and ameliorate temperature ranges by suitable arrangements of sheltering trees and shrubs (43).

The classical case of a local man-made climatic change is the conversion of a forest stand to pasture, followed by overgrazing and soil erosion, so that ultimately nothing will grow again. The extremes of temperature to which the exposed surface is subjected are very often detrimental to seedlings, so that they do not become established. Geiger pointed this out years ago. But not all grazing lands follow the cycle outlined above. Sometimes it is a change in the macroclimate that tilts the balance one way or another (44).

Since ancient times man has compensated for vagaries of the natural climates by means of various systems of irrigation. Irrigation not only offsets temporary deficiencies in rainfall but, again, affects the heat balance. It decreases the diurnal temperature ranges, raises relative humidities, and creates the so-called "oasis effect." Thornthwaite, only a decade and a half ago, categorically stated that man is incapable of deliberately causing any significant change in the climatic patterns of the earth. Changes· in microclimate seemed to him so local and trivial that special instrumentation was needed to detect them. However, "Through changes in the water balance and sometimes inadvertently, he exercises his greatest influence on climate" (45).

What happens when vast areas come under irrigation? This has taken place over 62×10^3 square kilometers of Oklahoma, Kansas, Colorado, and Nebraska since the 1930's. Some meteorologists have maintained that about a 10 percent increase in rainfall occurs in the area during early summer, allegedly attributable to moisture reevaporated from the irrigated lands (46). Synoptic meteorologists have generally made a good case for the importation, through precipitation, of moisture from marine sources, especially the Gulf of Mexico. Yet ^3H determinations have shown, at least for the Mississippi valley area, that two-thirds of the precipitated water derives from locally evaporated surface waters. Anyone who has ever analyzed trends in rainfall records will be very cautious about accepting apparent changes as real until many decades have passed. For monthly rainfall totals, 40 to 50 years may be needed to establish trends because of the large natural variations (47).

This century has seen, also, the construction of very large reservoirs. Very soon after these fill they have measurable influences on the immediate shore vicinity. These are the typical lake effects. They include reduction in temperature extremes, an increase in humidity, and small-scale circulations of the land- and lake-breeze ᐱtype, if the reservoir is large enough. Rarely do we have long records as a basis for comparing conditions before and after establishment of the reservoir. Recently, Zych and Dubaniewicz (48) published such a study for the 30-year-old reservoir of the Nysa Klodzka river in Poland, about 30 square kilometers in area. At the town of Otmuchow, about 1 kilometer below the newly created lake, a 50-year temperature normal was available (for the years 1881 to 1930). In the absence of a regional trend there has been an increase in the annual temperature of 0.7°C at the town near the reservoir. It is now warmer below the dam than above it, whereas, before, the higher stations were warmer because of the temperature inversions that used to form before the water surface exerted its moderating influence. It is estimated that precipitation has decreased, because of the stabilizing effect of the large body of cool water. Here, as elsewhere, the influence of a large reservoir does not extend more than 1 to 3 kilometers from the shore. Another form of deliberate man-controlled ᐧinterference with microclimate, with potentially large local benefits, is suppression of evaporation by monomolecular films. Where wind speeds are low, this has been a highly effective technique for conserving water. The reduction of evaporation has led to higher water surface temperature, and this may be beneficial for some crops, such as rice (49).

The reduction of fog at airports by seeding of the water droplets also belongs in this category of man-controlled local changes. In the case of supercooled droplets, injection of suitable freezing nuclei into the fog will cause freezing of some drops, which grow at the expense of the remaining droplets and fall out, thus gradually dissipating the fog. For warm fogs, substances promoting the growth or coalescence of droplets are used. In many cases dispersal of fog or an increase in visual range sufficient to permit flight operations can be achieved (50). Gratifying though this achievement is for air traffic, it barely qualifies as even a microclimatic change because of the small area and brief time scale involved. Similarly, the changes produced by artificial heating in orchards and vineyards to combat frosts hardly qualify as microclimatic changes.

Finally, a brief note on general weather modification is in order. Most of the past effort in this field has been devoted to attempts to augment rainfall and suppress hail. The results have been equivocal and variously appraised (51). The technique, in all cases, has been cloud seeding by various agents. This produces undoubted physical results in the cloud, but the procedures are too crude to permit prediction of the outcome. Thus, precipitation at the ground has been both increased and decreased (52). The most reliable results of attempts to induce rainfall have been achieved through seeding clouds forming in up-slope motions of winds across mountains and cap clouds (53). Elsewhere targeting of precipitation is difficult, and the effects of seeding downwind from the target area are not well known. No analysis has ever satisfactorily shown whether cloud seeding has actually caused a net increase in precipitation or only a redistribution. In any case, if persistently practiced, cloud seeding could bring about local climatic changes. But an ecological

question arises: If we can do it, should we? This point remains controversial.

Attempts to suppress hail by means of cloud seeding are also still in their infancy. Here the seeding is supposed to achieve the production of many small ice particles in the cloud, to prevent any of them from growing to a size large enough to be damaging when they reach the ground. The seeding agent is introduced into the hail-producing zone of cumulonimbus—for example, by ground-fired projectiles. Some successes have been claimed, but much has yet to be learned before one would acclaim seeding as a dependable technology for eliminating this climatic hazard (54).

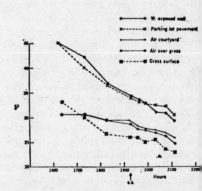

Fig. 3. A typical example of microclimatic heat island formation in incipient urbanization. The top two curves show radiative temperatures of wall and parking lot pavement on a clear summer evening (6 August 1968). The two middle curves show air temperatures (at elevation of 2 meters) in the paved courtyard and over an adjacent grass surface; from sunset (s.s.) onward, the courtyard is warmer than the air over the grass. The bottom (dashed) curve gives the radiative temperature of grass. The symbol at 2030 hours indicates the start of dew formation.

184

Hurricane modification has also been attempted. The objective is reduction of damage caused by wind and storm surges. Seeding of the outer-wall clouds around the eye of the storm is designed to accomplish this. The single controlled experiment that has been performed, albeit successfully in the predicted sense, provides too tenuous a basis for appraising the potential of this technique (55). Here again we have to raise the warning flag because of the possibility of simultaneous change in the pattern of rainfall accompanying the storm. In many regions tropical storm rain is essential for water supply and agriculture. If storms are diverted or dissipated as a result of modification, the economic losses resulting from altered rainfall patterns may outweigh the advantages gained by wind reduction (56). As yet such climatic modifications are only glimpses on the horizon.

General Urban Effects

By far the most pronounced and locally far-reaching effects of man's activities on microclimate have been in cities. In fact, many of these effects might well be classified as mesoclimatic. Some of them were recognized during the last century in the incipient metropolitan areas. Currently the sharply accelerated trend toward urbanization has led to an accentuation of the effects. The problem first simply intrigued meteorologists, but in recent years some of its aspects have become alarming. Consequently the literature in this field has grown rapidly and includes several reviews summarizing the facts (57).

We are on the verge of having a satisfactory quantitative physical model of the effect of cities on the climate.

It combines two major features introduced by the process of urbanization. They concern the heat and water balance and the turbulence conditions. To take changes in turbulence first, the major contributory change is an increase in surface roughness. This affects the wind field and, in particular, causes a major adjustment in the vertical wind profile so that wind speeds near the surface are reduced. The structural features of cities also increase the number of small-scale eddies and thus affect the turbulence spectrum.

The change in the heat balance is considerably more radical. Here, when we change a rural area to an urban one, we convert an essentially spongy surface of low heat conductivity into an impermeable layer with high capacity for absorbing and conducting heat. Also, the albedo is usually lowered. These radical changes in surface that accompany the change from rural to urban conditions lead to rapid runoff of precipitation and consequently to a reduction in local evaporation. This is, of course, equivalent to a heat gain —one which is amplified by radiative heat gain resulting from the lowering of the albedo. This heat is effectively stored in the stone, concrete, asphalt, and deeper compacted soil layers of the city. In vegetated rural areas usually more incoming radiation is reflected and less is stored than in the city. Therefore structural features alone favor a strongly positive heat balance for the city. To this, local heat production is added. The end result is what has been called the urban heat island, which leads to increased convection over the city and to a city-induced wind field that dominates when weather patterns favor weak general air flow.

Most of the features of the near-the-surface climatic conditions implied by this model have, over the years, been documented by comparisons of measurements made within the confines of cities and in their rural surroundings, mostly at airports. Such comparisons gave reasonably quantitative data on the urban effect, but some doubts remained. These stemmed from the fact that many cities were located in special topographic settings which favored the establishment of a city—such as a river valley, a natural harbor, or an orographic trough. They would by nature have a microclimate different from that of the surroundings. Similarly, airport sites were often chosen for microclimatic features favorable for aviation. Some of the uncertainties can be removed by observing atmospheric changes as a town grows. An experiment along this line was initiated 3 years ago in the new town of Columbia, Maryland. The results so far support earlier findings and have refined them (58).

Perhaps of most interest is the fact that a single block of buildings will start the process of heat island formation. This is demonstrated by air and infrared surface temperature measurements. An example is given in Fig. 3. The observations represented by the curves of Fig. 3 were made in a paved court enclosed by low-level structures which were surrounded by grass and vegetated surfaces. On clear, relatively calm evenings the heat island develops in the court, fed by heat stored in the daytime under the asphalted parking space of the court and the building walls. This slows down the radiative cooling process, relative to cooling from a grass surface, and keeps the air that is in contact with the surface warmer than that over the grass (59).

The heat island expands and intensifies as a city grows, and stronger and stronger winds are needed to overcome

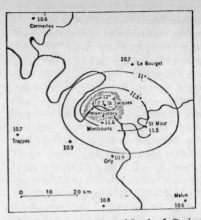

Fig. 4. The urban heat island of Paris, shown by mean annual isotherms in degrees Celsius. The region is characterized by minimal orographic complexity. [After Dettwiller (61)].

it (60). And although it is most pronounced on calm, clear nights, the effect is still evident in the long-term mean values. Figure 4 shows the isotherms in the Paris region, which is topographically relatively simple and without appreciable differences in elevation. A pronounced metropolitan heat island of about 1.6°C in the mean value can be seen. This is typical of major cities. In the early hours of calm, clear nights the city may be 6° to 8°C warmer than its surroundings. The Paris example is noteworthy because it has been demonstrated that the rise in temperature is not confined to the air but also affects the soil. It has been observed in a deep cave under the city, where temperatures have been measured for two centuries (61). Curiously enough, the cave temperature was once considered so invariant that the cave in question was proposed as one of the fixed points for thermometer scales. This artificially introduced trend in temperatures also plays havoc with the long-term temperature records from cities. They become suspect as guides for gaging the slow, natural climatic fluctuations.

Part of the rise in temperature must be attributed to heat rejection from human and animal metabolism, combustion processes, and air-conditioning units. Energy production of various types certainly accounts for a large part of it. In the urbanized areas the rejected energy has already become a measurable fraction of the energy received from the sun at the surface of the earth. Projection of this energy rejection into the next decades leads to values we should ponder. One estimate indicates that in the year 2000 the Boston-to-Washington megalopolis will have 56 million people living within an area of 30,000 square kilometers. The heat rejection will be about 65 calories per square centimeter per day. In winter this is about 50 percent, and in summer 15 percent, of the heat received by solar radiation on a horizontal surface (62). The eminent French geophysicist J. Coulomb has discussed the implications of doubling the energy consumption in France every 10 years; this would lead to unbearable temperatures (63). It is one of a large number of reasons for achieving, as rapidly as possible, a steady state in population and in power needs.

An immediate consequence of the heat island of cities is increased convection over cities, especially in the daytime. That has been beautifully demonstrated by the lift given to constant-volume balloons launched across cities (64). The updraft leads, together with the large amount of water vapor released by combustion processes and steam power, to increased cloudiness over cities. It is also a potent factor in the increased rainfall reported from cities, discussed below in conjunction with air pollution problems. Even at

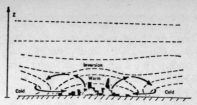

Fig. 5. Idealized scheme of nocturnal atmospheric circulation above a city in clear, calm weather. The diagram shows the urban heat island and the radiative ground inversions in the rural areas, a situation that causes a "country breeze" with an upper return current. (Dashed lines) Isotherms; (arrows) wind; Z, vertical coordinate.

night the heating from below will counteract the radiative cooling and produce a positive temperature lapse rate, while at the same time inversions form over the undisturbed countryside. This, together with the surface temperature gradient, creates a pressure field which will set a concentric country breeze into motion (65). A schematic circulation system of this type is shown in Fig. 5.

The rapid runoff of rainfall caused by the imperviousness of the surfaces of roads and roofs, as well as by the drainage system, is another major effect of cities. In minor rainfalls this has probably only the limited consequence of reducing the evaporation from the built-up area and thus eliminating much of the heat loss by the vaporization that is common in rural areas. But let there be a major rainstorm and the rapid runoff will immediately lead to a rapid rise of the draining streams and rivers. That can cause flooding and, with the unwise land use of flood plains in urban areas, lead to major damage. The flood height is linearly related to the amount of impervious area. For the 1- to 10-year recurrence intervals, flood heights will be increased by 75 percent for an area that has become 50 percent impervious, a value not at all uncommon in the usual urban setting. Observations in Hempstead, Long Island, have shown, for example, that, for a storm rainfall of 50 millimeters, direct runoff has increased from 3 millimeters in the interval from 1937 to 1943 to 7 millimeters in the interval from 1964 to 1966. This covers the time when the area changed from open fields to an urban community (66).

It is very difficult to document the decrease of wind speed over cities. Long records obtained with unchanged anemometer exposures at representative heights are scarce. Reasonable interpretations of available records suggest a decrease of about 25 percent from the rural equivalents. This is not unreasonable in the light of measurable increases in aerodynamic roughness. These are around 10 to 30 centimeters for meadows and cultivated fields and around 100 centimeters for woodland. There are several estimates for urban areas. I will give here a value calculated from the unique wind measurements on the Eiffel tower at a height of 316 meters, and from other wind records in the Paris region (67). These data yield values around 500 centimeters. They also suggest a decrease in wind at the top of the Eiffel tower from the interval 1890–1909 to the interval 1951–1960 of 0.4 meter per second, or 5 percent of the mean wind speed. In view of the height of this anemometer, this is quite a notable adjustment of the wind profile to the increase in terrain roughness.

Air Pollution Effects

Most spectacular among the effects of the city upon the atmospheric environment are those caused by air pollution. The catalogue of pollutants put into the air by man is long and has been commented upon in so many contexts that reference to the literature will have to suffice (68). Nor shall I dwell here on the special interactions of pollutants with the atmosphere in climatically and topographically specialized instances, such as the much investigated case of Los Angeles (69). I shall concentrate, instead, on the rather universal effects of pollutants on local climates.

Among these is the attenuation of solar radiation by suspended particulates. Although this affects the whole spectrum, it is most pronounced in the short wavelengths. The total direct radiation over most major cities is weakened by about 15 percent, sometimes more in winter and less in summer. The ultraviolet is reduced by 30 percent, on an average, and in winter often no radiation of wavelengths below 390 nanometers is received. The extinction takes place in a very shallow layer, as simultaneous measurements taken at the surface and from a tall steeple have shown (70).

Horizontally, the particulate haze interferes with visibility in cities. When shallow temperature inversions are present, the accumulation of aerosols can cause 80- or 90-percent reduction of the visual range as compared with the range for the general uncontaminated environment. The haze effect is accentuated by the formation of water droplets around hygroscopic nuclei, even below the saturation point. This is the more noteworthy because relative humidities near the surface are generally lower in cities than in the countryside. This is attributable partially to the higher temperatures and partially to the reduced evaporation. Nonetheless, fog occurs from two to five times as often in the city as in the surroundings. Fortunately, this seems to be a reversible process. Recent clean-up campaign have shown that, through the use of smokeless fuels, considerable lessening of the concentration of particulates, and hence of fog and of the attenuation of light, can be achieved. In London, for example, with the change in heating practices, winter sunshine has increased by 70 percent in the last decade, and the winter visibilities have improved by a factor of 3 since the improvements were introduced (71).

I have alluded above to the increase in cloudiness over cities. It is likely that the enormous number of condensation nuclei produced by human activities in and around cities contributes to this phenomenon. Every set of measurements made has confirmed early assessments that these constituents are more numerous by one or two orders of magnitude in urbanized regions than in the country (72). Every domestic or industrial combustion process, principally motor vehicle exhaust, contributes to this part of the particulate. Independent evidence suggests that there is more rainfall over cities than over the surrounding countryside. But the evidence that pollutants are involved is tenuous. There is little doubt that the convection induced by the heat island can induce or intensify showers. This has been demonstrated for London, where apparently thundershowers yield 30 percent more rain than in the surrounding area (73). Orographic conditions would lead one to expect more showers in hilly terrain. This is not the case. Although this buoyancy effect is certainly at work, it does not stand alone: in some towns there are observations of precipitation increases from supercooled winter stratus clouds over urban areas. Some well-documented isolated cases of snow over highly industrialized towns suggest a cloud-seeding effect by some pollutants that may act as freezing nu-

clei (74). Also the rather startling variation of urban precipitation in accordance with the pattern of the human work week argues for at least a residual effect of nucleating agents produced in cities. The week is such an arbitrary subdivision of time that artificial forces must be at work. Observations over various intervals and in various regions indicate increased precipitation for the days from Monday through Friday as compared with values for Saturday and Sunday. These increases usually parallel the increase in industrialization, and, again, there is evidence for a more pronounced effect in the cool season (75).

Although most studies indicate that the increase in precipitation in urban areas is around 10 percent—that is, close to the limit of what could still be in the realm of sampling errors—some analyses have shown considerably larger increases in isolated cases. These instances have not yet been lifted out of the umbra of scientific controversy (76). But we should note here that some industrial activities and internal combustion engines produce nuclei that can have nucleating effects, at least on supercooled cloud particles. In the State of Washington in some regions that have become industrialized there is evidence of a 30-percent increase in precipitation in areas near the pulp mills over an interval of four decades (77). There are also incontrovertible observations of cloud banks forming for tens of kilometers in the plumes of power plants and industrial stacks. This is not necessarily associated with increased precipitation but raises the question of how far downwind man's activities have caused atmospheric modifications.

In the absence of systematic three-dimensional observations, we have to rely on surface data. A recent study by

Band (78) throws some light on the conditions. He found that, for a heat island 3°C warmer than its surroundings, a small but measurable temperature effect was still notable 3 kilometers to leeward of the town. Similarly, a substantial increase in the number of condensation nuclei was noted 3 kilometers downwind from a small town. In the case of a major traffic artery, an increased concentration of nuclei was measurable to 10 kilometers downwind. For a major city, radiation measurements have suggested that the smoke pall affects an area 50 times that of the built-up region. These values, which are probably conservative, definitely indicate that man's urbanized complexes are beginning to modify the mesoclimate.

As yet it is very difficult to demonstrate that any far-reaching climatic effects are the results of man's activities. If man-made effects on this scale already exist or are likely to exist in the future, they will probably be a result of the vast numbers of anthropogenic condensation and freezing nuclei. Among the latter are effective nucleating agents resulting from lead particles in automobile exhaust. These particles have become ubiquitous, and if they combine with iodine or bromine they are apt to act as freezing nuclei. Schaefer and others have pointed out that this could have effects on precipitation far downwind (79). These inadvertent results would lead either to local increases in precipitation or to a redistribution of natural precipitation patterns. They are, however, among the reversible man-made influences. As soon as lead is no longer used as a gasoline additive—which, hopefully, will be soon—the supply of these nucleating agents will stop and the influence, whatever its importance, should vanish promptly because of the relatively short lifetime of these nuclei.

Perhaps more serious, and much more difficult to combat, is the oversupply of condensation nuclei. Gunn and Phillips pointed out years ago that, if too many hygroscopic particles compete for the available moisture, cloud droplets will be small and the coalescence processes will become inhibited (80). This could lead to decreases in precipitation, a view that has recently been confirmed (81).

There remains one final area of concern: pollution caused by jet aircraft. These aircraft often leave persistent condensation trails. According to one school of thought, these artificial clouds might increase the earth's albedo and thus cause cooling. Although on satellite pictures one can occasionally see cloud tracks that might have originated from these vapor trails, they seem to be sufficiently confined, with respect to space and time, to constitute a very minute fraction of the earth's cloud cover. The other view of the effect of these vapor trails, which change into cirriform clouds, is that ice crystals falling from them may nucleate other cloud systems below them and cause precipitation. Any actual evidence of such events is lacking. And then we have the vivid speculations concerning weather modifications by the prospective supersonic transport planes. For some time military planes have operated at the altitudes projected for the supersonic transports. The ozone layer has not been destroyed, and no exceptional cloud formations have been reported. The water vapor added by any probable commercial fleet would be less than 10^{-9} of the atmospheric water vapor; thus, no direct influence on the earth's heat budget can be expected. At any rate, it seems that the sonic boom is a much more direct and immediate effect of the supersonic transport than any possible impact it may have on climate (*82*).

There is little need to comment on the multitude of schemes that have been proposed to "ameliorate" the earth's climate. Most of them are either technologically or economically unfeasible. All of them would have side effects that the originators did not consider. The new trend toward thinking in ecological terms would lead us to require that much more thoroughgoing analyses of the implications of these schemes be made than have been made so far before any steps are taken toward their implementation (*83*).

Summary

Natural climatic fluctuations, even those of recent years, cover a considerable range. They can be characterized as a "noise" spectrum which masks possible global effects of man-caused increases of atmospheric CO_2 and particulates. Local modifications, either deliberate or inadvertent, measurably affect the microclimate. Some artificial alterations of the microclimate are beneficial in agriculture. Among the unplanned effects, those produced by urbanization on local temperature and on wind field are quite pronounced. The influences on rainfall are still somewhat controversial, but effects may extend considerably beyond the confines of metropolitan areas. They are the result of water vapor released by human activity and of the influence of condensation and freezing nuclei produced in overabundance by motor vehicles and other combustion processes. Therefore it appears that on the local scale manmade influences on climate are substantial but that on the global scale natural forces still prevail. Obviously this should not lead to complacency. The potential for anthropogenic changes of climate on a larger and even a global scale is real. At this stage activation of an adequate worldwide monitoring system to permit early assessment of these changes is urgent. This statement applies particularly to the surveillance of atmospheric composition and radiation balance at sites remote from concentrations of population, which is now entirely inadequate. In my opinion, man-made aerosols, because of their optical properties and possible influences on cloud and precipitation processes, constitute a more acute problem than CO_2. Many of their effects are promptly reversible; hence, one should strive for elimination at the source. Over longer intervals, energy added to the atmosphere by heat rejection and CO_2 absorption remain matters of concern.

References and Notes

1. L. V. Berkner and L. S. Marshall, *Advan. Geophys.* 12, 309 (1967); S. I. Rasool, *Science* 157, 1466 (1967).
2. The climatic consequences of an original single continent, continental drift, changing ocean size, and changing positions of the continents with respect to the poles are not discussed here.
3. M. I. Budyko, *Sov. Geogr.: Rev. Transl.* 10, 429 (1969); *J. Appl. Meteorol.* 9, 310 (1970). For a discussion and extension of Budyko's models, see W. D. Sellers, *ibid.* 8, 392 (1969); *ibid.* 9, 311 (1970).
4. For a recent review of the principal thoughts in this area, based primarily on work by C. E. P. Brooks (1951), W. D. Sellers (1965), and M. I. Budyko (1968), see H. L. Ferguson, *Atmosphere* 6, 133 (1968); *ibid.*, p. 145; *ibid.*, p. 151.
5. M. Milankovitch, "Canon of Insolation and the Ice-Age Problem," translation of *Kgl. Serbische Akad. Spec. Publ.* 132 (1941) by *Israel Program Sci. Transl.* (1969), *U.S. Dep. Comm. Clearing House Fed. Sci. Tech. Inform.*
6. C. Emiliani and J. Geiss, *Geol. Rundschau* 46, 576 (1957); C. Emiliani, *J. Geol.* 66, 264 (1958); *ibid.* 74, 109 (1966); *Science* 154, 851 (1966); W. S. Broecker, D. L. Thurber, J. Goddard, T.-L. Ku, R. K. Matthews, K. J. Mesolella, *ibid.* 159, 297 (1968).
7. M. I. Budyko, *Tellus* 21, 611 (1969); D. M. Shaw and W. L. Donn, *Science* 162, 1270

(1968).

8. J. R. Bray, *Science* **168**, 571 (1970).

9. F. Baur, *Meteorol. Abhandl.* 50, No. 4 (1967).

10. For a recent review of the many factors causing climatic changes, see *Meteorol. Monogr.* 8, No. 30 (1968); for a divergent view on the problem, see L. R. Curry, *Ann. Ass. Amer. Geogr.* 52, 21 (1962); for factors involved in artificially induced changes, see H. Flohn, *Bonner Meteorol. Abhandl. No. 2* (1963).

11. H. C. Fritts, *Mon. Weather Rev.* 93, 421 (1965).

12. G. Manley, *Quart. J. Roy. Meteorol. Soc.* 79, 242 (1953); F. Baur, in Linke's *Meteorologisches Taschenbuch, Neue Ausgabe*, F. Baur, Ed. (Akademische Verlagsgesellschaft Geest und Portig, Leipzig, 1962), vol. 1, p. 710; Y. S. Rubinstein and L. G. Polozova, *Sovremennoe Izmenenie Klimata* (Gidrometeorolgicheskoe Izdatelstvo, Leningrad, 1966); H. H. Lamb, *The Changing Climate* (Methuen, London, 1966); H. von Rudloff, in *Europa seit dem Beginn der regelmässigen Instrumentenbeobachtungen (1670)* (Vieweg, Brunswick, 1967); H. E. Landsberg, *Weatherwise* 20, 52 (1967); M. Konček and K. Cehak, *Arch. Meteorol. Geophys. Bioklimatol. Ser. B Allg. Biol. Klimatol.* 16, 1 (1968); T. Anderson, "Swedish Temperature and Precipitation Records since the Middle of the 19th Century," *National Institute of Building Research, Stockholm, Document D4* (1970); for the Far East a particularly pertinent paper is H. Arakawa, *Arch. Meteorol. Geophys. Bioklimatol. Ser. B Allg. Biol. Klimatol.* 6, 152 (1964).

13. H. E. Landsberg, C. S. Yu, L. Huang, "Preliminary Reconstruction of a Long Time Series of Climatic Data for the Eastern United States," *Univ. Md. Inst. Fluid Dyn. Appl. Math. Tech. Note BN-571* (1968); for other assessments of climatic fluctuations in the United States, see also E. W. Wahl, *Mon. Weather Rev.* 96, 73 (1968); D. G. Baker, *Bull. Amer. Meteorol. Soc.* 41, 18 (1960).

14. C. W. Hurley, Jr., *Mt. Washington News Bull.* 10, No. 3, 13 (1969).

15. W. S. Carlson, *Science* 168, 396 (1970).

16. J. Bjerknes, *Advan. Geophys.* 10, 1 (1964); S. I. Rasool and J. S. Hogan, *Bull. Amer. Meteorol. Soc.* 50, 130 (1969); N. I. Yakovleva, *Izv. Acad. Sci. USSR, Atm. Ocean. Phys. Ser.* (American Geophysical Union translation) 5, 699 (1969).

17. J. Namias, in *Proc. Amer. Water Resources Conf. 4th* (1968), p. 852; *J. Geophys. Res.* 75, 565 (1970).

18. The term *greenhouse effect*, which has been commonly accepted for spectral absorption by atmospheric gases of long-wave radiation emitted by the earth, is actually a misnomer. Although the opaqueness of the glass in a greenhouse for long-wave radiation keeps part of the absorbed or generated heat inside, the seclusion of the interior space from advective and convective air flow is a very essential part of the functioning of a greenhouse. In the free atmosphere such flow is, of course, always present.

19. S. Arrhenius, *Worlds in the Making* (Harper, New York, 1908), pp. 51–54.

20. G. S. Callendar, *Quart. J. Roy. Meteorol. Soc.* 64, 223 (1938).

21. G. N. Plass, *Amer. J. Phys.* 24, 376 (1956).

22. W. Bischof and B. Bolin, *Tellus* 18, 155 (1966); K. W. Brown and N. J. Rosenberg, *Mon. Weather Rev.* 98, 75 (1970).

23. G. S. Callendar, *Tellus* 10, 253 (1958); B. Bolin and C. D. Keeling, *J. Geophys. Res.* 68, 3899 (1963); T. B. Harris, *Bull. Amer. Meteorol. Soc.* 51, 101 (1970); *ESSA* [*Environ. Sci. Serv. Admin.*] *Pam. ERLTM-APCL9* (series 33, 1970).

24. H. Lieth, *J. Geophys. Res.* 68, 3887 (1963).

25. E. K. Peterson, *Environ. Sci. Technol.* 3, 1162 (1969).

26. R. Revelle and H. E. Suess, *Tellus* 9, 18 (1957); H. E. Suess, *Science* 163, 1405 (1969); R. Berger and W. F. Libby, *ibid.* 164, 1395 (1969).

27. S. Manabe and R. T. Wetherald, *J. Atmos. Sci.* 24, 241 (1967).

28. G. J. Symons, Ed., *The Eruption of Krakatoa and Subsequent Phenomena* (Royal Society, London, 1888).

29. W. J. Humphreys, *Physics of the Air* (McGraw-Hill, New York, ed. 3, 1940), pp. 587–618.

30. R. A. Ebdon, *Weather* 22, 245 (1967); J. M. Mitchell, Jr. [personal communication and presentation in December 1969 at the Boston meeting of the AAAS] attributes about two-thirds of recent hemispheric cooling to volcanic eruptions.

31. A. B. Meinel and M. P. Meinel, *Science* 155, 189 (1967); F. E. Volz, *J. Geophys. Res.* 75, 1641 (1970).

32. In the 1930's I made a large number of counts of Aitken condensation nuclei [see H. Landsberg, *Mon. Weather Rev.* 62, 442 (1934); *Ergeb. Kosm. Phys.* 3, 155 (1938)]. These gave a background of ~100 to 200 nuclei per cubic centimeter. Measurements made in the last decade indicate an approximate doubling of this number [see C. E. Junge, in *Atmosphärische Spurenstoffe und ihre Bedeutung für den Menschen* (1966 symposium, St. Moritz) (Birkhäuser, Basel, 1967)].

33. R. A. McCormick and J. H. Ludwig, *Science* 156, 1358 (1967).

34. J. T. Peterson and R. A. Bryson, *ibid.* 162, 120 (1968).

35. R. A. Bryson advocates this hypothesis. He states, in *Weatherwise* 21, 56 (1968): "All other factors being constant, an increase of atmospheric turbidity will make the earth cooler by scattering away more incoming sunlight. A decrease of dust should make it warmer." This remains a very simplified model, because "all other factors" never stay constant. See also W. M. Wendland and R. A. Bryson, *Biol. Conserv.* 2, 127 (1970). E. W. Barret in "Depletion of total short-wave irradiance at the ground by suspended particulates," a paper presented at the 1970 International Solar Energy Conference, Melbourne, Australia, calculates for various latitudes the depletion of radiation received at the ground because of dust. For geometrical reasons this is a more pronounced effect at higher than at lower latitudes. He therefore postulates that an order-of-magnitude increase in the amount of dust will redistribute the energy balance at the surface sufficiently to cause changes in the general circulation of the

atmosphere.

36. W. T. Roach, *Quart. J. Roy. Meteorol. Soc.* **87**, 346 (1961); K. Bullrich, *Advan. Geophys.* **10**, 101 (1964); H. Quenzel, *Pure Appl. Geophys.* **71**, 149 (1968); R. J. Charlson and M. J. Pilat, *J. Appl. Meteorol.* **8**, 1001 (1969).

37. H. Landsberg, *Bull. Amer. Meteorol. Soc.* **21**, 102 (1940); N. Georgievskii, *Sev. Morskoi Put. No. 13* (1939), p. 29; A. Titlianov, *Dokl. Vses. (Ordena Lenina) Akad. Sel'skokhoz. Nauk Imeni V. I. Lenina* **6**, No. 8, 8 (1941); A. I. Kolchin, *Les. Khoziaistvo* **3**, 69 (1950); *Les i Step* **3**, 77 (1951); G. A. Ausiuk, *Priroda (Moskva)* **43**, No. 3, 82 (1954).

38. F. F. Davitaya, *Trans. Soviet Acad. Sci. Geogr. Ser. 1965 No. 2* (English translation) (1966), p. 3.

39. M. R. Block, *Paleogeogr. Paleoclimatol. Paleoecol.* **1**, 127 (1965).

40. J. O. Fletcher, "The Polar Ocean and World Climate," *Rand Corp., Santa Monica, Calif., Publ. P-3801* (1968); "Managing Climatic Resources," *Rand Corp., Santa Monica, Calif., Publ. P-4000-1* (1969).

41. T. Jefferson, letter written from Monticello to his correspondent Dr. Lewis Beck of Albany, dated July 16, 1824.

42. R. Geiger, *Das Klima der bodennahen Luftschicht* (Vieweg, Brunswick, 1961), p. 503.

43. J. van Eimern, L. R. Razumova, G. W. Robinson, "Windbreaks and Shelterbelts," *World Meteorological Organ., Geneva, Tech. Note No. 59* (1964); J. M. Caborn, *Shelterbelts and Windbreaks* (Faber and Faber, London, 1965).

44. I. A. Campbell, according to a news item in *Arid Land Research Newsletter No. 33* (1970), p. 10, studied the Shonto Plateau in northern Arizona, where he found that all gullies were stabilized, remaining just as they were 30 years ago. Yet there are now far more sheep in the area. He concluded that accelerated erosion there was caused by climatic variations and not by overgrazing.

45. C. W. Thornthwaite, in *Man's Role in Changing the Face of the Earth*, W. L. Thomas, Jr., Ed. (Univ. of Chicago Press, Chicago, 1956), p. 567.

46. L. A. Joos, "Recent rainfall patterns in the Great Plains," paper presented 21 October 1969 before the American Meteorological Society; F. Begemann and W. F. Libby, *Geochim. Cosmochim. Acta* **12**, 277 (1957).

47. In this context it is important to stress again the inadequacy of the ordinary rain gage as a sampling device. With about one gage per 75 square kilometers, we are actually sampling 5×10^{-10} of the area in question. But precipitation is usually unevenly distributed, especially when rain occurs in the form of showers. Then the sampling errors become very high. Even gages close to each other often show 10 percent differences in monthly totals. It takes, therefore, a long time to determine whether differences are significant or trends are real. This same caveat applies to analyses of rainmaking or to changes induced by effects of cities. This problem is often conveniently overlooked by statisticians unfamiliar with meteorological instruments and by enthusiasts with favorite hypotheses [see H. E. Landsberg, *Physical Climatology* (Gray, Dubois, Pa., ed. 2, 1966), p. 324; G. E. Stout, *Trans. Ill. Acad. Sci.* **53**, 11 (1960)].

48. S. Zych and H. Dubaniewicz, *Zesz. Nauk. Univ. Lodz Riego Ser. II* **32**, 3 (1969); S. Gregory and K. Smith, *Weather* **22**, 497 (1967).

49. V. F. Pushkarev and G. P. Leochenko, *Sov. Hydrol. Select. Pap.* **3**, 253 (1967); M. Gangopadhyaya and S. Venkataraman, *Agr. Meteorol.* **6**, 339 (1969); R. Kapesser, R. Greif, I. Cornet, *Science* **166**, 403 (1969).

50. W. B. Beckwith, in "Human Dimensions of Weather Modification," *Univ. Chicago, Dep. Geogr. Res. Pap. No. 150* (1966), p. 195; B. A. Silverman, *Bull. Amer. Meteorol. Soc.* **51**, 420 (1970).

51. "Weather and Climate Modification, Problems and Prospects," *Nat. Acad. Sci. Nat. Res. Counc. Publ. No. 1350* (1966); M. Neiburger, "Artificial Modification of Clouds and Precipitation," *World Meteorol. Organ., Geneva, Tech. Note No. 105* (1969); "Weather Modification, a Survey of the Present Status with Respect to Agriculture," *Res. Branch, Can. Dep. Agr., Ottawa, Publ.* (1970); M. Tribus, *Science* **168**, 201 (1970).

52. L. Le Cam and J. Neyman, Eds., *Weather Modification Experiments* (Proceedings of the 5th Berkeley Symposium on Mathematical Statistics and Probability (Univ. of California Press, Berkeley, 1967).

53. J. R. Stinson, in *Water Supplies for Arid Regions*, F. L. Gardner and L. E. Myers, Eds. (Univ. of Arizona Press, Tucson, 1967), p. 10; U.S. Department of the Interior, Office of Atmospheric Water Resources, Project Skywater 1969 Annual Report, Denver (1970).

54. R. A. Schleusner, *J. Appl. Meteorol.* **7**, 1004 (1968); "Metody vozdeistviia na gradovye protsessy," in *Vysokogornyi Geofiz. Trudy 11* (Gidrometeorologicheskoe Izdatelstvo, Leningrad, 1968).

55. R. C. Gentry, *Science* **168**, 473 (1970).

56. G. W. Cry, "Effects of Tropical Cyclone Rainfall on the Distribution of Precipitation over the Eastern and Southern United States," *ESSA* [*Environ. Sci. Serv. Admin.*] *Prof. Pap. No. 1* (1967); A. L. Sugg, *J. Appl. Meteorol.* **7**, 39 (1968).

57. H. E. Landsberg, in *Man's Role in Changing the Face of the Earth*, W. L. Thomas, Jr., Ed. (Univ. of Chicago Press, Chicago, 1956), p. 584; A. Kratzer, *Das Stadtklima*, vol. 90 of *Die Wissenshaft* (Vieweg, Brunswick, 1956); H. E. Landsberg, in "Air over Cities," *U.S. Pub. Health Serv. R. A. Taft Sanit. Eng. Center, Cincinnati, Tech. Rep. A 62-5* (1962); J. L. Peterson, "The Climate of Cities: A Survey of Recent Literature," *Nat. Air Pollut. Contr. Admin., Raleigh, N.C., Publ. No. AP-59* (1969).

58. P. M. Tag, in "Atmospheric Modification by Surface Influences," *Dep. Meteorol., Penn. State Univ., Rep. No. 15* (1969), pp. 1–71; M. A. Estoque, "A Numerical Model of the Atmospheric Boundary Layer," *Air Force Cambridge Res. Center, GRD Sci. Rep.* (1962); L. O. Myrup, *J. Appl. Meteorol.* **8**, 908 (1969).

59. H. E. Landsberg, in "Urban Climates," *World Meteorol. Organ., Geneva, Tech. Note No. 108* (1970), p. 129.

60. T. R. Oke and F. G. Harnall, *ibid.*, p. 113.

61. J. Dettwiller, *J. Appl. Meteorol.* **9**, 178 (1970).

62. R. T. Jaske, J. F. Fletcher, K. R. Wise, "A national estimate of public and industrial heat rejection requirements by decades through

the year 2000 A.D.," paper presented before the American Institute of Chemical Engineers at its 67th National Meeting, Atlanta, 1970).

63. J. Coulomb, News Report, Nat. Acad. Sci. Nat. Res. Counc. 20, No. 3, 6 (1970).

64. W. A. Hass, W. H. Hoecker, D. H. Pack, J. K. Angell, Quart. J. Roy. Meteorol. Soc. 93, 483 (1967).

65. F. Pooler, J. Appl. Meteorol. 2, 446 (1963); R. E. Munn, in "Urban Climates," World Meteorol. Organ., Geneva, Tech. Note No. 108 (1970), p. 15.

66. W. H. K. Espey, C. W. Morgan, F. D. Marsh, "Study of Some Effects of Urbanization on Storm Run-off from Small Watersheds," Texas Water Develop. Board Rep. No. 23 (1966); L. A. Martens, "Flood Inundation and Effects of Urbanization in Metropolitan Charlotte, North Carolina," U.S. Geol. Surv. Water Supply Pap. 1591-C (1968); G. E. Seaburn, "Effects of Urban Development on Direct Run-off to East Meadow Brook, Nassau County, Long Island, N.Y.," U.S. Geol. Surv. Prof. Pap. 627-B (1969).

67. J. Dettwiller, "Le vent au sommet de la tour Eiffel," Monogr. Meteorol. Nat. No. 64 (1969).

68. See, for example, Air Pollution, A. C. Stern, Ed. (Academic Press, New York, ed. 2, 1968).

69. A. J. Hagen-Smit, C. E. Bradley, M. M. Fox, Ind. Eng. Chem. 45, 2086 (1953); J. K. Angell, D. H. Pack, G. C. Holzworth, C. R. Dickson, J. Appl. Meteorol. 5, 565 (1966); M. Neiburger, Bull. Amer. Meteorol. Soc. 50, 957 (1969); in "Urban Climates," World Meteorol. Organ., Geneva, Tech. Note No. 108 (1970), p. 248.

70. F. Lauscher and F. Steinhauser, Sitzungsber. Wiener Akad. Wiss. Math. Naturw. Kl. Abt. 2a 141, 15 (1932); ibid. 143, 175 (1934).

71. R. P. McNulty, Atmos. Environ. 2, 625 (1968); R. S. Charlson, Environ. Sci. Technol. 3, 913 (1969); R. O. McCaldin, L. W. Johnson, N. T. Stephens, Science 166. 381 (1969); C. G. Collier, Weather 25, 25 (1970); London Borough Association press release, quoted from UPI report of 14 Jan. 1970.

72. H. Landsberg, Bull. Amer. Meteorol. Soc. 18, 172 (1937).

73. B. W. Atkinson, "A Further Examination of the Urban Maximum of Thunder Rainfall in London, 1951–60," Trans. Pap. Inst. Brit. Geogr. Publ. No. 48 (1969), p. 97.

74. J. von Kienle, Meteorol. Rundschau 5, 132 (1952); W. M. Culkowski, Mon. Weather Rev. 90, 194 (1962).

75. R. H. Frederick, Bull. Amer. Meteorol. Soc. 51, 100 (1970).

76. S. A. Changnon, in "Urban Climates," World Meteorol. Organ., Geneva, Tech. Note 108 (1970), p. 325; B. G. Holzman and H. C. S. Thom, Bull. Amer. Meteorol. Soc. 51, 335 (1970); S. A. Changnon, ibid., p. 337.

77. G. Langer, in Proc. 1st Nat. Conf. Weather Modification, Amer. Meteorol. Soc. (1968), p. 220; P. V. Hobbs and L. F. Radke, J. Atmos. Sci. 27, 81 (1970); Bull. Amer. Meteorol. Soc. 51, 101 (1970).

78. G. Band, "Der Einfluss der Siedlung auf das Freilandklima," Mitt. Inst. Geophys. Meteorol. Univ. Köln (1969), vol. 9.

79. V. J. Schaefer, Science 154, 1555 (1966); A. W. Hogan, ibid. 158, 800 (1967); V. J. Schaefer, Bull. Amer. Meteorol. Soc. 50, 199 (1969); State University of New York at Albany, Atmospheric Sciences Research Center, Annual Report 1969; J. P. Lodge, Jr., Bull. Amer. Meteorol. Soc. 50, 530 (1969); G. Langer, ibid. 51, 102 (1970).

80. R. Gunn and B. B. Phillips, J. Meteorol. 14, 272 (1957).

81. P. A. Allee, Bull. Amer. Meteorol. Soc. 51, 102 (1970).

82. G. N. Chatham, Mt. Washington Observ. News. Bull. 11, No. 1, 18 (1970); P. M. Kuhn, Bull. Amer. Meteorol. Soc. 51, 101 (1970); F. F. Hall, Jr., ibid., p. 101; V. D. Nuessle and R. W. Holcomb, Science 168, 1562 (1970).

83. P. Dansereau, BioScience 14, No. 7, 20 (1964); in Future Environments of North America, S. F. Darling and J. P. Milton, Eds. (Natural History Press, Garden City, N.Y., 1966), p. 425; R. Dubos, "A theology of the earth," lecture presented before the Smithsonian Institution, 1969; M. Bundy, "Managing knowledge to save the environment," address delivered 27 Jan. 1970 before the 11th Annual Meeting of the Advisory Panel to the House Committee on Science and Astronautics.

84. The work discussed here has been supported in part by NSF grants GA-1104 and GA-13353.

RENEWING THE SOIL

By Judith G. Meyer

HE COMPOST PILE HAS LONG BEEN a feature of farms and backyard gardens. The pile provides for natural decay of organic wastes ranging from leaves to manure. The resulting product conditions the soil (as explained below) and returns valuable organic material to the nutrient cycle. Chemical fertilizers, on the other hand, promote short-term growth of crops at the cost of long-term environmental problems. In addition to the agricultural benefits, composting offers an attractive way to reduce pollution by making ecologically sound use of animal wastes, sludge from municipal sewage treatment plants, and wastes from food-processing factories. The difficulty is that composting for application to the soil costs more than alternative methods when it is attempted on a scale larger than the farmyard. The experience in industrialized countries has been that compost cannot compete economically with chemical fertilizers. One approach that warrants further examination is the development of integrated systems for composting and recycling municipal and agricultural wastes with support from local, state, and federal agencies and institutions concerned with waste disposal, conservation, and agriculture.

When plant and animal residues (such as leaves and animal droppings on the forest floor) are added to the soil, or are placed in compost piles, under favorable conditions of moisture and aeration, they are immediately attacked by a variety of organisms, including bacteria, fungi, worms, insect larvae, and molds. As a result, some of the contents of the materials pass into the air, others are used by the microorganisms for building microbial cell substance, and still others are gradually converted into a uniform, dark-colored, amorphous mass called humus[1] (compost is one type of humus).

This article is based in large part upon "The Potential of Composting in Resource Recovery," by Charles G. Gunnerson, presented at the 137th Annual Meeting of the American Association for the Advancement of Science, Chicago, December 1970.

ENVIRONMENT, Vol. 14, No. 2, pp. 22-24 ff.

Humus serves several purposes in the life of the soil, all of which contribute to soil fertility. The material supplies essential plant nutrients (such as nitrogen and phosphorus), the types and quantities of which depend on the composition of the wastes from which it was formed. In addition, it has important physical effects on the soil, making it a soil conditioner: The capacity of humus to hold moisture prevents soils from drying out too rapidly. The material also maintains sufficient pore spaces in the soil; these spaces permit both air circulation—which is essential for good root growth and development—and drainage of excess water.[2]

Composting, which is simply the process by which man speeds up the natural conversion of wastes to humus, is the oldest technology for recycling organic wastes. Quantities of these residuals in the United States are huge and include approximately half of the 260 million tons of municipal solid wastes collected in 1967 (or a potential of 150 million tons of cured compost); essentially all of the 550 million tons of inedible portions of crops (including forest slash) and the 1,560 tons of animal and poultry manures and carcasses produced annually in the U.S.; and locally significant amounts of food-processing wastes.

Despite the value of composting as a source of humus and as a method of waste disposal, it has not been able to compete economically with chemical fertilizers or with waste disposal methods such as landfills and incineration. In the U.S. compost has been economically unsuccessful because of its lack of steady markets; the high initial investment and operating costs of composting processes; and the necessity of handling and disposing of noncompostable wastes.[3] Furthermore, compost usually contains only small percentages of nutrients. In many cases, chemical nutrients are added to compost to beef up the nutrient content; data indicate that nitrogen fertilizer must be added to some composts to prevent nitrogen deficiencies in the soil and consequent decreased crop yields.

Table 1 shows that composting is one of the most expensive options for municipal refuse disposal. Some of the costs may be recovered by sales of compost or of other salvageable materials. However, income from recovery of paper, metals, and other materials or from sales of compost varies widely. Overenthusiastic estimates of such income have resulted in the disenchantment shown by abandoned compost plants in both the United States and Europe.

196

An estimate of composting costs based on operations funded by the U.S. Public Health Service at the Johnson City, Tennessee, and Gainesville, Florida plants[3] is presented in Table 2. Costs are per ton of refuse processed. These costs represent "economies of scale" (that is, the more material that is composted, the cheaper it is to compost each ton of waste), since plants serving larger communities can produce compost at a lower cost per ton. However, the size and type of community affect the economics of composting in other ways: Smaller communities (for example, rural communities) generating, say, 50 tons of refuse per day are more likely to be located within areas that can utilize the finished compost; on the other hand, significant markets for salvaged paper and other secondary

---

TABLE 1

DIRECT COSTS TO THE DISPOSER OF MUNICIPAL SOLID WASTES*

	Dollars per ton
Promiscuous dumping and littering	0.00**
Open dump, usually with burning	0.50 to 2.00
Sanitary landfill	1.00 to 3.50
Gas and odor control (estimated)	0.10 to 1.00
Water pollution control by encapsulation (estimated)	0.20 to 1.00
Landscaping	0.05 to 0.50
Incineration, current technology	8.00 to 14.00
Additional cost of air pollution control	1.00 to 2.00
Additional cost of heat recovery	2.00 to 4.00
Composting	8.00 to 30.00
Sea disposal of bulk material	1.00 to 10.00†
Sea disposal of baled, barreled, or otherwise contained material	7.00 to 50.00‡

*Costs are for the middle 80-percentile range for disposal only; they do not include collection, transportation, or indirect environmental costs.

**However, the cost to the public for removal and subsequent disposal is from approximately $40 to $4000 per ton.

†Wet weight basis; for example, sewage sludge at 95 percent moisture, dredging spoils, waste oils.

‡Costs are at dockside; higher costs are those associated with toxic or otherwise hard-to-handle wastes.

Source: Gunnerson, Charles G., "The Potential of Composting in Resource Recovery," presented at the 137th Annual Meeting of the American Association for the Advancement of Science, Chicago, December 1970.

TABLE 2

ESTIMATED COSTS FOR COMPOSTING MUNICIPAL SOLID WASTES

| | PLANT INPUT | |
Costs	50 tons/day	300 tons/day
Operating and capital	$10-20/ton	$8-12/ton
Income		
Paper, metal, and misc. salvage	$0-2/ton	$2-5/ton
Compost	$0-4/ton²	$0-2/ton°
Net Cost		
Range	$4-20/ton	$1-10/ton
Probable	$12/ton	$8/ton

°Costs per ton of refuse processed; assuming a typical 50 percent compost yield, break-even sale prices for the compost would be twice the values shown.

Source: Gunnerson, Charles G., "The Potential of Composting in Resource Recovery," presented at the 137th Annual Meeting of the American Association for the Advancement of Science, Chicago, December 1970.

materials are more likely to be found in the larger cities. At present, composting for profit can play a significant role in only a few communities.

The history of attempts to sell compost in the United States is indicated by Table 3, which shows that of eighteen plants built in the U.S. since 1951, only two—Altoona FAM, Inc., Altoona, Pennsylvania; and Ecology, Inc., Brooklyn, New York—were operating in November 1971. As of January 1971, four plants (Boulder, Houston, Mobile, and St. Petersburg) were operating on a demand basis in response to compost sales, and twelve plants had been closed.

An additional problem posed by composting is the presence in some wastes of heavy metals that are potentially toxic to plants and—once taken up into crops—to animals or to people eating the food. J. V. Lagerwerff[6] has warned of possible toxic concentrations in food or forage crops due to the presence in the wastes of aluminum, boron, cadmium, chromium, cobalt, copper, lead, manganese, mercury, nickel, or zinc. Some assurance concerning the metals' toxicity is afforded by T. D. Hinesly,[7] whose work with Chicago sewage sludge confirmed the accepted view that in neutral or alkaline soils the chemical characteristics of heavy metals cause them to be rather tightly bound by soil colloids and hence not readily available to plants. However, since not all soils are neutral or alkaline, this potential problem cannot be ignored. Careful monitoring of composting operations is required, and it may be necessary, where municipal wastes are to be disposed of in the soil, to exclude some types of wastes. The current trend toward this type of control is found in recently adopted provisons of the Los Angeles Municipal Code which forbid use of sewers for disposal of mercury or chlorinated hydrocarbons in industrial wastes.˙

Municipal Refuse Composting in Europe and the Middle East

Generally, the reasons for the failure of projects and proposals for composting in Europe and the Middle East are precisely those which have caused similar failures in the U.S.: The municipality or other operating agency is unable to provide the financial support necessary to cover costs of producing and distributing compost. Nevertheless, composting is more widely practiced in Europe than in the U.S. although the fraction of refuse which is composted is small —ranging from less than 1 percent in West Germany to 17 percent in Holland.˙ The Dutch operation is made possible by the historical use of humus in reclaiming submerged lands from the North Sea, the large percentage of agriculture devoted to high-value horticultural activities, and a well-managed sales and distribution system.

Reported costs of composting systems vary widely and are not uniformly derived. G. J. Kupchick[10] cites capital costs of from $0.55 to $1.91 per ton for windrow plants (described below) and $1.18 to $3.98 for digester plants (below); operating expenses of from $1.51 to $2.76 per ton; revenue from compost, zero to about $10 per ton, and revenue from salvage, zero to $0.79 per ton.

At twelve European plants serving 3,136,000 people, compost production was 45 percent of the refuse processed. About 70 percent of the product was sold at an average of $2.73 per ton of compost; this is equivalent to $0.90 per ton of refuse processed.[10] Conditions for favorable marketing of compost are rare, so that most European˙ cities have selected lower cost alternatives.

The cities of Buchs and Turgi, Switzerland illustrate the inability of composting projects to compete economically

TABLE 3

MUNICIPAL REFUSE COMPOSTING PLANTS IN THE UNITED STATES

Location	Company	Process	Capacity Ton/Day	Wastes	Began Operation	January 1971 Status
Altoona, Pa.	Altoona FAM, Inc.	Fairfield-Hardy	45	Garbage, paper	1951 1963	Operating
Boulder, Colo.	Harry Gorby	Windrow	100	Mixed refuse	1965	Operating on demand basis
Gainesville, Fla.	Gainesville Municipal Waste Conversion Authority (Grant from PHS)	Metro Waste Conversion	150	Mixed refuse, digested sludge	1968 1970	Closed 1971
Houston, Tex.	Metropolitan Waste Conversion Corp.	Metro Waste Conversion	360	Mixed refuse, raw sludge	1966	Operating on demand basis
Houston, Tex.	United Compost Services, Inc.	Snell	300	Mixed refuse	1966	Closed 1966
Johnson City, Tenn.	Joint USPHS-TVA	Windrow	52	Mixed refuse, raw sludge	1967	Closed 1971
Largo, Fla.	Peninsular Organics, Inc.	Metro Waste Conversion	50	Mixed refuse, digested sludge	1963	Closed 1967 (pilot plant)
Norman, Okla.	International Disposal Corp.	Naturizer	35	Mixed refuse	1959	Closed 1964
Mobile, Ala.	City of Mobile	Windrow (formerly briquetting process)	300	Mixed refuse, digested sludge	1966	Operating on demand basis
New York, N. Y.	Ecology, Inc.	Varro	150	Mixed refuse	1971	Operating
Phoenix, Ariz.	Arizona Biochemical Co.	Dano	300	Mixed refuse	1963	Closed 1965
Sacramento, Calif.	Dano of America, Inc.	Dano	40	Mixed refuse	1956	Closed 1963
San Fernando, Calif.	International Disposal Corp.	Naturizer	70	Mixed refuse	1963	Closed 1964
San Juan, P. R.	Fairfield Engineering Co.	Fairfield-Hardy	150	Mixed refuse	1969	Closed 1971
Springfield, Mass.	Springfield Organic Fertilizer Co.	Frazer-Eweson	20	Garbage	1954 1961	Closed 1962
St. Petersburg, Fla.	Westinghouse Corp.	Naturizer	105	Mixed refuse	1966	Operating on demand basis
Williamston, Mich.	City of Williamston	Riker	4	Garbage, raw sludge, corn cobs	1955	Closed 1962
Wilmington, Ohio	Good Riddance, Inc.	Windrow	20	Mixed refuse	1963	Closed 1965

Source: Breidenbach, A. W., et al., "Composting of Municipal Solid Wastes in the United States," U.S. Environmental Protection Agency Publication, Washington, D. C., 1971.

with other means of disposal. In these cities incineration is scheduled to replace composting, but the compost plants will remain operational.[9] In this way, the product will be available for those willing to pay the additional cost of composting over that of incineration.

Some of the recently proposed plants in Europe and the Middle East feature complicated materials handling or processing procedures which reflect intensive promotional efforts. There have even been commitments to pay a municipality for raw refuse. In Tehran (where construction on the partially completed plant was halted) and Istanbul (where construction never proceeded beyond the ground-breaking stage), published estimates of potential revenues from compost sales were overly optimistic.[10]

Although composting in Israel has had mixed results, the wide use of composting in Israel is *prima facie* evidence of a greater willingness to pay more for refuse processing and recycling than we find in the U.S. In five of the seven provinces either windrow (see below) or Dano composting plants process refuse from 43 percent of the total population. (The Dano process uses a long, slightly inclined rotating cylinder in which refuse is aerated and composted for about one week.) The largest operating plant in the world is the windrow plant at Tel Aviv; the newest is the Dano plant for 120,000 of Jerusalem's population. On the other hand, an existing windrow plant near Ashkelon is to be replaced by a sanitary landfill.[11]

Available cost figures from Europe and the Middle East are consistent with those reported for plants in the humid tropics; these include the one which was closed down at Kingston, Jamaica, and the operating one at Bangkok, Thailand.

The Composting Process

To understand the financial investment necessary for composting, a more detailed understanding of the process is necessary. Although, in simplest terms, the composting process involves piling wastes and allowing time for microorganisms to decompose it to compost, or humus, any composting process must satisfy the following requirements: provide for fairly rapid decomposition of the wastes (since large quantities are often involved); destroy disease-causing bacteria; prevent the presence of flies and hatching of their eggs (flies are important in the transmission of faecal-borne diseases); and produce no objectionable odors. Although there are several composting techniques, or processes, that are used throughout the world, there are certain general considerations, among which are the following:

First, the decomposition of organic matter occurs without the presence of oxygen (anaerobic conditions) or with oxygen present (aerobic conditions). Aerobic composting is the safest sanitary technique, since the temperatures produced when the carbon in the compost is oxidized to carbon dioxide rapidly destroy disease-producing bacteria. In addition, aerobic composting produces no objectionable odors. Anaerobic composting, on the other hand, usually results in only slow or partial disappearance of disease organisms and produces odors.[12]

Second, municipal wastes often contain salvageable and noncompostable materials and refuse that cannot later be shredded. In some composting processes these materials are segregated from the material that is to be composted by magnetic separators and screens.

Third, shredding or grinding of the waste material permits more rapid and uniform decomposition, makes the material more responsive to moisture control and aeration, provides insulation against heat loss, eases fly control, and facilitates quick and uniform application of the compost to the land.

Fourth, the decomposition process is slowed down if the ratio of carbon to nitrogen in the waste materials is higher than 40:1 or lower than 20:1; in addition, the carbon-nitrogen ratio affects the soil to which the compost is applied.

Fifth, the moisture content of the refuse must be controlled to ensure aerobic conditions. If the moisture is too great, air cannot get to the waste materials, and they become anaerobic with resulting odors, lower temperatures, and slower decomposition rates.[1]Insufficient moisture also produces lowered temperatures and slower reaction rates.

Sixth, aeration of the waste matter by turning it by hand or machines is essential for maintaining aerobic conditions.

Seventh, the method of stacking the waste material is crucial to the aeration. One of the most common arrangements is the windrow—a specially composed, elongated pile about four or five feet high, eight to twelve feet wide at the bottom, and any length. Another approach is the use of mechanized, enclosed digesters that promote more rapid decomposition and provide greater control over the end-product than do windrows.[13] Although digesters vary in their capabilities, an individual digester may allow control of such variables as oxygen supply, temperature, moisture, and mixing rates.

Eighth, after composting is completed, the product is often cured and/or dried to facilitate handling and transportation.

The yield of compost is from 40 to 60 percent by both weight and volume of the municipal refuse. The balance is made up of approximately equal amounts of one, water and carbon dioxide lost during decomposition; and two, noncompostable materials such as tires, appliances, metal, glass, and plastic, which ordinarily are separated from the compostable wastes and require separate handling and disposal.

Ecological Effects

Despite the economic problems in processing and distributing compost, the material has marked ecological advantages. Its soil-conditioning capabilities (mentioned earlier) are not easily duplicated by chemical fertilizers. A 50-year study of soil plots at the Sanborn Field at the Agricultural Experiment Station in Missouri revealed that although chemical fertilizers produced good yields, the physical condition of the soils deteriorated and the amount of organic matter decreased. These changes, in turn,

> prevented sufficient water from percolating into the soil and being stored for drought periods. Apparently a condition developed in the soil whereby the nutrients applied [were] not delivered to the plant when needed for optimum growth. . . . Evidently most of the nitrogen not used by the immediate crop [was] removed from the soil by leaching or denitrification . . . it is evident that heavy application of chemical fertilizers [gave] a very low efficiency of recovery.[14]

Thus, although chemical fertilizers may intensify crop production, they may also cause deterioration of soil structure.

Furthermore, substantial crop-yield increases have resulted from the sole use of compost, despite low nutritive content. In studies conducted over a nine-year period, compost increased production of oats, potatoes, and rye an average of 11.4 percent as compared to plots given equal amounts of nutrients in the form of chemical fertilizers.[4]

Another advantage of spreading compost on land is that it avoids the consequences of high local concentrations of wastes. When too much material is put onto one spot, the material may produce odors, and the material and toxic substances within it may drain into the groundwater and streams, causing water pollution. Compost from municipal refuse and other organic matter may be spread and farmed at rates of tens to hundreds of tons per acre per year, depending on local soil and cropping conditions.

Although chemical fertilizers, landfills, and incineration are presently more economically attractive, each has long-term environmental costs. The production of fertilizers requires use of great quantities of energy (for example, the electrical energy required to power huge compressors which create high pressures used in combining nitrogen with hydrogen to produce ammonia, a nitrogen fertilizer), the supply of which is becoming more and more scarce. The constituents of the fertilizers are often not held in the soil, but instead drain into and pollute waterways. Nitrates in the fertilizers contaminate water and food and in some cases pose a threat to human health.[15] The sanitary landfill, on the other hand, poses the danger of poisonous materials seeping into groundwater. This threat is particularly serious in humid areas and those regions, such as marshlands, where a high water table exists.[3] Also, landfill areas are becoming increasingly scarce. Incineration creates air pollution; abatement measures (which will increase the costs of incineration) will not eliminate the emissions but only bring them within legal limits. In addition, both dumping the potentially useful materials into landfills and destroying the materials in incinerators constitute a waste of resources.

Examples of Existing and Proposed Programs

To explore aspects of successful U.S. composting operations, let us examine the operations of the two U.S. composting plants still in full-time operation—one in Altoona, Pennsylvania, the other in Brooklyn. The Altoona project is aided by a municipal ordinance which requires that citizens separate glass and metal from refuse before it is collected.

A digester installed by the Fairfield Engineering Co. of Marion, Ohio then processes the compostable waste material in about five days. The plant's capacity is approximately 25 tons per day.[13]

The Ecology, Inc. plant in Brooklyn has been in operation for about a year and presents the most encouraging example of composting in the U.S. The company, which has been partially financed by the Economic Development Administration, processes about 150 tons of municipal refuse per day and turns out its own Ecology Fertilizer, a lawn-care product that is fortified with nutrients.

The Ecology, Inc. process is distinguished from other composting processes by several factors that give it a competitive advantage. First, the company's digester can compost refuse with a paper content of up to 90 percent (most composting plants send paper to landfills since they cannot process it). Second, noncompostable materials do not have to be separated from compostables before beginning the successive stages of the composting process; only ferrous metals (removed after shredding—an early stage) do not go through the digester. Third, the digester permits control of all of the variables in the decomposition process and consequently enables the company to produce a compost with uniform composition and almost any desired characteristics.[13]

The Ecology, Inc. compost is fortified with nutrients, compacted, and either pelletized or granulated. Since the market for the high-grade compost is limited, the company is investigating the use of its compost for wallboard manufacture. Although Stephen Varro, Jr., a civil engineer and the company's president, is optimistic about Ecology, Inc.'s future capability of economically handling a significant portion of New York City's municipal wastes, the city's officials doubt that there will be sufficient markets for such large quantities of compost.[13]

An example of cooperation between federal and state agencies in a regional, though limited, composting project is provided by New York State. The Cooperative Extension Service of New York State, which includes Cornell University, the State University of New York, and the U.S. Department of Agriculture, has participated with municipalities in promoting the composting of municipally collected leaves and brush trimmings.[16] Leaves can no longer be burned in Rockland County, New York, because of air pollution restrictions. Two municipalities collect leaves

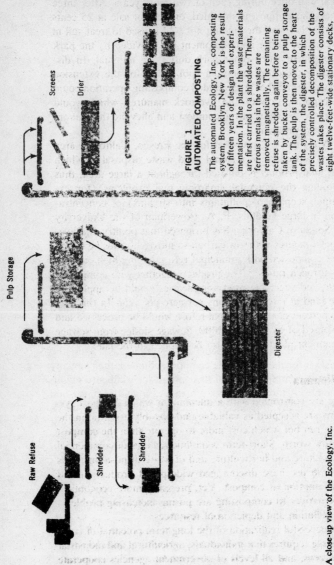

FIGURE 1
AUTOMATED COMPOSTING

The automated Ecology, Inc. composting system, Brooklyn, New York is the result of fifteen years of design and experimentation. In the plant the waste materials are first carried to a shredder. Then, ferrous metals in the wastes are removed magnetically. The remaining refuse is shredded again before being taken by bucket conveyor to a pulp storage tank. The pulp is then moved to the heart of the system, the digester, in which precisely controlled decomposition of the wastes takes place. The digester consists of eight twelve-feet-wide stationary decks, along which one-foot-deep layers of pulp are moved by chain-driven rakes. When tests indicate that the decomposition process is complete, the finished compost goes through screens, coolers, and driers. Finally, it is packaged for distribution.

Raw Refuse

Shredder

Shredder

Pulp Storage

Digester

Screens

Drier

A close-up view of the Ecology, Inc. compost fertilizer before bagging for distribution. Because the fertilizer is of uniform consistency (unlike the end-products of most other composting operations), it goes through fertilizer spreaders easily.

206

from the roadside on scheduled days, haul them to a composting site, pile them up, turn them twice during the first year and once during each of two more years. After three years the compost is shredded, offered for sale at 25 cents per bushel, and the amount not sold is used to treat soil in the parks. Labor and equipment are provided by the park department when other park duties are minimal. In discussing these operations, a spokesman for the extension service noted that an expanded composting operation could incorporate poultry and livestock manures, which would increase the value of the compost and alleviate the manure disposal problem.

A composting proposal for the Fresno, California area offers a method of regional solid waste disposal in which the final product is diffused throughout a large area, thus avoiding the potential environmental problems (for example, seepage of pollutants into streams) of concentration in large landfills. F. A. Bowerman of the University of Southern California has proposed that poultry and livestock manures with low carbon-to-nitrogen ratios be mixed and composted with municipal refuse having high carbon-to-nitrogen ratios.[17] The product, together with composted fruit and vegetable processing wastes would be applied to the land at rates of 75 tons per acre per year. In this way 20 percent of the municipal refuse would be processed and disposed of by the year 2000. Sewage sludge from sewage treatment plants would also be applied to the land.

Dilemma

We are confronted with a dilemma in which compost systems are accepted as valuable and possibly essential in the long run but which cost more to operate than the compost is now worth. Short-term economic realities of commercial agriculture and horticulture and of waste disposal methods now in use have discouraged widespread production and consumption of compost. Yet, presently more economical alternatives to composting are posing increasing problems of pollution and depletion of resources.

Successful realization of the long-term potential of composting requires that individuals, agricultural and industrial concerns, and all levels of government agencies cooperate in the production and utilization of compost. A model for effecting this cooperation exists in the U.S. Department of Agriculture's (USDA) Extension Service. A joint effort of

207

the federal Environmental Protection Agency and the USDA reaching to the county level, could be developed to ensure the recycling of organic wastes to the soil.

The lack of immediate financial return on composting is not a justification for withholding individual, municipal, state, or federal support. Just as health research programs that provide no initial return may later result in the saving of taxpayers' lives and dollars, support of compost production and utilization could, in the long run, prevent and reverse environmental damage wrought by presently economical soil-treatment and waste-disposal methods. □

NOTES

1. Waksman, Selman A., *Soil Microbiology*, John Wiley and Sons, Inc., New York, 1952, pp. 100-104.

2. *Ibid.*, pp. 144-146.

3. Carlson, Carl W., and J. D. Menzies, "Utilization of Urban Wastes in Crop Production," *BioScience*, 21(12):561, June 15, 1971.

4. *Ibid.*, p. 562.

5. Breidenbach, A. W., et al., "Composting of Municipal Solid Wastes in the United States," U.S. Environmental Protection Agency Publication, Washington, D.C., 1971.

6. Lagerwerff, S. V., "Heavy Metal Contamination of Soils," in *Agriculture and the Quality of the Environment*, N. C. Brady, ed., American Association for the Advancement of Science, 1967, pp. 343-364.

7. Hinesly, T. D., "Agricultural Benefits and Environmental Changes Resulting from the Use of Digested Sludge on Field Crops," Report to Metropolitan Sanitary District, Jan. 1970.

8. City of Los Angeles, Ordinances 142023 and 142186, May 6, 1971.

9. Hart, S. A., *Solid Waste Management/Composting, European Activity and Amercian Potential*, Public Health Service Publication No. 1826, U.S. Government Printing Office, Washington, D. C., 1968.

10. Kupchick, G. J., "Economics of Composting Municipal Refuse in Europe and Israel, with Special Reference to Possibilities in the U.S.A.," Bulletin of World Health Organization, 34:798-809, 1966.

11. Michaels, Abe, consulting sanitary engineer, New York, New York, personal communication.

12. For a description of the fundamentals of composting, see Gotaas, Harold B., *Composting, Sanitary Disposal and Reclamation of Organic Wastes*, World Health Organization, Geneva, Switzerland, 1956.

13. "Composting Municipal Solid Wastes," *Environmental Science and Technology*, 5(11):1090, Nov. 1971.

14. Smith, G. E., *Sanborn Field Bulletin 458*, University of Missouri, College of Agriculture, Agricultural Experiment Station, Columbia, Missouri, quoted in Commoner, Barry, "Nature Unbalanced. How Man Interferes with the Nitrogen Cycle," *Scientist and Citizen* [now *Environment*], Jan./Feb. 1968, p. 12.

15. Commoner, *ibid.*, pp. 12-17.

16. "The Disposal of Leaves, Brush, and Trees in Rockland County," Cooperative Extension Association of Rockland County, New York, New York, Oct. 3, 1967. Foss, E. W., *Considerations in Composting for Municipalities; A Progress Report*, Agricultural Engineering Extension Bulletin No. 378, Department of Agricultural Engineering, Cornell University, Ithaca, New York, June 1968.

17. Bowerman, F. A., *A System Study of Solid Waste Management in the Fresno Area*, Public Health Service Publication No. 1959, U.S. Government Printing Office, Washington, D. C., 1959.

Effect of Restricted Use of Phosphate-Based Detergents on Onondaga Lake

C. B. Murphy, Jr.

Abstract. *A marked decrease in the concentration of total inorganic phosphate in the epilimnion and hypolimnion of Onondaga Lake, New York State, has been observed during the 1½ years between July 1971 and January 1973. This decrease has been correlated to the implementation of phosphate-limiting legislation. The response of characteristic plankton species has been investigated.*

One of the tools available to environmental regulatory agencies in the control of cultural eutrophication is the establishment of composition limitations for waste-creating consumer products with high levels of nutrients. Detergents are the main consumer products contributing nutrients to aquatic environments. It has been estimated that 10^9 kg of phosphorus enters the nation's waters annually through the use of phosphate-based detergents; this accounts for 30 to 40 percent of the phosphorus entering the aquatic environment (1).

Sharp reductions in the concentration of condensed inorganic phosphorus have been observed in Onondaga Lake (north of Syracuse, New York) following the implementation of legislation limiting the percentage of phosphorus allowed in detergents. The legislation, which affects municipal discharges in the urban watershed influent to Onondaga Lake, was enacted both locally and by the state. The Common Council of the City of Syracuse first enacted legislation limiting the phosphate composition in detergents to 8.7 percent, effective on 1 July 1971. New York State, following the example of Syracuse (as well as Erie County, Suffolk County, and Bayville in other parts of the state), enacted similar legislation (2), effective on 1 January 1972. After each legislative implementation, reductions in condensed inorganic phosphorus in Onondaga Lake were observed (see Table 1).

A monitoring program for Onondaga Lake has been carried out since 1968 (3). Grab samples, collected every 2 weeks at 3-m intervals from the surface to the bottom at a station located in the southern basin, have shown decreases of 85 and 76 percent in the average condensed inorganic phosphate concentrations in the epilimnion and hypolimnion, respectively. The orthophosphate concentrations were found to decline by 47 and 15 percent, respectively, over the same period of time. The concentrations of condensed inorganic phosphate and orthophosphate from January 1970 to January 1973 are shown in Figs. 1 and 2.

Standard analytical procedures were used to determine the concentrations of total orthophosphate, total inorganic phosphate, and the derived value for total condensed inorganic phosphate (4). The determination of orthophosphate involved the formation of molybdophosphoric acid, which is subsequently reduced to the intensely colored molybdenum blue complex by stannous chloride. The concentration of molybdenum blue is determined by comparing

SCIENCE, October, 1973, Vol. 182, pp. 379-381.

210

the absorbance of the sample at 625 nm to that of prepared standards. For the determination of total inorganic phosphate the sample was digested with sulfuric acid in an autoclave for 30 minutes. The analysis of the resulting orthophosphate component was then conducted as outlined above. The analytical procedures were checked against standard samples and found to have a precision of approximately 2 percent and an accuracy within 5 percent. The same analyses were also periodically conducted by using the Technicon 94-70W method outlined for the AAII model. The method involves reduction of molybdophosphoric acid by ascorbic acid and subsequent spectrophotometric analysis. The analytical methods agreed within 5 percent.

Onondaga Lake is approximately 11.7 km^2 in area and has an approximate volume of 14×10^{10} liters and an average annual residence time for lake water of 122 days. Eight natural and man-made major tributaries discharge into the lake. Only the discharge from the Syracuse metropolitan sewage treatment plant showed a significant decrease in the load of condensed inorganic phosphorus. The concentration of total inorganic phosphate in the plant effluent declined from an average of 5.46 mg/liter in 1970 to 2.49 mg/liter in 1972. This decrease of 54.4 percent compares well with the 57.4 percent decline in the average total inorganic phosphate concentration in the lake over the same period. The other sources and sinks within Onondaga Lake were essentially the same before and after the legislation.

In the past 5 years, a characteristic seasonal succession of phytoplankton has been observed within the lake. There is little growth of plankton in the winter, when the lake is covered by ice;

a diatom population develops in the spring; and the green algae Chlorella, Scenedesmus obliquus, Scenedesmus quadricauda, and Oocystis parva dominate the summer period. Blue-green algae of the genus Aphanizomenon follow the die-off of the greens, and dominate the late summer and early fall.

In 1972, the first full growth season after the implementation of phosphate-limiting legislation, Aphanizomenon was absent in the succession. Instead, the green algae blooms continued through the summer and fall with cell counts comparable to those measured in previous years. The observed decline and subsequent elimination of blue-green algae when the concentration of condensed inorganic phosphate decreased 85 percent and the concentration of orthophosphate decreased 47 percent in the photic zone is consistent with results reported by Shapiro (5). Shapiro found that addition of CO_2 or lowering of the pH stimulates a shift in a mixed population from blue-green to green algae. He also indicated that the addition of nutrients resulted in dominance by blue-green algae. In Onondaga Lake, both the pH and the total inorganic carbon concentration were essentially unchanged after the phosphate-limiting legislation went into effect. In the photic zone the pH and total inorganic carbon were found to be 7.69 and 18.7 mg/liter, respectively. It therefore appears that the alteration of the phytoplankton seasonal succession is the result of reducing the phosphorus concentrations in the photic zone. Although there were climatological variations between 1970 and 1972, they do not seem to be of sufficient magnitude and intensity to account for the observed plankton variations.

It should be noted that the concentrations of inorganic and organic nitro-

Table 1. Change in the concentration of condensed inorganic phosphorus (P) in the epilimnion and hypolimnion of Onondaga Lake following the implementation of local and state legislation restricting phosphorus in detergents. The changes are from the baseline values, 0.73 and 0.81 mg/liter.

Period of observation	Dates	Epilimnion		Hypolimnion	
		P (mg/liter)	Change (%)	P (mg/liter)	Change (%)
Before legislation	1 January 1970 to 30 June 1971	0.73		0.81	
After urban legislation was implemented	1 July 1971 to 31 December 1971	0.22	− 69.8	0.58	− 28.4
After state legislation was implemented	1 January 1972 to 31 December 1972	0.11	− 84.9	0.19	− 76.5

gen, the total organic carbon, and the biochemical oxygen demand were essentially the same during the time period being evaluated.

An increase in the phytoplankton diversity index was also observed following the implementation of the detergent phosphate legislation. An increase in Margalef's (6) average diversity index from 0.695 to 0.801 most likely reflects a higher degree of stability within the phytoplankton community. This increase in the diversity of the phyto-

plankton community may indicate a general improvement in the trophic status of the lake. Most significant to the residents in the vicinity of the lake is the fact that the objectionable floating scums attendant with the presence of the blue-green algae might be eliminated from future plankton seasonal successions. This would also have the effect of increasing dissolved oxygen, which is removed from the epilimnion during aerobic decomposition of the nonviable algal mass. The green algae,

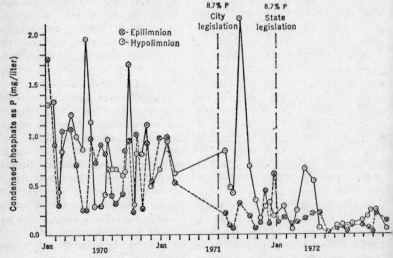

Fig. 1. Condensed inorganic phosphate concentration in Onondaga Lake.

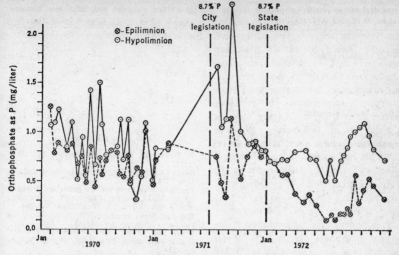

Fig. 2. Orthophosphate concentration in Onondaga Lake.

which are more acceptable ecologically because of their more direct linkage to the food chain, together with more uniform concentrations of dissolved oxygen may lead to the development of a more productive environment for higher aquatic organisms.

Caution must be taken in applying these results to other lakes, which may differ greatly from Onondaga Lake in water chemistry, chemical stratification, and stability of minerals (7). Onondaga Lake is dimictic in that it undergoes two periods of circulation per year; the major circulation occurs in the fall. Chemical contributions to the lake in the form of $CaCl_2$ and $NaCl$ from a soda ash manufacturer establish a density structure which impedes the rate of vertical mixing. Industrial and municipal point sources and natural nonpoint sources in the form of salt springs have established a steady-state concentration of chlorides of approximately 1750 mg/liter. Among lakes of its size in the East, Onondaga Lake has one of the highest concentrations of dissolved solids.

The high calcium concentrations are a major factor in the continuous formation of phosphate-bearing minerals such as hydroxylapatite $[Ca_5(PO_4)_3OH]$ and fluorapatite $[Ca_{10}(PO_4)_6F_2]$ throughout the lake. In addition, the lake is oversaturated with calcite ($CaCO_3$) throughout the year except during the middle and late winter when the pH falls below 7.

Since Onondaga Lake serves as a receptacle for an area that is almost entirely urban, there is little contribution of phosphorus from natural and agricultural sources. Preliminary estimates of the influent total inorganic phosphorus indicate that approximately 71 percent can be accounted for by municipal point-source discharges, 19 percent by municipal nonpoint sources (combined sewer overflows), 1 to 2 percent by industrial sources, and 8 to 9 percent by agricultural and natural sources (8). Natural sources have been

213

reported to account for 26 to 41 percent of the phosphorus discharged to the receiving water bodies in the continental United States. It has been predicted that elimination of phosphates from detergents might result in the reduction of the average total phosphorus concentrations in receiving waters from 0.26 to 0.18 mg/liter for a reduction of 37.7 percent (9). The legislation limiting phosphates in detergents has had a much more pronounced effect on Onondaga Lake, reducing the average concentration of total inorganic phosphorus from 1.74 to 0.74 mg/liter—a net change of 57.4 percent.

It is evident that the limitation of detergent phosphate composition to 8.7 percent phosphorus by weight has had a discernible effect on the chemical and biological composition of the lake. Perhaps, therefore, a harder look should be given to the use of this type of legislation by State and Federal regulatory agencies in the control of cultural eutrophication. Due to present domestic fiscal policy limitations, legislation of

this nature may be one of the effective methods of controlling eutrophication in the immediate future.

References and Notes

1. R. D. Grundy, *Environ. Sci. Technol.* **5**, 1184 (1971).
2. New York State Legislature, Laws of 1971, chap. 716.
3. The monitoring program was conducted jointly by Onondaga County Department of Public Works and O'Brien & Gere Engineers, Inc., Syracuse, New York.
4. *Standard Methods for the Examination of Water and Waste Water* (American Public Health Association, New York, ed. 12, 1965), pp. 234–237.
5. J. Shapiro, *Science* **179**, 382 (1973).
6. R. Margalef, *Perspectives in Ecological Theory* (Univ. of Chicago Press, Chicago, 1968), p. 111.
7. "Onondaga Lake study," report to the Water Quality Office of the Environmental Protection Agency, on EPA Project 11060 FAE (April 1971).
8. C. B. Murphy, unpublished results.
9. F. A. Ferguson, *Environ. Sci. Technol.* **2**, 188 (1968).

23 March 1973; revised 18 June 1973

Effects of Pollution on the Structure and Physiology of Ecosystems

Changes in natural ecosystems caused by many different types of disturbances are similar and predictable.

G. M. Woodwell

The accumulation of various toxic substances in the biosphere is leading to complex changes in the structure and function of natural ecosystems. Although the changes are complex, they follow in aggregate patterns that are similar in many different ecosystems and are therefore broadly predictable. The patterns involve many changes but include especially simplification of the structure of both plant and animal communities, shifts in the ratio of gross production to total resiration, and loss of part or all of the inventory of nutrients. Despite the frequency with which various pollutants are causing such changes and the significance of the changes for all living systems (1), only a few studies show details of the pattern of change clearly. These are studies of the effects of ionizing radiation, of persistent pesticides, and of eutrophication. The effects of radiation will be used here to show the pattern of changes in terrestrial plant communities and to show similarities with the effects of fire, oxides of sulfur, and herbicides. Effects of such pollutants as pesticides in the animal community are less conspicuous but quite parallel, which shows that the ecological effects of pollution correspond very closely to the general

"strategy of ecosystem development" outlined by Odum (1) and that they can be anticipated in considerable detail.

The problems caused by pollution are of interest from two viewpoints. Practical people—toxicologists, engineers, health physicists, public health officials, intensive users of the environment—consider pollution primarily as a direct hazard to man. Others, no less concerned for human welfare but with less pressing public responsibilities, recognize that toxicity to humans is but one aspect of the pollution problem, the other being a threat to the maintenance of a biosphere suitable for life as we know it. The first viewpoint leads to emphasis on human food chains; the second leads to emphasis on human welfare insofar as it depends on the integrity of the diverse ecosystems of the earth, the living systems that appear to have built and now maintain the biosphere.

The food-chain problem is by far the simpler; it is amenable at least in part to the pragmatic, narrowly compartmentalized solutions that industrialized societies are good at. The best example of the toxicological approach is in control of mutagens, particularly the radionuclides. These present a specific, direct hazard to man. They are

SCIENCE, April, 1970, Vol. 168, pp. 429-433.

215

much more important to man than to other organisms. A slightly enhanced rate of mutation is a serious danger to man, who has developed through medical science elaborate ways of preserving a high fraction of the genetic defects in the population; it is trivial to the rest of the biota, in which genetic defects may be eliminated through selection. This is an important fact about pollution hazards—toxic substances that are principally mutagenic are usually of far greater direct hazard to man than to the rest of the earth's biota and must be considered first from the standpoint of their movement to man through food webs or other mechanisms and to a much lesser extent from that of their effects on the ecosystem through which they move. We have erred, as shown below, in assuming that all toxic substances should be treated this way.

Pollutants that affect other components of the earth's biota as well as man present a far greater problem. Their effects are chronic and may be cumulative in contrast to the effects of short-lived disturbances that are repaired by succession. We ask what effects such pollutants have on the structure of natural ecosystems and on biological diversity and what these changes mean to physiology, especially to mineral cycling and the long-term potential for sustaining life.

Although experience with pollution of various types is extensive and growing rapidly, only a limited number of detailed case history studies provide convincing control data that deal with the structure of ecosystems. One of the clearest and most detailed series of experiments in recent years has been focused on the ecological effects of radiation. These studies are especially useful because they allow cause and effect to be related quantitatively at the ecosystem level, which is difficult to do in nature. The question arises, however, whether the results from studies of ionizing radiation, a factor that is not usually considered to have played an important role in recent evolution, have any general application. The answer, somewhat surprisingly to many biologists, seems to be that they do. The ecological effects of radiation follow patterns that are known from other types of disturbances. The studies of radiation, because of their specificity provide useful clues for examination of effects of other types of pollution for which evidence is much more fragmentary.

The effects of chronic irradiation of a late successional oak-pine forest have been studied at Brookhaven National Laboratory in New York. After months' exposure to chronic irradiation from a ^{137}Cs source, five well-defined zones of modification of vegetation had been established. They have become more pronounced through years of chronic irradiation (Fig. 1). The zones were:

1) A central devastated zone, where exposures were > 200 R/day and higher plants survived, although certain mosses and lichens survived up to exposures > 1000 R/day.

2) A sedge zone, where Carex pensylvanica (2) survived and ultimately formed a continuous cover (> 1 R/day).

3) A shrub zone in which two species of Vaccinium and one Gaylussacia survived, with Quercus ilicifolia toward the outer limit of the circle where exposures were lowest (40 R/day).

4) An oak zone, the pine having been eliminated (> 16 R/day).

5) Oak-pine forest, where exposures were < 2 R/day, and there was no obvious change in the number of species

although small changes in rates of growth were measurable at exposures as low as 1 R/day.

The effect was a systematic dissection of the forest, strata being removed layer by layer. Trees were eliminated at low exposures, then the taller shrubs (*Gaylussacia baccata*), then the lower shrubs (*Vaccinium* species), then the herbs, and finally the lichens and mosses. Within these groups, it was evident that under irradiation an upright form of growth was a disadvantage. The trees did vary—the pines (*Pinus rigida*) for instance were far more sensitive than the oaks without having a conspicuous tendency toward more upright growth, but all the trees were substantially more sensitive than the shrubs (*3*). Within the shrub zone, tall forms were more sensitive; even within the lichen populations, foliose and fruticose lichens proved more sensitive than crustose lichens (*4*).

The changes caused by chronic irradiation of herb communities in old fields show the same pattern—upright species are at a disadvantage. In one old field at Brookhaven, the frequency of low-growing plants increased along the gradient of increasing radiation intensity to 100 percent at > 1000 R/day (*5*). Comparison of the sensitivity of the herb field with that of the forest, by whatever criterion, clearly shows the field to be more resistant than the forest. The exposure reducing diversity to 50 percent in the first year was ∼ 1000 R/day for the field and 160 R/day for the forest, a greater than fivefold difference in sensitivity (*3*).

The changes in these ecosystems under chronic irradiation are best summarized as changes in structure, although diversity, primary production, total respiration, and nutrient inventory are also involved. The changes are similar to the familiar ones along natural gradients of increasingly severe conditions, such as exposure on mountains, salt spray, and water availability. Along all these gradients the conspicuous change is a reduction of structure from forest toward communities dominated by certain shrubs, then, under more severe conditions, by certain herbs, and finally by low-growing plants, frequently mosses and lichens. Succession, insofar as it has played any role at all in the irradiated ecosystems, has simply reinforced this pattern, adding a very few hardy species and allowing expansion of the populations of more resistant indigenous species. The reasons for radiation's causing this pattern are still not clear (*3, 6*), but the pattern is a common one, not peculiar to ionizing radiation, despite the novelty of radiation exposures as high as these.

Its commonness is illustrated by the response to fire, one of the oldest and most important disruptions of nature. The oak-pine forests such as those on Long Island have, throughout their extensive range in eastern North America, been subject in recent times to repeated burning. The changes in physiognomy of the vegetation follow the above pattern very closely—the forest is replaced by communities of shrubs, especially bear oak (*Quercus ilicifolia*), *Gaylussacia*, and *Vaccinium* species. This change is equivalent to that caused by chronic exposure to 40 R/day or more. Buell and Cantlon (*7*), working on similar vegetation in New Jersey, showed that a further increase in the frequency of fires resulted in a differential reduction in taller shrubs first, and a substantial increase in the abundance of *Carex pensylvanica*, the same sedge now dominating the sedge zone of the irradiated forest. The parallel is detailed; radiation and repeated fires both reduce the structure of the forest in similar ways, favoring low-growing hardy species.

The similarity of response appears to extend to other vegetations as well. G. L. Miller, working with F. McCormick at the Savannah River Laboratory, has shown recently that the most radiation-resistant and fire-resistant species of 20-year-old fields are annuals and perennials characteristic of disturbed places (8). An interesting sidelight of his study was the observation that the grass stage of long leaf pine (*Pinus palustris*), long considered a specific adaptation to the fires that maintain the southeastern savannahs, appears more resistant to radiation damage than the mature trees. At a total acute exposure of 2.1 kR (3 R/day), 85 percent of the grass-stage populations survived but only 55 percent of larger trees survived. Seasonal variation in sensitivity to radiation damage has been abundantly demonstrated (9), and it would not be surprising to find that this variation is related to the ecology of the species. Again it appears that the response to radiation is not unique.

The species surviving high radiation-exposure rates in the Brookhaven experiments are the ones commonly found in disturbed places, such as roadsides, gravel banks, and areas with nutrient-deficient or unstable soil. In the forest they include *Comptonia peregrina* (the sweet fern), a decumbent spiny *Rubus*, and the lichens, especially *Cladonia cristatella*. In the old field one of the most conspicuously resistant species was *Digitaria sanguinalis* (crabgrass) among several other weedy species. Clearly these species are generalists in the sense that they survive a wide range of conditions, including exposure to high intensities of ionizing radiation—hardly a common experience in nature but apparently one that elicits a common response.

With this background one might predict that a similar pattern of devastation would result from such pollutants as oxides of sulfur released from smelting. The evidence is fragmentary, but Gorham and Gordon (10) found around the smelters in Sudbury, Ontario, a striking reduction in the number of species of higher plants along a gradient of 62 kilometers (39 miles). In different samples the number of species ranged from 19 to 31 at the more distant sites and dropped abruptly at 6.4 kilometers. At 1.6 kilometers, one of two randomly placed plots (20 by 2 meters) included only one species. They classified the damage in five categories, from "Not obvious" through "Moderate" to "Very severe." The tree canopy had been reduced or eliminated within 4.8 to 6.4 kilometers of the smelter, with only occasional sprouts of trees, seedlings, and successional herbs and shrubs remaining; this damage is equivalent to that produced by exposure to 40 R/day. The most resistant trees were, almost predictably to a botanist, red maple (*Acer rubrum*) and red oak (*Quercus rubra*). Other species surviving in the zones of "Severe" and "Very severe" damage included *Sambucus pubens*, *Polygonum cilinode*, *Comptonia peregrina*, and *Epilobium angustifolium* (fire weed). The most sensitive plants appeared to be *Pinus strobus* and *Vaccinium myrtilloides*. The pine was reported no closer than 25.6 kilometers (16 miles), where it was chlorotic.

This example confirms the pattern of the change—first a reduction of diversity of the forest by elimination of sensitive species; then elimination of the tree canopy and survival of resistant shrubs and herbs widely recognized

218

as "seral" or successional species or "generalists."

The effects of herbicides, despite their hoped for specificity, fall into the same pattern, and it is no surprise that the extremely diverse forest canopies of Viet Nam when sprayed repeatedly with herbicides are replaced over large areas by dense stands of species of bamboo (11).

The mechanisms involved in producing this series of patterns in terrestrial ecosystems are not entirely clear. One mechanism that is almost certainly important is simply the ratio of gross production to respiration in different strata of the community. The size of trees has been shown to approach a limit set by the amount of surface area of stems and branches in proportion to the amount of leaf area (12). The apparent reason is that, as a tree expands in size, the fraction of its total surface devoted to bark, which makes a major contribution to the respiration, expands more rapidly than does the photosynthetic area. Any chronic disturbance has a high probability of damaging the capacity for photosynthesis without reducing appreciably the total amount of respiration; therefore, large plants are more vulnerable than species requiring less total respiration. Thus chronic disturbances of widely different types favor plants that are small in stature, and any disturbance that tends to increase the amount of respiration in proportion to photosynthesis will aggravate this shift.

The shift in the structure of terrestrial plant communities toward shrubs, herbs, or mosses and lichens, involves changes in addition to those of structure and diversity. Simplification of the plant community involves also a reduction of the total standing crop of or-

ganic matter and a corresponding reduction in the total inventory of nutrient elements held within the system, a change that may have important long-term implications for the potential of the site to support life. The extent of such losses has been demonstrated recently by Bormann and his colleagues in the Hubbard Brook Forest in New Hampshire (13), where all of the trees in a watershed were cut, the cut material was left to decay, and the losses of nutrients were monitored in the runoff. Total nitrogen losses in the first year were equivalent to twice the amount cycled in the system during a normal year. With the rise of nitrate ion in the runoff, concentrations of calcium, magnesium, sodium, and potassium ions rose severalfold, which caused eutrophication and even pollution of the streams fed by this watershed. The soil had little capacity to retain the nutrients that were locked in the biota once the higher plants had been killed. The total losses are not yet known, but early evidence indicates that they will be a high fraction of the nutrient inventory, which will cause a large reduction in the potential of the site for supporting living systems as complex as that destroyed—until nutrients accumulate again. Sources are limited: the principal source is erosion of primary minerals.

When the extent of the loss of nutrients that accompanies a reduction in the structure of a plant community is recognized, it is not surprising to find depauperate vegetation in places subject to chronic disturbances. Extensive sections of central Long Island, for example, support a depauperate oak-pine forest in which the bear oak, *Quercus ilicifolia*, is the principal woody species. The cation content of an extremely dense stand of this common community, which has a biomass equivalent to that of the more diverse late successional forest that was burned much less recently and less intensively, would be about 60 percent that of the richer stand, despite the equivalence of standing crop. This means that the species, especially the bear oak, contain, and presumably require, lower concentrations of cations. This is an especially good example because the bear oak community is a long-lasting one in the fire succession and marks the transition from a high shrub community to forest. It has analogies elsewhere, such as the heath balds of the Great Smoky Mountains and certain bamboo thickets in Southeast Asia.

The potential of a site for supporting life depends heavily on the pool of nutrients available through breakdown of primary minerals and through recycling in the living portion of the ecosystem. Reduction of the structure of the system drains these pools in whole or in part; it puts leaks in the system. Any chronic pollution that affects the structure of ecosystems, especially the plant community, starts leaks and reduces the potential of the site for recovery. Reduction of the structure of forests in Southeast Asia by herbicides has dumped the nutrient pools of these large statured and extremely diverse forests. The nutrients are carried to the streams, which turn green with the algae that the nutrients support. Tschirley (11), reporting his study of the effects of herbicides in Viet Nam, recorded "surprise" and "pleasure" that fishing had improved in treated areas. If the herbicides are not toxic to fish, there should be little surprise at improved catches of certain kinds of fish in heavily enriched waters adjacent to herbicide-treated forests. The bamboo thickets that replace the forests also reflect the drastically lowered potential

of these sites to support living systems. The time it takes to reestablish a forest with the original diversity depends on the availability of nutrients, and is probably very long in most lateritic soils.

In generalizing about pollution, I have concentrated on some of the grossest changes in the plant communities of terrestrial ecosystems. The emphasis on plants is appropriate because plants dominate terrestrial ecosystems. But not all pollutants affect plants directly; some have their principal effects on heterotrophs. What changes in the structure of animal communities are caused by such broadly toxic materials as most pesticides?

The general pattern of loss of structure is quite similar, although the structure of the animal communities is more difficult to chart. The transfer of energy appears to be one good criterion of structure. Various studies suggest that 10 to 20 percent of the energy entering the plant community is transferred directly to the animal community through herbivores (14). Much of that energy, perhaps 50 percent or more, is used in respiration to support the herbivore population; some is transferred to the detritus food chain directly, and some, probably not more than 20 percent, is transferred to predators of the herbivores. In an evolutionarily and successionally mature community, this transfer of 10 to 20 percent per trophic level may occur two or three times to support carnivores, some highly specialized, such as certain eagles, hawks, and herons, others less specialized, such as gulls, ravens, rats, and people.

Changes in the plant community, such as its size, rate of energy fixation, and species, will affect the structure of the animal community as well. Introduction of a toxin specific for animals, such as a pesticide that is a generalized nerve toxin, will also topple the pyramid. Although the persistent pesticides are fat soluble and tend to accumulate in carnivores and reduce populations at the tops of food chains, they affect every trophic level, reducing reproductive capacity, almost certainly altering behavioral patterns, and disrupting the competitive relationships between species. Under these circumstances the highly specialized species, the obligate carnivores high in the trophic structure, are at a disadvantage because the food chain concentrates the toxin and, what is even more important, because the entire structure beneath them becomes unstable. Again the generalists or broad-niched species are favored, the gulls, rats, ravens, pigeons and, in a very narrow short-term sense, man. Thus, the pesticides favor the herbivores, the very organisms they were invented to control.

Biological evolution has divided the resources of any site among a large variety of users—species—which, taken together, confer on that site the properties of a closely integrated system capable of conserving a diversity of life. The system has structure; its populations exist with certain definable, quantitative relationships to one another; it fixes energy and releases it at a measurable rate; and it contains an inventory of nutrients that is accumulated and recirculated, not lost. The system is far from static; it is subject, on a time scale very long compared with a human lifespan, to a continuing augmentive change through evolution; on a shorter time scale, it is subject to succession toward a more stable state after any disturbance. The successional patterns are themselves a product of the evolution of life, providing for systematic recovery from any acute disturbance. Without a detailed discussion of the theory of ecology, one can say that biological evolution, following a pattern approximating that outlined above, has built the earth's ecosystems, and that these systems have been the dominant influence on the earth throughout the span of human existence. The structure of these systems is now being changed all over the world. We know enough about the structure and function of these systems to predict the broad outline of the effects of pollution on both land and water. We know that as far as our interests in the next decades are concerned, pollution operates on the time scale of succession, not of evolution, and we cannot look to evolution to cure this set of problems. The loss of structure involves a shift away from complex arrangements of specialized species toward the generalists; away from forest, toward hardy shrubs and herbs; away from those phytoplankton of the open ocean that Wurster (15) proved so very sensitive to DDT, toward those algae of the sewage plants that are unaffected by almost everything including DDT and most fish; away from diversity in birds, plants, and fish toward monotony; away from tight nutrient cycles toward very loose ones with terrestrial systems becoming depleted, and with aquatic systems becoming overloaded; away from stability toward instability especially with regard to sizes of populations of small, rapidly reproducing organisms such as insects and rodents that compete with man; away from a world that runs itself through a self-augmentive, slowly moving evolution, to one that requires constant tinkering to patch it up, a tinkering that is malignant in that each act of repair generates a need for further repairs to avert problems generated at compound interest.

This is the pattern, predictable in broad outline, aggravated by almost any pollutant. Once we recognize the pattern, we can begin to see the mean-

Fig. 1. The effects of chronic gamma radiation from a 9500-curie ^{137}Cs source on a Long Island oak-pine forest nearly 8 years after start of chronic irradiation. The pattern of change in the structure of the forest is similar to that observed along many other gradients, including gradients of moisture availability and of exposure to wind, salt spray, and pollutants such as sulfur dioxide. The five zones are explained in the text. The few successional species that have invaded the zones closest to the source appear most conspicuously as a ring at the inner edge of zone 2. These are species characteristic of disturbed areas such as the fire weed, *Erechtites hieracifolia,* and the sweet fern, *Comptonia peregrina,* among several others. [The successional changes over 7 years are shown by comparison with a similar photograph that appeared as a cover of *Science (16)*].

ing of some of the changes occurring now in the earth's biota. We can see the demise of carnivorous birds and predict the demise of important fisheries. We can tell why, around industrial cities, hills that were once forested now are not; why each single species is important; and how the increase in the temperature of natural water bodies used to cool new reactors will, by augmenting respiration over photosynthesis, ultimately degrade the system and contribute to degradation of other interconnected ecosystems nearby. We can begin to speculate on where continued, exponential progress in this direction will lead: probably not to extinction—man will be around for a long time yet—but to a general degradation of the quality of life.

The solution? Fewer people, unpopular but increasing restrictions on technology (making it more and more expensive), and a concerted effort to tighten up human ecosystems to reduce their interactions with the rest of the earth on whose stability we all depend. This does not require foregoing nuclear energy; it requires that if we must dump heat, it should be dumped into civilization to enhance a respiration rate in a sewage plant or an agricultural ecosystem, not dumped outside of civilization to affect that fraction of the earth's biota that sustains the earth as we know it. The question of what fraction that might be remains as one of the great issues, still scarcely considered by the scientific community.

References and Notes

1. E. P. Odum, *Science* **164**, 262 (1969).
2. Plant nomenclature follows that of M. L. Fernald in *Gray's Manual of Botany* (American Book, New York, ed. 8, 1950).
3. G. M. Woodwell, *Science* **156**, 461 (1967); ——— and A. L. Rebuck, *Ecol. Monogr.* **37**, 53 (1967).
4. G. M. Woodwell and T. P. Gannutz, *Amer. J. Bot.* **54**, 1210 (1967).
5. ——— and J. K. Oosting, *Radiat. Bot.* **5**, 205 (1965).
6. ——— and R. H. Whittaker, *Quart. Rev. Biol.* **43**, 42 (1968).
7. M. F. Buell and J. E. Cantlon, *Ecology* **34**, 520 (1953).
8. G. L. Miller, thesis, Univ. of North Carolina (1968).
9. A. H. Sparrow, L. A. Schairer, R. C. Sparrow, W. F. Campbell, *Radiat. Bot.* **3**, 169 (1963); F. G. Taylor, Jr., *ibid.* **6**, 307 (1965).
10. E. Gorham and A. G. Gordon, *Can. J. Bot.* **38**, 307 (1960); *ibid.*, p. 477; *ibid.* **41**, 371 (1963).
11. F. H. Tschirley, *Science* **163**, 779 (1969).
12. R. H. Whittaker and G. M. Woodwell, *Amer. J. Bot.* **54**, 931 (1967).
13. F. H. Bormann, G. E. Likens, D. W. Fisher, R. S. Pierce, *Science* **159**, 882 (1968).
14. These relationships have been summarized in detail by J. Phillipson [*Ecological Energetics* (St. Martin's Press, New York, 1966)]. See also L. B. Slobodkin, *Growth and Regulation of Animal Populations* (Holt, Rinehart and Winston, New York, 1961) and J. H. Ryther, *Science* **166**, 72 (1969).
15. C. F. Wurster, *Science* **159**, 1474 (1968).
16. G. M. Woodwell, *ibid.* **138**, 572 (1962).
17. Research carried out at Brookhaven National Laboratory under the auspices of the U.S. Atomic Energy Commission. Paper delivered at 11th International Botanical Congress, Seattle, Wash., on 26 August 1969 in the symposium "Ecological and Evolutionary Implications of Environmental Pollution."

The Strategy of Ecosystem Development

An understanding of ecological succession provides
a basis for resolving man's conflict with nature.

Eugene P. Odum

The principles of ecological succession bear importantly on the relationships between man and nature. The framework of successional theory needs to be examined as a basis for resolving man's present environmental crisis. Most ideas pertaining to the development of ecological systems are based on descriptive data obtained by observing changes in biotic communities over long periods, or on highly theoretical assumptions; very few of the generally accepted hypotheses have been tested experimentally. Some of the confusion, vagueness, and lack of experimental work in this area stems from the tendency of ecologists to regard "succession" as a single straightforward idea; in actual fact, it entails an interacting complex of processes, some of which counteract one another.

As viewed here, ecological succession involves the development of ecosystems; it has many parallels in the developmental biology of organisms, and also in the development of human society. The ecosystem, or ecological system, is considered to be a unit of biological organization made up of all of the organisms in a given area (that is, "community") interacting with the physical environment so that a flow of energy leads to characteristic trophic structure and material cycles within the system. It is the purpose of this article to summarize, in the form of a tabular model, components and stages of development at the ecosystem level as a means of emphasizing those aspects of ecological succession that can be accepted on the basis of present knowledge, those that require more study, and those that have special relevance to human ecology.

Definition of Succession

Ecological succession may be defined in terms of the following three parameters (1). (i) It is an orderly process of community development that is reasonably directional and, therefore, predictable. (ii) It results from modification of the physical environment by the community; that is, succession is community-controlled even though the physical environment determines the pattern, the rate of change, and often sets limits as to how far development can go. (iii) It culminates in a stabilized ecosystem

SCIENCE, April, 1969, Vol. 164, pp. 262-270.

in which maximum biomass (or high information content) and symbiotic function between organisms are maintained per unit of available energy flow. In a word, the "strategy" of succession as a short-term process is basically the same as the "strategy" of long-term evolutionary development of the biosphere—namely, increased control of, or homeostasis with, the physical environment in the sense of achieving maximum protection from its perturbations. As I illustrate below, the strategy of "maximum protection" (that is, trying to achieve maximum support of complex biomass structure) often conflicts with man's goal of "maximum production" (trying to obtain the highest possible yield). Recognition of the ecological basis for this conflict is, I believe, a first step in establishing rational land-use policies.

The earlier descriptive studies of succession on sand dunes, grasslands, forests, marine shores, or other sites, and more recent functional considerations, have led to the basic theory contained in the definition given above. H. T. Odum and Pinkerton (2), building on Lotka's (3) "law of maximum energy in biological systems," were the first to point out that succession involves a fundamental shift in energy flows as increasing energy is relegated to maintenance. Margalef (4) has recently documented this bioenergetic basis for succession and has extended the concept.

Changes that occur in major structural and functional characteristics of a developing ecosystem are listed in Table 1. Twenty-four attributes of ecological systems are grouped, for convenience of discussion, under six headings. Trends are emphasized by contrasting the situation in early and late development. The degree of absolute change, the rate of change, and the time required to reach

a steady state may vary not only with different climatic and physiographic situations but also with different ecosystem attributes in the same physical environment. Where good data are available, rate-of-change curves are usually convex, with changes occurring most rapidly at the beginning, but bimodal or cyclic patterns may also occur.

Bioenergetics of Ecosystem Development

Attributes 1 through 5 in Table 1 represent the bioenergetics of the ecosystem. In the early stages of ecological succession, or in "young nature," so to speak, the rate of primary production or total (gross) photosynthesis (P) exceeds the rate of community respiration (R), so that the P/R ratio is greater than 1. In the special case of organic pollution, the P/R ratio is typically less than 1. In both cases, however, the theory is that P/R approaches 1 as succession occurs. In other words, energy fixed tends to be balanced by the energy cost of maintenance (that is, total community respiration) in the mature or "climax" ecosystem. The P/R ratio, therefore, should be an excellent functional index of the relative maturity of the system.

So long as P exceeds R, organic matter and biomass (B) will accumulate in the system (Table 1, item 6), with the result that ratio P/B will tend to decrease or, conversely, the B/P, B/R, or B/E ratios (where $E = P + R$) will increase (Table 1, items 2 and 3). Theoretically, then, the amount of standing-crop biomass supported by the available energy flow (E) increases to a maximum in the mature or climax stages (Table 1, item 3). As a consequence, the net community production, or yield, in an annual cycle is large in young nature and small or zero in mature nature (Table 1, item 4).

Comparison of Succession in a Laboratory Microcosm and a Forest

One can readily observe bioenergetic changes by initiating succession in experimental laboratory microecosystems. Aquatic microecosystems, derived from various types of outdoor systems, such as ponds, have been cultured by Beyers (5), and certain of these mixed cultures are easily replicated and maintain themselves in the climax state indefinitely on defined media in a flask with only light input (6). If samples from the climax system are inoculated into fresh media, succession occurs, the mature system developing in less than 100 days. In Fig. 1 the general pattern of a 100-day autotrophic succession in a microcosm based on data of Cooke (7) is compared with a hypothetical model of a 100-year forest succession as presented by Kira and Shidei (8).

During the first 40 to 60 days in a typical microcosm experiment, daytime net production (P) exceeds nighttime respiration (R), so that biomass (B) accumulates in the system (9). After an early "bloom" at about 30 days, both rates decline, and they become approximately equal at 60 to 80 days. the B/P ratio, in terms of grams of carbon supported per gram of daily carbon production, increases from less than 20 to more than 100 as the steady state is reached. Not only are autotrophic and heterotrophic metabolism balanced in the climax, but a large organic structure is supported by small daily production and respiratory rates.

While direct projection from the small laboratory microecosystem to open nature may not be entirely valid, there is evidence that the same basic trends that are seen in the laboratory are characteristic of succession on land and in large bodies of water. Seasonal successions also often follow the same pattern, an early seasonal bloom characterized by rapid growth of a few dominant species being followed by the development later in the season of high B/P ratios, increased diversity, and a relatively steady, if temporary, state in terms of P and R (4). Open systems may not experience a decline, at maturity, in total or gross productivity, as the space-limited microcosms do, but the general pattern of bioenergetic change in the latter seems to mimic nature quite well.

These trends are not, as might at first seem to be the case, contrary to the classical limnological teaching which describes lakes as progressing in time from the less productive (oligotrophic) to the more productive (eutrophic) state. Table 1, as already emphasized, refers to changes which are brought about by biological processes *within* the ecosystem in question. Eutrophication, whether natural or cultural, results when nutrients are imported into the lake from *outside* the lake—that is, from the watershed. This is equivalent to adding nutrients to the laboratory microecosystem or fertilizing a field; the system is pushed back, in successional terms, to a younger or "bloom" state. Recent studies on lake sediments (10), as well as theoretical considerations (11), have indicated that lakes can and do progress to a more oligotrophic condition when the nutrient input from the watershed slows or ceases. Thus, there is hope that the troublesome cultural eutrophication of our waters can be reversed if the inflow of nutrients from the watershed can be greatly reduced. Most of all, however, this situation emphasizes that

226

it is the entire drainage or catchment basin, not just the lake or stream, that must be considered the ecosystem unit if we are to deal successfully with our water pollution problems. Ecosystematic study of entire landscape catchment units is a major goal of the American plan for the proposed International Biological Program. Despite the obvious logic of such a proposal, it is proving surprisingly difficult to get tradition-bound scientists and granting agencies to look beyond their specialties toward the support of functional studies of large units of the landscape.

Food Chains and Food Webs

As the ecosystem develops, subtle changes in the network pattern of food chains may be expected. The manner in which organisms are linked together through food tends to be relatively simple and linear in the very early stages of succession, as a consequence of low diversity. Furthermore, heterotrophic utilization of net production occurs predominantly by way of grazing food chains—that is, plant-herbivore-carnivore sequences. In contrast, food chains become complex webs in mature stages, with the bulk of biological energy flow following detritus pathways (Table 1, item 5). In a mature forest, for example, less than 10 percent of annual net production is consumed (that is, grazed) in the living state (12); most is utilized as dead matter (detritus) through delayed and complex pathways involving as yet little understood animal-microorganism interactions. The time involved in an uninterrupted succession allows for increasingly intimate associations and reciprocal adaptations between plants and animals, which lead to the development of many mechanisms that reduce grazing—such as the develop-ment of indigestible supporting tissues (cellulose, lignin, and so on), feedback control between plants and herbivores (13), and increasing predatory pressure on herbivores (14). Such mechanisms enable the biological community to maintain the large and complex organic structure that mitigates perturbations of the physical environment. Severe stress or rapid changes brought about by out-side forces can, of course, rob the system of these protective mechanisms and allow irruptive, cancerous growths of certain species to occur, as man too often finds to his sorrow. An example of a stress-induced pest irruption occurred at Brookhaven National Laboratory, where oaks became vulnerable to aphids when translocation of sugars and amino acids was impaired by continuing gamma irradiation (15).

Radionuclide tracers are providing a means of charting food chains in the intact outdoor ecosystem to a degree that will permit analysis within the concepts of network or matrix algebra. For example, we have recently been able to map, by use of a radiophosphorus tracer, the open, relatively linear food linkage between plants and insects in an early old-field successional stage (16).

Diversity and Succession

Perhaps the most controversial of the successional trends pertain to the complex and much discussed subject of diversity (17). It is important to distinguish between different kinds of diversity indices, since they may not follow parallel trends in the same gradient or developmental series. Four components of diversity are listed in Table 1, items 8 through 11.

The variety of species, expressed as a species-number ratio or a species-area ratio, tends to increase during the

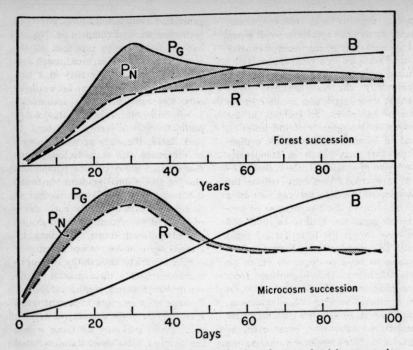

Fig. 1. Comparison of the energetics of succession in a forest and a laboratory microcosm. P_G, gross production; P_N, net production; R, total community respiration; B, total biomass.

early stages of community development. A second component of species diversity is what has been called equitability, or evenness (18), in the apportionment of individuals among the species. For example, two systems each containing 10 species and 100 individuals have the same diversity in terms of species-number ratio but could have widely different equitabilities depending on the apportionment of the 100 individuals among the 10 species—for example, 91-1-1-1-1-1-1-1-1-1 at one extreme or 10 individuals per species at the other. The Shannon formula,

$$- \Sigma \frac{ni}{N} \log_2 \frac{ni}{N}$$

where ni is the number of individuals

in each species and N is the total number of individuals, is widely used as a diversity index because it combines the variety and equitability components in one approximation. But, like all such lumping parameters, Shannon's formula may obscure the behavior of these two rather different aspects of diversity. For example, in our most recent field experiments, an acute stress from insecticide reduced the number of species of insects relative to the number of individuals but increased the evenness in the relative abundances of the surviving species (19). Thus, in this case the "variety" and "evenness" components would tend to cancel each other in Shannon's formula.

While an increase in the variety of

species together with reduced dominance by any one species or small group of species (that is, increased evenness) can be accepted as a general probability during succession (20), there are other community changes that may work against these trends. An increase in the size of organisms, an increase in the length and complexity of life histories, and an increase in interspecific competition that may result in competitive exclusion of species (Table 1, items 12–14) are trends that may reduce the number of species that can live in a given area. In the bloom stage of succession organisms tend to be small and to have simple life histories and rapid rates of reproduction. Changes in size appear to be a consequence of, or an adaptation to, a shift in nutrients from inorganic to organic (Table 1, item 7). In a mineral nutrient-rich environment, small size is of selective advantage, especially to autotrophs, because of the greater surface-to-volume ratio. As the ecosystem develops, however, inorganic nutrients tend to become more and more tied up in the biomass (that is, to become intrabiotic), so that the selective advantage shifts to larger organisms (either larger individuals of the same species or larger species, or both) which have greater storage capacities and more complex life histories, thus are adapted to exploiting seasonal or periodic releases of nutrients or other resources. The question of whether the seemingly direct relationship between organism size and stability is the result of positive feedback or is merely fortuitous remains unanswered (21).

Thus, whether or not species diversity continues to increase during succession will depend on whether the increase in potential niches resulting from increased biomass, stratification (Table 1, item 9), and other consequences of biological organization exceeds the countereffects of increasing size and competition. No one has yet been able to catalogue all the species in any sizable area, much less follow total species diversity in a successional series. Data are so far available only for segments of the community (trees, birds, and so on). Margalef (4) postulates that diversity will tend to peak during the early or middle stages of succession and then decline in the climax. In a study of bird populations along a successional gradient we found a bimodal pattern (22); the number of species increased during the early stages of old-field succession, declined during the early forest stages, and then increased again in the mature forest.

Species variety, equitability, and stratification are only three aspects of diversity which change during succession. Perhaps an even more important trend is an increase in the diversity of organic compounds, not only of those within the biomass but also of those excreted and secreted into the media (air, soil, water) as by-products of the increasing community metabolism. An increase in such "biochemical diversity" (Table 1, item 10) is illustrated by the increase in the variety of plant pigments along a successional gradient in aquatic situations, as described by Margalef (4, 23). Biochemical diversity within populations, or within systems as a whole, has not yet been systematically studied to the degree the subject of species diversity has been. Consequently, few generalizations can be made, except that it seems safe to say that, as succession progresses, organic extrametabolites probably serve increasingly important functions as regulators which stabilize the growth and composition of the ecosystem. Such metabolites may, in fact, be extremely important in preventing populations from overshooting the equilibrial density, thus in reducing oscillations as the system develops stability.

The cause-and-effect relationship between diversity and stability is not clear and needs to be investigated from many angles. If it can be shown that biotic diversity does indeed enhance physical stability in the ecosystem, or is the result of it, then we would have an important guide for conservation practice.

Preservation of hedgerows, woodlots, noneconomic species, noneutrophicated waters, and other biotic variety in man's landscape could then be justified on scientific as well as esthetic grounds, even though such preservation often must result in some reduction in the production of food or other immediate consumer needs. In other words, is variety only the spice of life, or is it a necessity for the long life of the total

Table 1. A tabular model of ecological succession: trends to be expected in the development of ecosystems.

Ecosystem attributes	Developmental stages	Mature stages
Community energetics		
1. Gross production/community respiration (P/R ratio)	Greater or less than 1	Approaches 1
2. Gross production/standing crop biomass (P/B ratio)	High	Low
3. Biomass supported/unit energy flow (B/E ratio)	Low	High
4. Net community production (yield)	High	Low
5. Food chains	Linear, predominantly grazing	Weblike, predominantly detritus
Community structure		
6. Total organic matter	Small	Large
7. Inorganic nutrients	Extrabiotic	Intrabiotic
8. Species diversity—variety component	Low	High
9. Species diversity—equitability component	Low	High
10. Biochemical diversity	Low	High
11. Stratification and spatial heterogeneity (pattern diversity)	Poorly organized	Well-organized
Life history		
12. Niche specialization	Broad	Narrow
13. Size of organism	Small	Large
14. Life cycles	Short, simple	Long, complex
Nutrient cycling		
15. Mineral cycles	Open	Closed
16. Nutrient exchange rate, between organisms and environment	Rapid	Slow
17. Role of detritus in nutrient regeneration	Unimportant	Important
Selection pressure		
18. Growth form	For rapid growth ("*r*-selection")	For feedback control ("*K*-selection")
19. Production	Quantity	Quality
Overall homeostasis		
20. Internal symbiosis	Undeveloped	Developed
21. Nutrient conservation	Poor	Good
22. Stability (resistance to external perturbations)	Poor	Good
23. Entropy	High	Low
24. Information	Low	High

ecosystem comprising man and nature?

Nutrient Cycling

An important trend in successional development is the closing or "tightening" of the biogeochemical cycling of major nutrients, such as nitrogen, phosphorus, and calcium (Table 1, items 15–17). Mature systems, as compared to developing ones, have a greater capacity to entrap and hold nutrients for cycling within the system. For example, Bormann and Likens (24) have estimated that only 8 kilograms per hectare out of a total pool of exchangeable calcium of 365 kilograms per hectare is lost per year in stream outflow from a North Temperate watershed covered with a mature forest. Of this, about 3 kilograms per hectare is replaced by rainfall, leaving only 5 kilograms to be obtained from weathering of the underlying rocks in order for the system to maintain mineral balance. Reducing the volume of the vegetation, or otherwise setting the succession back to a younger state, results in increased water yield by way of stream outflow (25), but this greater outflow is accompanied by greater losses of nutrients, which may also produce downstream eutrophication. Unless there is a compensating increase in the rate of weathering, the exchangeable pool of nutrients suffers gradual depletion (not to mention possible effects on soil structure resulting from erosion). High fertility in "young systems" which have open nutrient cycles cannot be maintained without compensating inputs of new nutrients; examples of such practice are the continuous-flow culture of algae, or intensive agriculture where large amounts of fertilizer are imported into the system each year.

Because rates of leaching increase in a latitudinal gradient from the poles to the equator, the role of the biotic community in nutrient retention is especially important in the high-rainfall areas of the subtropical and tropical latitudes, including not only land areas but also estuaries. Theoretically, as one goes equatorward, a larger percentage of the available nutrient pool is tied up in the biomass and a correspondingly lower percentage is in the soil or sediment. This theory, however, needs testing, since data to show such a geographical trend are incomplete. It is perhaps significant that conventional North Temperate row-type agriculture, which represents a very youthful type of ecosystem, is successful in the humid tropics only if carried out in a system of "shifting agriculture" in which the crops alternate with periods of natural vegetative redevelopment. Tree culture and the semiaquatic culture of rice provide much better nutrient retention and consequently have a longer life expectancy on a given site in these warmer latitudes.

Selection Pressure:
Quantity versus Quality

MacArthur and Wilson (26) have reviewed stages of colonization of islands which provide direct parallels with stages in ecological succession on continents. Species with high rates of reproduction and growth, they find, are more likely to survive in the early uncrowded stages of island colonization. In contrast, selection pressure favors species with lower growth potential but better capabilities for competitive survival under the equilibrium density of late stages. Using the terminology of growth equations, where r is the intrinsic rate of

231

increase and K is the upper asymptote or equilibrium population size, we may say that "r selection" predominates in early colonization, with "K selection" prevailing as more and more species and individuals attempt to colonize (Table 1, item 18). The same sort of thing is even seen within the species in certain "cyclic" northern insects in which "active" genetic strains found at low densities are replaced at high densities by "sluggish" strains that are adapted to crowding (27).

Genetic changes involving the whole biota may be presumed to accompany the successional gradient, since, as described above, quantity production characterizes the young ecosystem while quality production and feedback control are the trademarks of the mature system (Table 1, item 19). Selection at the ecosystem level may be primarily interspecific, since species replacement is a characteristic of successional series or seres. However, in most well-studied seres there seem to be a few early successional species that are able to persist through to late stages. Whether genetic changes contribute to adaptation in such species has not been determined, so far as I know, but studies on population genetics of Drosophila suggest that changes in genetic composition could be important in population regulation (28). Certainly, the human population, if it survives beyond its present rapid growth stage, is destined to be more and more affected by such selection pressures as adaptation to crowding becomes essential.

Overall Homeostasis

This brief review of ecosystem development emphasizes the complex nature of processes that interact. While one may well question whether all the trends described are characteristic of all types of ecosystems, there can be little doubt that the net result of community actions is symbiosis, nutrient conservation, stability, a decrease in entropy, and an increase in information (Table 1, items 20–24). The overall strategy is, as I stated at the beginning of this article, directed toward achieving as large and diverse an organic structure as is possible within the limits set by the available energy input and the prevailing physical conditions of existence (soil, water, climate, and so on). As studies of biotic communities become more functional and sophisticated, one is impressed with the importance of mutualism, parasitism, predation, commensalism, and other forms of symbiosis. Partnership between unrelated species is often noteworthy (for example, that between coral coelenterates and algae, or between mycorrhizae and trees). In many cases, at least, biotic control of grazing, population density, and nutrient cycling provide the chief positive-feedback mechanisms that contribute to stability in the mature system by preventing overshoots and destructive oscillations. The intriguing question is, Do mature ecosystems age, as organisms do? In other words, after a long period of relative stability or "adulthood," do ecosystems again develop unbalanced metabolism and become more vulnerable to diseases and other perturbations?

Relevance of Ecosystem Development Theory to Human Ecology

Figure 1 depicts a basic conflict between the strategies of man and of nature. The "bloom-type" relationships, as exhibited by the 30-day microcosm or

232

the 30-year forest, illustrate man's present idea of how nature should be directed. For example, the goal of agriculture or intensive forestry, as now generally practiced, is to achieve high rates of production of readily harvestable products with little standing crop left to accumulate on the landscape—in other words, a high P/B efficiency. Nature's strategy, on the other hand, as seen in the outcome of the successional process, is directed toward the reverse efficiency—a high B/P ratio, as is depicted by the relationship at the right in Fig. 1. Man has generally been preoccupied with obtaining as much "production" from the landscape as possible, by developing and maintaining early successional types of ecosystems, usually monocultures. But, of course, man does not live by food and fiber alone; he also needs a balanced CO_2–O_2 atmosphere, the climatic buffer provided by oceans and masses of vegetation, and clean (that is, unproductive) water for cultural and industrial uses. Many essential life-cycle resources, not to mention recreational and esthetic needs, are best provided man by the less "productive" landscapes. In other words, the landscape is not just a supply depot but is also the *oikos*—the home—in which we must live. Until recently mankind has more or less taken for granted the gas-exchange, water-purification, nutrient-cycling, and other protective functions of self-maintaining ecosystems, chiefly because neither his numbers nor his environmental manipulations have been great enough to affect regional and global balances. Now, of course, it is painfully evident that such balances are being affected, often detrimentally. The "one problem, one solution approach" is no longer adequate and must be replaced by some form of ecosystem analysis that considers man as a part of, not apart from, the environment.

The most pleasant and certainly the safest landscape to live in is one containing a variety of crops, forests, lakes, streams, roadsides, marshes, seashores, and "waste places"—in other words, a mixture of communities of different ecological ages. As individuals we more or less instinctively surround our houses with protective, nonedible cover (trees, shrubs, grass) at the same time that we strive to coax extra bushels from our cornfield. We all consider the cornfield a "good thing," of course, but most of us would not want to live there, and it would certainly be suicidal to cover the whole land area of the biosphere with cornfields, since the boom and bust oscillation in such a situation would be severe.

The basic problem facing organized society today boils down to determining in some objective manner when we are getting "too much of a good thing." This is a completely new challenge to mankind because, up until now, he has had to be concerned largely with too little rather than too much. Thus, concrete is a "good thing," but not if half the world is covered with it. Insecticides are "good things," but not when used, as they now are, in an indiscriminate and wholesale manner. Likewise, water impoundments have proved to be very useful man-made additions to the landscape, but obviously we don't want the whole country inundated! Vast man-made lakes solve some problems, at least temporarily, but yield comparatively little food or fiber, and, because of high evaporative losses, they may not even be the best device for storing water; it might better be stored in the watershed, or underground in aquafers. Also, the cost of building large dams is a drain on already overtaxed revenues. Although as individuals we readily recognize that we can have too many dams or other large-scale environmental changes, governments are so fragmented and lacking in systems-analysis capabilities that there is no effective mechanism whereby negative feedback signals can be received and acted on before there has been a serious overshoot. Thus, today there are governmental agencies, spurred on by popular and political enthusiasm for dams, that are putting on the drawing boards plans for damming every river and stream in North America!

Society needs, and must find as quickly as possible, a way to deal with the landscape as a whole, so that manipulative skills (that is, technology) will not run too far ahead of our understanding of the impact of change. Recently a national ecological center outside of government and a coalition of governmental agencies have been proposed as two possible steps in the establishment of a political control mechanism for dealing with major environmental questions. The soil conservation movement in America is an excellent example of a program dedicated to the consideration of the whole farm or the whole watershed as an ecological unit. Soil conservation is well understood and supported by the public. However, soil conservation organizations have remained too exclusively farm-oriented, and have not yet risen to the challenge of the urban-rural landscape, where lie today's most serious problems. We do, then, have potential mechanisms in American society that could speak for the ecosystem as a whole, but none of them are really operational (29).

The general relevance of ecosystem development theory to landscape planning can, perhaps, be emphasized by the

Table 2. Contrasting characteristics of young and mature-type ecosystems.

Young	Mature
Production	Protection
Growth	Stability
Quantity	Quality

"mini-model" of Table 2, which contrasts the characteristics of young and mature-type ecosystems in more general terms than those provided by Table 1. It is mathematically impossible to obtain a maximum for more than one thing at a time, so one cannot have both extremes at the same time and place. Since all six characteristics listed in Table 2 are desirable in the aggregate, two possible solutions to the dilemma immediately suggest themselves. We can compromise so as to provide moderate quality and moderate yield on all the landscape, or we can deliberately plan to compartmentalize the landscape so as to simultaneously maintain highly productive and predominantly protective types as separate units subject to different management strategies (strategies ranging, for example, from intensive cropping on the one hand to wilderness management on the other). If ecosystem development theory is valid and applicable to planning, then the so-called multiple-use strategy, about which we hear so much, will work only through one or both of these approaches, because, in most cases, the projected multiple uses conflict with one another. It is appropriate, then, to examine some examples of the compromise and the compartmental strategies.

Pulse Stability

A more or less regular but acute

physical perturbation imposed from without can maintain an ecosystem at some intermediate point in the developmental sequence, resulting in, so to speak, a compromise between youth and maturity. What I would term "fluctuating water level ecosystems" are good examples. Estuaries, and intertidal zones in general, are maintained in an early, relatively fertile stage by the tides, which provide the energy for rapid nutrient cycling. Likewise, freshwater marshes, such as the Florida Everglades, are held at an early successional stage by the seasonal fluctuations in water levels. The dry-season drawdown speeds up aerobic decomposition of accumulated organic matter, releasing nutrients that, on reflooding, support a wet-season bloom in productivity. The life histories of many organisms are intimately coupled to this periodicity. The wood stork, for example, breeds when the water levels are falling and the small fish on which it feeds become concentrated and easy to catch in the drying pools. If the water level remains high during the usual dry season or fails to rise in the wet season, the stork will not nest (30). Stabilizing water levels in the Everglades by means of dikes, locks, and impoundments, as is now advocated by some, would, in my opinion, destroy rather than preserve the Everglades as we now know them just as surely as complete drainage would. Without periodic drawdowns and fires, the shallow basins would fill up with organic matter and succession would proceed from the present pond-and-prairie condition toward a scrub or swamp forest.

It is strange that man does not readily recognize the importance of recurrent changes in water level in a natural situation such as the Everglades when similar pulses are the basis for some of his most enduring food culture systems (31). Alternate filling and draining of ponds has been a standard procedure in fish culture for centuries in Europe and the Orient. The flooding, draining, and soil-aeration procedure in rice culture is another example. The rice paddy is thus the cultivated analogue of the natural marsh or the intertidal ecosystem.

Fire is another physical factor whose periodicity has been of vital importance to man and nature over the centuries. Whole biotas, such as those of the African grasslands and the California chaparral, have become adapted to periodic fires producing what ecologists often call "fire climaxes" (32). Man uses fire deliberately to maintain such climaxes or to set back succession to some desired point. In the southeastern coastal plain, for example, light fires of moderate frequency can maintain a pine forest against the encroachment of older successional stages which, at the present time at least, are considered economically less desirable. The fire-controlled forest yields less wood than a tree farm does (that is, young trees, all of about the same age, planted in rows and harvested on a short rotation schedule), but it provides a greater protective cover for the landscape, wood of higher quality, and a home for game birds (quail, wild turkey, and so on) which could not survive in a tree farm. The fire climax, then, is an example of a compromise between production simplicity and protection diversity.

It should be emphasized that pulse stability works only if there is a complete community (including not only plants but animals and microorganisms) adapted to the particular intensity and frequency of the perturbation. Adaptation—operation of the selection process —requires times measurable on the evolutionary scale. Most physical stresses introduced by man are too sudden, too violent, or too arrhythmic for adaptation to occur at the ecosystem level, so severe

235

oscillation rather than stability results. In many cases, at least, modification of naturally adapted ecosystems for cultural purposes would seem preferable to complete redesign.

Prospects for a Detritus Agriculture

As indicated above, heterotrophic utilization of primary production in mature ecosystems involves largely a delayed consumption of detritus. There is no reason why man cannot make greater use of detritus and thus obtain food or other products from the more protective type of ecosystem. Again, this would represent a compromise, since the short-term yield could not be as great as the yield obtained by direct exploitation of the grazing food chain. A detritus agriculture, however, would have some compensating advantages. Present agricultural strategy is based on selection for rapid growth and edibility in food plants, which, of course, make them vulnerable to attack by insects and disease. Consequently, the more we select for succulence and growth, the more effort we must invest in the chemical control of pests; this effort, in turn, increases the likelihood of our poisoning useful organisms, not to mention ourselves. Why not also practice the reverse strategy—that is, select plants which are essentially unpalatable, or which produce their own systemic insecticides while they are growing, and then convert the net production into edible products by microbial and chemical enrichment in food factories? We could then devote our biochemical genius to the enrichment process instead of fouling up our living space with chemical poisons! The production of silage by fermentation of low-grade fodder is an example of such a procedure already in widespread use. The cultivation of detritus-eating fishes in the Orient is another example.

By tapping the detritus food chain man can also obtain an appreciable harvest from many natural systems without greatly modifying them or destroying their protective and esthetic value. Oyster culture in estuaries is a good example. In Japan, raft and long-line culture of oysters has proved to be a very practical way to harvest the natural microbial products of estuaries and shallow bays. Furukawa (33) reports that the yield of cultured oysters in the Hiroshima Prefecture has increased tenfold since 1950, and that the yield of oysters (some 240,000 tons of meat) from this one district alone in 1965 was ten times the yield of natural oysters from the entire country. Such oyster culture is feasible along the entire Atlantic and Gulf coasts of the United States. A large investment in the culture of oysters and other seafoods would also provide the best possible deterrent against pollution since the first threat of damage to the pollution-sensitive oyster industry would be immediately translated into political action!

The Compartment Model

Successful though they often are, compromise systems are not suitable nor desirable for the whole landscape. More emphasis needs to be placed on compartmentalization, so that growth-type, steady-state, and intermediate-type ecosystems can be linked with urban and industrial areas for mutual benefit. Knowing the transfer coefficients that define the flow of energy and the movement of materials and organisms (including man) between compartments, it should be possible to determine, through analog-computer manipulation, rational limits for the size and capacity of each compartment. We might start, for ex ample, with a simplified model, shown in Fig. 2, consisting of four compartments of equal area, partitioned according to the basic biotic-function criterion —that is, according to whether the area is (i) productive, (ii) protective, (iii) a compromise between (i) and (ii) or (iv), urban-industrial. By continually refining the transfer coefficients on the basis of real world situations, and by increasing and decreasing the size and capacity of each compartment through computer simulation, it would be possible to determine objectively the limits that must eventually be imposed on each compartment in order to maintain regional and global balances in the exchange of vital energy and of materials. A systems-analysis procedure provides at least one approach to the solution of the basic dilemma posed by the question "How do we determine when we are getting too much of a good thing?" Also it provides a means of evaluating the energy drains imposed on ecosystems by pollution, radiation, harvest, and other stresses (34).

Implementing any kind of compartmentalization plan, of course, would require procedures for zoning the landscape and restricting the use of some land and water areas. While the principle of zoning in cities is universally accepted, the procedures now followed do not work very well because zoning restrictions are too easily overturned by short-term economic and population pressures. Zoning the landscape would require a whole new order of thinking. Greater use of legal measures providing for tax relief, restrictions on use, scenic easements, and public ownership will be required if appreciable land and water areas are to be held in the "protective" categories. Several states (for example, New Jersey and California), where pollution and population pressure are beginning to hurt, have made a start in this direction by enacting "open space" legislation designed to get as much unoccupied land as possible into a "protective" status so that future uses can be planned on a rational and scientific basis. The United States as a whole is fortunate in that large areas of the country are in national forests, parks, wildlife refuges, and so on. The fact that such areas, as well as the bordering oceans, are not quickly exploitable gives us time for the accelerated ecological study and programming needed to determine what proportions of different types of landscape provide a safe balance between man and nature. The open oceans, for example, should forever be allowed to remain protective rather than productive territory, if Alfred Redfield's (35) assumptions are correct. Redfield views the oceans, the major part of the hydrosphere, as the biosphere's governor, which slows down and controls the rate of decomposition and nutrient regeneration, thereby creating and maintaining the highly aerobic terrestrial environment to which the higher forms of life, such as man, are adapted. Eutrophication of the ocean in a last-ditch effort to feed the populations of the land could well have an adverse effect on the oxygen reservoir in the atmosphere.

Until we can determine more precisely how far we may safely go in expanding intensive agriculture and urban sprawl at the expense of the protective landscape, it will be good insurance to hold inviolate as much of the latter as possible. Thus, the preservation of natural areas is not a peripheral luxury for society but a capital investment from which we expect to draw interest. Also, it may well be that restrictions in the use of land and water are our only practical means of avoiding overpopulation or too great an exploitation of resources, or both. Interestingly enough, restriction of land use is the analogue of a natural behavioral control mechanism known as "territoriality" by which many species of animals avoid crowding and social stress (36).

Since the legal and economic problems pertaining to zoning and compartmentalization are likely to be thorny, I urge law schools to establish departments, or institutes, of "landscape law" and to start training "landscape lawyers" who will be capable not only of clarifying existing procedures but also of drawing up new enabling legislation for consideration by state and national governing bodies. At present, society is concerned—and rightly so—with human rights, but environmental rights are equally vital. The "one man one vote" idea is important, but so also is a "one man one hectare" proposition.

Education, as always, must play a role in increasing man's awareness of his dependence on the natural environment. Perhaps we need to start teaching the principles of ecosystem in the third grade. A grammar school primer on man and his environment could logically consist of four chapters, one for each of the four essential kinds of environment, shown diagrammatically in Fig. 2.

Of the many books and articles that are being written these days about man's environmental crisis, I would like to cite two that go beyond "crying out in alarm" to suggestions for bringing about a reorientation of the goals of society. Garrett Hardin, in a recent article in *Science* (37), points out that, since the optimum population density is less than the maximum, there is no strictly technical solution to the problem of pollution caused by overpopulation; a solution, he suggests, can only be achieved through moral and legal

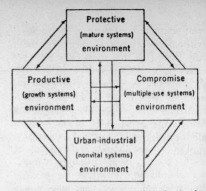

Fig. 2. Compartment model of the basic kinds of environment required by man, partitioned according to ecosystem development and life-cycle resource criteria.

means of "mutual coercion, mutually agreed upon by the majority of people."

Earl F. Murphy, in a book entitled *Governing Nature* (38), emphasizes that the regulatory approach alone is not enough to protect life-cycle resources, such as air and water, that cannot be allowed to deteriorate. He discusses permit systems, effluent charges, receptor levies, assessment, and cost-internalizing procedures as economic incentives for achieving Hardin's "mutually agreed upon coercion."

It goes without saying that the tabular model for ecosystem development which I have presented here has many parallels in the development of human society itself. In the pioneer society, as in the pioneer ecosystem, high birth rates, rapid growth, high economic profits, and exploitation of accessible and unused resources are advantageous, but, as the saturation level is approached, these drives must be shifted to considerations of symbiosis (that is, "civil rights," "law and order," "education," and "culture"), birth control, and the recycling of resources. A balance be-

een youth and maturity in the socioenvironmental system is, therefore, the
really basic goal that must be achieved
if man as a species is to successfully
pass through the present rapid-growth
stage, to which he is clearly well
adapted, to the ultimate equilibrium-
density stage, of which he as yet shows
little understanding and to which he
now shows little tendency to adapt.

References and Notes

1. E. P. Odum, *Ecology* (Holt, Rinehart &
   Winston, New York, 1963), chap. 6.
2. H. T. Odum and R. C. Pinkerton, *Amer.
   Scientist* 43, 331 (1955).
3. A. J. Lotka, *Elements of Physical Biology*
   (Williams and Wilkins, Baltimore, 1925).
4. R. Margalef, *Advan. Frontiers Plant Sci.* 2,
   137 (1963); *Amer. Naturalist* 97, 357 (1963).
5. R. J. Beyers, *Ecol. Monographs* 33, 281
   (1963).
6. The systems so far used to test ecological
   principles have been derived from sewage
   and farm ponds and are cultured in half-
   strength No. 36 Taub and Dollar medium
   [*Limnol. Oceanog.* 9, 61 (1964)]. They are
   closed to organic imput or output but are
   open to the atmosphere through the cotton
   plug in the neck of the flask. Typically,
   liter-sized microecosystems contain two or
   three species of nonflagellated algae and one
   to three species each of flagellated protozoans,
   ciliated protozoans, rotifers, nematodes, and
   ostracods; a system derived from a sewage
   pond contained at least three species of fungi
   and 13 bacterial isolates [R. Gordon, thesis,
   University of Georgia (1967)]. These cultures are thus a kind of minimum ecosystem
   containing those small species originally
   found in the ancestral pond that are able to
   function together as a self-contained unit
   under the restricted conditions of the laboratory flask and the controlled environment of
   a growth chamber [temperature, 65° to 75°F
   (18° to 24°C); photoperiod, 12 hours; illumi-
   nation, 100 to 1000 footcandles].
7. G. D. Cooke, *BioScience* 17, 717 (1967).
8. T. Kira and T. Shidei, *Japan. J. Ecol.* 17, 70
   (1967).
9. The metabolism of the microcosms was
   monitored by measuring diurnal pH changes,
   and the biomass (in terms of total organic
   matter and total carbon) was determined
   by periodic harvesting of replicate systems.
10. F. J. H. Mackereth, *Proc. Roy. Soc. London
    Ser. B* 161, 295 (1965); U. M. Cowgill and
    G. E. Hutchinson, *Proc. Intern. Limnol. Ass.*
    15, 644 (1964); A. D. Harrison, *Trans. Roy.
    Soc. S. Africa* 36, 213 (1962).
11. R. Margalef, *Proc. Intern. Limnol. Ass.* 15,
    169 (1964).
12. J. R. Bray, *Oikos* 12, 70 (1961).
13. D. Pimentel, *Amer. Naturalist* 95, 65 (1961).
14. R. T. Paine, *ibid.* 100, 65 (1966).
15. G. M. Woodwell, *Brookhaven Nat. Lab.
    Pub.* 924(*T-381*) (1965), pp. 1–15.

16. R. G. Wiegert, E. P. Odum, J. H. Schnell,
    Ecology 48, 75 (1967).
17. For selected general discussions of patterns
    of species diversity, see E. H. Simpson, *Na-
    ture* 163, 688 (1949); C. B. Williams, *J.
    Animal Ecol.* 22, 14 (1953); .G. E. Hutchin-
    son, *Amer. Naturalist* 93, 145 (1959); R.
    Margalef, *Gen. Systems* 3, 36 (1958); R.
    MacArthur and J. MacArthur, *Ecology* 42,
    594 (1961); N. G. Hairston, *ibid.* 40, 404
    (1959); B. C. Patten, *J. Marine Res. (Sears
    Found. Marine Res.)* 20, 57 (1960); E. G.
    Leigh, *Proc. Nat. Acad. Sci. U.S.* 55, 777
    (1965); E. R. Pianka, *Amer. Naturalist* 100,
    33 (1966); E. C. Pielou, *J. Theoret. Biol.*
    10, 370 (1966).
18. M. Lloyd and R. J. Ghelardi, *J. Animal Ecol.*
    33, 217 (1964); E. C. Pielou, *J. Theoret.
    Biol.* 13, 131 (1966).
19. G. W. Barrett, *Ecology* 49, 1019 (1969).
20. In our studies of natural succession following
    grain culture, both the species-to-numbers and
    the equitability indices increased for all
    trophic levels but especially for predators
    and parasites. Only 44 percent of the species
    in the natural ecosystem were phytophagous,
    as compared to 77 percent in the grain field.
21. J. T. Bonner, *Size and Cycle* (Princeton
    Univ. Press, Princeton, N.J., 1963); P. Frank,
    Ecology 49, 355 (1968).
22. D. W. Johnston and E. P. Odum, *Ecology*
    37, 50 (1956).
23. R. Margalef, *Oceanog. Marine Biol. Annu.
    Rev.* 5, 257 (1967).
24. F. H. Bormann and G. E. Likens, *Science*
    155, 424 (1967).
25. Increased water yield following reduction of
    vegetative cover has been frequently demon-
    strated in experimental watersheds throughout
    the world [see A. R. Hibbert, in *International
    Symposium on Forest Hydrology* (Pergamon
    Press, New York, 1967), pp. 527–543]. Data
    on the long-term hydrologic budget (rainfall
    input relative to stream outflow) are avail-
    able at many of these sites, but mineral
    budgets have yet to be systematically studied.
    Again, this is a prime objective in the "eco-
    system analysis" phase of the International
    Biological Program.
26. R. H. MacArthur and E. O. Wilson, *Theory
    of Island Biogeography* (Princeton Univ. Press,
    Princeton, N.J., 1967).
27. Examples are the tent caterpillar [see W. G.
    Wellington, *Can. J. Zool.* 35, 293 (1957)]
    and the larch budworm [see W. Baltens-
    weiler, *Can. Entomologist* 96, 792 (1964)].
28. F. J. Ayala, *Science* 162, 1453 (1968).
29. Ira Rubinoff, in discussing the proposed sea-
    level canal joining the Atlantic and Pacific
    oceans [*Science* 161, 857 (1968)], calls for
    a "control commission for environmental
    manipulation" with "broad powers of ap-
    proving, disapproving, or modifying all ma-
    jor alterations of the marine or terrestrial
    environments. . . ."
30. See M. P. Kahl, *Ecol. Monographs* 34, 97
    (1964).
31. The late Aldo Leopold remarked long ago
    [*Symposium on Hydrobiology* (Univ. of
    Wisconsin Press, Madison, 1941), p. 17] that
    man does not perceive organic behavior in
    systems unless he has built them himself.

Let us hope it will not be necessary to re-build the entire biosphere before we recognize the worth of natural systems!

32. See C. F. Cooper, *Sci. Amer.* 204, 150 (April 1961).
33. See "Proceedings Oyster Culture Workshop, Marine Fisheries Division, Georgia Game and Fish Commission, Brunswick" (1968), pp. 49-61.
34. See H. T. Odum, in *Symposium on Primary Productivity and Mineral Cycling in Natural Ecosystems*, H. E. Young, Ed. (Univ. of Maine Press, Orono, 1967), p. 81; ———, in *Pollution and Marine Ecology* (Wiley, New York, 1967), p. 99; K. E. F. Watt, *Ecology and Resource Management* (McGraw-Hill, New York, 1968).
35. A. C. Redfield, *Amer. Scientist* 46, 205 (1958).
36. R. Ardrey, *The Territorial Imperative* (Atheneum, New York, 1967).
37. G. Hardin, *Science* 162, 1243 (1968).
38. E. F. Murphy, *Governing Nature* (Quadrangle Books, Chicago, 1967).

Synergism of Insecticides by Herbicides

E. P. Lichtenstein, T. T. Liang, B. N. Anderegg

Abstract. *The herbicides atrazine, simazine, monuron, and 2,4-D (2,4-dichloro-phenoxyacetic acid) enhanced the toxicity of selected insecticides to* Drosophila melanogaster *Meigen,* Musca domestica *L., and larvae of* Aedes aegypti *L. The insecticides—nine organophosphorus compounds, two chlorinated hydrocarbons, and one carbamate—were used at dosages that resulted in low insect mortalities, while the herbicides by themselves were nontoxic. Atrazine was most effective. With increasing amounts of this herbicide and constant amounts of some insecticides, increasing mortalities of fruit flies were observed. Exposure of the insects for 24 hours to carbofuran (0.5 microgram), p,p'-DDT [1,1,1-trichloro-2,2-bis(p-chlorophenyl)ethane] (4 micrograms), parathion (0.35 microgram), and diazinon (0.2 microgram) alone resulted in mortalities of 7.5, 9.5, 8, and 10.5 percent, respectively. Based on dosage mortality curves obtained with increasing amounts of atrazine, mortalities of 50 percent of the insect populations would have been achieved with 23, 40, 6, and 10 micrograms of atrazine added to the above-mentioned dosages of carbofuran, DDT, parathion, and diazinon, respectively.*

The effects of pesticides or other synthetic chemicals on biological systems have usually been investigated by utilizing one particular test chemical. However, under actual environmental conditions, particularly in agricultural situations, a mixture of synthetic chemicals or their metabolites (or both) is present, and these chemicals may interact in biological systems. For example, detergents increase the persistence and toxicity in soils of the organophosphorus insecticides parathion and diazinon (1), reduce the penetration of parathion into pea roots, and inhibit the translocation of lindane into pea greens (2). Street (3) stressed the ecological significance of pesticide interactions, stating that "DDT and dieldrin are additive at low dosages in inducing testosterone metabolism in pigeon liver." Street et al. (4) compared the

effects of polychlorinated biphenyl compounds (PCB's) and organochlorine pesticides on the induction of hepatic microsomal enzymes. Tsao et al. (5) reported that Aroclor 5460 greatly increased the residual toxicity of lindane, although it had no toxic effect on Musca domestica L. by itself. They also indicated that this polychlorinated polyphenyl compound may have a synergistic effect with lindane. Lichtenstein et al. (6) demonstrated synergistic effects of PCB's on DDT [1,1,1-trichloro-2,2-bis(p-chlorophenyl) ethane] and dieldrin in insects, and Fuhremann and Lichtenstein (7) showed that PCB's increased in particular the toxicity of the oxygen analogs of organophosphorus insecticides to houseflies. Plapp (8) showed that the PCB Aroclor 1254 synergized a carbamate insecticide, carbaryl. Because of

SCIENCE, August, 1973, Vol. 181, pp. 847-849.

these interactions of pesticides with other environmental chemicals in biological systems, we investigated the effects of several herbicides on the toxicity of some commonly used insecticides and on some of their toxic metabolites.

Insects were exposed to herbicides or insecticides, alone or in combinations with each other. The herbicides used were analytical grade atrazine, simazine, monuron, and 2,4-D (2,4-dichlorophenoxyacetic acid). The insecticides and some of their potential metabolites used (see Table 2) were also analytical grade. The three insect species that were exposed to these chemicals were fruit flies (*Drosophila melanogaster* Meigen), a DDT-susceptible strain (CSMA-1948) of houseflies (*Musca domestica* L.), and mosquito larvae (*Aedes aegypti* L.). With *Drosophila*, 3-day-old flies were exposed to dry residues of the chemicals or combinations thereof in 4-ounce (~120-ml) test jars (9). Appropriate amounts of atrazine, simazine, or one of the insecticides in chloroform, and of monuron and 2,4-D in acetone were pipetted into the bioassay jars, and the solvents were evaporated. Fifty fruit flies were then placed in each jar containing the dry pesticide residues, and mortality counts were periodically made over a 24-hour exposure period. Each test was replicated four or eight times. With *Musca domestica* the pesticides in 2 μl of solvent were applied topically to the ventral portion of female houseflies. Insecticides or atrazine (or both) were applied in methanol and monuron and 2,4-D were applied in acetone. Simazine, because of its low solubility in these solvents, was not used with houseflies. Tests were conducted with four or eight replicates each consisting of 15 houseflies. In experiments with *Aedes aegypti* appropriate amounts of insecticides or herbicides (or both) in chloroform were added to tap water; 2,4-D was added in acetone. The solvents were removed from the water by evaporation under vacuum, the water was adjusted to volume, and 10-ml aliquots were placed in small glass vials. For each test, 15 third-instar mosquito larvae were introduced into the treated water and mortality counts were made over a 24-hour period; tests were replicated four or eight times. The results from

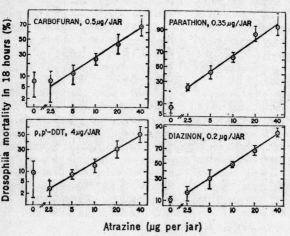

Fig. 1. Effects of increasing dosage of atrazine (0 to 40 μg per jar) in synergizing the toxicities of insecticides applied at constant dosages with the herbicide.

Table 1. Effect of herbicides on the toxicity of parathion and DDT to three insect species. Percent insect mortality is reported for a 24-hour exposure period; values are the means and standard deviations of four or eight replicate tests. In the ratio, $H + I$ is the mortality observed with herbicide plus insecticide, and I is the mortality observed with insecticide alone. For *Drosophila* the herbicide concentration was 40 µg per herbicide plus insecticide, and I is the mortality observed with insecticide alone. For *Musca* chemicals were applied topically; the herbicide concentration was 15 µg per fly; parathion, 0.02 µg per fly; DDT, 0.1 µg per fly. For *Aedes* chemicals were applied in water; the herbicide concentration was 10 ppm; parathion, 0.016 ppm; DDT, 0.18 ppm.

Insecticide	No herbicide Insect mortality (%)	Atrazine Insect mortality (%)	Atrazine Ratio $H + I$ / I	Simazine Insect mortality (%)	Simazine Ratio $H + I$ / I	Monuron Insect mortality (%)	Monuron Ratio $H + I$ / I	2,4-D Insect mortality (%)	2,4-D Ratio $H + I$ / I
				Drosophila melanogaster					
None	0	0		0		0		0	
Parathion	9 ± 5.0	48 ± 10*	5.3	23 ± 2†	2.6	24 ± 3.7†	2.7	15 ± 3	1.7
DDT	10 ± 2.5	22 ± 5.4†	2.2	25 ± 13§	2.5	17 ± 7.9	1.7	18 ± 4.5‡	1.8
				Musca domestica					
None	0	0				0		0	
Parathion	11 ± 3.4	45 ± 20*	4.1			40 ± 15*	3.6	15 ± 12	1.4
DDT	8 ± 5.6	25 ± 8.6*	3.1			20 ± 10†	2.5	7 ± 7	0.9
				Aedes aegypti					
None	0	0		0		0		0	
Parathion	15 ± 3.4	80 ± 11*	5.3	67 ± 5.4*	4.5	53 ± 9.4*	3.5	48 ± 8.4*	3.2
DDT	10 ± 8.6	12 ± 11	1.2	10 ± 3.8	1.0	13 ± 12	1.3	17 ± 3.9	1.7

Results significantly different from the control (no herbicide) at the * 0.1 percent level, † 1 percent level, ‡ 5 percent level, § 10 percent level.

Table 2. Increase in toxicity of insecticides to *Drosophila melanogaster* Meigen when atrazine is also present. The results are for 24-hour exposure periods; insect mortality values are means and standard deviations for four or eight replicated tests. The atrazine concentration was 40 μg per (4-ounce) jar. In the ratio, $H + I$ is the observed mortality with herbicide plus insecticide; I is the observed mortality with the insecticide alone.

Insecticide	Insecticide concentration (μg per jar)	Insect mortality (%) with		Ratio $\dfrac{H + I}{I}$
		No herbicide	Atrazine	
None	0.00	0	0	
Parathion	0.35	9 ± 8.4	77 ± 9.9*	8.6
Paraoxon	0.35	13 ± 2.5	52 ± 2.5*	4.0
Diazinon	0.20	9 ± 3.5	33 ± 11.7‡	3.7
Diazoxon	0.70	14 ± 2.3	82 ± 21†	5.9
Dyfonate	0.35	31 ± 6.8	73 ± 16‡	2.4
Dyfoxon	0.35	12 ± 9.1	33 ± 12§	2.8
Phorate	0.60	22 ± 4.4	52 ± 6.6†	2.4
Phorate sulfoxide	3.5	23 ± 5.3	86 ± 29‡	3.7
Phorate sulfone	2.2	18 ± 3.0	91 ± 14*	5.1
Carbofuran	0.7	43 ± 18	93 ± 4.8‡	2.2
DDT	2.0	17 ± 15	57 ± 12‡	3.4
Dieldrin	0.14	5 ± 4.1	36 ± 4.4*	7.2

Results significantly different from the control (no herbicide) at the * 0.01 percent level, † 0.1 percent level, ‡ 1 percent level, § 5 percent level.

all experiments were expressed as the mean and the standard deviation of the percentage mortalities observed after a specific period of exposure to the pesticides. The differences between mortalities due to insecticides and those due to insecticides plus herbicides were statistically analyzed by the *t*-test.

In the first experimental series, synergistic effects of herbicides on insecticides were studied by exposing fruit flies, houseflies, or mosquito larvae to parathion, *p,p'*-DDT, one of the four herbicides, or insecticide-herbicide combinations as indicated in Table 1. The insecticide dosages chosen were such that insect mortalities obtained after 24 hours of exposure to insecticides alone were relatively low. The results indicate (Table 1) that in most cases all four herbicides increased the toxicity of the insecticides. This increase was greater with parathion than with DDT. Atrazine was most effective, increasing significantly (at the 0.1 percent level) the toxicity of parathion to

fruit flies and mosquito larvae by a factor of 5.3, and to houseflies by a factor of 4.1. Least effective was 2,4-D, which increased insecticide toxicity in only two out of six cases (DDT toxicity with fruit flies and parathion toxicity with mosquito larvae). No synergistic effects on the toxicity of DDT toward mosquito larvae were observed with any of the herbicides. Although enough DDT was added to the water to give a concentration of 0.18 part per million (ppm), this concentration was probably never obtained because of its low water solubility (0.001 ppm). It is, therefore, questionable as to what an extent the larvae had a chance to come into contact with the insecticide.

In the second experimental series, the synergistic effects of atrazine on the toxicity of 12 insecticides were studied with fruit flies. The insecticides included nine organophosphorus compounds, one carbamate, and two chlorinated hydrocarbons (Table 2). Insects were exposed to dry deposits of atrazine, one of the 12 insecticides, or atrazine-insecticide combinations. Atrazine was always applied at 40 μg per bioassay jar and the insecticides in amounts as indicated in Table 2. The toxicity of all the insecticides was significantly increased by atrazine. This increase ranged from a factor of 2.2 to 8.6, depending on the insecticide present. From the data reported above (Tables 1 and 2) it appears that the phenomenon of synergism of insecticides by selected herbicides is rather general, therefore suggesting that the mode of action of the herbicides was not related to the blocking of specific detoxifying enzyme systems within the insect body. Other factors, such as an increase in insecticide penetration through the insect cuticle, could possibly have played a role in these phenomena.

In a third experimental series fruit flies were exposed to fixed amounts of insecticides (carbofuran, 0.5 μg; DDT, 4 μg; parathion, 0.35 μg; or diazinon, 0.2 μg) and increasing amounts of atrazine (from 2.5 to 40 μg per bioassay jar) in order to ascertain a potential dose-response relation of the synergistic effects of the herbicide. Results presented in Fig. 1 indicate that with increasing amounts of atrazine, increasing insect mortalities occurred during the 18-hour exposure period. Exposure of the fruit flies to carbofuran, DDT, parathion, or diazinon alone resulted in mortalities of 7.5, 9.5, 8, and 10.5 percent, respectively. The dosage-mortality curves indicate that 50 percent mortality of the insect populations would have been achieved with the addition of 23, 40, 6, and 10 μg of atrazine, respectively.

Results with fruit flies as shown in Tables 1 and 2 and Fig. 1 were obtained in different tests conducted over a period of several months. Since the susceptibility of the insects to pesticides fluctuates to some extent from week to week, quantitative differences in various data are due to these fluctuations.

This report further illustrates the necessity for continued investigations of the interactions of pesticides with other chemicals in biological systems. Although it is imperative to study the fate and behavior of single environmental chemicals, it is also apparent that these problems must be approached within the concept of a whole system in which chemicals can interact with each other.

References and Notes

1. E. P. Lichtenstein, *J. Econ. Entomol.* **59**, 985 (1966).
2. ———, T. W. Fuhremann, N. E. A. Scopes, R. F. Skrentny, *J. Agr. Food Chem* **15**, 864 (1967).
3. J. C. Street, *Ind. Med.* **38** (No. 11), 91 (1969).
4. ———, F. M. Urray, D. J. Wagstaff, A. D. Blau, 158th annual meeting of the American Chemical Society, Division of Pesticide Chemistry, Chicago, Illinois, 8 September 1969, abstract 017.
5. C. H. Tsao, W. N. Sullivan, I. Hornstein, *J. Econ. Entomol.* **46**, 882 (1953).
6. E. P. Lichtenstein, K. R. Schulz, T. W. Fuhremann, T. T. Liang, *ibid.* **62**, 761 (1969).
7. T. W. Fuhremann and E. P. Lichtenstein. *Toxicol. Appl. Pharmacol.* **22**, 628 (1972).
8. F. W. Plapp, Jr., *J. Environ. Entomol.* **5**, 580 (1972).
9. C. A. Edwards, S. D. Beck, E. P. Lichtenstein, *J. Econ. Entomol.* **50**, 622 (1957).
10. Special thanks are expressed to T. W. Fuhremann for assistance in statistical analyses. Supported by the College of Agricultural and Life Sciences, University of Wisconsin, Madison, and by NSF grant GB-35021. Contribution by project 1387 from the Wisconsin Agricultural Experiment Station as a collaborator under North Central Regional Cooperative Research Project 96 on "Environmental implications of pesticide usage."

245

SURVEYING HIGHWAY IMPACT

By James B. Sullivan and Paul A. Montgomery

THE TROUBLE BEGAN IN 1893. THE DURYEA BROTHERS IN SPRINGFIELD, MAS-
sachusetts had successfully road-tested their gasoline engine automobile, and
engineers held high hopes for the future of rubber tire transportation. According
to a 1910 engineering report:[1]

"It was quite generally believed by engineers before the introduction of
motor traffic that at least 60 percent of wear on roads was due to the action of
horses' feet; consequently, when the motor vehicle was first introduced, engineers and others having charge of roads 'welcomed this new type of vehicle,
believing the soft pneumatic tire would have rather a beneficial effect if any at
all, upon the road surface.

"The first effect observed from fast motor traffic was an excessive amount
of dust raised from the road surface; the other injurious effect is the shearing
stress of the driving wheels upon the road surface. The effect on a road subjected
to much fast traffic is to denude to the surface to a great extent of the fine bind-
ing material, which results in the larger stones in the road becoming loose."

In our present era of broad superhighways, undesirable side effects of the
horseless carriage have not yet been eliminated. It was predicted that in 1972,
a year of better road surfaces, flatter grades, and fewer curves, over 50,000
people would die and two million more would suffer disabling injuries on the
highways;[2] the leading cause of death for people between one and thirty-eight
years of age would be motor vehicle accidents.[3] Cities are now connected to
suburbs, to the countryside, to better places to live, work and play; yet of the
occupied land in the city's central area, almost half is roads and parking space.[4]
Each year 50,000 people are uprooted from their homes to clear the way for
federal-aid highways.[5] During a time of acute energy shortage, one-quarter of
total U.S. energy production is used by the automobile.[6] Rush hour traffic on
expressways is still so congested that noise pollution and air pollution are not
merely ecological phrases but persistent realities.

Increased awareness of these problems has caused citizens to ask that people
and their environment replace highly specialized engineering factors as the focus
of concern for highway builders. This article examines the mechanism established
by federal legislation to strengthen environmental concern: the environmental
impact statements required by the National Environmental Policy Act (NEPA).[7]

Signed into law on January 1, 1970, NEPA attempts to prevent environmental
neglect by reforming the way decisions are made. Section 102 of the act requires
all federal agencies to submit a detailed statement (referred to as a 102 state-

ENVIRONMENT, Vol. 14, No. 9, pp. 12-20.

ment), which assesses the impact on the human environment of any proposed action and discusses all possible alternatives, before the action is taken. The term "human environment" is interpreted in the broadest sense by Federal Highway Administration (FHWA) guidelines as ". . . the aggregate of all external conditions and influences (esthetic, ecological, biological, cultural, social, economic, historical, etc.) that effect the life of a human."*

Section 102(2)(C) of NEPA specifies that "to the fullest extent possible," all agencies of the federal government, utilizing a "systematic, interdisciplinary approach," shall assess: (1) the environmental impact of the proposed action; (2) any adverse environmental effects which cannot be avoided should the proposal be implemented; (3) alternatives to the proposed action; (4) the relationship between local, short-term uses of man's environment and the maintenance and enhancement of long-term productivity; and (5) any irreversible and irretrievable commitments of resources which would be involved in the proposed action should it be implemented.

If all these requirements were dealt with, the resulting 102 statement would indeed be action-forcing. By providing a broad base of objective data, the 102 statement would force road builders to consider more than just the economic and engineering issues that formerly dominated highway planning. At least these were the act's intentions.

In an attempt to find out how well the requirements of the law are being met, the authors conducted a survey of 76 final 102 statements, filed through June 1972, for proposed urban highway projects within cities of more than 50,000 population. The contents of each of the final urban 102 statements were checked against the list of federally required evaluations of certain problem areas. They were studied to see how these areas, in which a proposed highway facility could have a significant environmental impact, either harmful or beneficial, were treated in the statements.

The response of local highway agencies to these requirements was varied. Some of the 76 statements did not mention the prob-

lem area or denied that the proposed highway development would have any effect on it. Others affirmed that the highway would have a positive or negative impact on the environment but did not give any supporting evidence. A few reports listed the positive and negative impacts, along with the studies that had been done to determine the impact of the highway. The complete results of the survey, including a list of requirements for the content of a highway 102 statement, are contained in Table 1.

Indicative of the tenor of these local statements is their reliance on standardized phrases to dismiss potentially serious environmental degradation. One-third of the statements asserted without qualification that *all* highways increase the health and safety of the general public. Approximately one-third of the statements denied any but minor, temporary adverse effects. And while 91 percent of the statements affirmed the long-term productiveness of the proposed highway facility, only 4 percent provided data to substantiate this claim.

Some problem areas were neglected in a significant number of statements: 13 percent did not mention the problem of air pollution; 34 percent failed to consider the issue of community disruption; 44 percent did not discuss the disposition of citizen comments; 67 percent failed to mention the impact on taxes and the tax base; 86 percent did not consider mass transit alternatives; 18 percent failed to mention noise pollution; 54 percent failed to mention the impact on nearby property values; 58 percent did not consider the problems related to increased urbanization; and 33 percent did not consider the alternative of not building the project.

It almost goes without saying that 102 statements should be tailored to the specific highway situation at hand. A. E. Johnson, executive director of the American Association of State Highway Officials, assured the authors that every statement has been a customized product. Nevertheless, the survey uncovered the repetition of identical phrases, paragraphs, and even pages in impact statements for different urban highways. Highway engineers in St. Louis, for

TABLE I

FINAL ENVIRONMENTAL IMPACT STATEMENTS FOR URBAN HIGHWAYS: REQUIRED CONTENTS AND RESPONSES*

	Source	Not Mentioned	Impact Denied	Undocumented Positive Impact	Undocumented Negative Impact	Data Given Positive Impact	Data Given Negative Impact
A. Description of the proposed highway improvement and surroundings							
1. Number of trips per day for the design year	°°	41	—	3	—	57	—
2. Anticipated new trips generated two years after completion of highway section	°°	86	—	4	—	9	—
3. General description of surrounding terrain, existing and proposed land uses, etc.	°°	3	—	41	—	57	—
4. Present residential and neighborhood character	†	28	—	38	—	33	—
5. Maps, sketches, pictures, etc., sufficiently detailed for layman reviewer††	°°	3	—	36	—	62	—
B. The probable impact of the proposed development or improvement††							
6. Impact on economic activity; inventory of economic factors	°°†	34	4	53	3	7	0
7. Impact on employment	°°†	66	3	22	3	9	0
8. Impact on taxes; effect on local tax base	°°†	67	5	17	9	1	0
9. Impact on property values: residential	°°†	60	1	32	5	1	0
commercial		54	1	41	3	1	1
10. Problems relating to anticipated increase in urbanization	°°†	58	4	32	3	3	1
11. Probable impact of displacing families and businesses	°°†	59	19	13	8	2	3
12. Impact upon narrow band (about 1,000 feet) adjacent to the highway	°°	49	3	21	12	14	3
13. Problem of division or disruption of an established community	°°	34	47	4	7	4	4
14. Problem of division of existing uses (separating homes from shops, schools, etc.)	°°	37	39	7	7	1	9
15. Problem of increased urban congestion	°°†	36	3	51	7	5	0
16. Impact on air quality; air pollution	°°††	13	33	32	20	4	0
17. Impact on groundwater, flooding erosion, sedimentation; water pollution	°°††	26	49	8	11	5	1
18. Ambient noise levels for adjoining areas; noise pollution	°°††	18	22	18	29	7	5
19. Impact on public health and safety	°°	49	7	34	0	11	0
20. Effect upon 4(f) lands	†°						
21. Implications for population distribution	°°						
22. Impact on natural, ecological, cultural, scenic resources of significance							
23. Disruption of orderly planned development; inconsistency with local plans, goals							
24. Impact on recreation and parks	†						
25. Impact on esthetics	†						
26. Impact on wildlife and general ecology of the area	†						
27. Effect on natural and historic landmarks	†						
C. Any probable adverse environmental effects which cannot be avoided should the proposal be implemented							
28. Adverse effects, both those which cannot be reduced in severity, and those which can be reduced to an acceptable level	°°	4	32	—	57	—	8

248

D. Alternatives

		1	2	3	4	5	6
29. Probable beneficial and/or adverse effects of each alternative	• •†	68	3	22	3	3	1
30. Objective evaluation and analysis of estimated costs (social and transportation), including social service	• •						
31. Data supporting the selected alternative	• •‡	16	14	42	47	42	7
32. Consideration of "do-nothing" alternative: not going ahead with project		33	1	5	5	3	0
33. Consideration of the alternative of mass transit		86	—	—	—	—	—

E. The relationship between local short-term uses of man's environment and the maintenance and enhancement of long-term productivity

		1	2	3	4	5	6
34. Short-term uses as compared to the long-term effects	• •†	1	4	91	—	4	—
35. Impact on changes in traffic patterns	• •	45	1	45	3	7	0
36. Foreseen changes in land use (items that may limit or expand land use)	• •‡	38	4	49	4	5	0

F. Any irreversible and irretrievable commitments of resources which would be involved in the proposed action should it be implemented

		1	2	3	4	5	6
37. Commitments of resources; curtailing the range of beneficial uses of environment	• •†‡	5	47	—	43	—	4
38. Major related actions generated by highway which would be difficult to rescind	• • •	86	3	3	3	3	4
39. Future development in the area: residential	• • •	53	4	36	4	4	0
commercial	• •	37	4	53	4	3	0
industrial		66	1	30	0	3	0

G. Planning and measures taken and proposed to minimize harm from adverse effects

		1	2	3	4	5	6
40. Efforts to minimize impact: measures unique to a project discussed in detail	• •	28	4	53	0	16	0
41. Measures taken to insure proper rehousing of people and businesses relocated	• •†	32	3	50	—	18	2
42. Operation, use of existing facilities during construction, after completion	†	59	1	13	17	4	4
43. Operation, use of other transportation facilities during and after construction		87	0	5	4	3	0

H. Final statements shall incorporate all comments received on draft (including environmental comments contained in public hearing transcript) along with discussion of comments

		1	2	3	4	5	6
44. Discussion of problems and objections raised by citizens in the review process	• •†‡	14	10	30	—	41	—
45. The disposition of the comments and suggestions raised	• •‡	26	11	22	4	32	1

*The numbers in the table are percentages, rounded to the nearest whole number. Dashes indicate the category is not applicable. The 76 final 102 statements surveyed are listed according to city, date, and ELR order number in the report of the Center for Science in the Public Interest, James B. Sullivan and Paul A. Montgomery, Highways and the Environment, August 1972.

*Dept. of Transportation, FHWA, PPM 90-1, Appendix E, 2.(a-h), and Appendix F, 3. (a-d).

†Dept. of Transportation, FHWA, PPM 20-8, 4. c. (1.23).

††The problem areas listed in numbers 20-27 of this section were not part of the original survey; no statistics were gathered in these areas.

‡Dept. of Transportation. Office of the Secretary. Order 5610.1A. October 4, 1971.

example, described the positive attitude of the public toward their proposed urban highway in the identical words used by highway engineers in Omaha.[9]

In claiming that their proposed highways would not involve an irreversible or irretrievable commitment of natural resources, engineers in Reading, Pa.; Waterloo, Iowa; St. Louis, Mo.; Omaha, Neb.; Philadelphia, Pa.; Gadsden, Ala.; Tulsa, Okla.; and Chesapeake, Va.,[10] all used this same comment: "If the facility is no longer needed for transportation purposes or a greater need for the area it occupies arises, the roadway can be converted to the needed land use."

As a final example, in the local agencies' assessment of the relationship between short-term uses and long-term effects of the proposed highway, identical wording was used by the state engineers in Baltimore, Md.; Tulsa, Okla. (two highways); St. Louis, Mo.; Gadsden, Ala.; Omaha, Neb.; Chesapeake, Va.; and Madison, Wis.[11] According to one Department of Transportation (DOT) staff member who reviews these 102 statements, it is as though some states "turn in the same report for several projects and just change the names."[12]

The main inadequacy brought out by the survey of the 102 process is that few data are being collected at the local level on social, economic, and environmental issues. In place of data, generalities and assurances abound. Requiring government agencies to file 102 statements was intended to make environmental considerations as important as technological and economic factors in decision-making. But technical specialists at the state level are having a great deal of difficulty incorporating environmental considerations into their planning. This analysis of highway statements indicates that for many state highway officials a 102 statement is just additional procedural red tape.

Highway engineers interviewed by the authors, both within and outside of the DOT, were not surprised that compliance with the section 102 requirements of NEPA was not instantaneous and complete on the part of local highway departments. A 1971 DOT evaluation study of urban transportation planning reported that the states lack both the commitment and the resources to provide adequate environmental assessment.[13] Moreover, when NEPA was put into effect, the responsibility for preparing 102 statements was relegated to staff members trained primarily as engineers, not as social or environmental scientists.

The consequences could have been predicted. Lacking expertise and scientific studies, local highway agencies are resorting to form paragraphs and questionable generalities. The impact statements surveyed contain arguments rather than findings, opinions rather than studies, and generalities rather than facts. These generalities appear again and again in 102 statements as being applicable to each and every highway. They preclude further data-seeking and end inquiry by affirming the basic notion that a safer, more efficient highway facility has a positive effect on man's environment.

Although the urban highway 102 statements being filed are technically not fulfilling the requirements of NEPA and DOT, the roads are still being built. To understand why and to see what actions could be taken, we examined the political side of the 102 process.

Choosing Battles

Final concurrence or non-concurrence with highway environmental impact statements is the responsibility of DOT's Office of Environment and Urban Systems (called TEU). In TEU's Office of Environmental Quality (OEQ), a staff of readers goes through all the draft and final statements that have been reviewed by the FHWA and either concurs with the statements, offers comments on them, or rejects them. An inter-staff report, dated June 26, 1972, summarizes TEU's work to date:

"TEU has received 1,453 draft and 732 final statements from FHWA . . . TEU offered substantive comments on 21 percent of all drafts received . . . TEU returned a total of eleven FHWA final statements for revision."

More significantly, TEU spokesmen admit that the impact statement process has not succeeded in incorporating environmental concern into the highway planning process.

The spokesmen estimate that a systematic, interdisciplinary evaluation was in evidence in fewer than 50 projects. Although the 102 statements from state agencies have lately become more cognizant of social and environmental effects, the TEU staff says that the statements still "are a long way from being even partially satisfying."[14]

Because of the reliance on generalities, the 102 statements do not provide the detailed assessment required by law and technically could be rejected on that basis. However, only eleven final statements, 1.5 percent of those filed, have been rejected by TEU because of a variety of pressures on the OEQ office. The interdisciplinary staff of OEQ is relatively well qualified to assess highway 102 statements,[15] but it is too small and insecure an office to tackle the large and powerful FHWA. The FHWA recognizes the potential at OEQ; as a result, "every six months or so, there are battles royal about delegating [OEQ's] power to [FHWA's] office."[16]

Although the OEQ staff has a consensus opinion of the quality of the highway 102 statements, intramural fights with superiors in TEU occur regularly over the strength of impact statement criticisms. There are disagreements, the reviewers admit, especially with James Beggs, the under-secretary.[17] Other than the reality of political pressures, the most decisive argument brought forth against forceful commenting by OEQ is that of the FHWA administrators: "No citizens are complaining, so why are you?"

Therefore, when OEQ takes a stand, the staff members "choose their battles carefully, not on the basis of law, but on the basis of citizen support."[18] OEQ looks for citizen complaints at public hearings, in letters mailed to the OEQ office, and in threats of litigation by environmentalists. In the words of one veteran reviewer:[19]

"We don't look for a battle in, say, the middle of Utah where they're upgrading 0.6 miles of rural highway to two lanes. We look for the public hearing where there's twenty-five pages of battle, and every citizen who talks just blasts the project. We choose our battles very carefully."

When asked if NEPA's 102 process has been successful in stopping or altering harmful highways, one of the OEQ staff responded:[20]

"I'm not sure if it's due to NEPA or to citizen opposition and threats of litigation. NEPA or no NEPA, if there's public opposition, they'll change the route. The Highway Administration is subject to public pressure just like anybody else. But it takes so much!"

Questionable Assertions

Highway 102 statements frequently contain a number of somewhat stereotyped assertions that require careful analysis if one is to assess the statements in preparation for public hearings on proposed projects. In this section, eight representative arguments made by highway departments are presented, followed by a discussion of the points raised.

Relief of congestion. From an Amhurst, New York statement and DOT's 1972 Highway Act statement:

"Overall traffic capacity in the corridor would be increased with a corresponding decrease in congestion."[21] "New highways speed up and smooth out the flow of traffic as compared to traffic flows without the new highways."[22]

Actually it appears that urban highways only temporarily speed up and smooth out the flow of traffic as compared to traffic flows without the new highway. In the long run, they induce a larger number of people to buy and use automobiles as their major mode of travel. This increases congestion and stop-and-go traffic.

The new-highway inducement for greater reliance on private automobile transportation is widely accepted by highway and traffic engineers. For example, a 1970 study[23] by FHWA engineers showed that traffic generation amounted to a 7 percent annual average increase over the pre-freeway years in the corridors served by new freeways. Although the study was done mostly in rural areas, urban highways exhibit the same inducement pattern. A "before and after" study (1959 and 1961) of Chicago's Congress Street Expressway revealed a 21 percent increase in total vehicle miles of travel within the study area over

251

the two year period. This growth was three times the normal Chicago increase at that time, which was 3.5 percent per year or 7 percent for the two year period.[24]

It should be noted that new highways not only induce new traffic, but this traffic is also associated with longer trips. A study of the Baltimore area revealed that in 1926 the average work trip length was 2.6 miles; in 1946 it was about four miles; and by 1962 it had increased to more than five miles. The researchers ascribed this increase to improved highway facilities.[25]

Air pollution. From statements for an expressway in Gainesville, Florida; US 9W in Albany, New York; and DOT's 1972 Highway Act statement:

"Air pollution caused by exhaust emissions should present no problem."[26] "Upon completion of the project . . . traffic will be moving at higher and more uniform speeds, which according to studies causes less pollution from exhaust emissions than does stop-and-go and fast and slow traffic operations such as that caused by existing conditions."[27] "Two major categories of motor vehicle emissions, carbon monoxide and hydrocarbons, are reduced roughly as the square root of the increase in average traffic speeds. Emissions per vehicle-mile of travel of the third major category of motor vehicle emissions, nitrogen oxides, is statistically unrelated to changes in average traffic speed."[22]

Information which contradicts the above statements is given in an engineering study that attempts to answer this question in detail.[28] The study found that for steady-state speeds, typical of vehicles traveling on an uncongested and smoothly flowing highway, carbon monoxide emissions drop about 40 percent as speed is increased to 30 miles per hour, then increase greatly to over twice the 20 mph level as speed is increased to 70 miles per hour. Hydrocarbon emissions change very little, dropping off slightly as speed is increased to 30 and 40 miles per hour, then increasing slightly as speed is further increased to 70 mph.

Data show that nitrogen oxide emissions are not statistically unrelated to change in average traffic speeds but, rather, increase

drastically with speed. Smoothly flowing traffic at 60 mph emits approximately nine times as much nitrogen oxide as does traffic at 20 mph.

Citizens with engineering or science backgrounds can make approximate predictions of future air pollution levels directly near a new highway with the help of a Public Health Service publication, *Workbook of Atmospheric Dispersion Estimates* (available for $3.00 from the National Technical Information Service (NTIS), Springfield, Virginia, 22151).

The statement for I-78 in Allentown, Pennsylvania claims, "The wide right-of-way permits combustion emissions to dissipate readily which will help to prevent the building up of noxious fumes."[29]

This statement is incomplete because it considers only the pollution problem produced near the highway. In any given area, pollutants from all roads add up to produce a "background" pollution concentration that does not significantly depend on the traffic on any particular roadway. Thus, building a new road may temporarily decrease the traffic on a parallel arterial, but because the road will cause traffic increases over the whole area, average pollution levels will rise. After the new road has been open more than a few months, of course, congestion will increase on that road as well, so that pollution levels will be considerably higher. This area-wide "background" component of pollution becomes especially serious during atmospheric temperature inversions when stable air layers can trap pollutants and cause them to build up to two or three times their normal concentration.[30]

Air pollution studies indicate that suburban areas during the next decades will be subject to drastic pollution increases. Residential sections of Arlington County near Washington, D.C., for example, will be subjected to an estimated 348 percent increase in auto emissions during the period from 1964 to 1985 compared to a 109 to 193 percent increase in downtown Washington for the same time period. Areas twenty miles west of center-city Chicago will be subjected to a 709 percent increase from

1956 to 1980, while emission levels in the center-city area will remain static during that same time.[31]

Some idea of the degree to which auto emissions will increase in a neighborhood can be obtained from the local highway and traffic department traffic projections or from the air quality implementation plans prepared to satisfy requirements of the federal Clean Air Act.[32] (These are available from the U.S. Environmental Protection Agency.)

Noise pollution. From the statements for I-15 in San Bernardino, California; US 77 in Lincoln, Nebraska; and I-78 in Allentown, Pennsylvania:

"Noise intrusion would be relatively minor."[33] "The design for this highway project will provide for smooth flow of traffic which will minimize air and noise pollution created by motor vehicle operations."[34] "The wide right-of-way will permit traffic noise to disperse and spend itself to an acceptable decibel level."[35]

Since 1955 the amount of land exposed to objectionable levels of intrusive noise has grown from 100 to 2,000 square miles.[36] Most urban noise results from traffic; studies in London found that traffic produced a higher noise level than any other source at 80 percent of the sites measured.

Noise is most often measured in units called decibels (dBA). A car horn 3 feet away produces approximately 115 dBA; a heavy truck 50 feet away produces about 90 dBA, enough to cause hearing damage to anyone exposed to it for extended lengths of time. For a good summary of how these noise levels affect us see *Effects of Noise On People* (available from NTIS).

Highway engineers try to reduce this noise by various techniques, such as depressing the highway, planting trees and shrubbery, leaving wide right-of-way areas to disperse the noise. Some of these techniques are more effective than others. If noise in the roadway is 83 dBA, for example, a ten-foot barrier would reduce noise levels right next to the road to approximately 65 dBA, quite a noticeable decrease. Depressing the road would reduce levels next to the road to slightly over 70 dBA. An approximate rule of thumb for using distance to disperse noise is that doubling the distance from the noise subtracts 3 dBA, not a very effective method of noise reduction.

The trouble with these techniques is that in urban areas space limitations often make them impractical. In addition, devices to trap noise also trap air pollutants, thereby increasing pollution exposure for motorists on the roadway. Another difficulty is that noise control devices can only decrease noise on the freeway and not on the city streets which receive increased traffic produced by the freeway. To make some rough but easy calculations about noise levels from a proposed freeway, a useful aid is the Department of Housing and Urban Development's booklet *Noise*

TABLE 2

DEATH RATES FOR AUTOMOBILE, RAIL, AND AIR TRANSPORTATION
(per 100 million passenger miles)

	Death Rate	Comparison of Death Rate with Auto Rate (death rate/auto death rate)
Passenger automobiles and taxis—old roads	2.20	1.00
Passenger automobiles and taxis—freeways	1.17	0.53
Railroad passenger trains	0.09	0.041
Scheduled air transport	0.13	0.059

Assessment Guidelines.

Safety. From the statement for I-759 in Gadsden, Alabama: "One of the most significant benefits of the construction of this roadway, as well as all Interstate highways, is the accident reduction and safety record of this system. Smoother flow of traffic should reduce accidents that so often occur in stop-and-go traffic."[37]

This statement fails to consider the safer alternatives of non-highway forms of transportation. A comparison of death rates for automobiles with rates for other forms of travel indicates that highways are extremely unsafe (see Table 2).[38] Although the road death rate on freeways is only half that on older roads, this advantage is meager compared with the safety record for other modes of travel. For example, railroad passenger trains are almost 24 times safer per passenger mile than old highways and over 13 times safer than the interstate roads.

Some safety predictions can be calculated for a specific highway. Assume, for example, the proposed road will carry 30,000 vehicles per day over a stretch of six miles. Since commuter automobiles on the average carry 1.4 passengers each, this works out to approximately 92 million passenger miles on the road each year. Using the comparative mortality rates cited in Table 2 (1.17 for freeways versus 0.09 for railroads) this means theoretically that one life per year could be saved if rail transit rather than the highway carried the commuters.

Mobility and the indigent. A Wilmington, Delaware statement indicates that all income groups will benefit from the proposed highway:

"Every resident of the city stands to benefit from increased city financial programs and increased job opportunities."[39]

This statement overlooks the fact that large segments of the American population do not have an automobile or are unable to drive. Because of our reliance on the highway mode of travel and the accompanying neglect of public transportation, these people, who are primarily the poor, handicapped and aged, are left virtually immobile.

Census Bureau statistics reveal that 57 percent of households with incomes under $3,000 have no automobile; 14 percent in the $3,000 to $9,999 income range have none.[40] The DOT surveyed five cities—Baltimore, Md.; Milwaukee, Wis.; Springfield, Mass.; Richmond, Va.; and Columbia, S.C. —and found almost one out of four dwellings without a car.[41] A study of five Ohio cities revealed that 54.6 percent of households with the head of the household older than 65 years have no car, while 42 percent of these homes reported that they needed more transportation than was available.[42]

This problem of inadequate transportation has severe effects on the poor and the aged, ranging from inability to obtain employment, education, and health care—to the problem, once work is found, of excessive time spent commuting.

Land values and property tax. From a statement for a road in Bloomington, Illinois: "The lucrative economy provided by the highway raises the tax base of an area and the additional tax revenue provides for social service expenditures."[43]

This is not always so, according to the President's Council on Environmental Quality, which states:[44]

"Federally assisted highway construction has been the major determinant of growth patterns and development in this country since 1956 . . . Construction of suburban arteries can easily be justified as a short-range solution to pressing problems of congestion. Yet it can also spur new development far from the city core, reward land speculators, create a need for more public services, destroy natural areas, dump more cars into the central city and promote a pattern of suburban settlement that nearly precludes mass transit."

The effect of highways on land values is directly related to the availability of underdeveloped land. If the highway is in a position where it creates easier access to underdeveloped land and thus contributes favorable conditions for its development, then the value of this land may increase. If the land surrounding the highway is already fully developed, as in most central business districts, or if there is no possibility for development, as in remote farm land, new highways probably will not increase land values significantly.

A limited access highway will be of limited economic benefit to the urban or rural community through which it passes if there are no exits to that community. A clogged highway that accelerates the suffocation of an urban area can do little to enhance property value. Indeed, in the case of a congested city center, the opposite may well occur.

Two other forms of loss in property value often follow highways. In almost all cases, except near interchanges, studies show that residential land within one-half mile of superhighways decreases in value. And residential areas that do not qualify for urbanization (because of zoning or other reasons) also tend to lose value when disrupted.

Highways have raised property values in small cities, where roads attract major industry to an area that is not otherwise served by adequate transportation. Higher land values, however, do not automatically mean social benefit. Recent cost-benefit studies in Kentucky found that the cost of services that the local government had to provide for new industrial development outweighed the increase in revenues from property taxes on the higher land values.[15]

Even if highways aid the economic development of their locality, they may not transmit this new wealth to the cities. The new fringe of development may be out of the city's taxing jurisdiction, and, by opening up new areas for development, highways may attract existing industry from downtown areas. This not only reduces the tax base and adds to the unemployment rolls in cities, but also precipitates a cycle that pulls out other businesses and the affluent. Urban cores are then left with people and businesses unable to pay for requisite city services.

Relocation and community disruption. From the statement for a freeway in Louisville, Kentucky: "A roadway of this type must necessarily separate one neighbor from another, divide one farm into two, and produce slight inconveniences to minor travel in order to bring the County, State, and Nation as a whole into closer communication."[46]

In 1970 alone, 57,686 people were uprooted from their homes to clear the way for federal-aid highways.[5] These people belonged to 19,844 households.[5] The FHWA estimates that, during the next several years, displacements will rise to about 25,000 households annually.[5] During 1970 about 3,500 farms, businesses, and non-profit organizations were also evicted.

But gross statistics like these do not adequately describe the problem of relocation at the local level. For example, when the Watts-Century freeway in Los Angeles was built, it was decided that two highway interchanges in the heart of the Watts community were needed. These interchanges necessitated the displacement of 2,600 families. The housing units affected were low-cost, and half were occupied by the owners. Twenty percent of the occupants were retired and on fixed incomes. To find or build comparable housing at no additional cost to the occupants was impossible. The average value of the houses outside the Watts area is between $18,000 and $22,000.[17]

Relocation discriminates. In 1970, 18 percent of those dislocated were non-white, while only 12.5 percent of the population were non-white. Studies show black people also pay more for their relocation (see Table 3).[18]

TABLE 3
COST OF RELOCATION

	White	Black
Acquisition price	$5,905	$5,338
Replacement cost	8,357	9,234
Financial loss	2,454	3,896

In a survey of attitudes of people toward the north leg of the proposed Inner Loop in Washington, D.C., scientists found that involuntary moves are upsetting, that individuals with sentimental attachments to specific neighborhood features often crowd into adjacent, similar neighborhoods with losses to all, and that major physical neighborhood changes require major adjustments.[49]

These findings are consistent with another study of the impact of forced relocation on the lives of the working class in Boston's West End project. The researcher found that forced relocation is a highly disruptive and disturbing experience, a crisis with potential danger to mental health for many people. All the symptoms of the grief syndrome are often present, and grief reaction is strongest among the working class, particularly those having a strong commitment to their neighborhood. Reactions are expressed in terms of painful loss, continued longing and depression, sense of helplessness, and psychological or social distress.[49]

In a companion study, another scientist concluded that "the deleterious effects of the uprooting experience, the loss of familiar places and persons, and the difficulties of adjusting to and accepting new living environments may be far more serious issues than are changes in housing status."[49]

Use of natural resources. From a statement for a freeway in Waterloo, Iowa: "The elements which go into highway construction cannot be classified as irreversible or irretrievable commitments of resources. If the facility is no longer needed as a transportation network or if a greater need arises for the area it occupies, the roadway can be converted to the needed land use."[50]

Highways use vast quantities of materials. One favorite statistic touted by road builders is dramatic: all of the crushed stone, sand, and gravel used in the construction of the Interstate system could build a wall 50 feet wide and 9 feet high completely around the world.[51]

For any individual highway project, resources used can be calculated from the DOT use-factors listed in Table 4.[52] For example, a $100 million highway segment would use 68,000 x 100 = 6,800,000 man-hours of labor and 49,000 x 100 = 4,900,000 board feet of lumber.

When resources used for all the roads constructed each year are added up, it is clear that highways consume a significant portion of our natural resources. In 1969 highway construction used 24.6 percent of cement produced in the U.S. and 51.3 percent of the sand and gravel. Autos used 19.5 percent of our steel[53] (highways used an additional 4 percent),[54] 71.7 percent of natural rubber,[55] and 24.4 percent of total U.S. energy output. The amount of land paved

TABLE 4

MATERIALS AND LABOR REQUIRED FOR HIGHWAY CONSTRUCTION*

Material	Unit	Number of Units Per Million Dollars of Construction Cost
Cement	Barrels	13,600
Bituminous Material	Tons	856
Aggregates		
Purchased by Contractor	Tons	42,000
Produced by Contractor	Tons	30,000
Steel		
Structural	Tons	182
Reinforcing	Tons	230
Lumber	Board feet	49,000
Petroleum Products	Gallons	125,000
Labor	Man-hours	68,000

*Costs of right-of-way acquisition and engineering are not taken into account.

over for highways is equivalent to the total area of Vermont, New Hampshire, Massachusetts, Connecticut, and Rhode Island—about half of New England.[55]

These uses of natural resources involve deep-seated issues (for example, see "Lost Power," *Environment*, April 1972) that cannot logically be glossed over by simply suggesting that one can always convert the highway right-of-way for some other purpose.

These and similar arguments appear in many 102 statements, although they vary in context from statement to statement. Citizens, whether as individuals or in groups, usually cannot do a complete and detailed assessment of the environmental impact of a new highway; that is rightly the role of government. What citizens can and have done in many cities is to make certain that those responsible for this assessment actually carry it out in adequate detail. Hopefully, public action of this sort will induce transportation planners to develop the commitment necessary to supply realistic environmental analyses. Our present assessment techniques are hardly worthy of this country's technical sophistication. ☐

NOTES

1. Page, Logan W., quoted in **Engineering Record**, Feb. 26, 1910.

2. **Accident Facts,** National Safety Council, 1971, p. 3.

3. **Ibid.,** p. 8.

4. **The Collapse of Commuter Service,** American Municipal Association, 1960, p. 12.

5. U.S. Dept. of Transportation, Federal Highway Administration, Office of Right-of-way, Relocation Division.

6. Hirst, E., "Energy Consumption for Automobiles," unpublished report, Oak Ridge National Laboratory, 1972, Table 3.

7. Public Law 91-190.

8. **Policy and Procedure Memorandum 90-1,** U.S. Dept. of Transportation, Federal Highway Administration.

9. References to impact statements are given by their **Environmental Law Reporter** (ELR) number, in this case ELR 1831 (St. Louis) and 309 (Omaha).

10. The 102 statements, in order, are: ELR 1820, 978, 1831, 3097, 4151, 4274, 1284, 976.

11. In order, ELR, 972, 1284 and 1596, 1831, 4274, 3097, 3015, and 976.

12. Personal interview, July 19, 1972. To protect confidentiality, names are omitted.

13. **An Evaluation of Urban Transportation Planning,** U.S. Dept. of Transportation, Office of the Secretary, Feb. 1971.

14. Personal interview, July 14, 1972.

15. "Interdisciplinary Nature of Staff Members," staff report. The fields within the TEU office are: public administration, political science, economics, law, urban systems, planning, civil engineering, environmental health, social sciences, health education, environmental design, real estate appraisal.

16. Personal interview, July 21, 1972.

17. **Ibid.**

18. **Ibid.**

19. **Ibid.**

20. **Ibid.**

21. ELR 450.

22. **Draft Environmental Impact Statement on the Proposed Federal-Aid Highway and Mass Transportation Act of 1972,** U. S. Dept. of Transportation, p. 19.

23. "Reduced Congestion On Old Routes," U.S. Dept. of Transportation, Federal Highway Administration, unpublished report, Mar. 19, 1970.

24. Chicago Area Transportation Study Paper, prepared for presentation at the 42nd Annual Meeting of the Highway Research Board, Washington, D.C., Jan. 1963.

25. Voorhees, A. M., **et al.,** "Traffic Patterns and Land Use Alternatives," presented at the 41st Annual Meeting of the Highway Research Board, Jan. 1962.

26. ELR 1319.

27. ELR 4269.

28. "Effect of Speed on Emissions," Project M-220, unpublished report, California Air Resources Board, Mar. 1971.

29. ELR 1662.

30. "The Automobile and Air Pollution: A Program for Progress, Part II," U.S. Dept. of Commerce, Dec. 1967, p. 18.

31. "Calculating Future Carbon Monoxide Emissions and Concentrations From Urban Traffic Data," U.S. Dept. of Health, Education, and Welfare, Public Health Service, June 1967, p. 12.

32. 42 U.S.C., 1857 et seq.

33. ELR 1642.

34. ELR 1355.

35. ELR 1662.

36. Ruckelshaus, William D., Administrator, U.S. Environmental Protection Agency, Statement before the Subcommittee on the Environment, Senate Committee on Commerce, Apr. 7, 1972, p. 51.

37. ELR 4274.

38. **Accident Facts,** op. cit., p. 75.

49. ELR 1277.

40. "Consumer Buying Indicators," **Series P-65, No. 18,** U.S. Bureau of the Census, Aug. 11, 1967, p. 5.

41. Wilbur Smith & Associates, **Patterns of Car Ownership, Trip Generation and Trip Sharing In Urbanized Areas; A Report to the Bureau of Public Roads,** U.S. Dept. of Transportation, 1968, p. 100.

42. "Older Americans and Transportation," U.S. Senate Committee on Aging, 1970, pp. 10-11.

43. ELR 4640.

44. **First Annual Report**, Council on Environmental Quality, Aug. 1970, p. 194.

45. "Impact of New Industry on Local Government Finances in Five Small Towns in Kentucky," **Agricultural Economic Report 191**, U.S. Dept. of Agriculture, Sept. 1970.

46. ELR 328.

47. "Transportation and Community Values," **Special Report 105**, Highway Research Board, 1969, p. 117.

48. "Community Values and Socioeconomic Impact," **Highway Research Record 277**, Highway Research Board, 1969, p. 7.

49. "Relocation: Social and Economic Aspects," **Special Report 110**, Highway Research Board, 1969, p. 20.

50. ELR 978.

51. "The Highway Transportation Story in Facts," National Highway Users Conference, Sept. 1969, p. 21.

52. **Highway Statistics/1969**, U.S. Dept. of Transportation, Federal Highway Administration, p. 104.

53. 1971 Automobile Facts and Figures, Automobile Manufacturers Association, p. 25.

54. Calculated from above usage statistics.

55. **Highway Statistics/1969**, loc. cit., calculated from mileage and road width statistics.

Environmental Protection in the City of New York

Urban pollution control presents problems of great technical, legal, and political complexity.

Merril Eisenbud

The City of New York, by reason of its size, its geographic position in the midst of the world's most densely populated region, and decades of neglect, has been beset acutely with environmental problems. As has been generally true at all levels of government, a comprehensive approach to environmental protection had been handicapped in the past by traditional organizational separation of responsibilities, with inadequate coordination among the organizational units. To provide a unified approach, Mayor John V. Lindsay created the Environmental Protection Administration (EPA) in March 1968 to consolidate former administratively separate functions concerned with environmental hygiene. With its formation, EPA became responsible for street sanitation, water supply, water pollution control, air pollution, and noise abatement. It is an organization of more than 20,000 employees, with an annual operating budget of about $275 million, and a construction program of more than $2 billion during the next 5 years.

This article will deal with some of the pitfalls and successes of the program during its first 2 years of existence. Although no two communities are alike in all respects, the pollution problems of all cities do have many characteristics in common, and one generalization that can surely be made is that problems of urban pollution control present aspects of enormous legal, technical, sociological, and political complexities. No substantial progress can be made without huge expenditures of money and many years of sustained effort.

Air Pollution Control

The present active program of air pollution control began in the mid-1960's in response to widespread public interest. In 1965 Councilman Robert Low and the then mayoral candidate Lindsay began campaigns to strengthen the local laws governing air pollution control. A series of hearings before the City Council developed the first comprehensive report (1) of the problems of air pollution control in New York City, and early in 1966 a second report was published by a mayoral task force

SCIENCE, November, 1970, Vol. 170, pp. 706-712.

chaired by Norman Cousins (2). These two reports laid the groundwork for the energetic program developed by Commissioner Austin N. Heller, who headed the Department of Air Resources (3) from the late spring of 1966 until February 1970.

A new air pollution control law (Local Law 14) was passed by the City Council early in 1966 and mandated certain basic requirements among which were the following. (i) The sulfur content of all fuels burned in New York City would be limited to 1 percent by the 1969 to 1970 heating season. (ii) No incinerators could be installed in newly constructed buildings. (iii) All existing apartment house incinerators were to be shut down or upgraded according to a specified timetable. (iv) Emission controls were to be installed as soon as possible on all municipal incinerators. (v) All open burning of leaves, refuse, and building demolition materials would be banned within city limits.

The overall emissions of sulfur dioxide to the city's atmosphere were reduced by 56 percent by the end of 1969. This has been reflected by progressive reductions in the hourly peak concentration of SO_2 (Fig. 1). The annual maximum hourly concentration, which was 2.2 parts per million (ppm) in 1965, was reduced to 0.8 ppm by 1969, and further improvement has been observed in the early months of 1970.

Dust and soot are the most annoying form of air pollution in many cities. The sources of the particulate emissions in New York City are shown in Table 1, which indicates that space heating, municipal incineration, apartment house incineration, and power generation ac-

count for about 80 percent of the 69,100 tons (1 ton = 907 kilograms) emitted per year to the atmosphere as of November 1969.

During 1969, three of the city's eleven municipal incinerators were shut down, and another is scheduled to be closed as soon as alternate means of handling refuse can be arranged in the next year or two. The remaining seven incinerators are sufficiently modern so that air-cleaning equipment can be installed at a cost of about $12 million. However, because no equipment manufacturer would offer performance warranties, and in the absence of experience, an experimental program was designed to obtain the information needed to make the required engineering decisions. In addition to pilot plant tests of various air-cleaning techniques, full-scale installations have been made of two electrostatic precipitators and one Venturi scrubber. The early experience at these installations has been encouraging (Fig. 2), but, because of the corrosive nature of the effluents and the generally arduous service to which equipment of this kind must be put, many months of testing will be necessary. These are the first installations of this type in the United States, and the information being obtained will be generally useful to communities throughout the country.

The largest single source of particulate emissions to the air of New York City is space heating from about 30,000 apartment houses that burn No. 6 residual fuel oil. The black smoke that one sees curling up from apartment house rooftops during the heating season is usually the result of improper operation of residual fuel oil boilers. Local Law 14 mandates installation of equipment modifications that will result in increased combustion efficiency and less particulate emission, and these are working well in about 1,500 furnaces where the change has been made.

The second largest source of particulates is apartment house incinerators, about 17,000 of which were constructed between about 1947 and 1967.

The improvements required for incinerators and residual oil burners proved practical, but the apartment owners nevertheless brought suit against the city, charging that the law was unconstitutional and imposed unreasonable hardships on the landlords. This suit has stalled compliance with the provisions of Local Law 14 that pertain to apartment house oil burners and incinerators.

The city has installed an aerometric

Table 1. Sources of particulate emissions to the atmosphere of New York City in November 1969 [from (3)].

Source	Amount (ton/year)	Per-cent
Space heating	22,300	32.3
Municipal incineration	13,330	19.3
On-site incineration	12,690	18.4
Mobile sources	9,900	14.3
Power generation	6,400	9.2
Industrial sources	4,500	6.5
Total	69,120	100.0

network consisting of 38 stations that began operation in late 1968. Data from ten of the stations are telemetered directly to the laboratory, and the others are manually operated. The Department of Air Resources has also developed an alert warning system that mandates progressively more stringent steps to reduce contaminant emissions in the event of an air pollution emergency. Should the SO_2, particulate, or CO concentrations reach predetermined values, various controls would go into effect, including reduction of municipal incineration, shifts to the less polluting fuels, and, if necessary, a gradual reduction of industrial processes, power generation, and incineration. The diminution that is continuing to take place in sulfur and particulate emissions makes it increasingly unlikely that stringent curtailment of activities will ever be necessary.

The internal combustion engine is the main source of CO in urban atmospheres at the present time. The concentration of CO exceeds the air quality target of 15 ppm near some heavily used streets, but it is not known to what extent people are exposed to these concentrations on a continuing basis. It is commonly believed that the automobile is the main source of urban pollution. This is certainly true in some

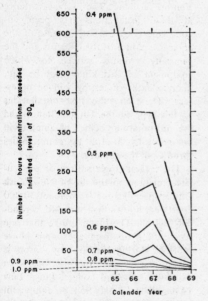

Fig. 1. The number of hours the concentration of SO_2 exceeded the indicated level, 1965–69 [from (3)].

localities where photochemical reactions involving components of automobile exhausts are known to contribute in a major way to the irritating smog characteristic of Los Angeles and certain other cities. However, this phenomenon has been less of a problem in New York City, where the subjective complaints due to air pollution can more properly be ascribed to sulfur oxides and particulates.

Another popular misconception is that the automobile is the main polluter because its emissions are greater in quantity than any other source of air pollution. Thus in New York City in 1967 it was estimated that automobiles discharged 1.7 million tons of CO per year. The next largest pollutant was SO_2, which was being emitted to the atmosphere at a rate of 828,000 tons per year. However, SO_2 is far more noxious than CO, for which the tentative air quality criterion is 15 ppm in New York State, as compared to about 0.1 ppm for SO_2. Thus the SO_2 emissions, though only about 48 percent of the CO emissions, are far more significant because its permissible concentration is less than 1 percent of that for CO.

The main source of CO exposure of city dwellers is apt to be cigarettes, the CO content of mainstream smoke being over 40,000 ppm (4). Smoking one pack of cigarettes per day is said to be equivalent to continuous exposure to 50 ppm of CO in ambient air.

As the air of our cities gradually becomes cleaner, many communities will have to answer the questions, "How clean is clean?" or "How much is clean air worth?" Unfortunately, there is often insufficient basic knowledge with which to answer such questions intelligently. Air pollution imposes economic losses due to soiling and corrosion and also causes health effects. The economic losses due to air pollution include shorter shelf life of many types of goods, higher cleaning costs, and corrosion of certain materials. The economic loss in large urban areas is thought to average $65 per person per year, but there have been no studies as to how these costs can be apportioned among the various sources of air pollution.

One could argue that every city should have the cleanest air possible. The problem is that air pollution abatement measures cost a good deal of money, and the costs increase exponentially as the goals become more strict. The measures that must be adopted in New York City to implement the present provisions of the air pollution control law will cost about $500 million by about 1972. If the economic losses due to air pollution are as high as has been estimated, this is obviously a good investment, since the city's 8 million residents would receive a return on their investment of more than 100 percent per year, assuming the estimated economic loss to be $65 per capita.

There are many epidemiological studies in the literature, but there is as yet no satisfactory way of appraising the health effects of air pollutants at the concentrations experienced where reasonable abatement procedures are in effect. The results of these studies are highly equivocal at the levels of atmospheric pollution that will be reached when the present control program is fully implemented in 1972 to 1973. Should pressures develop for a higher degree of abatement than is now contemplated by Local Law 14, one would be justified in asking at what point any further investment would be less wisely spent on air pollution control than on housing, elimination of lead poisoning in the ghettos, better nutrition, better hospital service, or any other of the unlimited number of ways by which one can benefit the public health. We will see that this question arises again in connection with current policies on water pollution control.

For lack of a cost-benefit approach to the hygiene of urban atmospheres, we are doing surprisingly little about one class of particularly noxious pollutants, the aero-allergens. There are few data on the societal costs of disability from hay fever, but one source (5) estimates that 8 million people suffer from hay fever in the United States, that prescribed medicines for treatment of this affliction cost $65 million in this country in 1964, and that 25 million days are lost from work. The aero-allergens probably impose a greater cost in impairment of health than can be ascribed to any of the atmospheric pollutants for which control measures are now being developed. As noted earlier, about $500 million will be spent in New York City to implement the provisions of the air pollution law. This money will be spent over about a 5-year period and will be followed by increased annual operating costs of many millions of dollars per year. Nationwide, the Department of Health, Education, and Welfare estimates (6) that the annual cost of sulfur and particulate control in the United States, based on the use of 1 percent sulfur oil, will be about $500 million in 1971. In contrast, the total budget for ragweed control in New York City is about $5000 per year, which allows hardly enough to answer an occasional complaint.

If expenditures for ragweed control were of the same order of magnitude as for other pollutants, it might be feasible to control the pollen in a variety of ways. For example, specific herbicides might be developed, or the growth of ragweed might be controlled by some ecological process such as by adjusting the quality of soil in vacant fields and other areas where ragweed tends to grow. Or, as a last resort, the ragweed could be pulled out by hand, which would provide much needed summer employment for city youths. No doubt more meaningful control techniques would be suggested if there had been adequate research into the subject. Here clearly is an example of an environmental factor that deserves a higher priority.

Asbestos is an example of a relatively new contaminant of urban atmospheres, and there are ominous indications of the need for stringent controls (7). When sprayed on structural steel, asbestos makes an excellent fire-retardant material, but it contaminates the urban atmosphere at the time of application and again when the building is demolished. It is known that inhaled asbestos can produce a rare form of cancer, mesothelioma, after long incubation periods, but there is as yet no information about the relation of the incidence of this disease to the concentration of asbestos in urban air. There is evidence that mesotheliomas are now being seen more frequently in the general population, and it has been suggested that this may be due to asbestos pollution. Cases being seen today may be due to exposure two or three decades ago, when exposure was presumably much less than it is today. However, today's exposure may not produce cases for 20 or 30 years. Thus, the people living in today's cities may be committed to a higher incidence of mesothelioma in the future. A thorough study of the use of asbestos in the building trades is needed, and recommendations must be developed to minimize urban exposure or to find a substitute for the asbestos.

This is being done in New York City, and rules for the safe handling of asbestos are about to be issued.

When most people complain about air pollution they are referring to the dust that settles on furniture and other surfaces. Chemical and optical techniques must be developed that make it possible to apportion the settled dust among the various possible sources of pollution. Sometimes the sources are obvious, but sometimes not, and techniques are needed that would make it possible to ascertain if oil burners, incinerators, demolition dust, or natural dust is the offender in any given instance. Only with such information can one intelligently design a program of particulate emissions control.

The long-range prospects for clean air in New York, as in other large cities, are good and will be achieved in part as a by-product of the development of nuclear power. These plants are relatively pollution-free and will in time replace the fossil fuel plants unless the very existence of nuclear power as an alternative to fossil fuels causes the latter to undertake research and development that leads to a high degree of air pollution control. Recent developments in sulfur removal suggest that this may already be happening.

Whether the electrical generators operate on nuclear power or pollution-free fossil fuels, the central stations are destined to provide an increasing percentage of the energy needs of the community. Truly clean air will not be achieved until the thousands of inefficient individual space-heating boilers are eliminated in favor of steam or electric heat supplied from well-controlled central generating stations.

Noise Abatement

The law that established the Environmental Protection Administration specified that it should develop a noise abatement program, the broad outlines of which were developed by a task force that spent 3 years preparing a thoughtful analysis of the noise problems of the city together with recommendations for the future program (8).

A program of noise abatement in any large city is destined to be a long and arduous one. High on the list of priorities should be construction machinery, automotive equipment, aircraft, rooftop air conditioners, sirens, horns, and subways. A model noise abatement law, similar to the law dealing with air pollution control, must be developed, and rules and regulations must be adopted for enforcement purposes. Finally, new technological approaches must be developed.

Some progress has already been made in New York City in a small way. From the joint efforts of the Task Force, industry, and the Department of Sanitation, have come improvements now being incorporated into New York City's purchasing specifications which allow a marked reduction in the noise levels from sanitation trucks. Progress has also been made in the partial quieting of diesel compressors used in construction work.

Step by step it should be possible to provide a more quiet city. However, many of the sources of noise are beyond a city's powers to control. For example, all automotive equipment is subject to State control. The acoustic standards established by New York State call for a limit of 88 decibels, 50 feet (1 foot

264

= 0.3 meter) from a truck. This may be satisfactory for a throughway in the open country, but is not acceptable for a truck passing through city streets where people are located closer than 50 feet and where the sound reverberates from buildings. Accordingly, state legislation is being prepared that will mandate acoustic specifications for motor vehicles that are more appropriate for urban needs.

Aircraft noise, so troublesome to many communities, is preempted by the federal government, and the city's role is therefore limited to persuasion or such influence as can be mounted by the collected efforts of legislators from urban areas.

Water Supply

The City of New York is blessed with a supply of excellent water carried in deep rock tunnels from reservoirs located on watersheds as far away as 125 miles. The city must provide water for its own needs, and is also required by state law to provide water to eight upstate counties.

The per capita demand for water has been rising steadily from about 25 gallons per day (gpd) (1 gallon = 3.8 liters) in the early 19th century to more than 150 gpd at present. The demand for water by the people living in the area served by the system is now 1400 million gallons per day (mgd) and is expected to increase to 2200 mgd by 2020, at which time the extrapolated per capita daily consumption would be about 185 gpd. Present projections indicate that the demand for water will exceed the dependable yield of the present system by sometime in the late 1980's unless steps are taken to conserve the use of water.

Fig. 2. Effectiveness of electrostatic participation for removal of visible emissions from a municipal incinerator. The structures shown are a cooling tower and precipitator for one furnace. Two furnaces were in operation · at the time of the photograph, one on each stack. There are four furnaces at this incinerator, thus requiring that the installation illustrated be quadrupled to clean the particulate emissions from the four furnaces. [Courtesy American Wheelbrator Company]

The extent to which water can be conserved is not fully understood. Intensive educational campaigns during past periods of drought have reduced water use by about 150 mgd, but public cooperation to this extent can reasonably be expected only during periods of near emergency—not under normal conditions. In the future, water conservation should be sought by adoption of a program of universal water metering and encouragement of plumbing manufacturers to develop fixtures that use less water.

New York is almost alone among the larger cities in not having a system of universal water metering. About 170,000 meters have been installed in commercial buildings and in about 20,000 residences, but this accounts for only about 23 percent of all water accounts. Nevertheless, the per capita rate of water use is not excessive. Of the eleven largest cities in the United States, among which the per capita consumption of water ranges from 132 to 235 gpd, only three cities consume water at a rate lower than that of New York City. The reason for the wide range of per capita consumption among the various cities is not understood.

With metering, water charges could be adjusted to discourage the unnecessary use of water. Rating systems presently charge less for water as the use increases. A system must be devised that will not be punitive and will not discourage the use of water for sanitary or other purposes within reasonable limits, but that will result in increasing unit costs for water as the use increases. Before this can be done, it will be necessary to know much more than we do about the way in which water is used in the household and the minimum quantities that can be used for various purposes.

A major objective of the water management program should be to stabilize, and possibly reduce, the per capita demand. In order to do this, one must first undertake studies designed to elucidate the reasons why the per capita demand is increasing. Second, there is a need to design plumbing fixtures that use less water. An excellent example is the toilet flush tank which in most cases uses about 6 gallons per flush. Assuming that the average person flushes the toilet four times per day (and there

aren't even good data on this), this use would consume 24 gallons per day, or about 15 percent of the per capita consumption. Flush tanks are available that perform their function in a satisfactory manner with only 2 gallons per flush. The gradual changeover to more efficient tanks in the years ahead would thus reduce the per capita consumption of water by about 10 percent or more. This kind of innovation is also needed in kitchen faucets, shower baths, laundry machines, and other household or commercial plumbing fixtures.

Unless the use of water can be stabilized, additional sources of supply will be necessary in the decades ahead. Recent studies suggest that the Hudson River, which is now in the process of rehabilitation, could be used as a source of water in the latter part of this century. It will be necessary to assure that the freshwater flow is adequate to keep the saltwater tidal intrusion well below the proposed intakes presently planned for Hyde Park, and for this purpose water stored in Adirondack Mountains reservoirs would be released to the Hudson River during the dry summer months.

It is possible that, in time, reuse of water will become feasible on a scale suitable for large cities, or that large-scale desalination will be possible. Every effort should be made to further technology in these areas, but for potable water in the quantities required by large cities, no practical choice other than impoundment of surface water is available for the foreseeable future in many parts of the country.

Water Pollution Control

New York City currently provides some degree of secondary treatment for about 75 percent of the 1300 mgd of sewage generated. About 325 mgd of raw sewage continue to be discharged into the estuary, mainly from the west side of Manhattan. With the aid of the New York State Pure Waters Bond Issue, which provides for 60 percent reimbursement of expenditures for sewage plant construction, a $1.2-billion program has been started by New York City which, when completed in 1975, will provide high-degree secondary treatment for all its dry-weather waste water.

When the new plants are completed, there will remain the problem created by the fact that New York City, like many communities, uses combined sewers to collect both sanitary and storm drainage. The storm waters overwhelm the capacity of the sewage treatment plants, causing overflow of untreated sewage into the estuary. This problem is particularly acute in the 30-square-mile Jamaica Bay, which drains major portions of Brooklyn and Queens and which is intended to be included in the Gateway National Park, the first national park to be located within a city. Following completion of secondary sewage treatment facilities, a second program, not likely to be completed until the mid- or late 1980's, will provide for treatment of storm waters. In preparation, a $1-million ecological study of Jamaica Bay, financed by the Federal Water Pollution Control Administration, has been undertaken to provide a quantitative understanding of the hydrological, biological, and chemical characteristics of the bay. A demonstration storm water treatment plant is being built on the shore of Jamaica Bay and will serve as a prototype for a ring of several additional plants that will ultimately be built on its periphery. These plants will im-

pound storm water which will be degritted, filtered, and chlorinated before being discharged into the estuary. Additional plants of this type will be constructed in the East Bronx. It is anticipated that by the late 1980's the estuary will have been sufficiently restored so that virtually the total shoreline of New York City may be available for recreational bathing.

The purpose of estuarine pollution control is to protect the water quality for recreational purposes, seafood harvesting, and wildlife preservation. Chemical indices of pollution such as biochemical oxygen demand (BOD), concentrations of nutrient ions and toxic substances, as well as biological indicators, such as the concentration of coliform organisms, are necessary adjuncts to a water pollution control program, but many of the standards currently in use have little basis, either theoretical or empirical, despite the fact that the standards have a fundamental influence on the design of sewage treatment plants and their cost. In most cases there is inadequate information about the hydrological and ecological characteristics of an estuary, and hence the design of water pollution control plants cannot be optimized in relation to the nature of the receiving waters. Sewage sent to plants located in one part of an estuary may require a higher degree of treatment than that treated in a plant located elsewhere. Moreover, the location and design of outfalls may influence the treatment requirements, and these designs should be based on the characteristics of the estuary. In the New York estuary, as in most places throughout the country, sufficient information does not exist. This is unfortunate because hundreds of millions of dollars are involved in decisions as to whether a plant should be designed, for example, for removal of either 67 or 90 percent of the BOD. There may, in fact, be no ecological or health gain in going to the higher value in one place, whereas in other cases a need for the highest possible secondary or even tertiary treatment might be indicated.

Each estuary should be studied thoroughly so that as complete as possible a mathematical model of the hydrological and biological characteristics can be developed. Such a program might take as much as 10 years to complete, and it should be financed out of the appropriations for capital construction.

Bathing water standards for saline waters are long overdue for reexamination; as in the case of certain of the air quality criteria, there is a need for extensive epidemiological research to provide a more quantitative understanding of the relation of various amounts of pollution to the public health. Recent literature (9) has suggested that the U.S. approach to the subject has been too conservative. The British, on the basis of studies of the health of bathers at a number of beaches in the United Kingdom, have concluded that marine beaches can be used for bathing if the water is esthetically acceptable! As earlier, we are faced with the question, "How clean is clean?"

Solid Waste Management

The City of New York is faced with enormous crises because of the burgeoning volume of solid waste. The streets are increasingly dirty, and the city will run out of disposal sites by the mid-1970's.

New York City's 8 million people live on 6000 miles of streets. They are joined each workday by an influx of more than 2 million people, approximately the population of the nation's second largest city, who come from outlying suburbs to earn their living. The rate of solid waste generation is increasing 2 to 4 percent per year and is currently about 5 pounds per capita per day. Depending on the part of town, the cost of collecting refuse varies from $15 to $30 per ton, and has increased steadily in recent years. The sanitation industry is one of the few in which wages have increased during the past decades without a commensurate increase in the productivity of labor, and it is frequently said that the only change in the technology of **garbage collection is that the internal combustion engine has replaced the horse.**

The garbage can is one of the principal impediments to higher efficiency and is long overdue for replacement. Numerous options are available as alternatives that will make the job easier for the sanitation man, thus increasing his productivity and making it possible to provide cleaner streets at less cost. Experiments conducted during 1969 demonstrated that plastic or paper bags are an efficient and sanitary alternative and that their use should be encouraged. The main advantage is that the sanitation man is no longer required to pick up a heavy can and laboriously shake the refuse from it. Bags have found to be popular with both the householder and the men, and their use is increasing. The cost to the householder at the present time is approximately 8¢ per day per bag, and this will undoubtedly decrease as the bags are made available in mass distribution.

New high-rise apartment houses are still being built with no provision for refuse handling other than the garbage can. One large housing complex was planning to use 400 cans per day. While plastic or paper bags offer a suitable alternative for private homes or small multidwelling buildings, a whole spectrum of still more efficient alternatives are available for the larger buildings. These range from containers of 1-yard capacity that can be handled manually, to large 10-yard containers which are handled mechanically by special trucks. The building codes should be changed to require all future buildings to incorporate efficient methods of handling solid waste.

Toward the close of 1969, the federal government agreed to support a demonstration of a vacuum system for handling solid refuse within a large housing complex. When completed in 1971, the housewife will drop her refuse into a conveniently located hopper from which the garbage will be transported pneumatically to a central location where it can be compacted and mechanically loaded for removal by the Sanitation Department.

Another possibility for more efficient waste handling might utilize the existing or proposed subway systems. One can visualize that all buildings along a subway route might drop their refuse to compactors below street grade with provision for transfer to special subway cars that would be used for hauling containerized wastes during the night hours. Still another method, which might be suitable for buildings located near the waterfront, would be to transfer the refuse pneumatically or by some other methods to hoppers that could discharge directly into barges. This would be an excellent objective at the proposed Battery Park City, which will accommodate 50,000 people and will generate approximately 1,235 tons of garbage a day. There is no reason why the streets of a city should be used for the transport of garbage if some other means can be found, especially if the alternate means are cheaper, cleaner, and more efficient.

The streets of a city become littered partly because of inefficient garbage collection activities and partly because of the high population density and the style of life in big cities. The origins of street litter are found deeply rooted in the complex technical and social system that comprises the metropolis. Economic trends, social mores, the complexities of the criminal courts system used to enforce the sanitary laws, and vehicular traffic congestion are all part of the problem.

The scrap automobile is a case in point. Until a few years ago the market for scrap steel was such that a scrap car could be disposed of by its owner at a price that offered incentive for him to arrange for its removal from the city streets. Changes in economics of the steel industry have altered this situation to the extent that in most parts of the city it costs more to remove a car than the car is worth. This has resulted in automobiles being abandoned on the streets of New York at an increasing rate—the total in 1969 was more than 57,000. The city has recently franchised scrap dealers to collect these cars from various parts of the city. In some cases, the scrap dealer is subsidized by the city and in others he pays the city a small price for the car. It is illegal to abandon a car in the city streets, but when the last owner removes the license plates and files off the engine number, it becomes prohibitively costly to trace him.

The nonreturnable bottle and its close relative the aluminum and steel can are another costly and offensive form of litter that owes some of its origins to the economics of our times.

The beverage distributors insist that until recently a deposit bottle made as many as 30 round trips between the distributor and the customer, but that because of the indifference of the consumers to even a 5¢ deposit, the number of round trips in many communities gradually diminished to as few as four or five before the bottle was discarded. This is given as the reason for the shift from deposit bottles. There is little question that the consumer prefers the nonreturnable container, as does the supermarket, some of which will no longer handle deposit bottles. The result of this is an enormous net increase in the volume of solid waste imposed on the city and a very considerable amount of additional litter. The nonreturnable bottle and the abandoned vehicle are examples of problems that can only be solved by the local community with the greatest of difficulty. National policies are needed that apply uniform rules on a countrywide basis.

Vehicular congestion contributes as much to the littered appearance of streets as any other factor. Because it is prohibitively expensive to sweep streets by hand, most large cities have acquired mechanical brooms which are effective only when the curb is clear. In New York City, alternate side of the street parking rules have been promulgated that theoretically should make it possible to sweep the curbs mechanically, but these rules are honored as much in the breach as in their acceptance. The basic problem is that for lack of comfortable mass transportation there are too many cars in the city. Fewer cars would make the city a far more pleasant place, would avoid the enormous economic waste of traffic congestion, and would reduce air pollution. It would, incidentally, make the streets easier to clean.

The difficulties of enforcing alternate side of the street parking rules illustrate some of the frustrations of city government. For one reason or another the Police Department was unable to enforce the parking rules with sufficient stringency, and the mayor attempted to obtain authority for the uniformed Sanitation Department officers, of whom there are about 1000, to issue summonses for parking violations. However, the state law specified that only a police officer could issue a summons. When city-sponsored legislation was introduced in Albany to make it possible for the Sanitation Department to issue summonses, its passage failed for two consecutive years. During the third year the law was passed, and late in 1969 the Sanitation Department began to issue summonses at a rate of about 5000 per week. However, within only a few months the new procedure, which was working very satisfactorily, was frustrated in the courts by a legal technicality. The ruling of the court in this case was so broad that it successfully blocked all the enforcement agents of the Environmental Protection Administration from issuing any summonses. No longer could the Sanitation Department officers issue summonses for littered sidewalks or could be the air pollution inspectors issue summonses for violation of local air pollution control laws. This matter has not as yet been resolved.

The Waste Disposal Crisis

This is a major problem to New York City because its refuse disposal sites will be exhausted by the mid-1970's. Ever since colonial days the city has followed the common practice of disposing of its solid wastes by filling its lowlands, and at the present time about 11 percent of the present land area of the city has been created in this way, including some of the most valuable commercial and recreational areas.

The largest land fill in the world is at Fresh Kills on Staten Island, but this will be completely filled by 1975. Smaller land fills exist in other parts of the city, and they too will be exhausted by that time.

The city at present produces about 21,000 tons of refuse per day, of which about 7,000 tons pass through municipal incinerators before going to the land fills. A basic strategy, therefore, must be to increase the municipal incineration capacity to reduce the volume of waste and to convert the refuse to a less offensive and more manageable form. A $200-million capital program has been begun, and construction of four giant incinerators is now contemplated; this will reduce the mass of refuse by about 75 percent, leaving a relatively innocuous ash that will occupy about 10 percent of the original volume. The present generation of municipal incinerators is one of the principal sources of atmospheric particulates. However, as noted earlier, these incinerators are being equipped with air cleaning equipment, and all new units will be provided with modern stack cleaning equipment. Since contemporary refuse has a heat value of about 5000 British thermal units per pound, every effort should be made to dispose of the heat either for power production or for generation of steam. It is estimated that the city can in this way recover about $2 per ton of refuse burned or as much as $12 million per year. The basic economics of such heat recovery is sound, assuming that the incinerators can be built near a market for the steam, and this practice is desirable from the conservation point of view.

In the long range, one must stabilize or, better yet, reverse the rising trend in the per capita production of refuse and use of water and other resources. To accomplish this will require development of new technology, changes in the habits of people, and new kinds of governmental regulation and participation. For example, New York City disposes of 350,000 tons of newsprint per year, at great cost in dollars, air pollution, and litter. From every point of view, including conservation of resources, it would be desirable to recycle this paper. By processing the paper in a modern, pollution-free plant for reuse by the newspaper industry, the streets and skies of New York would benefit, the tax dollar would go further, distant streams would be less polluted by effluents from paper mills, and extensive woodland areas would be conserved. Other examples could be given to illustrate the ways in which our economy must close on itself to reuse the products of its industry. This objective is one of the great technological challenges of the 1970's.

Conclusion

Before ending this account of the status of environmental protection in the nation's largest city, some additional thoughts may be desirable.

First, it should be stressed that in the long run environmental protection must go beyond pollution and must ultimately deal with other pressing problems including population control, poverty, raw materials conservation, vehicular traffic management, and land planning. A city that has clean air, clean streets, and clean water will not bring true quality to the way of life of its citizens until these and other monumental socioenvironmental problems are solved.

Second, it must be recognized that deficiencies in the political apparatus of communities have traditionally frustrated an orderly solution to complex problems, and it is hoped that this factor will not be an impediment to effective environmental rehabilitation. The elected officials, the bureaucracy of government, the unions, the community action groups, and the newspapers are important components of the social substrate from which all governmental programs must be developed and nourished. Professional environmental health specialists can define the objectives, develop the timetables, estimate the costs, and, as we have seen earlier, be given substantial sums of money with which to do the job. But factors that are related to the peculiar needs of the individual components of the political apparatus frequently cause issues to arise that seem extraneous to the job that must be done. The original objectives are sometimes overlooked, and priorities become misaligned. An important function of government is to permit the development of thoroughly considered plans of action that can be implemented by professional leaders who are given authority commensurate with the responsibilities assigned to them. A community that allows itself to fail in these respects will be unable to deal successfully with the ecological problems that face it.

References and Notes

1. Special Committee of the City Council of the City of New York to Investigate Air Pollution, "Air Pollution in New York City: An Interim Technical Report," *The City Record*, 24 June 1965.
2. Mayor's Task Force on Air Pollution in the City of New York, *Freedom to Breathe* (City of New York, New York, 1966).
3. Department of Air Resources, *Annual Report* (Environmental Protection Administration, New York, 1968).
4. Advisory Committee to The Surgeon General of the Public Health Service, *Smoking and Health* (U.S. Government Printing Office, Washington, D.C. 1964).
5. H. Finkelstein, *Air Pollution Aspects of Aero-allergens* (National Air Pollution Control Administration, Washington, D.C., 1969), contract PH-22-68-25.
6. Department of Health, Education, and Welfare, *The Cost of Clean Air* (U.S. Government Printing Office, Washington, D.C., 1969).
7. J. G. Thomson and W. M. Graves, *Arch. Pathol.* 81, 458 (1966).
8. Mayor's Task Force on Noise Control, *Toward a Quieter City* (City of New York, New York, 1970).
9. J. M. Henderson, *Proc. Amer. Soc. Civil Engrs.* 94, 1253 (1968).
10. The program described here was the coordinated work of a large staff. Although it is impractical to acknowledge all of their contributions individually, I wish to thank Commissioners M. Feldman (Water Resources), A. N. Heller (Air Resources), and G. L. Moeller (Sanitation) who provided the technical leadership for their respective departments.

SECTION IV

PUTTING LAW, CULTURE AND RESOURCES TOGETHER

Human Population and the Global Environment

John P. Holdren
Paul R. Ehrlich

Three dangerous misconceptions appear to be widespread among decision-makers and others with responsibilities related to population growth, environmental deterioration, and resource depletion. The first is that the absolute size and rate of growth of the human population has little or no relationship to the rapidly escalating ecological problems facing mankind. The second is that environmental deterioration consists primarily of "pollution," which is perceived as a local and reversible phenomenon of concern mainly for its obvious and immediate effects on human health. The third misconception is that science and technology can make possible the long continuation of rapid growth in civilization's consumption of natural resources.

We and others have dealt at length with the third misconception elsewhere (1). In this paper, we argue that environmental deterioration is a much more subtle, pervasive, and dangerous phenomenon than is implied by the narrow view of "pollution" alluded to above. We show further that population size and the rate of population growth, in rich countries as well as in poor ones, have been and continue to be im-

portant contributing factors in the generation of environmental disruption.

Environmental problems can be classified according to the nature of the damage to human beings:

1. Direct assaults on human welfare, including obvious damage to health (e.g. lead poisoning or aggravation of lung disease by air pollution), damage to goods and services (e.g. the corrosive effects of air pollution on buildings and crops), social disruption (e.g. displacement of people from their living areas by mining operations and hydroelectric projects), and other direct effects on what people perceive as the "quality of life" (e.g. congestion, noise, and litter).

2. Indirect effects on human welfare through interference with services provided for society by natural biological systems (e.g. diminution of ocean productivity by filling estuaries and polluting coastal waters, crop failure caused by pests whose natural enemies have been exterminated by civilization, and acceleration of erosion by logging or overgrazing).

Most of the attention devoted to

AMERICAN SCIENTIST, May/June, 1974, Vol. 62, No. 3, pp. 282-292.

environmental matters by scientists, politicians, and the public alike has been focused on the *direct* effects and, more particularly, on their acute rather than their chronic manifestations. This is only natural. It would be wrong, however, to interpret limited legislative and technical progress toward ameliorating the acute symptoms of environmental damage as evidence that society is on its way to an orderly resolution of its environmental problems. The difficulty is not merely that the discovery, implementation, and enforcement of treatment for the obvious symptoms is likely to be expensive and difficult, but also that the long-term human consequences of chronic exposure to low concentrations of environmental contaminants may be more serious—and the causes less amenable to detection and removal—than the consequences of exposure to acute pollution as it is perceived today.

The most serious threats of all, however, may well prove to be the indirect ones generated by mankind's disruption of the functioning of the natural environment—the second category listed above, to which we will devote most of our attention here.

Natural services

The most obvious services provided for humanity by the natural environment have to do with food production. The fertility of the soil is maintained by the plants, animals, and microorganisms that participate in the great nutrient cycles—nitrogen, phosphorus, carbon, sulfur. Soil itself is produced from plant debris and weathered rock by the joint action of bacteria, fungi, worms, soil mites, and insects. The best protection against erosion of soil and flooding is natural vegetation.

At many stages of the natural processes comprising the nutrient cycles, organisms accomplish what humans have not yet learned to do—the complete conversion of wastes into resources, with solar energy captured by photosynthesis as the driving energy source. Human society depends on these natural processes to recycle many of its own wastes, from sewage to detergents to industrial effluents (reflect on the term "biodegradable"). In the course of the same cycles, the environmental concentrations of ammonia, nitrites, and hydrogen sulfide—all poisonous—are biologically controlled (2, 3).

Insects pollinate most vegetables, fruits, and berries. Most fish—the source of 10 to 15 percent of the animal protein consumed by mankind—are produced in the natural marine environment, unregulated by man. (As is well known, animal protein is the nutrient in shortest supply in a chronically malnourished world.) Most potential crop pests—one competent estimate is 99 percent—are held in check not by man but by their natural enemies and by characteristics of the physical environment such as temperature, moisture, and availability of breeding sites (3). Similarly, some agents of human disease are controlled principally not by medical technology but by environmental conditions, and some carriers of such agents are controlled by a combination of environmental conditions and natural enemies (4).

275

Finally, the natural environment in its diversity can be viewed as a unique library of genetic information. From this library can be drawn new food crops, new drugs and vaccines, new biological pest controls. The loss of a species, or even the loss of genetic diversity within a species, is the loss forever of a potential opportunity to improve human welfare.

These "public-service" functions of the global environment cannot be replaced by technology now or in the foreseeable future. This is so in some cases because the process by which the service is provided is not understood scientifically, in other cases because no technological equivalent for the natural process has yet been devised. But in the largest number of cases, the sheer size of the tasks simply dwarfs civilization's capacity to finance, produce, and deploy new technology.

The day is far away when food for billions is grown on synthetic nutrients in greenhouses free of pests and plant diseases, when the wastes of civilization are recycled entirely by technological means, and when all mankind lives in surroundings as sterile and as thoroughly managed as those of of an Apollo space capsule. Until that improbable future arrives—and it may never come—the services provided by the orderly operation of natural biological processes will continue to be irreplaceable as well as indispensable.

Some elements of ecology

How many of these natural services are actually threatened by human activities? Any of them? All of them? These questions call for a closer look at the operation of the biological systems that provide the services.

Productivity. Plant communities are at the base of all food webs and are thus the basis of all life on earth. The fundamental measure of performance of a plant community is the rate at which solar energy is captured by photosynthesis to be stored in chemical bonds. In this context, *gross primary productivity* refers to the total rate of energy capture; *net primary productivity* is the total minus the rate at which captured energy is used to sustain the life processes of the plants themselves. Thus, net primary productivity measures the rate at which energy is made available to the remainder of the food web. *Net community productivity* is what remains after the other organisms in the biological community have used part of the net primary productivity to sustain their own life processes. The net community productivity may be exported (for example, in the form of grain from a wheat field) or it may remain in the community in the form of an enlarged standing crop of plants and animals. A community in balance may have no net community productivity at all—that is, the net primary productivity may be entirely burned up by the animals and microorganisms within the community. The productivities of various kinds of ecosystems are shown in Table 1 (5).

A critical point concerning energy flow in ecosystems is that each step in a food chain results in the eventual loss (as heat) of a substantial fraction of the energy transferred. A

276

Table 1. Productivity of various ecosystems (in kilocalories of energy per square meter per year)

Ecosystem	Net primary productivity	Net community productivity
Alfalfa field	15,200	14,400
Pine forest	5,000	2,000
Tropical rain forest	13,000	little or none
Long Island Sound	2,500	little or none

Source: Odum (5)

good rule of thumb for the loss is 90 percent. This means it takes 10,000 kilocalories of corn to produce 1,000 kcal of steer and, more generally, that available energy diminishes 10-fold at each higher trophic level. Thus, the food web is often described as an energy pyramid. Gains in production of animal protein come at high cost in primary calories, and the yield of prized food fishes such as cod and tuna is limited by their position on the fourth or fifth trophic level of the oceanic food web.

Complexity and stability in ecosystems. The intricate interlacing of most biological food webs provides a form of insurance against some kinds of disruptions. If one species of herbivore in a complex community is eradicated by disease or drought, the primary carnivores in the community may survive on other kinds of herbivores that are less susceptible to the disease. If a population of predators dwindles for one reason or another, an outbreak of the prey species is unlikely if there are other kinds of predators to fill the gap. Species diversity is one of a number of forms of biological complexity believed by many ecologists to impart stability to ecosystems.

Exactly what is meant by ecological stability? One definition is the ability of an ecosystem that has suffered an externally imposed disturbance to return to the conditions that preceded the disturbance. A more general meaning is that a stable ecosystem resists large, rapid changes in the sizes of its constituent populations. Such changes (called fluctuations or instabilities, depending on the circumstances) entail alteration of the orderly flow of energy and nutrients in the ecosystem. Usually this will mean disruption of the "public-service" functions of the ecosystem, whether or not the instability is severe enough to cause any extinctions of species.

What kinds of complexity can influence stability, and how? Species diversity, already mentioned, presumably imparts stability by providing alternative pathways for the flow of nutrients and energy through the ecosystem. Another possible advantage of a large number of species in a community is that there will then be few empty

277

niches—and thus few opportunities for invasion by a new species from outside the community, with possible disruptive effect. Sheer number of species is not the only determining factor in this type of complexity, however: a degree of balance in population sizes among the species is also required if the capacity of the alternative pathways is to be adequate and the niches solidly occupied. Measures of complexity exist at the population level as well as at that of the community. One is genetic variability, which provides the raw material for resistance against new threats. Another is physiological variability, in the form of a mixed age distribution. (Here the advantage of complexity manifests itself when threats appear that are specific to a particular stage in the organism's life cycle—say, a disease that strikes only juveniles.) There are other forms of complexity as well, including physical complexity of habitat and variety in the geographic distribution of a given species.

The causal links between complexity and stability in ecological systems are by no means firmly established or well understood, and exceptions do exist (6). The evidence of a general correlation between these properties is growing, however, and consists of theoretical considerations of the sort summarized above, general observations of actual ecosystems of widely varying complexity (the relatively simple ecosystem of the boreal coniferous forest—the "north woods"—is observed to be less stable than the complex tropical rain forest), and a limited number of controlled laboratory and field experiments.

Time scales of ecological change. Ecological stability does not mean constancy or stagnation, and ecological change can take place over much longer time spans than the month-to-month or year-to-year time scale of fluctuations and instabilities. Ecological *succession* refers to the orderly replacement of one community in an area with other communities over periods often measured in decades. *Evolution* refers to changes in the genetic characteristics of species, brought about by natural selection over time periods ranging from a few generations to hundreds of millions of years. Note that, in terms of human beings, evolution is not the solution to pollution. When significant evolutionary change does take place on the short time scale of a few generations, it is necessarily at the expense of the lives of a large fraction of the population.

History of human ecological disruption

Ecological disruption on a large scale by human beings is not a new phenomenon. Even before the advent of agriculture, man as a hunter is thought to have contributed to a reduction in the number of species of large mammals inhabiting the earth (7). Much more significant, however, was the era of abuse of soils and habitat that was initiated by the agricultural revolution about 10,000 years ago and has continued up to the present.

One of the best known early examples is the conversion to desert of the lush Tigris and Euphrates valleys, through erosion and salt accumulation resulting from faulty irrigation practices (8). In essence, the downfall of the great Mesopotamian civilization appears to have been the result of an "ecocatastrophe." Overgrazing and poor cultivation practices have contributed over the millennia to the expansion of the Sahara Desert, a process that continues today; and the Rajasthan desert in India is also believed to be partly a product of human carelessness and population pressure (9).

Much of Europe and Asia were deforested by preindustrial men, beginning in the Stone Age; heavy erosion, recurrent flooding, and nearly permanent loss of a valuable resource were the result. Overgrazing by the sheep of Navajo herdsmen has destroyed large tracts of once prime pastureland in the American Southwest (10). Attempts to cultivate too intensively the fragile soils of tropical rain-forest areas are suspected of being at least in part responsible for the collapse of the Mayan civilization in Central America and that of the Khmers in what today is Cambodia (11). (The famous temples of Angkor Wat were built partly of laterite, the rock-like material that results when certain tropical soils are exposed to the air through cultivation.)

The practice of agriculture —even where quality of soils, erosion, or salt accumulation do not pose problems—may encounter ecological difficulties. The most basic is that agriculture is a simplifier of ecosystems, replacing complex natural biological communities with relatively simple man-made ones based on a few strains of crops. Being less complex, agricultural communities tend to be less stable than their natural counterparts: they are vulnerable to invasions by weeds, insect pests, and plant diseases, and they are particularly sensitive to extremes of weather and variations in climate. Historically, civilization has attempted to defend its agricultural communities against the instabilities to which they are susceptible by means of vigilance and the application of "energy subsidies"— for example, hoeing weeds and, more recently, applying pesticides and fungicides. These attempts have not always been successful.

The Irish potato famine of the last century is perhaps the best-known example of the collapse of a simple agricultural ecosystem. The heavy reliance of the Irish population on a single, highly productive crop led to 1.5 million deaths when the potato monoculture fell victim to a fungus. To put it another way, the carrying capacity of Ireland was reduced, and the Irish population crashed.

Contemporary man as an ecological force

Agriculture. Advances in agricultural technology in the last hundred years have not resolved the ecological dilemma of agriculture; they have aggravated it. The dilemma can be summarized this way: civilization tries to manage ecosystems in such a way as to maximize productivity, "nature" manages ecosystems in such a way as to maximize stability, and the two goals are incompatible. Ecological succession proceeds in the direction of increasing complexity. Ecological research has shown that the most complex (and stable) natural ecosystems tend to have the smallest *net* community productivity; less complex, transitional ecosystems have higher net community productivity; and the highest net community productivities are achieved in the artificially simplified agricultural ecosystems of man (see Table 1). In short, productivity is achieved at the expense of stability.

Of course, mankind would have to practice agriculture to support even a fraction of the existing human population. A tendency toward instability in agricultural ecosystems must be accepted and, where possible, compensated for by technology. However, the trends in modern agriculture—associated in part with the urgent need to cope with unprecedented population growth and in part with the desire to maximize yields per acre for strictly economic reasons—are especially worrisome ecologically. There are four major liabilities.

1. As larger and larger land areas are given over to farming, the unex-

ploited tracts available to serve as reservoirs of species diversity and to carry out the "public-service" functions of natural ecosystems become smaller and fewer (see Table 2) (12).

2. Pressure to expand the area under agriculture is leading to destructive attempts to cultivate land that is actually unsuitable for cultivation with the technologies at hand. For example, the expansion of agriculture to steep hillsides has led to serious erosion in Indonesia (13), the increasing pressure of slash-and-burn techniques is destroying tropical forests in the Philippines (14), and attempts to apply the techniques of temperate-zone agriculture to the tropical soils of Brazil and Southern Sudan have led to erosion, loss of nutrients, and laterization (15). Overlogging of tropical forests has had similar effects.

3. Even in parts of the world where

Table 2. World land use, 1966 (in millions of km^2)

	Total	Tilled	Pasture	Forest	Other*
Europe	4.9	1.5	0.9	1.4	1.1
U.S.S.R.	22.4	2.3	3.7	9.1	7.3
Asia	27.8	4.5	4.5	5.2	13.7
Africa	30.2	2.3	7.0	6.0	15.0
North America	22.4	2.6	3.7	8.2	7.9
South America	17.8	0.8	4.1	9.4	3.5
Oceania	8.5	0.4	4.6	0.8	2.7
Total†	134.2	14.3	23.6	40.2	51.2
Percentage	100%	10.6%	21.3%	29.9%	38.2%

* Deserts, wasteland, built-on land, glaciers, wetlands
† Less Antarctica

Source: Borgstrom (12)

land area under agriculture is constant or (for economic reasons) dwindling, attempts to maximize yields per acre have led to dramatic increases in the use of pesticides and inorganic fertilizers, which have far-reaching ecological consequences themselves (2).

4. The quest for high yields has led also to the replacement of a wide range of traditional crop varieties all over the world with a few, specially bred, high-yield strains. Unprecedented areas are now planted to a single variety of wheat or rice. This enormous expansion of monoculture has increased the probability and the potential magnitude of epidemic crop failure from insects or disease (16).

Effects of pollution on ecosystems. The expansion and intensification of agriculture has been accompanied by a continuing industrial revolution that has multiplied many times over both the magnitude and variety of the substances introduced into the biological environment by man. It is useful to classify these substances as *qualitative pollutants* (synthetic substances produced and released only by man) and *quantitative pollutants* (substances naturally present in the environment but released in significant additional amounts by man).

Well-known qualitative pollutants are the chlorinated hydrocarbon pesticides, such as DDT, the related class of industrial chemicals called PCB's (polychlorinated biphenyls), and some herbicides. These substances are biologically active in the sense of stimulating physiological changes, but since organisms have had no experience with them over evolutionary time the substances are usually not easily biodegradable. Thus, they may persist in the environment for years and even decades after being introduced and may be transported around the globe by wind and water (17). Their long-term effects will be discovered only by experience, but their potential for disruption of ecosystems is enormous.

Within the category of quantitative pollutants, there are three criteria by which a contribution made by mankind may be judged significant.

1. Man can perturb a natural cycle with a large amount of a substance ordinarily considered innocuous, in several ways: by overloading part of the cycle (as we do to the denitrifying part of the nitrogen cycle when we overfertilize, leading to the accumulation of nitrates and nitrites in ground water) (18); by destabilizing a finely tuned balance (as we may do to the global atmospheric heat engine, which governs global climate, by adding CO_2 to the atmosphere via combustion of fossil fuels); or by swamping a natural cycle completely (as could happen to the climatic balance in the very long term from man's input of waste heat).

2. An amount of material negligible compared to natural global flows of the same substance can cause great damage if released in a sensitive spot, over a small area, or suddenly (for example, the destruction of coral reefs in Hawaii by silt washed from construction sites).

3. *Any* addition of a substance that can be harmful even at its naturally occurring concentrations must be considered significant. Some ra-

dioactive substances fall in this category, as does mercury.

The most general effect of pollution of all kinds on ecosystems is the loss of structure or complexity (19). Specifically, food chains are shortened by pollution via the selective loss of the predators at the top, because predators are more sensitive to environmental stresses of all kinds—pesticides, industrial effluents, thermal stress, oxygen deficiency—than are herbivores. This increased sensitivity results from several mechanisms: the predator populations are usually smaller than those of the prey species, so the predator populations tend to have a smaller reservoir of genetic variability and, hence, less probability of evolving a resistant strain; top predators are often exposed to higher concentrations of toxic substances than organisms at lower trophic levels, owing to the phenomenon of biological concentration of pollutants as they move up the food chain; and, finally, the direct effects of pollution on predators are compounded by the fact that pollutants may reduce the size of the prey population to the point where the predator population cannot be supported. Loss of structure may also occur at lower trophic levels when, for a variety of reasons, one species of herbivore or lower carnivore proves especially sensitive to a particular form of environmental stress. The food web does not have to be eradicated from top to bottom to show significant differential effects.

The adverse effects of loss of structure on the "public-service" functions performed by ecosystems are varied and serious. The vulnerable top predators in marine ecosystems are generally the food fishes most highly prized by man. The loss of predators on land releases checks on herbivorous pests that compete with man for his supply of staple crops. Damaging population outbreaks of these pests—the classic "instability"—are the result. (A good example of the outbreak phenomenon is the experience with pesticides and cotton pests in Peru's Canete Valley (20).) The loss of structure of ecosystems also increases the load on the aquatic food webs of decay, which are already heavily stressed by the burden of mankind's domestic and agricultural wastes. The resulting overload precipitates a vicious progression: oxygen depletion, a shift from aerobic to less efficient anaerobic bacterial metabolism, the accumulation of organic matter, and the release of methane and hydrogen sulfide gas (19).

Vulnerability of the sea. The ocean, presently indispensable as a source of animal protein, may be the most vulnerable ecosystem of all. Its vast bulk is deceiving. The great proportion of the ocean's productivity—over 99%—takes place beneath 10% of its surface area, and half of the productivity is concentrated in coastal upwellings amounting to only 0.1% of the surface area (21). The reason is that productivity requires nutrients, which are most abundant near the bottom, and sunlight, available only near the top. Only in the coastal shelf areas and in upwellings are nutrients and sunlight both available in the same place.

The coastal regions, of course, also receive most of the impact of man's activities—oil spills, fallout from atmospheric pollutants generated on the adjacent land, and river outflow bearing pesticide and fertilizer residues, heavy metals, and industrial chemicals. Almost perversely, the most fertile and critical components in the ocean ecosystem are the estuaries into which the rivers empty; estuaries serve as residence, passage zone, or nursery for about 90% of commercially important fish (3). To compound the problem of pollution, the salt marshes that are an integral part of estuarine biological communities are being destroyed routinely by landfill operations.

Overfishing is almost certainly also taking a heavy toll in the ocean, although it is difficult to separate its effect from that of pollution and destruction of the estuarine breeding grounds and nurseries. The combined result of these factors is clear, however, even if the blame cannot be accurately apportioned. Since World War II, the catches of the East Asian sardine, the California sardine, the Northwest Pacific salmon, the Scandinavian herring, and the Barents Sea cod (among others) have entered declines from which there has been no sign of recovery (2).

The 1972 world fisheries production of somewhat over 60 million metric tons was already more than half of the 100 million that some marine biologists consider to be the maximum sustainable yield (21). But recent interruptions in the pattern of continuously increasing yields since World War II (22), declining catches per unit effort, and increasing international friction over fishing rights make it seem unlikely that theoretical maximum yields will even be approached.

Flows of material and energy. Many people still imagine that mankind is a puny force in the global scale of things. They are persuaded, perhaps by the vast empty spaces visible from any jet airliner in many parts of the world, that talk of global ecological disruption is a preposterous exaggeration. The question of the absolute scale of man's impact, however, is amenable to quantitative investigation. Natural global flows of energy and materials can be reasonably calculated or estimated, and these provide an absolute yardstick against which to measure the impact of human activities.

The results are not reassuring. As a global geological and biological force, mankind is today becoming comparable to and even exceeding many natural processes. Oil added to the oceans in 1969 from tanker spills, offshore production, routine shipping operations, and refinery wastes exceeded the global input from natural seepage by an estimated 20-fold; the minimum estimate for 1980, assuming all foreseeable precautions, is 30 times natural seepage (23). Civilization is now contributing half as much as nature to the global atmospheric sulfur burden, and will be contributing as much as nature by the year 2000 (24). In industrial areas, civilization's input of sulfur (as sulfur dioxide) so overwhelms natural removal processes that increased atmospheric concentrations and acidic surface water are found hundreds to thousands of kilometers downwind (25). Combustion of fossil fuels has increased the global atmospheric concentration of carbon dioxide by 10% since the turn of the century (26). Civilization's contribution to the global atmospheric burden of particulate matter is uncertain: estimates range from 5 to 45% of total annual input (26). Roughly 5% of all the energy captured by photosynthesis on earth flows through the agricultural ecosystems supporting the metabolic consumption of human beings and their domestic animals—a few out of some millions of species (27). The rates at which mankind is mobilizing critical nutrients and many metals (including the most toxic ones) considerably exceeds the basic geological mobilization rates as estimated from river flows (see Table 3) (3). Such figures as these do not prove that disaster is upon us, but, combined with the ecological perspective summarized above, they are cause for uneasiness. In terms of the scale of its disruptions, civilization is for the first time operating on a level at which global balances could hinge on its mistakes.

Some of the forms of disruption just described are, of course, amenable in principle to elimination or drastic reduction through changes in technology. Civilization's discharges of oil, sulfur dioxide, and carbon dioxide, for example, could be greatly reduced by switching to energy sources other than fossil fuels. In the case of these pollutants, then, the questions involve not whether the disruptions *can* be managed but whether they *will* be, whether the measures will come in time, and what social, economic, and new environmental penalties will accompany those measures. At least one environmental problem is intractable in a more absolute sense, however, and this is the discharge of waste heat accompanying all of civilization's use of energy. We refer here not simply to the well-publicized thermal pollution at the sites of electric generating

Table 3. Mankind's mobilization of materials (in thousands of metric tons per year)

Element	Geological rate (river flow)	Man's rate (mining and consumption)
Iron	25,000	319,000
Nitrogen	3,500	30,000
Copper	375	4,460
Zinc	370	3,930
Nickel	300	358
Lead	180	2,330
Phosphorus	180	6,500
Mercury	3	7
Tin	1.5	166

Source: Institute of Ecology (2), SCEP (3)

plants, but to the fact that all the energy we *use*—as well as what we waste in generating electricity—ultimately arrives in the environment as waste heat. This phenomenon may be understood qualitatively by considering the heat from a light bulb, the heat from a running automobile engine and the heat in the exhaust, the heat from friction of tires against pavement and metal against air, or the heat from the oxidation of iron to rust—to name a few examples. Quantitatively, the ultimate conversion to heat of all the energy we use (most of which occurs near the point of use and almost immediately) is required by the laws of thermodynamics; the phenomenon cannot be averted by technological tricks.

The usual concern with local thermal pollution at power plants is that the waste heat, which is usually discharged into water, will adversely affect aquatic life. Most of the waste heat from civilization's energy use as a whole, by contrast, is discharged directly into the atmosphere, and the concern is disruption of climate. Again, it is instructive to compare the scale of human activities with that of the corresponding natural processes, in this case the natural energy flows that govern climate. One finds that the heat production resulting from (and numerically equal to) civilization's use of energy is not yet a significant fraction of the solar energy incident at the earth's surface on a global average basis (see Table 4); even if the present 5% per annum rate of increase of global energy use persists, it will take another century before civilization is discharging heat equivalent to 1% of incident solar energy at the surface worldwide (28).

Considerably sooner, however, as indicated in Table 4, mankind's heat production could become a significant fraction of smaller natural energy transfers that play a major role in the determination of regional and continental climate (e.g. the kinetic energy of winds and ocean currents and the poleward heat fluxes) (29). It is especially important in this connection that civilization's heat production is and will continue to be very unevenly distributed geographically. Human heat production already exceeds 5% of incident solar radiation at the surface over local areas of tens of thousands of square kilometers, and will exceed this level over areas of millions of square kilometers by the year 2000 if present trends persist (26). Such figures could imply substantial climatic disruptions. In addition to the effects of its discharge of heat, civilization has the potential to disrupt climate through its additions of carbon dioxide and particulate matter to the atmosphere, through large-scale alteration of the heat-transfer and moisture-transfer properties of the surface (e.g. agriculture, oil films on the ocean, urbanization), through cloud formation arising from aircraft contrails, and, of course, through the combined action of several or all of these disruptions.

Much uncertainty exists concerning the character and imminence of inadvertent climate modification through these various possibilities. It is known that a global warming of a few degrees centigrade would melt the icecaps and raise sea level by 80 meters, submerging coastal plains and cities. A few degrees in the opposite direction would initiate a new ice age. Although such

Table 4. Energy flows (in billion thermal kilowatts)

Civilization's 1970 rate of energy use	7
Global photosynthesis	80
15 billion people at 10 thermal kilowatts/person	150
Winds and ocean currents	370
Poleward heat flux at 40° north latitude	5,300
Solar energy incident at earth's surface	116,000

Sources: Woodwell (27), Sellers (29), Hubbert (29)

global warming or cooling is certainly possible in principle, a more complicated alteration of climatic *patterns* seems a more probable and perhaps more imminent consequence of the very unevenly distributed impacts of civilization's use of energy. It is particularly important to note that the consequences of climatic alteration reside not in any direct sensitivity of humans to moderate changes in temperature or moisture, but rather in the great sensitivity of food production to such changes (30) and, perhaps, in the possible climate-related spread of diseases into populations with no resistance against them (4).

The effect of climate on agriculture was once again dramatically demonstrated in early 1973. Because of "bad weather," famine was widespread in sub-Saharan Africa and was starting in India. Southeast Asia had small rice harvests, parts of Latin American were short of food, and crops were threatened in the United States and the Soviet Union. If there is another year of monsoon failure in the tropics and inclement weather in the temperate zones, the human death rate will climb precipitously. A telling symptom of overpopulation is mankind's inability to store sufficient carry-over food supplies in anticipation of the climatic variations that are a regular feature of the planet Earth.

Role of population

It is beyond dispute that a population too large to be fed adequately in the prevailing technological and organizational framework, as is the case for the globe today, is particularly vulnerable to environmental disruptions that may reduce production even below normal levels. More controversial, however, are the roles of the size, growth rate, and geographic distribution of the human population in *causing* such environmental disruptions, and it is to this issue that we now turn.

Multiplicative effect. The most elementary relation between population and environmental deterioration is that population size acts as a multiplier of the activities, consumption, and attendant environmental damages associated with each individual in the population. The contributing factors in at least some kinds of environmental problems can be usefully studied by expressing the population/environment relation as an equation:

environmental disruption =
population × consumption per
person × damage per unit
of consumption

Needless to say, the numerical quantities that appear in such an equation will vary greatly depending on the problem under scrutiny. Different forms of consumption and technology are relevant to each of the many forms of environmental disruption. The population factor may refer to the population of a city, a region, a country, or the world, depending on the problem being considered. (This point, of course, raises the issue of population *distribution*.) The equation, therefore, represents not one calculation but many.

For problems described by multiplicative relations like the one just given, no factor can be considered unimportant. The consequences of the growth of each factor are amplified in proportion to the size and the rate of growth of each of the others. Rising consumption per person has greater impact in a large population than in a small one— and greater impact in a growing population than in a stationary one. A given environmentally disruptive technology, such as the gasoline-powered automobile, is more damaging in a large, rich population (many people own cars and drive them often) than in a small, poor one (few people own cars, and those who do drive them less). A given level of total consumption (population times consumption per person) is more damaging if it is provided by means of a disruptive technology, such as persistent pesticides, than if provided by means of a relatively nondisruptive one,

such as integrated pest control.

The quantitative use of the population/environment equation is best illustrated by example. Suppose we take as an index of environmental impact the automotive emissions of lead in the United States since World War II. The appropriate measure of "consumption" is vehicle-miles per person, which increased twofold between 1946 and 1967. The impact per unit of consumption in this case is emissions of lead per vehicle-mile, which increased 83%, or 1.83-fold, in this period (*31*). Since the U.S. population increased 41%, or 1.41-fold, between 1946 and 1967, we have,

relative increase in
emissions =
1.41 × 2.0 × 1.83 = 5.16 or 416%

Note that the dramatic increase in the total impact arose from rather moderate but simultaneous increases in the multiplicative contributing factors. None of the factors was unimportant—if population had *not* grown in this period, the total increase would have been 3.66-fold rather than 5.16-fold. (Contrast this result with the erroneous conclusion, arising from the assumption that the contributing factors are additive rather than multiplicative, that a 41% increase in population "explains" only one-tenth of 416% increase in emissions.)

Calculations such as the foregoing can be made for a wide variety of pollutants, although with frequent difficulty in uncovering the requisite data. Where data are available, the results show that the historical importance of population growth as a multiplicative contributor to

287

widely recognized environmental problems has been substantial (32).

Between 1950 and 1970, for example, the world population increased by 46%. By regions, the figures were: Africa, 59%; North America, 38%; Latin America, 75%; Asia, 52%; Europe, 18%; Oceania, 54%; Soviet Union, 35% (33). On the assumption (which will be shown below to be too simplistic) that the patterns of technological change and rising consumption per capita that were experienced in this period would have been the same in the absence of population growth, one can conclude that the absolute magnitudes of damaging inputs to the environment in 1970 were greater *by these same percentages* than they would have been if population had remained at its 1950 value. Another way of saying this is that, under our simplistic assumption, the magnitude of damaging inputs to the global environment in 1970—a very large figure—would have been only 68% as large if population had not grown between 1950 and 1970. (This follows from the relation: 1970 inputs in absence of population growth equal actual 1970 inputs times 1950 population divided by 1970 population.)

Not only has population growth been important in *absolute* terms as a contributor of environmental damage, but it has been important *relative* to other sources of such damage. Perhaps the best way to illustrate this fact is with statistics for energy consumption per person, probably the best aggregate measure of both affluence and technological impact on the environment. One finds that energy consumption per person worldwide increased

Table 5. Percentage increases in population and energy consumption per capita between 1950 and 1970

	Population (%)	Energy/ person (%)
World	46	57
Africa	59	73
North America	38	43
Latin America	75	122
Asia	52	197
Europe	18	96
Oceania	54	54

Source: United Nations (33, 34)

57% between 1950 and 1970 (33, 34). By this measure then, and under our simple assumption that population growth and trends in affluence and technology were independent, one finds that population growth in the period 1950-1970 was almost equal to the *combined* effect of rising affluence and technological change as a contributor of damaging inputs to the environment. (The comparison of population growth and energy consumption broken down by major geographical regions is given in Table 5.) We shall argue, moreover, that the effect of the simplistic assumption of independence of population and other factors is more probably to *underestimate* the role of population than to overestimate it.

Nonlinear effects. While it is useful to understand what proportion of the historical increase in specific environmental problems has been directly attributable to the multiplier effect of population growth. there is a more difficult and perhaps more important question than this historical/arithmetical one. Specifically, under what circumstances may nonlinear effects cause a small increase in population to generate a disproportionately large increase in environmental disruption? These effects fall into two classes. First, population change may *cause* changes in consumption per person or in impact upon the environment per unit of consumption. Second, a small increase in impact upon the environment generated in part by population change and in part by unrelated changes in the other multiplicative factors—may stimulate a disproportionately large environmental change.

An obvious example in the first category is the growth of suburbs in the United States at the expense of central cities, which has had the effect of increasing the use of the automobile. Another is the heavy environmental costs incurred in the form of large water projects when demand (population times demand per person) exceeds easily exploited local supplies. Still another example is that of diminishing-returns phenomena in agriculture, in which increases in yield needed to feed new mouths can be achieved only by disproportionate increases in inputs such as fertilizer and pesticides.

Many phenomena that have the effect of generating disproportionate consequences from a given change in demographic variables cannot easily be expressed in the framework of a single equation. One such class of problems involves techno-logical change—the substitution of new materials or processes for old ones that provided the same types of material consumption. Obvious examples are the substitution of nylon and rayon for cotton and wool, of plastics for glass and wood and metals, of aluminum for steel and copper. Such substitutions may be necessitated by increasing total demand, or they may be motivated by other factors such as durability and convenience. Substitutions or other technological changes that are motivated by the pressure of increased total demand, and that lead to increases in environmental impact per unit of consumption, should be considered as part of the environmental impact of population growth.

Environmental disruption is not, however, measured strictly by man's inputs *to* the environment—what *we* do to *it*. Equally important is how the environment responds to what we do to it. This response itself is often nonlinear: a small change in inputs may precipitate a dramatic response. One example is the existence of thresholds in the response of individual organisms to poisons and other forms of "stress." Fish may be able to tolerate a 10° rise in water temperature without ill effect, whereas a 12° rise would be fatal. Carbon monoxide is fatal to human beings at high concentrations but, as far as we know, causes only reversible effects at low concentrations. Algal blooms in overfertilized lakes and streams are examples of exceeding a threshold for the orderly cycling of nutrients in these biological systems.

Another nonlinear phenomenon on the response side of environmental problems involves the simultaneous action of two or more inputs. A disturbing example is the combined effect of DDT and oil spills in coastal waters. DDT is not very soluble in sea water, so the concentrations to which marine organisms are ordinarily exposed are small. However, DDT is very soluble in oil. Oil spills therefore have the effect of concentrating DDT in the surface layer of the ocean, where much of the oil remains and where many marine organisms spend part of their time (23). These organisms are thus exposed to far higher concentrations of DDT than would otherwise be possible, and as a result, the combined effect of oil and DDT probably far exceeds their individual effects. Many other synergisms in environmental systems are known or suspected: the interaction of sulfur dioxide and particulate matter in causing or aggravating lung disease; the interaction of radiation exposure and smoking in causing lung cancer; the enhanced toxicity of chlorinated hydrocarbon pesticides when plasticizers are present (35).

The exact role of population change varies considerably among the various forms of nonlinear behavior just described. A nonlinearity in the environment's response to growing total input—such as a threshold effect—increases the importance of all the multiplicative contributors to the input equally, whether or not population and the other contributors are causally related. Some other forms of nonlinearity, such as diminishing returns and certain substitutions, would occur eventually whether population or consumption per capita grew or not. For example, even a constant demand for copper that persisted for a long time would lead eventually to increasing expenditures of energy per pound of metal and to substitution of aluminum for copper in some applications. In such instances, the role of population growth—and that of rising consumption per capita—is simply to accelerate the onset of diminishing returns and the need for technological change, leaving less time to deal with the problems created and increasing the chances of mistakes. With respect to other phenomena, such as the effects of population concentration on certain forms of consumption and environmental impact, population change is clearly the sole and direct cause of the nonlinearity (e.g. additional transportation costs associated with suburbanization).

Time factors

The pattern of growth. All rational observers agree that no physical quantity can grow exponentially forever. This is true, for example, of population, the production of energy and other raw material, and the generation of wastes. But is there anything about the 1970s—as opposed, say, to the 1920s or 1870s—that should make this the decade in which limits to growth become apparent? It should not be surprising that, when limits do appear, they will appear suddenly. Such behavior is typical of exponential growth. If twenty doublings are possible before a limit is reached in an exponentially growing process (characterized by a fixed doubling time if the growth rate is constant), then the system will be less than half "loaded" for the first nineteen doublings—or for 95% of the elapsed time between initiation of growth and exceeding the limit. Clearly, a long history of exponential growth does not imply a long future.

But where does mankind stand in its allotment of doublings? Are we notably closer to a limit now than we were 50 years ago? We are certainly moving faster. The number of people added to the world population each year in the 1970s has been about twice what it was in the 1920s. And according to one of the better indices of aggregate environmental disruption, total energy consumption, the annual increase in man's impact on the environment (in absolute magnitude, not percentage) is ten times larger now than then (33, 36). We have seen, moreover, that man is already a global ecological force, as measured against the yardstick of natural processes. While the human population grows at a rate that would double our numbers in 35 years, ecological impact is growing much faster. The 1970 M.I.T.-sponsored Study of Critical Environmental Problems estimated that civilization's demands upon the biological environment are increasing at about 5% per year, corresponding to a doubling time of 14 years (3). Continuation of this rate would imply a fourfold increase in demands on the environment between 1972 and the year 2000. It is difficult to view such a prospect with complacency.

Momentum, time lags, and irreversibility. The nature of exponential growth is such that limits can be approached with surprising suddenness. The likelihood of overshooting a limit is made even larger by the momentum of human population growth, by the time delays between cause and effect in many environmental systems, and by the fact that some kinds of damage are irreversible by the time they are visible.

The great momentum of human population growth has its origins in deep-seated attitudes toward reproduction and in the age composition of the world's population—37% is under 15 years of age. This means there are far more young people who will soon be reproducing—adding to the population—than there are old people who will soon be dying—subtracting from it. Thus, even if the momentum in attitudes could miraculously be overcome overnight, so that every pair of parents in the world henceforth had only the number of children needed to replace themselves, the imbalance between young and old would cause population to grow for 50 to 70 years more before leveling off. The growth *rate* would be falling during this period, but population would still climb 30% or more during the transition to stability. Under extraordinarily optimistic assumptions about when replacement fertility might *really* become the worldwide norm, one concludes that world population will not stabilize below 8 billion people (37).

The momentum of population growth manifests itself as a delay between the time when the need to stabilize population is perceived and the time when stabilization is actually accomplished. Forces that are perhaps even more firmly entrenched than those affecting population lend momentum to growth in per capita consumption of materials. These forces create time lags similar to that of population growth in the inevitable transition to stabilized levels of consumption and technological reform. Time delays

291

between the initiation of environmental insults and the appearance of the symptoms compound the predicament because they postpone recognition of the need for any corrective action at all.

Such environmental time delays come about in a variety of ways. Some substances persist in dangerous form long after they have been introduced into the environment (mercury, lead, DDT and its relatives, and certain radioactive materials are obvious examples). They may be entering food webs from soil, water, and marine sediments for years after being deposited there. The process of concentration from level to level in the food web takes more time. Increases in exposure to radiation may lead to increases in certain kinds of cancer only after decades and to genetic defects that first appear in later generations. The consequences of having simplified an environmental system by inadvertently wiping out predators or by planting large areas to a single high-yield grain may not show up until just the right pest or plant disease comes along a few years later.

Unfortunately, time lags of these sorts usually mean that, when the symptoms finally appear, corrective action is ineffective or impossible. Species that have been eradicated cannot be restored. The radioactive debris of atmospheric bomb tests cannot be reconcentrated and isolated from the environment, nor can radiation exposure be undone. Soil that has been washed or blown away can be replaced by natural processes only on a time scale of centuries. If all use of persistent pesticides were stopped tomorrow, the concentrations of these substances in fish and fish-eating birds might continue to increase for some years to come.

Vigorous action needed

The momentum of growth, the time delays between causes and effects, and the irreversibility of many kinds of damage all increase the chances that mankind may temporarily exceed the carrying capacity of the biological environment. Scientific knowledge is not yet adequate to the task of defining that carrying capacity unambiguously, nor can anyone say with assurance how the consequences of overshooting the carrying capacity will manifest themselves. Agricultural failures on a large scale, dramatic loss of fisheries productivity, and epidemic disease initiated by altered environmental conditions are among the possibilities. The evidence presented here concerning the present scale of man's ecological disruption and its rate of increase suggests that such possibilities exist within a time frame measured in decades, rather than centuries.

All of this is not to suggest that the situation is hopeless. The point is rather that the potential for grave damage is real and that prompt and vigorous action to avert or minimize the damage is necessary. Such action should include measures to slow the growth of the global population to zero as rapidly as possible. Success in this endeavor is a necessary but not a sufficient condition for achieving a prosperous yet environmentally sustainable civilization. It will also be necessary to develop and implement programs to alleviate political tensions, render nuclear war impossible, divert flows of resources and energy from wasteful uses in rich countries to necessity-oriented uses in poor ones, reduce the environmental impact and increase the human benefits resulting from each pound of material and gallon of fuel, devise new energy sources, and, ultimately, stabilize civilization's annual throughput of materials and energy.

There are, in short, no easy single-faceted solutions, and no component of the problem can be safely ignored. There is a temptation to "go slow" on population limitation because this component is politically sensitive and operationally difficult, but the temptation must be resisted. The other approaches pose problems too, and the accomplishments of these approaches will be gradual at best. Ecological disaster will be difficult enough to avoid even if population limitation succeeds; if population growth proceeds unabated, the gains of improved technology and stabilized per capita consumption will be erased, and averting disaster will be impossible.

References

1. See, e.g., National Research Council/ National Academy of Sciences. 1969. *Resources and Man.* San Francisco: W. H. Freeman and Co. Paul R. Ehrlich and John P. Holdren. 1969. Population and panaceas: a technological perspective. *BioScience* 12:1065–71.

2. Institute of Ecology. 1972. *Man in the Living Environment.* Madison: University of Wisconsin Press.

3. Report of the Study of Critical Environmental Problems (SCEP). 1970. *Man's Impact on the Global Environment: Assessment and Recommendations for Action.* Cambridge: M.I.T. Press.

4. Jacques M. May. 1972. Influence of environmental transformation in changing the map of disease. In *The Careless Technology: Ecology and International Development,* M. Taghi Farvar and John P. Milton, eds. Garden City, N.Y.: The Natural History Press.

5. Eugene P. Odum. 1971. *Fundamentals of Ecology.* 3rd ed. Philadelphia: Saunders, p. 46.

6. E. O. Wilson and W. A. Bossert. 1971. *A Primer of Population Biology.* Stamford, Conn: Sinauer Associates; and Brookhaven National Laboratory. 1969. Diversity and stability in ecological systems. *Brookhaven Symposia in Biology,* N. 22, BNL 50175 C-56. Upton, N.Y.: Brookhaven National Laboratory.

7. P. S. Martin and T. E. Wright, Jr., eds. 1957. *Pleistocene Extinctions: The Search for a Cause.* New Haven: Yale University Press.

8. Thorkild Jacobsen and Robert M. Adams. 1958. Salt and silt in ancient Mesopotamian agriculture. *Science* 128:1251–58.

9. M. Kassas. 1970. Desertification versus potential for recovery in circum-Saharan territories. In *Arid Lands in Transition.* Washington, D.C.: American Association for Advancement of Science. B. R. Seshachar. 1971. Problems of environment in India. In *International Environmental Science.* Proceedings of a joint colloquium before the Committee on Commerce, U.S. Senate, and the Committee on Science and Astronautics. House of Representatives, 92nd Congress. Washington, D.C.: U.S. Government Printing Office.

10. Carl O. Sauer. 1956. The agency of man on earth. In *Man's Role in Changing the Face of the Earth.* William L. Thomas, Jr., ed. Chicago: University of Chicago Press, p. 60.

11. Jeremy A. Sabloff. 1971. The collapse of classic Maya civilization. In *Patient Earth,* John Harte and Robert Socolow, eds. New York: Holt, Rinehart and Winston, p. 16.

12. Georg Borgstrom. 1969. *Too Many.* N.Y.: Macmillan.

13. Albert Ravenholt. 1974. Man-land-productivity microdynamics in rural Bali. In *Population: Perspective, 1973.* Harrison Brown, John Holdren, Alan Sweezy, and Barbara West, eds. San Francisco: Freeman-Cooper.

14. Albert Ravenholt. 1971. The Philip-

pines. In *Population: Perspective, 1971,*
Harrison Brown and Alan Sweezy, eds.
San Francisco: Freeman-Cooper, pp.
247–66.

15. Mary McNeil. 1972. Lateritic soils in
distinct tropical environments: Southern Sudan and Brazil. In *The Careless
Technology,* op cit., pp. 591–608.

16. O. H. Frankel et al. 1969. Genetic dangers in the Green Revolution. *Ceres*
2(5): 35–37 (Sept.–Oct.); and O. H.
Frankel and E. Bennett, eds. 1970. *Genetic Resources in Plants—Their Exploration and Conservation.* Philadelphia:
F. A. Davis Co.

17. See, e.g., R. W. Risebrough, R. J.
Huggott, J. J. Griffin, and E. D. Gold-
berg. 1968. Pesticides: Transatlantic
movements in the northeast trades.
Science 159:1233–36. G. M. Woodwell,
P. P. Craig, and H. A. Johnson. 1971.
DDT in the biosphere: Where does it
go? *Science* 174:1101–07.

18. D. R. Keeney and W. R. Gardner. 1970.
The dynamics of nitrogen transforma-
tions in the soil. In *Global Effects of
Environmental Pollution,* S. F. Singer,
ed. New York: Springer Verlag, pp. 96–
103.

19. G. M. Woodwell. 1970. Effects of pollution on the structure and physiology of
ecosystems. *Science* 168:429–33.

20. Teodoro Boza Barducci. 1972. Ecological
consequences of pesticides used for the
control of cotton insects in Canete Valley, Peru. In *The Careless Technology,*
op. cit., pp. 423–38.

21. John H. Ryther. 1969. Photosynthesis
and fish production in the sea. *Science*
166:72–76.

22. FAO. 1972. *State of Food and Agriculture 1972.* Rome: Food and Agriculture
Organization.

23. Roger Revelle, Edward Wenk, Bostwick
Ketchum, and Edward R. Corino. 1971.
Ocean pollution by petroleum hydrocar-
bons. In *Man's Impact on Terrestrial
and Oceanic Ecosystems,* William H.
Matthews, Frederick E. Smith, and Ed-
ward D. Goldberg, eds. Cambridge:
M.I.T. Press, p. 297.

24. W. W. Kellogg, R. D. Cadle, E. R.
Allen, A. L. Lazrus, and E. A. Martell.
1972. The sulfur cycle. *Science* 175:587.

25. Gene E. Likens, F. Herbert Bormann,
and Noye M. Johnson. 1972. Acid rain.
Environment 14(2):33.

26. Report of the Study of Man's Impact on
Climate. 1971. *Inadvertent Climate
Modification.* Cambridge: M.I.T. Press,
pp. 188–92.

27. George M. Woodwell. 1970. The energy
cycle of the biosphere. *Scientific American* 223(3):64–74.

28. John P. Holdren. 1971. Global thermal
pollution. In *Global Ecology,* J. P. Holdren and P. R. Ehrlich, eds. New York:
Harcourt Brace Jovanovich.

29. William D. Sellers. 1965. *Physical Climatology.* Chicago: University of Chicago Press. M. King Hubbert. 1971. Energy resources. In *Environment,* William
Murdoch, ed. Stamford, Conn.: Sinauer
Associates.

30. Sherwood B. Idso. 1971. Potential effects
of global temperature change on agriculture. In *Man's Impact on Terrestrial
and Oceanic Ecosystems,* op. cit., p.
184.

31. Barry Commoner. 1972. The environmental cost of economic growth. In *Population Resources and the Environment,*
Vol. 3 of the Research Reports of the
Commission on Population Growth and
the American Future. Washington
D.C.: U.S. Government Printing Offic
p. 339.

32. Paul R. Ehrlich and John P. Holdre
1972. One-dimensional ecology. *Science
and Public Affairs: Bull. Atomic Sci.*
28(5):16–27.

33. United Nations Statistical Office. 1972.
Statistical Yearbook, 1971. N.Y.: United
Nations Publishing Service.

34. United Nations Statistical Office. 1954.
Statistical Yearbook, 1953. N.Y.: United
Nations Publishing Service.

35. American Chemical Society. 1969.
*Cleaning Our Environment: The Chem-
ical Basis for Action.* Washington, D.C.:
American Chemical Society. U.S. Con-
gress. Joint Committee on Atomic En-
ergy. 1967. *Hearings on Radiation Expo-
sure of Uranium Miners,* Parts 1 and 2.
Washington, D.C.: U.S. Government
Printing Office. E. P. Lichtenstein, K.
R. Schulz, T. W. Fuhremann, and T. T.
Liang. 1969. Biological interaction be-
tween plasticizers and insecticides. *J.
Econ. Entom.* 62(4):761–65.

36. Joel Darmstadter et al. 1971. *Energy in
the World Economy.* Baltimore: Johns
Hopkins Press.

37. Nathan Keyfitz. 1971. On the momentum of population growth. *Demography*
8(1):71–80.

294

A Procedure for Evaluating Environmental Impact

By Luna B. Leopold, Frank E. Clarke, Bruce B. Hanshaw, and James R. Balsley

PREAMBLE

In a recent article in "Science" discussing the Environmental Policy Act of 1969, Gillette (1971) states "The law's instructions for preparing an impact report apparently are not specific enough to insure that an agency will fully or even usefully, examine the environmental effects of the projects it plans." This report contains a procedure that may assist in developing uniform environmental impact statements. The Department of the Interior and the Council on Environmental Quality will appreciate comments on the procedure here proposed.

The heart of the system is a matrix which is general enough to be used as a reference checklist or a reminder of the full range of actions and impacts on the environment that may relate to proposed actions. The marked matrix also serves as an abstract of the text of the environmental assessment to enable the many reviewers of impact reports to determine quickly what are considered to be the significant impacts and their relative importance as evaluated by the originators of the impact report.

Many exhaustive studies of the use of matrices for environmental studies are now being undertaken. (See Sorensen, 1971.) This comparatively simple system is intended as a guide for the many people who are faced with the evaluation and preparation of environmental impact reports before the results of these studies have been completed. It should be borne in mind that there is presently no uniformity in approach or agreement upon objectives in an impact analysis and this generalized matrix is a step in that direction.

The procedure does not limit the development of detail in any specific aspect of the environment; a separate expanded matrix for any environmental aspect can easily be developed within the framework provided.

INTRODUCTION

In any proposal for construction or development, it is the usual practice, both from the standpoint of engineering and economics, to prepare an analysis of the need for the development and the relationship between its monetary costs and monetary benefits. More recently, society has recognized that in addition to these customary economic analyses and discussions of need, there should be a detailed assessment of the effect of a proposed development on the environment and thus its ecological, separate from its monetary, benefits and costs; put together, these assessments comprise an Environmental Impact Statement. The preparation of a Statement should be done by a team of physical and social scientists and engineers; likewise, reviews of statements will generally require an interdisciplinary team effort.

The Environmental Policy Act of 1969 directs all agencies of the Federal Government to "identify and develop methods and procedures which will insure that presently unquantified environmental amenities and values are given appropriate consideration in decision-making along with economic and technical considerations". The Council on Environmental Quality, in furtherance of Section 102 of the Act, has set forth guidelines for the preparation of the required environmental statements. It is recommended in these guidelines that the second item to be included in the statement is "the probable impact of the proposed action on the environment".

This circular suggests an approach to accomplish that specific requirement by providing a system for the analysis and numerical weighting of probable impacts. This type of analysis does not produce an overall quantitative rating but portrays many value judgments. It can also serve as a guide in. preparing the statement called for under Section 102(2) (c) of the Act. A primary purpose is to insure that the impact of alternative actions is evaluated and considered in project planning.

USGS CIRCULAR 645, pp. 1-13.

295

Evaluating the environmental impact of an action program or proposal is a late step in a series of events which can be outlined in the following manner. Figure 1 is a flow chart of the recommended sequence of events which result in an environmental impact statement. The sequence is discussed briefly below and that portion which deals with impact assessment is expanded in more detail later in the text:

A. A statement of the major objective sought by the proposed project.

B. The technologic possibilities of achieving the objective are analyzed.

C. One or more actions are proposed for achieving the stated objective. The alternative plans which were considered as practicable ways of reaching the objective are spelled out in the proposal.

D. A report which details the characteristics and conditions of the existing environment prior to the proposed action is prepared. In some cases, this report may be incorporated as part of the engineering proposal.

E. The principal engineering proposals are finalized as a report or series of separate reports, one for each plan. The plans ordinarily have analyses of monetary benefits and costs.

F. The proposed plan of action, usually the engineering report, together with the report characterizing the present environment, sets the stage for evaluating the environmental impact of the proposal. If alternative ways of reaching the objective are proposed in C and if alternative engineering plans are detailed in the engineering report, separate environmental impact analyses must deal with each alternative. If only one proposal is made in the engineering report, it is still necessary to evaluate environmental impacts.

The environmental impact analyses require the definition of two aspects of each action which may have an impact on the environment. The first is the definition of the *magnitude* of the impact upon specific sectors of the environment. The term *magnitude* is used in the sense of degree, extensiveness, or scale. For example, highway development will alter or affect the existing drainage pattern and may thus have a large *magnitude* of impact on the drainage. The second is a weighting of the degree of *importance* (i.e. significance) of the particular action on the environmental factor in the specific instance under analysis. Thus the overall *importance* of impact of a highway on a particular drainage pattern may be small because the highway is very short or because it will not interfere significantly with the drainage. Depending upon the thoroughness and scope of the report inventorying existing environmental conditions, the analysis of *magnitude* of impact, though in some details subjective, can nevertheless be factual and unbiased. It should not include weights which express preference or bias.

The *importance* of each specific environmental impact must include consideration of the consequences of changing the particular condition on other factors in the environment. Again, the adequacy of the report under D would affect the objectivity in the assignment of the values for specific environmental conditions. Unlike *magnitude* of impact, which can be more readily evaluated on the basis of facts, evaluation of the *importance* of impact generally will be based on the value judgment of the evaluator. The numerical values of *magnitude* and *importance* of impact reflect the best estimates of pertinence of each action.

G. The text of the environmental impact report should be an assessment of the impacts of the separate actions which comprise the project upon various factors of the environment and thus provide justification for the determinations presented in F. Each plan of action should be analyzed independently.

H. The Environmental Impact Statement should conclude with a summation and recommendations. This section should discuss the relative merits of the various proposed actions and alternative engineering plans and explain the rationale behind the final choice of action and the plan for achieving the stated objective.

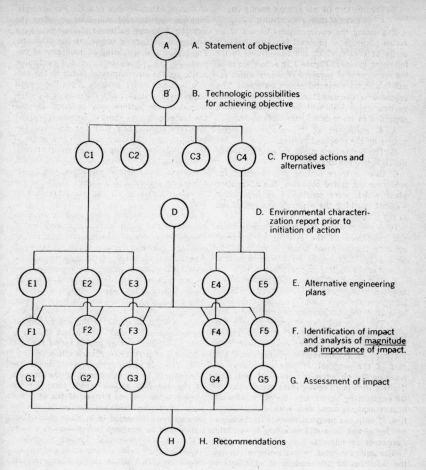

A. Statement of objective

B. Technologic possibilities for achieving objective

C. Proposed actions and alternatives

D. Environmental characterization report prior to initiation of action

E. Alternative engineering plans

F. Identification of impact and analysis of _magnitude_ and _importance_ of impact.

G. Assessment of impact

H. Recommendations

FIGURE 1.—Flow chart for development of action programs.

THE ENVIRONMENTAL IMPACT STATEMENT

A complete environmental impact statement consists of four basic items:

1. A complete analysis of the need for the proposed action. This would include parts A, B, and C of the Generalized Procedures;

2. An informative description of the environment to be involved, including a careful consideration of the boundaries of a project. For example, every drainage crossed by a highway can be affected at that point of crossing but may also be affected downstream as well owing to erosion. Therefore, these effects beyond the right-of-way should be described in part D of the Generalized Procedures;

3. A discussion of the pertinent details of the proposed action—part E of the Generalized Procedures;

4. An assessment of the probable impacts of the variety of specific aspects of the proposed action upon the variety of existing environmental elements and factors—parts F and G of the Generalized Procedures—and a summary or recommendation—part H—which would include the rationale supporting the selected plan of action.

The analysis of need, item (1) above, should be a justification which considers the full range of values to be derived, not simply the usual cost-benefit analysis. It should include a discussion of the overall objectives and of possible alternatives to meet them.

The characterization of the existing environment, item (2) above, should be a detailed description of the existing environmental elements and factors, with special emphasis on those rare or unique aspects, both good and bad, that might not be common to other similar areas. It should provide sufficient information to permit an objective evaluation of the environmental factors which could be affected by proposed actions. The description should include all the factors which together make up the ecosystem of the area. The vertical margin of the enclosed matrix can be used as a checklist in preparing this section.

The details of proposed action, item (3) above, should include discussion of possible alternative engineering methods or approaches to accomplish the proposed development (item 1). This should be done in sufficient detail so that all actions that may have impact upon the environment (item 2) can be checked. The horizontal margin of the matrix can be used as a checklist in preparing this section.

The environmental impact assessment, item (4) above, should consist of three basic elements:

a. A listing of the effects on the environment which would be caused by the proposed development, and an estimate of the *magnitude* of each.

b. An evaluation of the *importance* of each of these effects.

c. The combining of *magnitude* and *importance* estimates in terms of a summary evaluation.

In preparing this circular, it is not the intent to deal at length with items (1) through (3), and it is assumed that generalized procedures for their preparation are commonly followed since these items have been incorporated in many engineering feasibility studies and benefit-cost analyses of past projects. Rather, the primary intent is to focus on the new requirement and, therefore to address primarily the preparation of item (4)—the environmental impact assessment.

ENVIRONMENTAL IMPACT ASSESSMENT
MATRIX

The analysis embodied in a, b, and c above is made with a matrix (Plate 1) including on one axis the actions which cause environmental impact and on the other existing environmental conditions that might be affected. This provides a format for comprehensive review to remind the investigators of the variety of interactions that might be involved. It helps the planners to identify alternatives which might lessen impact. The number of actions listed horizontally in this sample matrix is 100 and the vertical list of environmental characteristics contains 88, which give a total of 8,800 possible interactions. Within such a matrix, only a few of the interactions would be likely to involve impacts of such *magnitude* and *importance* that they deserve comprehensive treatment. Although the items listed represent most of the basic actions and environmental factors likely to be involved in the full range of developments

298

which require impact reporting, not all would apply to every project proposal. Even this large matrix may not contain all elements necessary to make a full analysis of every project proposal encountered. However, the coding and format are designed for easy expansion to include additional items. Preliminary trials suggest that the number of applicable interactions for a typical project analysis usually will be between 25 and 50.

The most efficient way to use the matrix is to check each action (top horizontal list) which is likely to be involved significantly in the proposed project. Generally, only about a dozen actions will be important. Each of the actions thus checked is evaluated in terms of *magnitude* of effect on environmental characteristics on the vertical axis, and a slash is placed diagonally from upper right to lower left across each block which represents significant interaction. In marking the matrix, it is important to remember that actions may have major short-term impact (for a year or so) which are ameliorated in a few years and thus of minor or negligible importance in a long time frame. Conversely, other actions with lesser initial impact may produce more significant and persistent secondary effects and, therefore, have major impact in a long time frame. In the text, which discusses the matrix, one should indicate whether he is assessing short-term or long-term impact. As an example, oil drilling rigs are commonly considered noisy and nonaesthetic but they are on location for short periods of time—generally one to six months per site, whereas untreated spoil banks may silt and acidify streams for many years after completion of a project.

In marking the boxes, unnecessary replication can be avoided by concentrating on first-order effects of specific actions. For example, "mineral processing" would not be marked as affecting "aquatic life", even if the waste products are toxic in aquatic environments. The aquatic impact would be covered under "emplacement of tailing", "spills and leaks", or other processing operations which may lead to degradation of aquatic habitat.

After all the boxes which represent possible impact have been marked with a diagonal line, the most important ones are evaluated individually. Within each box representing a significant interaction between an action and an environmental factor, place a number from 1 to 10 in the upper left-hand corner to indicate the relative *magnitude* of impact; 10 represents the greatest magnitude and 1, the least. In the lower right-hand corner of the box, place a number from 1 to 10 to indicate the relative *importance* of the impact; again 10 is the greatest.

As an example, assume that a particular engineering proposal recommends construction of highways and bridges. The proposed action is item II.B.d. on the matrix. "Highways and bridges" might have environmental impacts through effect on "erosion" and related "deposition and sedimentation", among other things. "Erosion" and "deposition-sedimentation" occur under the main heading "Physical and Chemical Characteristics of the Environment" on the left side (ordinate) of the matrix and in the horizontal rows I.A.4.b. and I.A.4.c., respectively.

In this example, it might be that bridges will cause an important amount of bank erosion, because geologic materials in the area are poorly consolidated. This may lead the investigator to mark the *magnitude* of impact of highways and bridges on erosion 6 or more. If, however, the streams involved already have high sediment loads and appear to be capable of carrying such loads without objectionable secondary effects, the effective *importance* of bridges through increased erosion and sedimentation might be considered relatively small and marked 1 or 2 in the lower righthand corner of the block. This would mean that while *magnitude* of impact is relatively high, the *importance* of impact is not great.

In the assessment of accidents (II, J) such as "spills and leaks", it would be desirable to have some guide which would be helpful in determining the probability and effect of accidents. In this matter, the inclusion of controls which would reduce the probability of an accident would lower the matrix entry of *magnitude*, but it would have no influence on the evaluation of *importance* of impact.

The next step is to evaluate the numbers which have been placed in the slashed boxes. At this point, it is convenient to construct a simplified or reduced matrix which consists of only those actions and environmental characteristics which have been identified as interacting. Special note may be taken of boxes with exceptionally high individual numbers, as by circling the box. Although not used in this circular, we have found it convenient, when comparing alternatives in an action program, to identify the beneficial impacts with +, because alternate action plans may have different degrees of both beneficial and possibly detrimental impacts. However, in most cases the preparer will consider all impacts to be potentially deleterious because all the + factors would have been covered in the engineering report. Other investigators may wish to devise their own numerical rating methods; hence, the marginal boxes of Plate I are simply titled "computations".

It must be emphasized that no two boxes on any one matrix are precisely equatable. Rather, the significance of high or low numbers for any one box only indicates the degree of impact one type of action may have on one part of the environment. If alternative actions are under consideration, and a separate matrix is prepared for each action, identical boxes in the two matrices will provide a numerical comparison of the environmental impact for the alternatives considered.

Assignment of numerical weights to the *magnitude* and *importance* of impacts should be, to the extent possible, based on factual data rather than preference. Thus, the use of a rating scheme such as the one suggested here discourages purely subjective opinion and requires the author of an environmental impact statement to attempt to quantify his judgment of probable impacts. The overall rating allows the reviewers to follow the originators' line of reasoning and will aid in identifying points of agreement and disagreement. The matrix, is in fact, the abstract for the text of the environmental assessment.

TEXT

The text of an environmental impact assessment should be a discussion of individual boxes marked with the larger numerical values for *magnitude* and *importance*. Additionally, those columns which cause a large number of actions to be marked, regardless of their numerical values, should be discussed in detail. Likewise, those elements of the environment (rows) which have relatively large numbers of boxes marked should be addressed. The discussion of these items should cover the following points as put forth in the Council on Environmental Quality's guidelines published in the Federal Register (1971):

(i) a description of the proposed action including information and technical data adequate to permit careful assessment of impact. (This has been covered as items C and E in fig. 1.)

(ii) the probable impact of the proposed action on the environment

(iii) any probable adverse environmental effects which cannot be avoided

(iv) alternatives to the proposed action

(v) the relationship between local short-term uses of man's environment and the maintenance and enhancement of long-term productivity

(vi) any irreversible and irretrievable commitments of resources which would be involved in the proposed action should it be implemented, and

(vii) where appropriate, a discussion of problems and objections raised by other Federal, State, and local agencies and by private organizations and individuals in the review process and the disposition of the issues involved. This section may be added at the end of the review process in the final text of the environmental statement.

All of these points itemized above can be covered as part of a discussion of the matrix.

The text that accompanies the completed matrix should be primarily a discussion of the reasoning behind the assignment of numerical values for the *magnitude* of impact effects and their relative *importance*. The text should include a discussion of those actions which have significant impact and should not be diluted by discussions of obviously trivial side issues.

To be fully understandable, the discussion of the *magnitude* and *importance* of applicable impacts and responses will require some discussion in the text of the principal characteristics, physical and ecological, of the environment itself and some of the important characteristics of the proposed action which govern its environmental impact. The environmental impact assessment thus relies on and refers to the data incorporated in items 1, 2, and 3 (p. 4) —the full description of the geography, physical setting, vegetation, climate, and other facts about the environment and the physical and engineering aspects of the proposed development. This explanation is inserted here to caution that the environmental impact assessment need not be burdened nor should it be padded with descriptions of the project and the environment per se. It should include only such details as are needed for evaluating the environmental impact. The completed environmental impact assessment, together with items (1), (2), and (3), comprises the finished Environmental Impact Statement; all four items are required for review purposes.

In order to test the usefulness of the matrix approach, a matrix for an actual proposed mineral extraction and processing operation has been prepared and included as an appendix. This example is solely a model used for demonstration purposes and is not intended to be an impact assessment of the example project. A brief synopsis of the justification, regional setting, and general plan of operation extracted from a report which covers items (1), (2), and (3) of an environmental impact statement is included. In addition, for each of the boxes with entries, there is a brief discussion of the impact rating including the reasoning behind the assignment of values.

CONCLUDING STATEMENT

Obviously, the wide variety of projects and actions have such differing impact on environmental factors that no scheme of impact assessment will be universally applicable. However, greatest need is not for a single and universally applicable assessment method, but rather for a simple way of summarizing which impacts are considered of greatest moment by the people making the assessment. Different assessors will seldom come to identical conclusions, but it would be useful to know the basis for the difference.

The advantage of a matrix is in its use as a checklist or reminder of the full range of actions and impacts. The proposed manner of using the matrix is aimed at separating as far as possible factual information on *magnitude* of each type impact from the more subjective evaluation of the *importance* of the impact, the latter involving preference or bias to some degree. This separation of fact from preference is highly desirable.

Finally, the matrix and suggested method of use is presented as a draft, subject to improvement, expansion, and change. Because it is impractical to circulate unpublished manuscripts widely, this manuscript is being submitted for review by potential users as a U.S. Geological Survey circular, a series used for tentative, incomplete, or preliminary statements.

The authors acknowledge with thanks the cooperation of Robert H. Twiss for sharing his experience in matrix construction and for his thoughtful review of this manuscript. The help furnished through discussion, manuscript revision, and suggestions by Elmer Baltz and George Davis is also gratefully acknowledged.

APPENDIX: IMPACT ASSESSMENT OF A PHOSPHATE MINING LEASE BY MATRIX ANALYSIS

A phosphate deposit estimated to include 80 million tons of crude ore of an average content of 8.7 percent P_2O_5 is located in Los Padres National Forest, Ventura County, California. The ore consists of sand-size pellets of phosphorite occurring in a sequence of sandstones and siltstones of late Miocene age. The beds crop out on hillslopes along a strike length of about 5 miles. The beds dip approximately 30° north. The mineable beds are 90 feet thick with an overburden varying from 0 to 200 feet.

Application for a prospecting permit was made in February 1964, and a permit was granted in November 1964. A 3-year extension of the permit was approved in October 1966. The company made an application for a Preference Right Phosphate Lease in April 1969. The background material needed for the present analysis is contained in the company's report. Parts of the report are abstracted below for purposes of this circular.

The regional environment.—The deposit occurs in a semiarid region receiving 23 inches of annual percipitation, most of which occurs in the period November through April. The principal drainage system in the area is Sespe Creek; its headwaters are about 5 miles west of the Lease Application. In its upper reaches, Sespe is an ephemeral stream. The proposed mining operation would be 2 miles north of the Sespe. Vegetation ranges from sparse to medium heavy, is of a chaparral type including oak, manzanita, and mountain mahogany, and with a low density ground cover of grass.

Access to the area is by means of California State Highway 33, a black-topped paved road which runs from Ventura to Bakersfield. The prospect is within one to two miles of this highway; present access is over a temporary unpaved road. To develop the property, about 1½ miles of permanent paved road would have to be built.

The region is sparsely settled. In a 5-mile radius of the proposed mine, there are six year-round residents plus 10 summer residences. The nearest towns are Meiners Oaks and Ojai, 25 miles to the south, and New Cuyama about 35 miles to the north.

General mining plans.—The ore crops out as a narrow band about 5 miles long. Test core drilling indicated that the rock is too unstable to support underground workings and the company proposes to develop the mine by open-pit methods. The strike is approximately perpendicular to the local stream channels which drain toward Sespe Creek. The small canyons cut across the ore zone every 2,000 to 3,000 feet along the strike. In order to prevent damage to the watershed, the company envisions a mining operation which would not dam or interrupt these channels. Therefore, over the life of the mining operation a series of open pits would be dug parallel to the strike and terminated short of the tributary valleys which cross the ore body. The dimensions of the proposed open pits will be determined by the interval between adjacent canyons. Pit width would be a function of the amount of overburden which could be removed economically. In the downdip direction, mining would extend only so far as economics of overburden removal would allow.

The planned open pit geometry is V-shaped. One limb would follow the foot wall of the ore zone at approximately 30° from the horizontal. The high wall would be cut at 45° to the horizontal. Such a pit would be worked in a series of 20-foot high benches running parallel to the strike.

Ore processing.—An ore-processing plant would be constructed at the mine site to crush the ore. After crushing, the phosphate would be leached out with acid. The resultant pregnant liquor would be neutralized with quicklime to precipitate dicalcium phosphate in a granular form.

The tailings from the leach process is quartz sand which would be washed, dewatered, and stored in the open pit areas where mining had been completed.

The phosphate in the form either of granular solids or liquid would be transported to market via trucks. The major raw materials required to be brought in are quicklime and sulphur, the latter being converted to sulphuric acid at the mine site. Water required for the processing is small and is to be supplied by a 1,000-foot deep well already drilled.

Watershed and environmental values.—There are two principal environmental values which require consideration in this area as well as many subsidiary ones. A primary consideration is the effect on the California condor, a rare and endangered species present in the general region. The second major consideration is location of the mine lease close to the center of a large block of National Forest land. Pertinent to the latter is the fact that the total lease, 2,434 acres, is small by comparison with the total Forest. The site is 15 miles east-southeast along the mountain ridge from the edge of the San Rafael Wilderness so that no designated wilderness lands are involved. However, the need for recreational use of undeveloped public lands in California to relieve population pressure is relatively great and any commercial operation in an undeveloped area would have an effect on such use.

The Sespe Condor Sanctuary, located in the National Forest, lies 15 miles to the east of the mining area. From this sanctuary, the condors are said to range along the crestline to the northwest, across the center of the whole National Forest area. The ordinary flight or soaring patterns for condors would pass through the general region of the proposed mine site. One condor nest, apparently now abandoned, has been noted a few miles west of the mining site. The other known condor nests all lie within the condor sanctuary.

Among the subsidiary environmental impacts which the mining operation might cause, a few are mentioned briefly below and are discussed in more detail in connection with the impact matrix.

The possibility of water pollution from the phosphate itself is minimized by the fact that the phosphate ore is quite insoluble as shown by water quality analyses on surface water in the area. The mining operation would not increase the soluble phosphate content of the water resource. The effectiveness of erosion control measure applied within the mining area will determine the quantity of particulate phosphate mineral and other sediments added to Sespe Creek. The liquid chemicals handled at the plant are to be confined within dikes. Except for possible leakage from these dikes, or in case of spills on the highway, water pollution from processing chemicals and products should not occur.

Increased soil erosion and related sediment load to stream channels will depend upon the manner in which the stream channels crossing the ore body are protected from the open-pit mining operation.

Some level of air pollution is possible from noxious gases emanating from the plant in the form of fluorine from the ore, SO_2 gas from the manufacture of sulphuric acid, and fuel combustion products. Blasting, drilling, and equipment noise will have some environmental impact. Mining equipment will be diesel-powered and controlled by conventional mufflers.

The power requirements of the plant are estimated to be 5,000 KVA. The mine would require the construction of 14 miles of transmission lines which is to be erected on wooden poles on the right-of-way of State Highway 33. Natural gas would be taken from a pipeline already in the area which passes within 3 miles

of the proposed plant site using either overhead or buried lines.

The impact on vegetation and wildlife is influenced by the fact that, over the life of the mine, only 400 acres will be subjected to actual mining. The mining operation would involve an annual excavation of 4 to 5 acres with reclamation following closely in the mined-out area. A total of about 40 acres thus would be disturbed at any given time.

The brief summary above shows the main aspects of the planned mining operation for which environmental impact is being evaluated. More details on these and other aspects of the area and the project plan are contained in the company's report.

Using material contained in the company's report, an information matrix analysis was completed in the manner described in the previous section of this circular. The outcome of the analysis is recapitulated in reduced form as figure 2. The explanations which follow indicate the reasoning followed in this example.

The mining plan calls for a small "alternation of drainage" so that effects on "erosion" and "sedimentation" should be minor as compared with the effect of "highways and bridges" and "emplacement of tailings." "Modification of habitat" and "alteration of ground cover" are not likely to be important impacts because the total mined area is relatively small. "Industrial buildings" and "construction of highways" are considered to be among the more important impacts. The "blasting and drilling" under "construction" (II. B. q.) will be short term and have limited impact, but "drilling and blasting" for "resource extraction" (II. C. a.) will continue sporadically over the life of the project and, therefore, is relatively important. "Surface excavation" and "mineral processing" appear to have relatively important impact potential. On detailed consideration, "product storage" and "erosion control" are viewed as less important than some of the construction and resource extraction items noted above. Changes in traffic owing to the increase in "trucking" rather than increase in "automobile traffic" is considered to be capable of producing important impact. The

		Industrial sites and buildings II B.b.	Highways and bridges II B.d.	Transmission lines II B.h.	Blasting and drilling II C.a.	Surface excavation II C.b.	Mineral processing II D.f.	Trucking II G.c.	Emplacement of tailings II H.c.	Spills and leaks II J.b.
I A.2.d.	Water quality					2/2	1/1		2/2	1/4
I A.3.a.	Atmospheric quality						2/3			
I A.4.b.	Erosion	2/2				1/1			2/2	
I A.4.c.	Deposition, Sedimentation	2/2				2/2			2/2	
I B.1.b.	Shrubs					1/1				
I B.1.c.	Grasses					1/1				
I B.1.f.	Aquatic Plants					2/2			2/3	1/4
I B.2.c.	Fish					2/2			2/2	1/4
I C.2.e.	Camping and hiking					2/4				
I C.3.a.	Scenic views and vistas	2/3	2/1	2/3		3/3		2/1	3/3	
I C.3.b.	Wilderness qualities	4/4	4/4	2/2	1/1	3/3	2/5	3/5	3/5	
I C.3.h.	Rare and unique species		2/5		5/10	2/4	5/10	5/10		
I C.4.b.	Health and safety							3/3		

FIGURE 2.—The reduced matrix for a phosphate mining lease.

"emplacement of tailings" would occur throughout the life of the project and could have significant effects if poorly controlled. "Liquid effluent discharge" would be small during all phases of the project, and, therefore, would be relatively unimportant by comparison. "Spills and leaks" owing to accidents could be important within the mining operation area depending on the effectiveness of diking. Accidents would be especially significant on the highways over which new materials and finished products must be hauled.

With such consideration, the number of proposed actions considered important enough for discussion was reduced to 9. Under each of these items in the vertical column existing characteristics and conditions of the environment were inspected individually. Where the interaction was deemed sufficiently important, the impact was numerically evaluated in terms of *magnitude* and *importance*. The resulting codification appears in the completed matrix (fig. 2). The types of impact are discussed below in order of the items listed on the left-hand side of figure 2.

Water quality (I. A. 2. d.).—Water quality could be affected by the "surface excavation," by "emplacement of tailings," and by the possibility of "accidental spills and leaks." The planned "surface excavation" is off-channel and was, therefore, assigned *magnitude* 2. Because of the ephemeral nature of the streams, the *importance* of the excavation in affecting water quality was rated 2 also.

The same reasoning applies to the "emplacement of tailings" which are off-channel and not of a noxious character. "Spills and leaks" were considered sufficiently rare to be assigned *magnitude* 1, but *if* they occurred, they would be moderately *important* and, therefore, given a value of 4.

In actual practice, any of the identified impacts can be expanded to produce secondary matrices which can cover greater detail than is possible on plate I or figure 2 if the analysts or reviewer feels the need to do so. As an example, expanding the matrix items related to "water quality," the relative *magnitude* and *importance* of different specific actions may be more clearly shown than by merely using the main headings in the matrix. The example (fig. 3) indicates how expansion may show details pertinent to the individual situation. Additionally, water quality could also be expanded into subcategories such as pH, dissolved oxygen, turbidity, etc.

Atmospheric quality (I. A. 3. a.).—"Mineral processing" would be the principal source of degradation in atmospheric quality. Its *magnitude* was rated 2 owing to the small size of the plant and the absence of other industrial operations. Its *importance*, however, was rated 3 because of the sulphuric nature of the gases produced.

Erosion (I. A. 4. b.) and deposition (I. A. 4. c.).—Some "erosion" and thus some channel "deposition" will be caused by the construction of "highways and bridges" and by the "emplacement of tailings." The sandy nature of the washes in the area and thus naturally high sediment loads give both "erosion" and "deposition" caused by the project a relatively low importance. The *magnitude* and *importance* of each were relatively low owing to the fact that the mining operation would involve the construction of less than 2 miles of new roads and that protection against erosion is included in the design of the mining operation.

Shrubs (I. B. 1. b.) and grasses (I. B. 1. c.).—The disturbance of native "shrubs" and "grasses" is important only on the area which is going to be physically disturbed by the mining. Because vegetation change would occur only on parts of the 2,434 acre lease over the life of the project and revegetation is part of the scheduled project, the *magnitude* and *importance* are both rated low.

Aquatic plants (I. B. 1. f.).—"Aquatic plants" do not occur in the ephemeral streams near the plant site but do occur in the portion of the main stream some miles down valley where Sespe Creek is perennial. Any effect on "aquatic plants" reaching that far downstream would come from "excavation" and from "emplacement of tailings." The distance to the perennial stream indicated low values for *magnitude*, but a moderate value for *importance* in the case of "spills."

Fish (I. B. 2 c.).—The same reasoning that governed the assessment of impact on "aquatic plants" applies also to "fish" which persists only some miles downstream where Sespe Creek is perennial and the probable impacts are rated low.

Camping and Hiking (I. C. 2. e.).—The only alteration involving "camping and hiking" is caused by "surface excavation." Owing to the small area to be affected, its *magnitude* is rated 2, but its *importance* was considered moderate and rated 4 because any environmental change that interrupts recreational use of public land in a highly populated State is relatively important.

Scenic Views and Vistas (II. C. 3. a.).—This is one of the characteristics that is most seriously impacted by the proposed development. "Scenic views" are impaired in quality owing to "industrial buildings," "highways and bridges," "transmission lines," "surface excavation," "trucking," and "emplacement of tailings." All these have a low to moderate value of *magnitude* and generally a somewhat higher figure for *importance*. Compared with any of the previous items, the actions impacting "scenic views and vistas" are more numerous.

Wilderness qualities (I. C. 3. b.).—The item "wilderness and open space" (I. B. 1. a.) as a land use is not important in this area be-

	Industrial sites and buildings				Highways and bridges		Transmission lines		Surface excavation			Mineral processing			Trucking	Emplacement of tailings			Spills and leaks			
	Waste water	Sewage	Washing	Runoff from paving	Runoff during construction	Runoff from finished road	Sediment from cleared zone	Construction sediment	Sediment from fill	Effects of ore exposures	Effects of deep seepage	Sulfuric acid use	Acidity of yard runoff	Spilled sulfur compounds		Erosion of fill	Deep seepage	Acidity of seepage	Highway truck spills	Tailings pond leak	Tailings dams washout	Plant spills of acid
Water quality	3/3	3/3	1/1	1/2	1/1	1/2	1/1	1/1	2/2	1/1	1/1	1/1	1/3	1/4	3/3	1/2	1/2	1/3	1/3	1/1	1/1	1/1

FIGURE 3.—Expanded matrix showing actions which would impact water quality.

cause it is not designated wilderness; accordingly, it was not rated. What is important is the aesthetic and human interest item—"wilderness qualities." Thus, a distinction is made between wilderness as a "land use," not important in this area, and the "quality" of wild land which is considered highly important in the area. "Wilderness qualities" would be impacted under the proposed project primarily by "industrial buildings," "highways and bridges," "surface excavation," "trucking," and "emplacement of tailings." The impact of each on "wilderness qualities" is rated moderate with respect to both *magnitude* and *importance*. The result of this is that the degradation of "wilderness qualities" may be considered a potentially important impact caused by the proposed development.

Rare and unique species (I. C. 3. h.).—Possibly the most important environmental impact of the proposed development is its potential effect on the condor. A distinction is made between the biological conditions of fauna, "endangered species" (I. B. 2. g.), and the item under "aesthetics and human interest," "rare and unique species." The condor could be covered under either of these two, but should not

be under both. As a matter of choice then, the condor problem is specified under the item of "aesthetics and human interest."

Consideration was given to the fact that the main nesting area for the condors is some miles to the southeast and that a Naval training camp involving much heavy equipment is already operating near that nesting area. It is believed that the effect of the proposed development on condors would come about primarily from the "blasting" and from the increase in "truck traffic." For both of these actions, the *magnitude* is considered moderate and rated 5, but the *importance* of the survival of condors was considered to be great and thus any impact is of high importance. Those two items were, therefore, given an *importance* score of 10. Also the sulphur fumes from "mineral processing" might be an important deterrent to the use of this part of the range by condors. The effect on the birds is unknown, but it is conceivable that air pollution would keep them from landing to catch prey wherever the smell and smoke occurred. The *magnitude* of impact of this action was assessed as 5 and *importance* as 10.

Health and safety (I. C. 4. b.).—"Health and safety" would be impacted primarily by the increase in "trucking" on the highway as a result of mine operation.

Summary.—Inspection of figure 2 immediately gives the essence of the matrix analysis: the proposed actions which have the most environmental impacts are the construction of "highways and bridges," the "blasting," "surface excavation," "mineral processing," "trucking," and the "emplacement of tailings." The environmental characterisites most frequently impacted are those of "scenic views and vista," "wilderness qualities," and "rare and unique species."

As an outcome of this matrix analysis, the reviewers could ask the petitioners for the phosphate project "What actions can you take to reduce these possible impacts to lower levels?" if the impact is deemed sufficiently great. As an example, assume that the company, in light of the comparative values shown in the simplified matrix, decided to substitute for daytime trucking, a night-time only schedule for moving supplies and products. If it were known that condors soar only during the day and would be unaffected by night-time traffic, that *magnitude-importance* impact might be significantly reduced. Assume also that as another step to reduce impact, the company decided to mat the ground surface prior to any rock blasting. If this step were deemed effective, matrix entry of 5/10 of blasting on rare and unique species might perhaps reduce the entry at 1/10. These changes may, in one sense, appear to be minor, but in fact would cause a significant reduction in impact on the specific environmental factor shown to be most affected.

REFERENCES

Council on Environmental Quality, 1971, Statements on proposed Federal actions affecting the environment: Federal Register, v. 36, no. 19, p. 1398-1402 and no. 79, p. 7724-7729.

Gillette, Robert, 1971, Trans-Alaska pipeline: Impact Study Receives Bad Reviews: Science, v. 171, Mar. 19.

Sorensen, J. C., 1971, A framework for identification and control of resource degradation and conflict in the multiple use of the coastal zone: Univ. of Calif., Berkeley, Dept. of Landscape Architecture, M. S. thesis, p. 42; in press, Univ. of Calif. Press. (Contains a state-of-the-art review of matrix use in environmental studies)

Environmental Impact: Controlling the Overall Level

A rationing system may control environmental impact, while maximizing personal choice.

Walter E. Westman and Roger M. Gifford

Recent observations on the genesis of current environmental problems suggest that they stem from the interaction of three elements: the size and rate of growth of the human population (1), the growing per capita consumption of products (2), and the increasing use of products and technologies that are more pollution-generating and wasteful of resources (3). While people have disagreed on the relative contributions of each of these factors toward the overall impact of man's activities on his environment (4), there seems little doubt that the combined effect gives reason for concern. The Club of Rome report (5) is one of several (6, 7) which puts the case vividly that unchecked growth of each of these elements of environmental impact is incompatible with the perpetuation of human civilization.

It seems to be true of all dynamic systems that negative feedbacks must come into play if a long-term steady-state is to be achieved. If natural environmental feedbacks in the system of the biosphere were to come to exert full force, resulting in some variant of the Malthusian crash, much hardship would no doubt occur. There is disagreement about the extent to which improvements in technology can mitigate the crises predicted by a Malthusian analysis of the limits to growth (8). Quite apart from the question of the degree to which technological improvements can postpone behavioral changes, however, there seems to be general agreement that negative environmental feedbacks in some form will be necessary. To minimize the social hardships that will otherwise occur, and to spread them as evenly as possible across the populace, while giving each person the maximum freedom of choice of activity possible, a mechanism is needed for purposefully instituting environmental feedbacks before the more inhumane natural ones come into play. Furthermore, it is important that these feedbacks operate sufficiently rapidly to avoid fluctuations around the steady-state level sought. In this article, we describe an equitable system of resource allocation that could be made to act as such a rapid, anticipatory feedback system, while placing an artificial cap on the overall impact that society is making on the environment. The proposal involves establishing trade-offs between alternative activities by means of a new pricing unit in such a way that governments could control environmental impact, and at the same time provide a large measure of choice for individuals and organizations.

SCIENCE, August, 1973, Vol. 181, pp. 819-825.

Several points should be recognized from the outset. First, the system could be used to set the rate of environmental decay at any level within a wide range; that is, it is possible that governments may decide, using this natural resource policy, to set incentives that would lead to a rapid decline in environmental quality (9). It is our hope that, if implemented, the scheme would be used to prevent such a decline, but we wish to emphasize its fundamental independence from any particular set of sociopolitical priorities or ideologies.

Second, we recognize that, on theoretical grounds, no activity is without its environmental impact. If nothing else, our activities are increasing the entropy of the biosphere, or releasing heat. Numerous authors (10) have discussed the limited capacity of air, water, and land to absorb pollutants without degradation. Similarly, some resources are more readily renewed than others. Ultimately, life on earth will come to an end by one or another of the natural entropic processes, if not by some earlier catastrophe. What we seek is a method for prolonging the stay of human civilization on earth within these ultimate constraints, while sharing the stewardship of earth equitably.

The system we describe would, in practice, begin by limiting those resource uses and activities whose adverse effects on the environment are most severe and irreversible. The system could only be phased in gradually, starting with emphasis on the most destructive activities.

Third, some restriction of personal freedom is inherent in all regulations. It is likely that policies which lead to very low levels of environmental impact will require greater restrictions on personal freedom than we experience today. Thus, the policy we describe will almost certainly not receive immediate acceptance. On the other hand, the predictions of environmentalists, as summarized in the Club of Rome report, are too dire to ignore. As environmental impact increases, the changing conditions themselves may force upon governments an awareness of the need for comprehensive regulation, and upon the public a realization of the necessity to accept control.

We intend to initiate discussion of the implications and usefulness of the suggested scheme, to encourage tests of its properties with simulation models, and to help elucidate the kinds of data that need to be collected if such a scheme were to be implemented. It is our hope that such studies might lead to a series of detailed and pretested suggestions for regulating environmental impact when the public is willing to accept such controls. We suspect that a comprehensive national resource policy such as described here might be more protective of individual choice than the haphazard accumulation of governmental restrictions currently being imposed as particular environmental problems force themselves into the public arena. Although we are not prepared to propose the implementation of this system, we feel it deserves consideration.

The Natural Resource Unit:
The Essence of the Scheme

The proposal is basically a rationing mechanism in which a single unit—the natural resource unit (NRU)—is expendable on a range of goods, services, and activities that have an impact on the environment. These NRU's would be allocated equally to all individuals and, by special means, to firms, nonprofit organizations, and governmental departments. The government would establish the overall level of environmental impact for the country by fixing both the total annual allocation of NRU's and the NRU price of each good, service, and activity. The NRU system would not replace, but would complement, the existing money-based system. The government policy of total NRU releases and prices would reflect existing data on levels and trends in environmental impact, as well as social priorities.

The kinds of environmental impact that might be rationed by this scheme can be grouped as follows: (i) pollution of air, water, and land; (ii) destruction or disturbance of valued species' habitats, ecosystems, and scenery; (iii) extraction and use of recyclable and nonrecyclable physical resources; (iv) contribution to human population pressure; and (v) transitory, immediately reversible disturbance to individuals' local environment (for example, noise).

The activities leading to these environmental impacts vary in their importance to different people. Impacts cannot be regulated fairly by levying a uniform tax, because some people and firms would feel the impact of particular taxes more acutely than others—depending (i) on the value they place on the particular resource and (ii) on their initial financial status (11). The first of these difficulties is normally circumvented by applying an excise tax on the product or activity. In this sense, NRU's act like excise taxes. The second difficulty, the inequality of wealth, is inevitable in a competitive system; yet, with regard to impact on the biosphere, we see no reason why the rich should be allowed to ruin the environment more than the poor.

The NRU and the Individual

In our system, all individuals would be allocated an equal number of NRU's. The rich could spend their excess money on activities that have low levels of environmental impact. The NRU's would not be transferable, nor could they be bought with money. Unspent NRU's could be saved from year to year, but would become invalid when the individual died.

In his pattern of spending NRU's, a citizen could express his own preferences in his life-style, while being held to a maximum overall level of environmental impact equal to the potential impact of any other citizen. A person's life-style—for example, where he goes on a vacation or how many cars he owns—is already severely constrained by many aspects of his physical, social, and economic environment. A main difference that NRU's would make would be that some of the constraints would be imposed by society with a view to benefiting future citizens. The individual's life-style would be fashioned in part by a series of environmental trade-offs of his own choosing.

Perhaps the most important and controversial example of an activity that is costly in terms of environmental resources and that has a different value to different people is childbearing. For some, the right to have a large family may far outweigh the decrement in open space and resources that may result. For others, a self-imposed limit on family size might readily be undertaken in return for the use and conservation of wilderness and other resources. Unlike a financial tax on childbearing, an NRU system would not financially penalize citizens who wanted to have large families. Instead, they would have to weigh a large family against alternative uses of the environment. Through saving, parents could spread the NRU cost of bearing a child over a number of years. A child could be assigned

310

NRU's annually from birth, perhaps starting at a low allocation and increasing to the adult number in the midteens.

Such a system for regulating population growth might help settle a particularly knotty conflict of interest between current supporters of zero population growth and some members of racial minorities who rightly point out that an across-the-board limit to population growth would freeze their relative numbers in the population at the level of a perpetual minority (12). The NRU system would permit such persons to raise large families without threatening the overall level of environmental impact, although not without some personal sacrifice in spending on other environmentally costly items.

It would be highly desirable for NRU's not to be borrowed from future allocations. Such a restriction would ensure that the rate of spending of NRU's could be controlled, that per capita allocation of NRU's would remain uniform, and that accounting processes would be relatively streamlined. As with money, the supply of NRU's would have to be regulated by the available resource base and could not be allowed to increase at will. However, as with money, it is inevitable that some persons would outspend their existing capital of NRU's—by having an unintended child, for example. The philosophy of the NRU system is based on control of such resource spending, but clearly society may decide, on humanitarian grounds, that it will suspend the rigidity of NRU control to avoid imposing involuntary abortion. In such a case, borrowing against the future could be allowed. Severe and persistent NRU indebtedness, however, would presumably not be honored with loans. Such a policy is harsh, but it has its direct parallels among the down-and-

outs in our money-based society. In either case, society must reach some compromise between the rules of its resource control system and the "welfare" system.

The all-important complement to the distribution of NRU's among individuals would be a national "fiscal" policy to control the rate of consumption of resources and the rate of pollution generation. By setting NRU prices and determining annual rationing levels on the basis of existing data on environmental degradation and social priorities, the government would continuously control the overall level of environmental impact.

The NRU and the Organization

Industrial corporations and other organizations that play a role of their own in contributing to the welfare of society would have to be assigned NRU's on a separate basis. Of the several criteria that could be used (for example, size of work force, auction to least-polluting producer, and investment in R & D to reduce pollution), the following appears worthy of further consideration: an industry as a whole could be allowed to use up a set number of NRU's each year to offset the resources harvested by it and the total amount of pollutants released. The NRU allotment would be determined by the government on the basis of calculated allowable rates of resource consumption and pollution generation. Within a given industry, NRU's would be rationed to companies on the basis of existing plant capacity, using a standard production : NRU ratio set by the government. Obviously, a company that could devise ways during the year of increasing its production "efficiency" in relation to pollution generated and resources used (that is, increasing its production : NRU ratio) would be able to achieve higher production and possibly higher profits. The incentive is thus provided for improvement in pollution technology and resource conservation, while maintaining overall control of the pollutants generated and resources used each year.

In the following year, the company's NRU allocation would increase in proportion to its increased relative share of the industry's output. We recognize the tendency of this method to encourage amalgamation into larger companies to achieve efficiencies of scale. The proposed system would have to be used in conjunction with antitrust legislation, to the extent that amalgamation is considered undesirable.

Similar principles of resource allocation would apply to certain retail organizations, such as restaurants, with, perhaps, volume-of-trade : NRU ratios. Criteria closely related to the pollution-generating activity (for example, amount of grease burned as kitchen smoke) would be desirable, but in practice may be more difficult to measure. Most retail organizations generating simply sewage would be paying NRU's directly with their sewerage bills.

Nonprofit service organizations, such as public hospitals, churches, schools, and government departments themselves, engage in overhead activities that may warrant partial or total subsidization. In these cases, the administering agency of government would have to allocate an additional sum of NRU's to applying organizations, based on judgments of social priorities. The government's own NRU budget would have to be subjected to full public scrutiny, as is its money budget.

Certain goods and services accrue environmental impact costs at several stages between raw resource and fin-

ished product. These goods and services could be charged NRU's at each stage of the process. Thus a nonreturnable metal can would have accrued a certain NRU cost to the mining company in extracting the ore, another NRU cost in refining, another in manufacture, and another in sale. If the can were returnable and recyclable, the NRU cost at the retail level would be unnecessary (13). Note that in this system the "cost of pollution" is not wholly transferred to the consumer. The example of the metal can has, in fact, its precedent in the recent attempts in New York City to encourage recycling of containers through monetary incentives. Jerome Kretchmer, head of New York's Environmental Protection Agency, has said (14):

The philosophy behind the tax [on nonrecyclable containers] is important. It purpose is not to bring in revenues to the city but to establish economic incentives to manufacturers and wholesaler to recycle. It is a direct attempt on our part to reverse the economic realities in our society, to make recycled goods competitive in the marketplace.

The tax [on nonrecyclable containers] imposes a one- to three-cent levy on rigid and semi-rigid paper, glass, metal and plastic containers for all nonfood item sold at retail. Any container made of a prescribed percentage of recycled material is allowed a one cent credit against the tax. Wholesalers purchasing products from manufacturers reusing old containers would receive an additional one cent credit per container. As a result of the combinations of credits, all taxes are avoidable on paper, glass and single-metal cans. The per unit tax rate for each material is based on current estimates of the degree of difficulty of disposing and the feasibility of recycling for that material.

Administration and Politics
of a National Resource Policy

The effective formulation of such

national resource "fiscal" policy would require a large data base and constant input from the private sector concerning spending patterns. We envision a separate department (or departments) within the government, to be charged with the tasks of assembling the data on existing NRU and resource reserves, population size, and state-of-the-art of pollution technology, and of monitoring rates of change in these parameters. This would require, of course, extensive computer facilities and more extensive and frequent surveys than are now undertaken. These data would be used by the administering agency to adjust NRU rations annually and NRU prices annually or semiannually.

A primary function of such a department would be to determine whether the environmental impact of the community needs to be lessened, held the same, or could afford to be increased. Part of this decision would be based on direct polling of public opinion, and part would be based on the philosophy of environmental conservation of the political party in office. Another important decision would concern the distribution of units among government departments and agencies, profit-making organizations, nonprofit organizations, and individuals. Again, the allocation of total environment impact would be a matter of party political philosophy to some extent. The constant monitoring of NRU spending patterns, however, should improve the precision with which the government can assay priorities on environmental issues at any time.

We envision NRU currency as held and used in the form of personal credit cards. Retailers could record spending on the account, and daily or weekly intake would be transferred through regional to central computer banks. As with money, customer credit could be checked through local bank records. It is principally through this regular inflow of data to the central data bank that current social priorities would be gauged. Only through constant data input could sensitive adjustments in NRU prices and levels be made.

The number of NRU's rationed and the number spent each year would be recorded on a computer; the exact number saved each year would therefore be known. Since NRU's are nontransferable, but capable of being saved from year to year, the number saved after the system had been running for some time would be, in part, a function of the age distribution of the population.

Initially, the social value of those amenities that do not have a money price but that do have an environmental impact would have to be estimated by relatively qualitative means. But the NRU accounting system would generate quantitative data on cost and benefit of many more intangible items than are now priced. Once the system was in operation, this feedback mechanism should enable fairly workable NRU prices to be obtained by successive approximation; like any iterative method, however, the first estimate would only be a best guess based on anticipated spending patterns and supplies of resources. Although we recognize the difficulty in such a task, we think this proposal provides one publicly responsive way of allocating such costs. In fact, experience persuades us that, until many environmental costs and benefits—the so-called externalities —are assigned a quantitative value, their importance will be consistently underestimated in the cost-benefit analyses upon which so many social decisions are currently based.

Although spending patterns in NRU's

would serve to monitor community attitudes toward a wider range of social goods than financial records now do, the system of judging social priorities would still require much direct administrative and public discussion. We would still envision an annual NRU budget to be submitted by the administering agency to full public scrutiny and discussion and subjected to the equivalent of congressional or parliamentary checks. We would envision the persistence of lobby groups to argue the case for differential assignments of NRU's to various sectors of the resource economy. We acknowledge that the bookkeeping involved in processing two budgets instead of one is a bureaucratic bugaboo, but we would question whether the existing single economic budgeting accounts adequately for many of the important transactions and changes to which the natural resources of a country are currently subjected. A planned economy requires more data as a base for decisions; but the present alternative to such planning is a system in which the time lag between initial recognition of a problem with respect to a resource and the implementation of effective controls may be so long as to risk catastrophes (15).

The kinds of estimates of predicted environmental impact we will need will require computer simulation skills that are only now being developed. Computer modeling of the resources of wilderness areas, for example, has permitted estimation of the capacity of a park to sustain varying levels of human trampling (16). A number of workers (17) have developed the use of systems analysis in resource management, and recently a study group (18) has attempted to apply the technique to the State of California. Town and regional planners, resource economists, ecologists, and others (19) have developed skills in computer modeling, resource survey, and environmental impact assessment that are obvious tools in a resource policy system such as that presented. The National Environmental Center Bill (S. 1113) that passed the U.S. Senate last year already outlines as tasks the monitoring of environmental impact, the assessment of the effects of new technology, the study of current impacts on the environment, and the development of new methods for controlling environmental impact (20).

We emphasize again that the NRU system would apply at first to a limited number of the most environmentally costly activities and resources and would be gradually expanded as the data base, and public acceptance, increased. Lest phasing-in be slow, however, it should be borne in mind that the more items of environmental impact to be included in the NRU pricing system, the more equitable will become the distribution of true environmental impact throughout the population. Personal freedom (freedom from NRU pricing) is often inversely proportional to social freedom (freedom from environmental exploitation by others), as the "tragedy of the commons" (21) so compellingly illustrates.

Some Historical and Philosophical Roots

The system described above, of course, has its roots in the history of resource allocation theory. Economic systems are the obvious parallel to the system proposed here. In financial systems, all goods, services, and resources are given values in terms of a common monetary unit. Monetary transfer and resource allocation may occur freely, through supply and demand, or with partial or total government regulation of the means of production, distribution, and acquisition of resources and supply of monetary units. The NRU differs from money in that it is nontransferable; its system differs from Adam Smith's laissez-faire capitalism in its strong reliance on governmental adjustment of NRU prices and regulation of supply of the value units; it differs from a mixed economy (Western capitalism, for example) in its annual planning and governmental regulation of resource utilization; and it differs from a command economy (for example, that in the U.S.S.R.) in its stronger emphasis on consumer choice in the allocation of resources among the population. The reliance of this system on a strong fiscal policy is intended to dampen oscillations between resource spending (environmental impact) and resource saving (environmental conservation), although mild oscillations will probably occur. Note, too, that the NRU system differs from all economic systems in the very fact that it *coexists* with the economic system in a dual resource allocation scheme. The proper testing of the feasibility, stability, and effectiveness of a socioeconomic-NRU system requires, of course, considerable work.

The present proposal resembles that suggested by Edward Bellamy, in the 19th-century utopian novel *Looking Backward* (*22*), in its equal distribution of units to each individual each year. Bellamy's units were essentially nontransferable in that it was assumed that there would be an excess and no need to hoard; they differ from NRU's, however, in that the unspent excess dollars in Bellamy's utopia would be resumed at the end of the year, whereas we are proposing that NRU's remain usable and capable of being saved throughout the individual's life-

time. This capacity for saving should help increase the options open to an individual in choosing his life-style within an overall constraint.

The proposal is also related to various systems of rationing used in many countries during wartime and other stressful periods. In fact, the U.S. government has exercised fiscal control over a variety of resource uses, such as the rate of domestic oil consumption and the amount of farm land cultivated. The 1972 Federal Water Pollution Control Act Amendments impose a proportional charge on factories for wastes they send to a sewage treatment plant (*23*). Bills pending in Congress would permit government control of absolute amounts of toxic substances entering the environment and would establish national guidelines for land use (*24*). Still closer to the NRU idea is a passage in President Nixon's 1971 economic report (*25*):

Another alternative would be an environmental usage certificate system. It would limit the amount of pollutants directly, but allow the price for pollution to be set indirectly. Under this system, as under a system of pollution standards, a Government agency would set a specific limit on the total amount of pollutants that could be emitted. It would then issue certificates which would give the holder the right to emit some part of the total amount. Such certificates could be sold by the Government agency at auction and could be resold by owners. The Government auction and private resale market would thus establish a price on use of the environment. The more pollution a user engaged in, the more certificates he would have to buy. Groups especially concerned about the environment, such as conservation groups, would have a direct method of affecting the environment. They could themselves buy and hold some of the certificates, thus directly reducing the amount of emissions permitted and increasing the cost of pollution.

The Nixon scheme differs from ours

in that it is within the monetary framework and, as such, retains the existing financial inequalities. Not only would small industries be less able to compete for pollution certificates because of failure to achieve economies of scale, but poor citizens would have less control over the sale and use of pollution certificates than rich ones. Most conservation groups have no real means of competing with industry in the purchase of pollution certificates and, moreover, are acting at a level above pure self-interest. It is an important part of the NRU scheme to eradicate these initial inequalities.

Senator William Proxmire (D–Wis.) is one who has for several years suggested the application of effluent charges on the volume of water pollutants discharged by industry (26, 27). The charges for dumping pollutants would be set higher than the cost of employing pollution control technology, so that the industry would have an economic incentive to minimize the amount of pollutants discharged. Other proposals for effluent taxation have also been much discussed (28). We have pointed out above how, in a competitive monetary system, a uniform pollution tax allows those individuals and firms who are initially rich to purchase "licenses" to pollute the common environment to a degree that may be out of proportion to the value of their service to society. The NRU system would avoid this problem by establishing an upper limit on the NRU's distributed to individuals and corporations. However, both tax and NRU systems suffer from the difficulties of estimating the appropriate initial price or tax level needed to achieve the desired degree of control.

Some International Implications

One of the major problems of our time is the gap in resource use between industrialized nations and the Third World. Writers on the global environmental crisis (29) anticipated the bitter differences in attitude toward resource allocation and environmental pollution between developed and developing nations some time before they were highlighted by the 1972 U.N. Conference on the Human Environment at Stockholm. The complaints by the developing countries are analogous to those of minorities in more developed countries: if environmental impact (or population growth) is frozen uniformly at the present level, we (the Third World) will retain our underprivileged position in terms of ability to purchase resources. Since the industrialized nations attained their control over resources without controlling pollution, the developing countries, it is argued, should be allowed to do the same. The difficulty is that, under existing conditions of international competition, there is little reason to be confident that the differential cost of pollution control will be sufficient hindrance to industrialized nations to close the economic (and resource) gap between nations. Indeed, we suspect that the only likely way in which developing countries could obtain their proportionate share of the world's critical resources would be to allocate them on the basis of population size, independent of money, in an internationally administered natural resource rationing scheme (30). By analogy with a national NRU system, in order to establish equality of access to resources, one must divorce it from existing financial inequalities. Along with the global redistribution of resource wealth to individuals would be the ability of an internationally administered body to set overall limits on the rate of environmental impact on the biosphere—the rate of world population growth, resource utilization, and pollution. We will readily admit, however, that global acceptance of such regulation is extremely unlikely at present. We will, therefore, briefly consider the implications of only one nation's adopting an NRU rationing policy.

Since resources would continue to be purchased from abroad, the more highly industrialized countries would continue to absorb a disproportionate share of the world's resources. Existing means of redistribution (that is, foreign aid) would continue the attempt to close the gap with the Third World. The difficulties with the foreign aid approach would remain virutally unchanged (*31*).

On the other hand, the NRU limit placed on production by a developed country at home would provide an incentive for companies to increase investment abroad. To the extent that the countries receiving those foreign investments regarded them as undesirable, they would impose on the investor increasing export tariffs on products and profit taxes on investments. To the extent that the country with the NRU policy felt threatened by decreased investment at home, it would be likely to impose import quotas and tariffs (including tariffs in NRU's) and offer tax concessions for domestic investment. It seems inevitable that the overall effect of an isolated policy of environmental impact control would be a self-imposed cramp in the rate of growth of the country's material wealth. It is partly for this reason, of course, that international cooperation in coping with problems of pollution of the biosphere is being sought by industrialized nations (*32*).

Feasibility and Acceptability of the NRU Scheme

We do not believe that public attitudes in the industrialized nations are at a stage where the NRU scheme would be acceptable. Nor do we regard increased regulation as desirable in the absence of demonstrated need. We do believe, however, that, as public awareness of environmental and resource problems increases, pressure will mount for steps to be taken to regulate population growth, levels of pollution, and rates of resource use. In phase with environmental education, it will be important to point out that regulations of resource supply and pollution imply consequent restrictions in personal freedom. As the inevitability of this becomes more widely acknowledged, and if public concern continues to increase with increasing environmental impact, public attitudes toward comprehensive resource pricing may well change. We could hope that the overall level of environmental impact will gracefully stabilize at a desirable level entirely because of laissez-faire adjustments in social behavior. But, as current trends in the growth of environmental impact do not offer much reassurance in this regard, we feel that discussions of possible future regulatory systems should begin now.

It is of prime importance that the feasibility of the NRU scheme, and others like it, be tested extensively. It seems to us a logical development from Jay Forrester's (*15*) computer modeling of world dynamics that attempts be made to simulate the problems and potentials of comprehensive resource-control systems. To do so, and as a first step in implementation, it is necessary to continue to collect data on existing environmental impacts and their effects, and on existing and predicted sizes of populations and resource pools. At the present stage of our knowledge, we regard the current proposal simply as a useful conceptual model to be discussed and tested, and then refined or

317

discarded.

Summary

It is suggested that, by assigning to every resource use and activity (including childbirth) that causes environmental impact a price in money-independent units (NRU's), a new system of environmental trade-offs can be established—one which maintains maximum personal choice within overall environmental constraint. The social equality of the system in relation to resource exploitation would be enhanced by distributing NRU rations equally among the population each year. Special means of controlling industrial and organizational use of resources through NRU's are also discussed. The system is believed to offer a more sensitive means of gauging social priorities in relation to resource use than that achieved by an exclusively monetary system. Although involving more planning and more governmental regulation than is currently deemed feasible or acceptable, we believe the mechanism would lead to less restriction of personal freedom in a steady-state society than would the current trend toward unsystematic imposition of governmental regulations.

References and Notes

1. P. R. Ehrlich and J. P. Holdren, *Science* 171, 1212 (1971). Also see P. R. Ehrlich, *The Population Bomb* (Ballantine, New York, 1968); W. E. Howard, *BioScience* 19, 779 (1969); *Population Reference Bureau Data Sheet* (Population Reference Bureau, Washington, D.C., 1971); *United Nations Statistical Yearbook* (United Nations, New York, 1971).
2. For example, G. Borgstrom, *The Hungry Planet* (Collier-Macmillan, New York, 1965); *Too Many—An Overview of Earth's Limitations* (Collier-Macmillan, New York, 1969); National Academy of Sciences–National Research Council, *Resources and Man* (Freeman, San Francisco, 1969).
3. See especially B. Commoner, *The Closing Circle—Nature, Man and Technology* (Knopf, New York, 1971).
4. P. R. Ehrlich and J. P. Holdren, *Bull. At. Sci.* 28 (No. 5), 16 (1972); B. Commoner, *Environment* 14, (No. 3), 23 (1972); R. G. Ridker, *Science* 176, 1085 (1972).
5. D. H. Meadows, D. L. Meadows, J. Randers, W. W. Behrens, *The Limits to Growth* (Universe, New York, 1972).
6. E. Goldsmith, R. Allen, M. Allaby, J. Davoll, S. Lawrence, *Ecologist* 2, 1 (1972).
7. P. R. Ehrlich and A. H. Ehrlich, *Population, Resources, Environment* (Freeman, San Francisco, ed. 2, 1972).
8. R. Boyd, *Science* 177, 516 (1972).
9. Indeed, it is possible that an administering agency, following in the steps of a body such as the International Whaling Commission, would set the level of environmental impact so high that catastrophic situations would develop. See G. L. Small, *The Blue Whale* (Columbia Univ. Press, New York, 1971); R. Payne, quoted by P. R. Ehrlich and A. H. Ehrlich (7, pp. 130–131).
10. For example, W. E. Westman, *Amer. Sci.* 60, 767 (1972); P. R. Ehrlich, J. P. Holdren, R. W. Holm, Eds., *Man and the Ecosphere* (Freeman, San Francisco, 1971).
11. See also H. E. Daly, Ed., *Toward a Steady-State Economy* (Freeman, San Francisco, 1973).
12. R. Buckhout, *Environ. Behav.* 3, 322 (1971); S. Love, *Environ. Action* 4 (No. 6), 3 (1972).
13. An alternative policy would be to charge NRU's to every purchaser of metals each time he buys metal in any form. When the metal is resold, the NRU units that were charged would be made available again to the seller through the accounting system. This, however, would constitute a form of borrowing that has the disadvantages discussed in the text.
14. J. Kretchmer, quoted in *Environ. Action* 3 (No. 24), 5 (1972).
15. J. W. Forrester, *World Dynamics* (Wright-Allen, Cambridge, Mass., 1971).
16. R. F. Burden and P. F. Randerson, *J. Appl. Ecol.* 9, 439 (1972).
17. For example, K. E. F. Watt, *Ecology and Resource Management* (McGraw-Hill, New York, 1969) and ——, Ed., *Systems Analysis in Ecology* (Academic Press, New York, 1966).
18. A. Heller, Ed., *The California Tomorrow Plan* (Kaufmann, Los Altos, Calif., 1972).
19. For example, J. W. Forrester, *Urban Dynamics* (M.I.T. Press, Cambridge, Mass., 1969); L. B. Leopold, F. E. Clarke, B. B. Hanshaw, J. R. Balsley, *U.S. Geol. Surv. Circ.* 645, 1 (1971); L. P. Kadanoff, *Amer. Sci.* 60, 74 (1972); J. N. R. Jeffers, Ed., *Mathematical Models in Ecology* (Blackwell, Oxford, 1972); G. P. Patil, E. C. Pielou, W. E. Waters, Eds., *Many-Species Populations, Ecosystems, and Systems Analysis* (Pennsylvania State Univ. Press, University Park, 1971).
20. U.S. Senate Committee on Public Works, *National Environmental Center Act of 1971, Report No. 92-518* (Government Printing Office, Washington, D.C., 1971).
21. G. Hardin, *Science* 162, 1243 (1968).
22. E. Bellamy, *Looking Backward, 2000–1887* (Belknap, Cambridge, Mass., 1967).
23. *Federal Water Pollution Control Act Amendments of 1972* (Government Printing Office, Washington, D.C., 1972).
24. Bills (92nd Congress) on toxic substances in manufactured products: S. 573 and S. 1478; on national land use policy, S. 632 and S. 921.
25. *Economic Report of the President, 1971* (Government Printing Office, Washington, D.C., 1971), p. 118.

26. Such a system, or variants of it, are in use
in Otsego, Mich.; Springfield. Mo.; the state
of Vermont; and the Ruhr Valley in West
Germany (27, p. 187).

27. U.S. Senate Committee on Public Works,
Water Pollution Hearings (Government Printing Office, Washington, D.C., 1970), part 1.

28. See, for example, H. C. Wallich, *Fortune*
(October 1972), p. 114. For an illuminating
debate on the subject of effluent charges for
water pollution, see *Congr. Rec.* (2 November
1971), p. S17425; also (27, pp. 187–200; 346–
365).

29. For example, G. Myrdal, *Challenge of World
Poverty: A World Anti-Poverty Program in
Outline* (Pantheon, New York, 1970).

30. There is obviously room for debate on what
constitutes a country's "proportionate share"
of critical world resources. If population
size were to be the criterion, it is possible
that some other distribution of population
by nation than the current one would be
used by the international administering body

31. For accounts of difficulties with past foreign
aid programs, see I. Illich, *Celebration of
Awareness: A Call for Institutional Revolu-
tion* (Doubleday, Garden City, N.Y., 1970);
M. T. Farvar and J. P. Milton, Eds., *The
Careless Technology—Ecology and Interna-
tional Development* (Natural History Press,
New York, 1972).

32. See L. K. Caldwell, *In Defense of Earth—
International Protection of the Biosphere*
(Indiana Univ. Press, Bloomington, 1972)
and the resolutions of the United Nations
Conference on the Human Environment,
Stockholm, 1972.

33. We acknowledge the inspiration for ideas in
this article provided by discussions with the
late Joseph F. Hodgson, and with D. Ritchey
and D. Kass of Cornell University. We are
grateful to A. Costin, P. Ellyard, J. T. O.
Kirk, M. M. Scurrah, M. R. Scurrah, G.
Smith, and J. Zwar for their comments on
drafts of this article.

ENVIRONMENTAL MATRIX

A Conceptual Tool to Help

Unravel the Environmental Tangle

The "environmental matrix" shown on the next two pages incorporates in a single table many of the basic conclusions of *To Live on Earth*, a recent Resources for the Future study of man's relation to the natural environment. At the same time it reflects the method by which those findings were derived.

In *To Live On Earth* Sterling Brubaker analyzes the major forces — population, economic activity, and technology — behind the tangle of problems relating to environmental quality, weighs the seriousness of the wide variety of threats to human well-being and even survival, and explores ways of dealing with the disparate hazards. Unique to the study is the systematic approach by which environmental problems are classified in order of gravity, by salient characteristics, and by appropriate methods of treatment.

To cover so much ground in a book of well under 300 pages in itself calls for concentrated presentation. The matrix that conveys the essence of the whole book is necessarily set down in a kind of shorthand. The first of its ten columns presents problems by their seriousness, in ascending order from effects on amenities to effects on the earth's capacity to support life. The next four columns list the principal causes of each problem, the nature of the threat it poses, its place on the time scale, and the size of the area affected. The sixth column suggests appropriate levels of management. The last four columns concern possible avenues of action, ranging from comparatively simple adjustments in technology and management to slow and hard-to-achieve changes in social values.

"The matrix serves best," Brubaker cautions, "if attention is centered on the captions rather than on the entries in each box.

Reprinted from the 1972 Annual Report of Resources for the Future, Inc. pp. 1-4.

The entries are very impressionistic and are not defended too ardently. . . . Nonetheless, the matrix points up where problems fall on the scale of gravity and what kinds of things can be done about them. . . .

"As we move toward graver possible consequences we tend to find that the effects are deferred in time and enlarged in scope, that the appropriate administrative unit becomes larger, and that the remedies are more likely to be dependent on value changes. By contrast, many of the less grave threats to health or the amenities . . . are subject to control on a smaller scale and can be managed by extension of regulation or revision of incentive. . . . Sensible strategy will weight the graver threats differently, for we can take few chances with disaster."

The matrix is reproduced from the final chapter of *To Live On Earth* (copyright 1972 by The Johns Hopkins University Press) published in cloth by Hopkins at $6.95 and in paper by the New American Library.

Environmental problems by order of gravity	Causative factors 1. size of population 2. concentration of population 3. per capita income level 4. consumption pattern 5. technology	Character of insult 1. temporary insult 2. cumulative insult 3. reversible damage 4. permanent damage (human time scale) 5. synergistic potential	Problem threshold 1. continuing 2. now or soon 3. one generation 4. more than one generation	Area affected 1. local 2. regional 3. national 4. international 5. global
Amenity considerations				
Litter	4,3	1,2	1	1,2
Noise	2,5	1	1	1
Odor	5	1	1	1
Air, visibility aspects	2,5,4,	1	1	1,2
Water quality, recreational aspects	5,2,1	1,2,3,5	1	1,2,4
City, aesthetic aspects	4,5	N	1	1
City, convenience and efficiency aspects	2,4	3	1,2	1
Country, aesthetic aspects	5,4,1	2,4	1,2	1,2,3
Access to country and nature	4	2,3	1,2	1,2
Human health effects				
Air pollution – combustion products	5,4,2,3	1,3,5	1,2,3	1,2
Water pollution:				
Pathogens	2,5	1,3	2,3	1,2,4
Nitrates	5	2,3	2,3	1,2
Industrial chemicals	5	All	2,3	1,2,4
Pesticides (via food chain)	5,1,3	2,3	3	2,4,5
Radioactivity	5,3	2,4	3	1,2
Heavy metals	5	2,4	All	1,2,4
Human genetic and reproductive effects				
Radioactivity	5,3	4	3,4	3,5
Pesticides	5,1,3	4	N	3
Industrial chemicals	5	4	2,3,4	1,2,5
Effects on ecological system and the earth's life-supportive capacity				
Human occupancy of biospace	5,1,3,4	2,4,5	All	3,5
Ocean threats:				
Pesticides	5	2,4,5	3	5
Oil	3,4	3,5	3	5
Other chemicals	5	2,4	3,4	5
Erosion	5,1,3	2,4	1,4	1,2,5
Fertilizers and damage to mineral cycling	5	3	4	1,5
CO_2, albedo, and climate	5,1,3	2,5	4	5
Heat rejection:				
Local aspect	5,2	1,5	2,3	2,4
Global aspect	3,1	3,5	4	5

Irrespective of source of financing   N = none, unknown, uncertain, not applicable, negligible

Appropriate management level[a]	Possible economic approaches	Possible institutional approaches	Possible technological approaches	Efficacy of possible value change bringing:
1. local 2. regional authority 3. national 4. multinational agreement or authority 5. global	1. environmental charge 2. tax on material 3. subsidy	1. laws and regulations 2. enlarged systems management or planning 3. court actions	1. containment at source 2. neutralization of objectionable discharges 3. reduction in discharge volume via process and material changes 4. increased recycling	1. reduced population growth 2. slower income and more equal distribution 3. less burdensome consumption patterns 4. curtailment of property rights
1 2	1,3	1,2	4,3	3,2
1	N	1	3,1	N
1	N	1	2	N
1,2	1,3	1,2	3,2	2,3
1,2,4	All	All	All	2,1
1	2,3	1,2	N	4,3
1,2	All	2	N	4,3,2
2,3	3	All	N	4,2,3,1
1,2,3	2,3	2	N	3,1
2,3,4	All	1,2	All	3,2
1,2,4	3	1,2	2	1
1,2	2,3	1	3,1	3,4
1,2,4	1,2	1,2	All	2,1
3,4	2	1	3,1	3
3	N	1	3,1	2,1
2,3,4	N	1	3,1	N
3,5	N	1	3,1	2,1
3	2	1	3,1	N
3,4	1,2	1,2	All	2,3
3,5	All	All	1	2,3,1
5	2	1	3	N
5	1	1	3,2,1	2,3
5	1,2	1,2	All	2,3
1,3	3	1	3	4,2,1
1,3	2	1	N	2,1
3,5	N	1,2	3	2,1
2,3,4	1,3	All	2	3
5	N	1	3	2,3,1

The Michigan
Environmental Protection Act of 1970

Act 127 P.A. 1970, Mich. Comp. Laws, Ann. §§691-1201-1207
(West's 3 Mich. Leg. Serv. 1970)

AN ACT to provide for actions for declaratory and equitable relief for protection
the air, water and other natural resources and the public trust therein; to prescribe t
rights, duties and functions of the attorney general, any political subdivision of the sta
any instrumentality or agency of the state or of a political subdivision thereof, any pers
partnership, corporation, association, organization or other legal entity; and to provi
for judicial proceedings relative thereto.

The People of the State of Michigan enact:

Sec. 1. This act, shall be known and may be cited as the "Thomas J. Anderson, Gord
Rockwell environmental protection act of 1970".

Sec. 2. (1) The attorney general, any political subdivision of the state, any inst
mentality or agency of the state or of a political subdivision thereof, any person, partn
ship, corporation, association, organization or other legal entity may maintain an action
the circuit court having jurisdiction where the alleged violation occurred or is likely
occur for declaratory and equitable relief against the state, any political subdivision there
any instrumentality or agency of the state or of a political subdivision thereof, any p
son, partnership, corporation, association, organization or other legal entity for the prot
tion of the air, water and other natural resources and the public trust therein fr
pollution, impairment or destruction.

(2) In granting relief provided by subsection (1) where there is involved a standard
pollution or for an anti-pollution device or procedure, fixed by rule or otherwise, by
instrumentality or agency of the state or a political subdivision thereof, the court ma

(a) Determine the validity, applicability and reasonableness of the standard.

(b) When a court finds a standard to be deficient, direct the adoption of
standard approved and specified by the court.

Sec. 2a. If the court has reasonable ground to doubt the solvency of the plaint
or the plaintiff's ability to pay any cost or judgment which might be rendered against h
in an action brought under this act the court may order the plaintiff to post a sure
bond or cash not to exceed $500.00.

Sec. 3. (1) When the plaintiff in the action has made a prima facie showing t
the conduct of the defendant has, or is likely to pollute, impair or destroy the air, wa
or other natural resources or the public trust therein, the defendant may rebut the pri
facie showing by the submission of evidence to the contrary. The defendant may also sh
by way of an affirmative defense, that there is no feasible and prudent alternative
defendant's conduct and that such conduct is consistent with the promotion of the pub
health, safety and welfare in light of the state's paramount concern for the protection
its natural resources from pollution, impairment or destruction. Except as to the affirmat
defense, the principles of burden of proof and weight of the evidence generally applica
in civil actions in the circuit courts shall apply to actions brought under this act.

(2) The court may appoint a master or referee, who shall be a disinterested pers
and technically qualified, to take testimony and make a record and a report of his fi
ings to the court in the action.

(3) Costs may be apportioned to the parties if the interests of justice require.

Sec. 4. (1) The court may grant temporary and permanent equitable relief, or may impose conditions on the defendant that are required to protect the air, water and other natural resources or the public trust therein from pollution, impairment or destruction.

(2) If administrative, licensing or other proceedings are required or available to determine the legality of the defendant's conduct, the court may remit the parties to such proceedings, which proceedings shall be conducted in accordance with and subject to the provisions of Act No. 306 of the Public Acts of 1969, being sections 24.201 to 24.313 of the Compiled Laws of 1948. In so remitting the court may grant temporary equitable relief where necessary for the protection of the air, water and other natural resources or the public trust therein from pollution, impairment or destruction. In so remitting the court shall retain jurisdiction of the action pending completion thereof for the purpose of determining whether adequate protection from pollution, impairment or destruction has been afforded.

(3) Upon completion of such proceedings, the court shall adjudicate the impact of the defendant's conduct on the air, water or other natural resources and on the public trust therein in accordance with this act. In such adjudication the court may order that additional evidence be taken to the extent necessary to protect the rights recognized in this act.

(4) Where, as to any administrative, licensing or other proceeding, judicial review thereof is available, notwithstanding the provisions to the contrary of Act No. 306 of the Public Acts of 1969, pertaining to judicial review, the court originally taking jurisdiction shall maintain jurisdiction for purposes of judicial review.

Sec. 5. (1) Whenever administrative, licensing or other proceedings, and judicial review thereof are available by law, the agency or the court may permit the attorney general, any political subdivision of the state, any instrumentality or agency of the state or of a political subdivision thereof, any person, partnership, corporation, association, organization or other legal entity to intervene as a party on the filing of a pleading asserting that the proceeding or action for judicial review involves conduct which has, or which is likely to have, the effect of polluting, impairing or destroying the air, water or other natural resources or the public trust therein.

(2) In any such administrative, licensing or other proceedings, and in any judicial review thereof, any alleged pollution, impairment or destruction of the air, water or other natural resources or the public trust therein, shall be determined, and no conduct shall be authorized or approved which does, or is likely to have such effect so long as there is a feasible and prudent alternative consistent with the reasonable requirements of the public health, safety and welfare.

(3) The doctrines of collateral estoppel and res judicata may be applied by the court to prevent multiplicity of suits.

Sec. 6. This act shall be supplementary to existing administrative and regulatory procedures provided by law.

Sec. 7. This act shall take effect October 1, 1970.

This act is ordered to take immediate effect.

Environmental Impact Review
Notification System for Conservation Commissions

Prepared by Paul D. Ammerman

INTRODUCTION

The systematic review of capital construction projects and other projects or activities for their potential effect on the environment is a new and important conservation tool. The basic idea is quite positive in that it forces everyone to stop and think about the environmental implications of their actions. The intent of these reviews is to promote environmental responsibility, not to block projects completely even though in some instances this may be the end result.

In New York State, a number of the county environmental management councils are heavily involved in environmental impact review work. In Monroe County, for example, the Council has published a number of studies and have prepared their own environmental impact statements for particular projects. In Suffolk the Environmental Quality Council, created by county charter revision, has responsibility by law for reviewing and coordinating the preparation of draft environmental impact statements by county agencies whose work affects the environment.

Local procedures have been developed, too. The Town of Hungtington has subdivision regulations which require all land developers to submit a detailed and specific environmental impact statement for any development they may propose. A number of towns on Long Island and elsewhere require the issuance of permits for any development affecting wetlands. The Town of Pound Ridge in Westchester County has water control regulations which require permits for any usage or modification of wetlands, lakes or ponds, reservoirs, or rainfall drainage systems. Conservation commissions usually have been in the forefront on the initiation of legislation of this kind

In 1971 the State enabling legislation (Art. 12-F, GML) for conservation advisory councils (conservation commissions) was amended to incorporate a new section, 239-y, authorizing the redesignation of a council as a conservation board following completion and submittal of an open lands inventory and map to the local governing body. A specific environmental impact review authority goes with this redesignation in that all proposals for development or use of any of the land or water in the official open areas index must be forwarded to the conservation board by the local agency that receives them. The board must issue a report within 45 days to the referring agency, with a copy to the local governing body.

A number of commissions have converted to board status and others are planning to do so. It must be pointed out, however, that while Section 239-y of Article 12-F provides a framework authorizing a board to conduct these reviews, the board must work out effective administrative procedures with appropriate local agencies and the local governing body to really make the review system work. It also must develop guidelines for conducting a comprehensive and thorough environmental review.

While this important State law for conservation commissions gives strong legislative backing for conduct of these reviews, a number of conservation commissions with good support from their local governing body have not waited to convert to conservation board status before assuming project review functions. This can be worked out administratively in any municipality as a wholly allowable activity for a conservation commission under their general responsibility of advising the local governing body on environmental problems and issues.

Bureau of Community Assistance, Division of Educational Services, New York State Department of Environmental Conservation, June, 1973, pp. 1-8.

In the same vein, the Bureau of Community Assistance has been working recently with various units in the Department of Environmental Conservation and with other State agencies to systematically improve communication with local conservation commissions and county environmental management councils in the area of environmental impact review. It is important that commissions and councils receive prompt notification from the originating agency or unit regarding any activity that affects their community environment. The Bureau, working with DEC's Office of Environmental Analysis which has primary responsibility within the Department for environmental impact review coordination and studies, therefore has undertaken preparation of the following description of the principal review, permit, and hearing notification systems so that local commissions and county councils may have a better understanding of their role in these systems.

Each agency and unit, as described, will be given an updated listing every three months of the names and addresses of all chairmen of commissions and councils as a basis for making direct mailings of the various notices. These names and addresses are supplied in the form of duplicated copies of computer printout listings. It is planned to expand this arrangement to include Federal agencies, particularly the Environmental Protection Agency.

The success of this system will depend upon the level and quality of response by conservation commissions and county environmental management councils. The notices received in the mail by the commission and council chairmen must be handled promptly. The lead time for response often is only 30 to 60 days. The chairman must alert other members; the review schedule often will require a special meeting.

Also, the notice may seem insignificant but may really be very important. (In a number of cases, for example, an application to DEC for a water supply permit for a few dwelling units has been the opening wedge for development of several thousand acres.) Explanation or interpretation may be required. Call the originating agency or unit. The commission should have a good working relationship with the Environmental Analysis Unit in the DEC Regional Office. This is absolutely essential if an effective contribution is going to be made by the commission. Call the head of the unit for a discussion. (After awhile he even may be calling you first!) Begin to develop similar contacts in other State agencies which may have a basic responsibility for a particular type of project.

Although the Bureau of Community Assistance has been and will continue to try to improve communications in the important area of environmental impact review, there are two local sources of information which councils and commissions should monitor. First, almost all activities described herein must be advertised locally in newspapers, for periods up to four weeks, before permits or grants are issued. This is done so that interested parties will be made aware of matters which concern them. Legal notices of intent to apply for stream protection permits and other DEC permits, OGS land grants and others are published, for example. Careful monitoring of the legal notices in local newspapers is necessary if conservation commissions are to stay abreast of potential impact situations.

The second source is your local government -- municipal clerk, supervisor or mayor, often the municipal attorney. Regional clearinghouses, as well as DEC headquarters and regional units advertise permit applications, send notices of hearings, A-95 and EIS notices and other information routinely to these people. Often these notices are disposed of routinely since they do not seem important to anyone. Conservation commissions should express interest in seeing such notices to review them for environmental implications. Ask that copies be routed to the commission. This also will help to prepare other local officials to receive comments on the projects from the commission.

FEDERAL REQUIREMENTS

National Environmental Policy Act. The impact of capital construction and other projects on the environment has been of concern to environmentalists for a long time. This concern for the environment per se as a matter to be considered in planning was formalized by Congress and the President in the National Environmental Policy Act (NEPA) of 1969.

Under NEPA all Federal agencies are required to prepare an environmental impact statement (EIS) discussing in detail proposed actions and projects which will have significant environmental effects. The governor of each state designates clearinghouses to distribute draft EIS. In New York, draft EIS are sent to the State Clearinghouse in the Office of Planning Services and to regional clearinghouses in the 12 regional planning agencies in the State. (See list attached.) The Governor has also designated that the Department of Environmental Conservation coordinate and prepare the State's response to draft EIS except for power transmission lines, which are reviewed by the Department of Public Service.

Notification of the availability of EIS are sent out by the State Clearinghouse to state agencies with an information copy to the appropriate regional clearinghouse. There are eight counties -- Columbia, Fulton, Greene, Montgomery, Schoharie, Sullivan, Ulster and Wyoming -- which are not covered by a clearinghouse. These counties receive notices directly from the State Clearinghouse.

Federal agencies are not uniform in their notification procedures, and it is hoped that this system will help unify the process. A list of Federal agency contacts is attached, and they may be contacted for copies of their EIS.

Circular A-95. State and regional clearinghouses are also recipients of A-95 notices. Circular A-95, distributed initially by the U.S. Bureau of the Budget and now by its successor, the U.S. Office of Management and Budget, implements section 204 of the Demonstration Cities and Metropolitan Development Act of 1966 and Title IV of the Intergovernmental Cooperation Act of 1968. It establishes a Project Notification and Review System (PNRS) which provides for early communication between applicants for Federal aid and the State and local governments in the applicant's vicinity. The purpose is to encourage a process of intergovernmental coordination and review of proposed projects. Notification of intent to apply for federal funding assistance under any of the approximately 100 programs covered by circular A-95 are sent to the State Clearinghouse which in turn distributes copies to other State agencies and to the appropriate regional clearinghouses. Regional clearinghouses, then, notify local agencies of proposed projects.

The Bureau of Community Assistance now regularly provides copies of the computerized mailing list for the chairmen of local conservation commissions and county and regional environmental management councils to the State Clearinghouse and, in cooperation with the administrator of the State Clearinghouse, to each regional clearinghouse. The importance of including commissions and councils in the notification system has been emphasized by the State Clearinghouse and by the Bureau. The commissions and councils now should be routinely receiving notices under both the A-95 program and the NEPA/EIS program. If there appears to be any gap or difficulty with this system, the regional clearinghouse and the Bureau of Community Assistance should be informed at once.

NYS DEPARTMENT OF TRANSPORTATION

The Federal Highway Administration (FHWA) delegated responsibility for preparation of draft EIS to the State Department of Transporation (DOT). Notification is handled through the system described above.

Additionally, however, FHWA is requiring states to develop an Environmental Action Plan, a document which describes the procedures and organizational assignments of responsibility to be utilized in developing Federally aided highway projects, and assuring that potential adverse social, economic and environmental effects of such projects are fully considered in the decision-making process. Input from Federal, state and local agencies, officials, special interest groups and the public is desired. Commissions and councils were surveyed in early 1973 as to whether they were interested in participating in the development of the action plan. (Only about 25 percent responded.) The action plan must be approved by November 1, 1973, and implemented by November 1, 1974.

DOT currently issues Project Information Reports (PIR-I, PIR-II) for proposed projects. A PIR-I is an "early warning" document which presents the generalities of a new proposed project. A PIR-II is a detailed analysis for a new project location approval. The latter statement is submitted in lieu of a draft EIS if it is determined that environmental impact will not be significant.

The Bureau of Community Assistance has worked with the Planning Division of DOT to have DOT Regional Offices send all PIR-I and PIR-II or draft EIS, whichever of the latter two is prepared, to commissions and councils (a list of DOT regional offices is attached). This procedure will be supplanted by the Action Plan mechanism, but under that system coordination and communication most likely will be broader because DOT is not limiting project statements to those partially funded by FHWA, nor will they be limited to highway construction projects only.

NYS OFFICE OF GENERAL SERVICES

The State Office of General Services (OGS) has three programs of potential interest to commissions and councils. Surplus State lands are offered for sale periodically at public auction. The Bureau of Community Assistance mailing list has been sent to OGS and sale notices will be sent to the pertinent local agencies.

Also, the State owns the land under water in major lakes and rivers. Grants and easements are issued by OGS for construction or shoreline alterations affecting such lands. Applicants for such grants or easements must advertise their intention for four weeks locally before a formal application is made. OGS has agreed, because they encourage local interest in these grants, to notify commissions and councils in affected areas.

OGS is "general contractor" for many State buildings and facilities. The Design and Architecture units will notify commissions and councils in affected localities when construction is considered. Again, local interest is encouraged.

NYS DEPARTMENT OF HEALTH

Of secondary interest, but of potential periodic importance, is health facilities planning. The Bureau of Community Assistance, with the cooperation of the State Department of Health, regularly will send copies of the mailing list to the seven Regional Health Planning Councils and to the six regional health directors (a list is attached). Councils and commissions should make contact with their regional health council and director.

NYS DEPARTMENT OF PUBLIC SERVICE

The Bureau of Community Assistance also is working with the Office of Environmental Planning of theDepartment of Public Service (DPS) to facilitate more communication between councils and commissions and the Public Service Commission (PSC) on environmental proceedings. At present, notice of such proceedings is served on the chief executive officers of the counties, towns, cities and villages directly affected by scheduled proceedings.

Article VII of the Public Service Law requires electric and gas utility companies to obtain certification of major electric or gas transmission lines before construction can begin. The Commission conducts an extensive environmental investigation into the proposed transmission line route and evaluates alternatives proposed by DPS staff and intervenors. DPS staff and the Commission encourage the active participation of local government and environmental interest groups. DPS staff holds pre-hearing seminars upon request to provide citizens with substantive information about the case issues and methods for actively intervening in a case. The final Commission certification of a route, when granted, can override local land use controls and overrides or displaces State permits otherwise required.

The recently enacted Article VIII of the Public Service Law requires certification of new major steam-electric generation facilities by the NYS Board on Electric Generating Siting and the Environment. The Board will conduct an in-depth environmental investigation of proposed facilities and sites. The law actively encourages local citizen and government participation in these proceedings also. DPS staff will hold briefings on request to apprise citizens of the Article VIII process. The final Board certification of a facility and site, when granted, is all that is required of the applicant. Local permit and control requirements are no longer controlling.

Section 149-b of Article VIII of the Public Service Law requires that private electric utility companies serving New York State annually file their long-range electric system plans with the Public Service Commission. Subsequently the Commission conducts public hearings at which interested parties may query the companies on their plans. The first such hearings may be held in late summer 1973.

Other activities of interest include the review by DPS staff of company rate increase applications. DPS invites public participation in these electric rate cases. The regulatory power for adjusting rates is a major tool for encouraging environmental responsibility by the utility companies. The recent landmark work by PSC on rules and regulations for undergrounding stemmed from the agencies authority to adjust rates.

Questions about the environmental regulatory activities of DPS should be directed to the Director of the Office of Environmental Planning, 44 Holland Ave., Albany 12208.

NYS DEPARTMENT OF ENVIRONMENTAL CONSERVATION

The State Department of Environmental Conservation (DEC) offers many opportunities for public involvement in environmental programs. To improve communications, several additions to DEC mailing lists have been made, and others are anticipated. For example county councils have been added to the list to receive all DEC press releases. They, in turn, have been asked to communicate with local commissions about pertinent news items. This will serve to improve notification on special hearings, such as the State Environmental Plan and rules and regulations, as well as on enforcement and permit hearings.

Part 615. Using Part 615 of Title Six of the Codes, Rules and Regulations of New York State, DEC may call full environmental impact hearings for major developments on the basis of an application for only one of a number of permits. Most of these might stem from water supply applications, although the recent hearing on the proposed Okwari Park was called on the basis of an application to build a dam.

Hearing unit. Except for special hearings such as those which might be held on the issuance of new regulations, and for enforcement hearings, most hearings, and especially permit hearings, are being centralized in a new unit in DEC's General Counsel's Office. It is planned that councils and commissions will be placed on the regular list to receive pertinent local, regional or statewide notices. These will include air discharge, pesticide, water supply and stream protection hearings.

Enforcement hearings. Enforcement hearings are called by DEC's Enforcement Counsel, whose staff includes the attorneys in the nine regional offices. Some enforcement hearings are called from the regional office. Enforcement Counsel and the regional attorneys will be provided with the mailing list of council and commission chairmen so as to expand the notification system.

Stream protection. Each DEC regional office also has an Environmental Analysis Unit (EAU) whose major workload involves the stream protection permit program. Applications for permits to do work which will cause stream bank and bed disturbance, to work in navigable waters or in wetlands contiguous to same or to build dams and docks are reviewed by the regional EAU. About 1,500 such permits are issued each year and about 25 hearings on these permits are called. Hearings are called from DEC headquarters. It is planned that councils and commissions will be placed on the notification list for these hearings. Regional office EAU's have other information important to councils and commissions, and the list of chairmen will be sent to them to expand their communications (a list of DEC regional offices is attached).

Community relations staff. Regional office community relations staff also will get the mailing list regularly and have been prompted to keep information flowing to commissions and councils.

Water discharge permits. One area of major importance is currently unresolved. The 1972 amendments to the Federal Water Pollution Control Act have totally revised the system of permits for discharges to streams. Unresolved is the question of which agency will issue permits -- the U.S. Environmental Protection Agency (EPA) or DEC. Thus, the system of public notification is also unresolved. However, a part of every application for federal assistance for sewage treatment works will now require that an environmental assessment statement (EAS) be written by the applicant. Included in the EAS must be minutes of a locally called public hearing on the project. On the basis of the EAS, EPA or DEC (whichever eventually assumes responsibility) may determine that an EIS is necessary. EPA will prepare the EIS.

Water management. The Division of Water Management Planning has three major activities of interest to local environmental commissions and councils. These activities are: water quality management planning, regional water resources planning board programs, and the Federal-State water resources studies and interstate compact commission activities. Basin and area-wide water quality management plans are being developed in the State to meet the requirements of the 1972 amendments to the Federal Water Pollution Control Act. Regional water and related land resources plans are being developed by ten regional water resources boards across the State, and the Erie-Niagara Board has completed its plan for the Erie-Niagara Basin. The Division provides staff support to the regional boards.

The Regional Water Resources Planning Boards provide a unique opportunity for local participation in water management planning (a list is attached). The Board meetings are open to the public and councils and commissions are invited to attend and take part in discussions and planning activities.

The Division has responsibility for coordination of and for providing State input to Federal-State water resources studies and to interstate compact commission activities.

The Division also is involved in the review and coordination of EIS, EAS, and A-95 PNRS for projects having impact on State water resources and water quality to determine possible conflicts and compatibility with existing or proposed water resources measures for the area in which the project is located.

ANATOMY OF A HEARING

League of Women Voters

"Why vote? Things stay the same or get worse, no matter who wins."
"If the trash isn't collected, I don't know where to complain."
"You can't trust anyone in government any more."
"Nobody cares about what I think or what I need."
"Nobody listens."

People try in many ways to influence government—to get some-one to listen. Besides exercising their vote in choosing their offi-cials, they take part in party politics...they vote to choose offi-cials...they write letters to them...organize and sign petitions for changes they want...start, or work with, pressure groups...stage protest marches and parades...boycott businesses or public ser-vices...even resort to violence.

The public hearing is yet another way to influence public de-cisions. A hearing gives a citizen or a group a chance for person-to-person exchange. Because it is usually geared to one issue or one area of concern, the dialog can be sharply focused. Hearings are a viable and useful part of the democratic process at every level of government—local, regional, state and national. Here, if any-where, someone is listening.

WHY HOLD HEARINGS?

Government officials or advisory bodies hold hearings for a good many different reasons. Sometimes they really want to hear from citizens; sometimes the law requires that they do so. Some witnes-ses are asked to appear because they can supply special knowledge, some because they represent a known point of view, some because of their status in the community. Individuals or groups that want to testify can ask to be put on the agenda. In some cases, anyone who wishes to be heard can simply appear during a time set aside for citizen comment. For example, in many open city council meet-ings the presiding officer may routinely ask if anyone present wants to speak. Any citizen or group that responds gets a hearing.

IN GENERAL, TO COMMUNICATE   In a hearing, a citizen has a chance to take part in a profitable face-to-face experience, if the real purpose of the hearing is to communicate: to find out what citizens think, to get expert analyses and data, to highlight the issue for better public understanding. The citizen can learn

what other citizens think and why;
what the attitudes of officials are;

LEAGUE OF WOMEN VOTERS, Phamphlet Publication No. 108, pp. 1-15.

what facts he has not considered or has not known;

where to get more information;

what gaps there were in his own statement or viewpoint.

TO RUBBER-STAMP   Officials may, however, hold a hearing merely to substantiate a decision they have already made. Then citizen opinion may get little or no consideration. There are often clues to indicate that the hearing panel is not seriously inviting citizens' views and that the real goal is to discourage citizen participation. When these symptoms exist, it's likely that the hearing is just an exercise:

√ Invited witnesses represent only one point of view.

√ Questions asked bring out only one kind of response.

√ Persons giving different points of view are passed over quickly, asked no questions or perfunctory ones.

√ Public notice of the meeting is short and announcements inconspicuous.

√ The hearing room is too small to accommodate all who want to attend.

TO INFORM AND EDUCATE   Governmental bodies may also hold hearings to inform the public about an issue. For example, the planning department may hold an open meeting to explain the master plan already approved by the city council. Or legislators may want to educate the public about an issue, so that, when laws are passed or proposals are put on the ballot, citizens will understand the problem and the chosen solutions. Questions and discussion may follow the explanation. Such a hearing, if it is well attended and if citizens have had a chance to study the plan beforehand, may bring about change even in an already approved plan.

TO LEARN   Some hearings are held to get help in drafting laws or ordinances, to find out whether or not a law is needed to solve a particular problem. City councils or legislative committees may want to find out:

- what the dimensions of the problem to be solved are;
- what kind of law, if any, ought to be drafted;
- what it ought to contain;
- what effect a law to solve this problem would have on other areas of concern;
- how the law ought to be implemented; how it would or would not work;

334

- what the social and other costs will be, if there is legislation, and if there is not.

EXAMPLE The Army Corps of Engineers often conducts public meetings around the country as they search for solutions of specific problems, like improvements for flood control in certain areas, future water and land re- source needs and problems of a river basin, etc. These hearings are open to all citizens. Sometimes the notices outline specific considerations and solicit surveys and reports that may have been made.

EXAMPLE A city commission is considering whether or not to change from electing the commission at large to electing from districts of equal population. It may have a committee to investigate. This committee may hold hearings to get citizen views.

TO TEST ALTERNATIVES Besides hearings related to drafting laws (legislative hearings), some hearings are held to find out what people think about a proposed action that is already authorized by law (administrative hearings).

EXAMPLE A new highway is to be built through or around a community. Where should it go?

EXAMPLE The citizens have voted money in a bond issue for a new library. Where shall it be built? What kinds of services should it provide?

TO GET FEEDBACK Officials may hold hearings to find out how well something is working, how the administration of a program is filling the need for which it was set up. Or a program is threatened with a reduction or a cut-off. And sometimes hearings are prompted by noisy dissatisfaction with procedures, an excessive number of complaints, or extensive publicity.

EXAMPLE A change in location is proposed for food stamp distribution. A clamor begins from those affected and sympathetic organizations. The newspaper runs a series of articles on the problems. The welfare depart- ment may respond by holding a hearing.

WHAT ARE THE RULES FOR HEARINGS?

Hearings that are required by law often must comply with certain specific rules: how much notice must be given; where and how notice is to be publicized.

Sometimes such regulations are ignored, but alert citizens can insist upon adequate notice, publicize failure to follow either requirements or traditions about hearings on important issues. Sometimes it is hard to find what the rules are, if any exist. An inquiry at the city or state attorney's office about hearing rules may produce results.

WHO TESTIFIES AT HEARINGS?

All citizens can and should use hearings to make their ideas known. An informal statement by a single citizen can be dramatic and effective. Sometimes the direct, forthright words of one person can begin the process of change.

However, testimony from an organization of like-minded citizens may carry more weight, simply because it represents the voices of many people. But "group" statements run the risk of being bland and general—although they should and need not be—because the spokesman is trying to reflect a broad, general agreement of his organization.

Suppose there is to be a hearing on converting some open space into a site for a city parking lot, and your group objects. What should your group do?

Should you testify? Some questions to consider are:

Would it be better to prepare joint testimony with another group with similar views?

Would separate but similar statements be stronger? Will yours supply a special emphasis?

Do you have an effective spokesman, especially good at answering questions?

Can you supply good substantiating data: the opinions of citizens who live nearby? locations and costs of other sites? comparison of open space and parks in your city with other nearby or comparable communities? effect of loss of this open space? who uses the open space area and for what?

Perhaps you may decide your group can be more useful by giving staff or technical assistance to the panel holding the hearing; by getting out a crowd; by publicizing the hearing. Or perhaps you could suggest a survey or sampling-of-opinion poll and offer help on designing and conducting it.

Should you involve others? Whether or not you testify, is the issue important enough to your group to warrant the time and effort necessary to encourage others? You probably know who your friends are on this issue. For most of them, a telephone call to be sure they know about the time and place and an expression that you hope they will appear is all you will need to do.

What if no hearings are scheduled? Let's say you hear about a decision to put a parking lot on an open space area, but no hearings have been held or scheduled. You and others can insist on a hearing so that both those supporting and those opposing can be heard. Approach the chairman of the council, the city planner, the park commission or director, the city manager. Ask that there be a hearing with adequate notice. Work with your media contacts. The news media will usually publicize the importance of a hearing, especially if enough people seem to want one.

You decide to testify. There are many pluses for testifying. It may result in the change you want. It may gain respect for you or your organization if you make an effective statement. The hearing, hopefully your testimony, can highlight the issues involved and thus educate citizens generally about them.

Make the most of the opportunity. Your statement is much more likely to make news if:

- the issue is controversial, the testimony and questions lively;
- there is a sizable attendance, indicating wide interest;
- new points of view and/or new facts are uncovered.

If you are really concerned, you will try to see that at least one of these newsworthy events takes place.

The hearing is a learning experience, not only for you but for the panel members as well. It lets them know what citizens think. An official may learn in some other way that there is opposition or support for a policy or proposal, but he has no way to assess or produce the visible political pressure that a hearing can generate.

You want to get the best possible mileage out of your effort. Even if you don't convince the panel, you can establish that you are a reliable and useful witness or that your point of view has merit.

Learn from watching and listening to this or other hearings before the same body: What seem to be good points to make? Which witnesses are listened to most attentively? Can you tell why? What kinds of questions are asked? What are the responses and attitudes of the panel members? You can pick up good pointers for now and for next time.

STEPS TO FOLLOW

How to get on
Schedule your appearance. Ask to be invited — simply telephoning your wish to testify often will do it.

For opportunities provided for informal statements in some city council or school board meetings, go early enough to get a seat near the front.

Rules
Find out what the hearing rules are and follow them.

Who writes the statement?
Choose the best person to write the draft. You may need two people — a good writer and the one who knows most about the particular issue. Writing ability and depth in subject matter are sometimes, but not necessarily, found in the same person.

What to include in the draft
Decide on what you want to include. A short, pithy statement, with attached facts and figures, is more effective than a long, rambling one. See that the attachments follow the pattern of the statement.

Select the most important and telling points. Consider both the issue and what you know about the panel members. Don't put in everything you know. Exercise restraint. You are trying not only to *inform* but also to *persuade*.

What not to include
Know your panel's attitudes. If your group is part of a national organization and you are testifying on a local issue, you may turn the panel off by explaining the national position and its application to the local scene. Start right off on the local issue.

Avoid cliches and repetitive language.

338

Don't explain how your organization functions, how it comes to support or oppose issues. The *reasons* should be apparent from what you say—otherwise you are wasting your and the panel's time. Tell what you did: "We made a survey of the library facilities in the high school, the book collection, the uses to which the facilities are put. We interviewed teachers, students, librarians...We found that..." Then highlight the basic findings and what you therefore recommend.

Options for developing your arguments

Begin with a clear statement of what you support or oppose (avoid overuse of these two words); then offer your reasons. Or start with the reasons and then your proposal.

Make one point at a time with back-up data; or describe the problem as you see it, then how you see the way to solution.

If you oppose a proposal, specify why you think it won't work. For example, if the issue is improved coordination among environmental agencies, you may agree with that overall *goal* but think the *plan* is full of holes. Get off to a good positive start by agreeing with the goal. Then pick out a key sentence in the proposal: "Implementation of flood plain management would be the duty of local authorities." Point out the weakness: "How many local governments are there in the river basin that have the power to establish such zoning? Only four out of twenty (better to say than 20 per cent). How will they cooperate so that regulations will not vary substantially? How will duplication of effort or working at cross purposes be avoided?" The *questions* reveal the holes. If you can give examples of what might happen if Town A did thus and Town B so, so much the better.

If you agree with parts of a proposal but oppose others, begin with the positive. Example: "The legislature has, we believe, taken some important steps in improving its procedures." List them. Then get on to what else needs doing. "The average citizen knows and cares little about the state legislature; sometimes he does not even know who represents him there. Perhaps it needs to become more visible —by TV and radio coverage of floor sessions and of

339

hearings; by..." For each suggestion, you might expand on how that particular change could increase visibility and citizen interest.

If you oppose the whole proposal, you still may agree that a *problem exists*. Then you might begin by describing the dimensions of that problem, giving the best data you have. Select carefully the facts and figures you use. Too many may give the panel indigestion. Be careful not to distort by your selection of statistics—your credibility and accuracy are important assets. You may want to draw on them in the future.

Point out consequences of inaction or "inadvisable" action. What has happened elsewhere is good evidence. Possible effects on other areas or on other problems are telling points. For example, a new library site is under discussion. *Where* the building is to go is important. Who used the old building? To whom was it accessible? Did the users live nearby? Are the proposed sites hard for them to get to—transportation? costs? traffic? Has a present-user survey been made? What effect will removal of the library have on the neighborhood?

Form of the statement
The statement should have a heading that includes before whom you are testifying, the date, your name (and the organization you represent, if any):

TESTIMONY BEFORE THE CITY COUNCIL
ON THE MASTER PLAN
By John E. Jones, President
Chamber of Commerce
April 10, 1972

Type double spaced, without errors, on one side of the paper. Leave even and adequate right- and left-hand margins. Make enough copies for all hearing panelists, press and media, and ten extra copies for other witnesses and interested observers. Sometimes rules require delivery of copies in advance—usually three or four days—to allow the panel members to read them before you appear. Find out what the rules are and follow them.

Check your statement
The president, executive committee, or whoever is authorized checks statements made in the name

of an organization. You as spokesman are thus protected from the wrath of members who misinterpret the organization's policy or what you said. There can be corrections in language that might be misunderstood or that does not reflect accurately the organization's position.

Informal testimony

If you plan to speak without written testimony at a city commission or school board meeting, where opportunities for informal views are offered, make an outline of what you want to say. Your views will come off better if you do.

How to Put the Panel to Sleep

"The Junior Chamber *wishes to take this opportunity to express* its approval.."

Go ahead. Express! "We approve..."

"We are concerned that periodically for some time problems involved in voter registration have come to the attention of this committee." .

Meet it head on! "Over and over you have listened to problems citizens face in registering."

"*It was evident* from our interview with Mr..."

Better: "We learned from Mr..."

"*We would like to ask* how many..."

You don't need permission. Ask! "How many..." (Posing questions that ought to be answered is an effective technique.)

"We *want to go on record as in opportion to...*" or "We *want to express our stand in opposition to...*"

You want more than "to be on record" or to "express our stand." You want something to happen. "We do not approve...because..."

"We *wish to take this opportunity to thank you for...*"

Jargon again! "Thank you for..."

"The Neighbors for Denton Park Expansion *wish to express their interest in and approval of the city council's announcement of...*"

Needs pruning. "The Neighbors for Denton Park Expansion heartily favor..." and follow by stating simply what the Neighbors approve — surely not just the announcement!

Select the spokesman carefully. A hearing calls for persuasiveness, good delivery, public relations skills. A good voice, ability to think quickly, poise, a good sense of humor, unflappability are assets.

Choose the person early on. Include him in the writing—he should feel easy with the language and format. He may want to make changes to suit his own style. He does not need to be the most knowledgeable member in your organization on the subject matter; for that very reason, he may want to ask some questions.

Speakers develop skills with practice. Bring in new witnesses. New leadership will not develop if the "old," experienced hands make all the appearances. For the first-time witness, practice before sympathetic critics is useful. The critics should remember that new approaches, individual and different styles of delivery, while they may not be the way "we've always done it," may be very effective. An organization can get in a rut.

Lively Testimony Makes News

An old ploy, but effective A woman appeared before a city council to complain about the pollution of a stream that ran by her home. In her own words, without other facts or figures, she said the stream was dirty, and produced a quart of water dipped from it. She insisted that the stream be cleaned up!

Leading up to a climax One organization, before testifying for public and nonprofit housing, conducted a tour of areas where such housing already existed, was being constructed and was proposed. Its members telephoned and paid for an ad in support of the most crucial site, giving the hearing time and place. They urged those who were to benefit to come. There was a crowd.

Just the facts Another group, checking a local annual recreation budget, found that a sizable amount of money seemed to be missing between one bank account and another. It testified before the recreation board. The result of publicity over this newsworthy fact—a state audit and tighter bookkeeping procedures.

WHAT ABOUT THE QUESTIONS?

Be prepared to answer questions. You may want someone to appear with you to help you answer. Heads of agencies routinely are attended by staff. There is no reason why citizen groups should not use similar techniques.

Questions from the panel are often a compliment. Your input is important, or the panel wouldn't bother. Even if some questions seem hostile, at least you are important enough to elicit them. You will win points if you are cool and collected under fire.

On the other hand, no questions may mean that the panel agrees with you or finds your testimony compelling.

If you cannot answer the question, say so. Or say you will get the information for the panel, if you think it possible.

You might be asked, "Would your organization support *this* change in..." Here you must be careful. You may not be sure. If you are absolutely certain, yes or no, say so. If you are not sure or think the proposed change deserves careful weighing, say that your organization would want to consider it to see what the implications or effects might be.

WHAT CAN YOU LEARN FROM HEARINGS?

Observe as well as participate. What should you look for? The following list may help:

Which panel members are present? which absent? If you have been present for more than one day of hearings, are some consistent absentees? always present?

What kinds of questions does each panel member ask? Do they indicate special interests or concerns? Keep track.

Who or what organizations testify? on what issues? with what points of view? Are certain kinds of questions asked consistently of certain groups? If so, can you determine why? Are there variations in the reception given witnesses?

Who are your potential allies? on what issues? For those with opposing views, can you determine why they differ? (You may already know, but you may get additional useful clues from careful observation.)

What kinds of issues draw a large audience? Why? Is the attendance because of wide-spread interest or strong emotional feeling? in response to efforts for a large number of bodies there?

Was the room chosen for the hearing big enough? Or was the interest in the issue a surprise to the panel? Who comes to listen? Does attendance differ according to the issue? status of witnesses? stature of the panel?

What indications do you see of effectiveness of hearings? (Keep notes.) What happens as a result? Nothing? A change? If a change, because of what aspect of the hearing—size and nature of the audience? status of witnesses? cogency and/or amount of testimony in favor of the change made? some dramatic incident? news coverage?

Consistent monitoring and reporting of hearings or meetings can provide useful data for either an individual or an organization. The data can be thermometers for timing action on an issue. They can indicate best possible points to make in subsequent testimony or compaigns and in selecting materials to highlight issues. They offer clues for approaches to individual officials and to those in the community who support or oppose your views. From both the hearings and media reporting, there are tips on what is newsworthy.

NEED BANDAIDS FOR EMERGENCY USE?

You want, of course, to put your organization's best foot forward. Unless you are a veteran spokesman, the approach to your first experience may be like a visit to the dentist—the worst part—the anticipation. Keep remembering that here is your chance for a face-to-face exchange, much more satisfying than writing or telephoning. Remember that you have a right to be heard.

As in any other venture, the unexpected can happen, and sometimes does. The panel chairman may suddenly notice that time is running out and announce abruptly, "The last three witnesses (you are one of those) will be limited to three minutes each." You were scheduled for 15—so cut! You can present the full statement "for the record" or "for the committee's use." The reason for the lack of time may be that earlier witnesses took more than 15 minutes each—or the panel asked questions and got speeches instead of succinct answers. (Sometimes the first paragraph or two of a statement can be a short summary of the principal thrust you want to make. When the time is short, you can use just the opening.)

So you spill the glass of water at the witness table over your testimony. There are extra copies; don't panic. If not and you don't have a handy extra in your brief case, while you're mopping up the water, ask the panel if one of its members will lend you his "dry" copy.

Or the microphone you're to use doesn't work or stops in the middle of your remarks. Raise your voice! If you're sitting, stand up and proceed; your voice will carry better. Don't spend five minutes of your time fiddling with the equipment, unless you're an electronics expert.

The speaker just ahead of you makes a point in almost the same language of a paragraph in your testimony. Take advantage! When you get to that place in your statement, say, "Mr. Peters has already expressed very well that..." and abbreviate what he said. You will get points from the panel, and from Mr. Peters, for having listened.

One witness before local boards and commissions, becoming a veteran and liking the experience, had these comments to make:

On fringe benefits: "I was awarded a tuition-free two-year course in how to give public testimony."

On a particular hearing: "This hearing was the only one which had limits on speaking time, but unfortunately they didn't apply to the department's own witnesses."

On effectiveness: "It is very hard to gauge the effect of testifying. Sometimes there is an immediate vote, sometimes questions are asked, sometimes action is postponed. Sometimes the committee sits unmoving through a whole hearing. However, as far as I can tell, their eyes are usually open."

As a witness, you will learn from your experiences, too. You may see ways to improve the hearing process, to make it more accessible to citizens, to make committees and commissions and government more responsive to what citizens think. It is a vehicle for participation. It can be made a more responsible bridge than it is between people and their governments.

And remember ... somebody may be listening! □